PARIS NOW AND THEN

Memoirs, Opinions, and a Companion
to the City of Light for the Literate Traveler

by

Brewster Chamberlin

The Vineyard Press
Port Jefferson, NY

BY THE SAME AUTHOR

*Kultur auf Trümmern. Berliner Berichte der
amerikanische Information Control Section, Juli bis
Dezember 1945* (1980)

A Piece of Paris: The Grand XIVth (1996)

For
Lynn-Marie Smith
with whom I share life and Paris

and

In Memory of

Karlheinz Schwaner
Rose Sklar
Eugène Fidler
André Corman
and
Warren Smith

each of whose Paris was much
different from ours.

Vineyard Press
106 Vineyard Press
Port Jefferson, NY 11777

An earlier, shorter version of the section
on the 14th Arrondissement was
published under the title
A Piece of Paris: The Grand XIVth
(1996, Masurovsky Publishing Co.
Washington, D.C.)

cover photo: Robert DeMaria (1961)

The price of purity is purists.
"Hometown Boy"

Paris, tu n'as pas changé, mon vieux
Paris, tu n'as pas changé - tant mieux!
Tu n'as pas maigri;
Tu n'as pas grossi.
Tu est toujours le même Paris.

--Old song, occasionally bellowed
with gusto by emigrés in The Edge Bar

Table of Contents

Acknowledgements

Several people found themselves dragooned into reading the text and have offered helpful comments, many of which I have gratefully incorporated and occasionally elaborated.

I would like to publicly express my thanks to Dean Chamberlin, Gregory Masurovsky, Marc Masurovsky, Elizabeth Koenig, Aaron Kornblum and Ronald Weitzel.

Several years ago, Lydia Perry planned to visit Paris and asked for suggestions as to hotels and restaurants. Little did she, or I for that matter, suspect this book would be the long-term result of her request for a few recommendations.

Clearly none of these helpful people are in any way responsible for my opinions scattered throughout the work.

Lynn-Marie Smith has contributed so much to this volume that her name almost deserves to be on the title page as co-author. However, I could not in good conscience thus so imply that she shares the more bizarre of my opinions. Nonetheless, the "we" refers of course to the two of us.

I remember the cantankerous, but erudite, elderly barkeep in The Edge Bar, his unruly gray-white hair sticking out at the back of his head, nodding in what he thought of as "a sage manner," leaning back away from the bar to proclaim, "Paris has been here in one form or another for a good long time. We've always enjoyed it, learned a bit from it, breathed in all its smells, gawked at all its glories, but no matter how hard we try we lose it in the end, and no matter how hard the French try to ruin it, the city remains for the next generation and those after that to discover, albeit differently, again and again. How's that for an epigram? A shade litry, maybe, but deeply felt and elegantly expressed, eh? Just the thing for Paris: so very French, but not too French."

Paris – Key West, December 2001

DEFINITIONS AND OTHER INTRODUCTORY MATTERS

A Dog's Life in Paris, 9 – L'Académie Française: The French and Their Language with Some Useful Definitions, 13

Yes, sweetheart, we'll always have Paris.
Rick to Ilse, 1941

This is not meant to be a traditional guide to the city. It is an entertainment, a commentary on things Parisian, a collection of anecdotes and chunks of history meant to amuse as well as instruct. Consider it a companion, meant to be both pleasurable and useful.

It began innocently enough several years ago as two pages of restaurant and hotel names followed by a few descriptive phrases for our English-speaking friends. It has gradually metamorphosed into the comparatively voluminous piece you hold in your hand. This is not all for the worse since the expansion allowed us to wallow in our own and others' memories of Paris without guilt or embarrassment. Of this most welcome opportunity we took full advantage. And to be honest we did a smattering of equally welcome research when our memories failed.

One or two things I know about her are not discussed in any detail or at all here, such as the wooded extravaganza of the Bois de Boulogne, the Avenue des Champs Élysées, the Musée de Louvre, and the massive pile of Nôtre-Dame (which belongs more to Victor Hugo, Charles Laughton, Lon Chaney, and Gina Lollobrigida than to the quotidian world), all of which everybody knows about already and which we either know very little about or find boring.

Lionel Abel has said that, "New York City is still the most living of all the great dying cities of the world." No

1

doubt he has his reasons. I, too, once lived in New York whilst it was still bearable, but would I live there today? On the other hand, Abel notes that, when he returned a decade later, he found Paris so changed from the period 1948-1951 that he no longer felt comfortable there.

But what had changed so much? "People were better dressed, had more money to spend, and were much less friendly than between '48 and '52." Oh yes, exactly during those years when the US dollar reigned unchallenged and sovereign, when Europe struggled to dig itself out of the ruins of the most destructive European war in history. Oh yes, the time when a young Ami with dollars could feel really into Paris intellectual life. Oh yes, how interesting poverty is in others, it makes them, ummm, so much more real. "... I found they now had refrigerators, automobiles, and money in the bank." How disappointing.

It is true that each generation sees the Paris of its youthful follies as somehow "better," somehow more "real" than the city becomes as that generation totters on into middle age. The city, of course, has no middle age. For those readers interested, you may read about it in Abel's *The Intellectual Follies: A Memoir of the Literary Venture in New York and Paris* (1984). Most of the book is not as silly as the passages cited above.

Before making your trip to the City of Light, you may find it worthwhile to read the latest edition of Patricia Wells' *A Food Lovers Guide to Paris* (1993); Ian Littlewood's *Paris: A Literary Companion* (1988); and, for general background, John Russell's *Paris* (1983) and Roger Shattuck's *The Banquet Years: The Origins of the Avant Garde in France 1885 to World War I* (1968); and Ernest Hemingway's memoirs, *A Moveable Feast* (1964), not for the facts, since large parts are fiction, but for the evocative milieux-descriptions and the references to cafés and bistros, and his powerfully, if sentimentally, expressed feeling for the city. Brian N. Morton's *Americans in Paris. An*

Anecdotal Street Guide (1984) will give you brief entries relating to the subject.

Of course, there were no such discrete events as World War I and World War II; the latter is simply the violently expanded continuation of the former with a brief period of respite between them. The Great 20th Century War would be a more accurate name for the conflict fought out across the soil and soul of Europe. One common, characteristic of all villages in France is the monument to the 20th century war dead: the list of those who fell in the 1914-18 phase is endlessly longer than that of those who died in the 1939-45 phase, which signifies less about the technology of war than about what the historian Marc Bloch called "the strange defeat" of France in 1940, which means that the French found themselves unable to fight the Germans and gave up. If, as Thomas Mann enthused in 1914, "war is purification, liberation and an enormous hope," we have in this century experienced a surfeit of cleansed, optimistic freedom costing millions of lives and the destruction of an incalculable amount of art.

The essential green *Guide Michelin* to Paris will give you a wealth of detail about places you may visit and, very important, will tell you the days the museums close. Keep in mind, however, that occasionally the Michelin people issue a new guide that often radically shifts geographical concentration. For example, the 1985 edition contains a large section dealing with the environs of Paris, but the 1990 edition drops all mention of Versailles and other sites near to the city. Consequently, whenever the text below refers to the green guide, the edition is cited to make references easier to find.

Equally important is a Paris street map indicating the métro and bus stops; pick one whose print is large enough to read quickly. The *Paris par Arrondissement* is useful but bulky; we prefer the *Plans-Guide Blay*, of which we've worn out three or four. Unfortunately, the print is exceedingly small; otherwise it is fine, once you have discarded the cardboard covers, except for the one with the métro system on it. Save this for future reference. Guard well your shoulder bag in the métro and, in fact, everywhere else.

Indeed, as one who suffered the humiliation of being both successfully and unsuccessfully pickpocketed on the métro, allow me to write a few words of advice. If a person is standing next to you with his or her arm in a large shoulder bag, move. The bag has no bottom and the hand at the end of the arm is moving toward your own bag or pocket. If you feel you might be a target of this form of theft on the métro, simply move to away from the doors or find a seat. Pickpockets usually tour in groups of three in the area of the train doors, one to abscond with your goods, two to block your way should you notice what has happened. Taking elemental precautions in subway safety will preclude you becoming a victim. If at the top of an escalator you are suddenly surrounded by a small mob of loud and vehemently energetic children who appear to be in the process of roughing you up, you are being pickpocketed and, short of throwing the little creeps down the steps, a measure frowned upon by most unmolested people, there isn't much you can do except tightly grasp your wallet and stride purposefully forward until their interest flags. If you happen to accidentally step on a few of the little charmers, so much the better, but do not fool yourself into thinking you have taught them anything. In the future, they will be more agile about staying out from under foot.

The annual red *Guide Michelin* offers information about hotels and restaurants, with a complex rating system to help guide your choices. We have never known the red Michelin to make a factual error, though we disagree occasionally with its ratings. On the whole, this is a most dependable guide.

4

Speaking of transportation, you should be aware that if you are going to be in the city for a week or more, you might wish to purchase a "carte de semaine," a weekly card available in the métro stations. The card allows you to make as many trips on as many buses and métros as you wish within the time specified. Indeed, traveling about the city by bus not only moves one from point to point, but one experiences the city quite differently from the underground. (And did you know that, since it opened on July 19, 1900 carrying a single passenger, the Paris métro has moved twenty times the world's population through 297 stations?) One can also purchase a "carnet" with ten métro and bus tickets for less than ten individual tickets.

The name métro is a shortened version of the full name: métropolitain, which you can still see in its original art deco style above the entrances to some of the stations around the city, as well as in the one imported to the USA at the Museum of Modern Art in New York City. In terms of symmetry, it should be at the Metropolitan Museum of Art in the same city, but what can one do? Life is asymmetrical.

Most of the métro stations have names, which comes as no surprise; they reflect a street (Ménilmontant), a square (Victor Hugo), an intersection (Réamur Sébastopol), an institution (Chambre des Députés), a gate to the city (Porte des Lilas), and the like. But several are more mysterious in their origin, such as Stalingrad, Malakoff, Jasmin, Ranelagh, Colonel Fabien, Bonne Nouvelle, and my favorite, Ourcq.[1]

The métro is operational from 5.30 AM to 12.30 AM, so plan your early morning or late night outings accordingly. One Sylvester's Eve (December 31), Lynn-Marie and I forgot the time in the pleasurable chaos of the celebration on the Champs Élysées and had to walk from there to the Gare du Nord, an interesting adventure at one-thirty in the morning! The trains and the buses are labeled according to their end destinations or final stops on the line. And since 1991 those relatively empty first-class yellow cars in which the inspector could catch and fine you for not having paid for a first-class ticket no longer exist, and now we all travel second class.

By now it is a commonplace to say that the French approach the notion of food and its preparation differently than most other societies, especially those of North America and other Anglo-Saxon, English-speaking national groups. This is not to say that the cuisine of Costa Rica or Nepal cannot be boring in their narrow palates of ingredients and methods, but the comparison of these cuisines with the French will have little meaning for most readers of this volume. Furthermore, it is not necessarily a matter of ingredients and methodology or talent, though obviously these are important; rather it is a question of approach, of stance, of how one views and integrates food and its preparation into one's life; in short, the value one places on it vis à vis other values.

I have eaten meals in truck stops and gas station beaneries in France that compare with solid bourgeois restaurants in the USA and the Britain; however, do not expect an extravaganza in such places. Indeed, with the increasing uniformity of mediocre food spreading throughout France and elsewhere due to the expanding ubiquity of such electronic "kitchen helpers" as the microwave oven and the ever-extending concentration of capital in restaurant chains, it becomes ever more difficult to find these places. In any case, as the late Elizabeth David somewhere in her incomparable work cautions, eat the daily special and do not ask the overworked staff to prepare anything not on the daily menu. One can eat badly in France, but one must be astoundingly unlucky to do so.

Speaking of Mrs. David, who died at the age of 78 in June 1992, you can find no better resource about French cooking, not just recipes but also her clearly written

English, beginning with the marvelous *French Provincial Cooking*, first published in 1960. In the last two decades we have worn out two copies of the Penguin paperback edition; fortunately, several years ago I found an English hardcover reprint and one voluptuous Sunday transferred to it all the handwritten comments we'd made in the paperbacks, discovering anew the incredible variety of both French cooking and Mrs. David's wit and learning. Imagine a brilliantly bright, warm day in the early afternoon, bathing in a shaded pool of cool Perrier water, sipping cold sparkling white wine, nibbling on Beluga caviar and water crackers, whilst discussing your favorite things with a few close friends. The Sunday with Mrs. David closely resembled that voluptuous image.[2]

The only writer who equals Mrs. David's interest in French food, and who writes equally as well if in a much different prose style (think of the difference between T.S. Eliot and Lawrence Durrell) is the unfortunately late MFK Fisher (known in our house as Mary-Frances), to whom Wysten Auden referred as "a national treasure" and to whom I turn when I need not only knowledge but also, perhaps primarily, inspiration. Mrs. Fisher died in her eighties in June 1992, a bad month for world culture. Her work is readily available, for which we can be grateful, and is not all about the French and their cooking, but those subjects she handles best because she loves them best. Fortunately, five of her books on food and eating are collected in one volume called *The Art of Eating* (1976), which I highly recommend for both its style and content.[3]

Which leads us back to France, where one eats better for less money that anywhere else I know. With the lunatic French lust for most things American (a national trait, the recognition of which is severely repressed by French innerschrecktuals of the left and the right), the mass introduction and acceptance of fast food methods is gradually changing this situation in that a generation of culinary know-nothings will be adults all to soon. Where will the market for quality and variety be then? But let us not waste time on that darkened corner of the future. One will, one fervently hopes, always find a small bistro in the city or a small restaurant in the countryside where the cook takes pride in her or his products and where, bien arrosé (well-watered) by a choice wine, a meal will be a gustatory revelation as exciting to the taste buds as it is pleasing to the purse.

France is, after all, the nation which produced Antoine Carême, the great 19th century chef, who proclaimed the cook to be "a god on earth," and the nation which has always made the best out of lousy food situations: an herb there, a scented sauce there. For instance, during the German attempt to starve Paris in the Winter of 1870-1871, Parisians who could afford the prices ate not only horse and mule, but also cats, dogs and rats (the latter at two francs a piece), then turned to the city zoo, where after such delicacies as camel kidney, tiger filet, wolf and antelope steaks, and kangaroo and elephant stew appeared on certain menus. The well-known Café Voisin reputedly listed on its menu "chat accompagné de rats," but this may have been a perverse joke.

Food shortages have similar effects regardless of the historical time in which they occur. In one of his books, Roger Peyrefitte cites a notice that appeared in the Paris newspapers during the harsh winter of 1940-1941.

> Attention Cat Eaters!
> Due to the shortage of food, certain hungry people have not been above capturing stray cats and making stew out of them. These people obviously are unaware of the risk they run. Cats, in their natural function of killing rats, which are the carriers of some of the most dangerous bacilli, can prove especially deadly to humans....

At least Peyrefitte *says* this appeared in the newspapers at the time. Hunger is the great leveler of all sentient beings.

When the world whimpering ends, the last places on earth one will be able to find superb if simple food will be France and Italy - but let us not blab this about! There will be little enough room as it is. Think about it: if D. H. Lawrence had learned to appreciate good food, would he have been any less of an emotional fascist?

Be that as it may be, except those of historical interest, restaurants are not included in this book for several reasons, the most important of which is the possibility of irrelevance: by the time you read this it is, alas, possible that one or another of those restaurants we might cite may have changed chefs or owners, or closed since we ate in them, as for instance the marvelous little Vietnamese place called Chez Tim, down the street from the Saint-Julien-le-Pauvre church where the loudmouthed, grinning German gave unasked for advice about Berlin, a city we knew better than he; or the elegant Monsieur Boeuf where one rainy new year's eve an elderly couple sat, their lapdog with its own plate from which madame fed the little beast tidbits of her own dinner. Nor are hotels noted unless they have some historic meaning or interest.

A Dog's Life in Paris. Dogs in restaurants. Lots of dogs in lots of restaurants. Especially lapdogs in higher priced establishments, but larger dogs in less splendid surroundings -- all over France. French traditions of public hygiene and pet care are strikingly different from the German or the American varieties. Curiously enough, one rarely sees cats in French restaurants unless they belong to the owners, and then only in the smaller, family-owned and run cafés and bars. (For an interesting story about the French, specifically working-class Parisians, and cats during the early 18th century, see Robert Darnton's fascinating essay "Workers Revolt: The Great Cat Massacre of the Rue Saint-Séverin" in his book *The Great*

Cat Massacre and Other Episodes in French Cultural History [1984].)

Why the French cannot leave Finette and Fido at home when they eat out is a matter for speculation and debate; we have not yet resolved the question. We once saw a parrot-like bird on the shoulder of a customer in a restaurant, but that hardly qualifies as a tradition.

Michael Bond has written a series of amusing mystery novels about a former policeman who reviews restaurants for a fictional publication called *Le Guide* and inevitably becomes involved in a kinky crime he must solve. His name is Aristide Pampelmousse and his companion, who assists him in reviewing and mystery-solving, is a dog named Pommes Frites. Bond has also written an entertaining, if occasionally inaccurate, guide called *The Pleasures of Paris. A Gastronomic Companion* (1987), which is worth your attention.

Dogs, not birds, in restaurants is the tradition, so do not be surprised to see one of the little beasts' heads resting on the table, expecting to be well-fed, while its owner, in whose lap it sits, chatters away about Leonardo or Regis Debray. Symptomatic of this tradition is a 1976 guide to Paris restaurants that lists not only the usual information, but also whether or not dogs are allowed. Needless to say, the overwhelming majority of them do allow.

Arnold Bennett spent some time in Paris during that splendidly optimistic period before 1914, during the year 1910 to be exact. In his *Paris Nights and Other Impressions of People and Places* (1913), he tells of overhearing the following statement made by a woman to another man "smiling at him mysteriously." "Do you know, I have made a strange discovery today. Paris gives more towards the saving of lost dogs than towards the saving of lost women. Very curious, is it not?" The curious tradition goes back generations.

Samuel Putnam, who lived in France during the 1920s, mentions in his memoirs, *Paris Was Our Mistress* (1947), "the new dog restaurant that had just been opened in Paris, where they served a ten-franc meal for canines..." But this may have been apocryphal.

The French love of canines and their (the French, not the canines) inability or unwillingness to curb them (the canines, not the French) has resulted in the invention of a curious looking mobile, battery-powered poop-scoop driven by civil servants in bright green uniforms. The driver arranges the machine, which resembles a motorcycle with a large white box behind the saddle, over the offending turds, lowers the box to cover them, presses a button, et voila! The offense disappears. Actually, Parisian taxpayers support a variety of such implements, all based on the vacuum principle, to the tune of about 42 million francs in 1991 (about $8.4 million in mid-1992 dollars). How much is that doggy in the boulevard? Only in Paris have we seen such a contraption; they should be standard equipment for all urban centers until humans can be taught the rudiments of modern sanitary procedures required for healthy city dwelling.

In the meantime, non-doggy-owning Parisians raised such a stink, so to speak, about the canine crap covering the city sidewalks and the stupendous cost to clean it up that city officials finally, in the summer of 1992, passed a regulation forbidding doggies from punctuating the walkways with their unamusing bowel movements. *Hot dog!* one might exclaim. But passing a regulation is one thing, enforcing it is something else entirely. There are an estimated 250,000 dogs in Paris, some of them liberated from the constraints of human owners; the undercover police doggy enforcement squad, empowered to issue FF 500 tickets to offenders' owners, number all of forty. There is very little chance that this, or any other similarly well meant but futile measure, will motivate Parisian dog owners to curb their animals.

If they did, however, the problem would be greatly alleviated because the city washes down the gutters daily. Civil servants in bright green overalls open strategically placed spigots, channel the rushing water into the sewer system with conveniently located rags (which no one ever seems to steal) and thusly purge the streets of the inevitable result of a consumer society wherein dogs are not on the menus but in restaurant chairs.

This form of public hygiene indicates progress when compared with the medieval form, which consisted of allowing pigs free run of the city streets to consume the dreck and offal that humans cavalierly tossed on to the pavement. This methods held a double attraction for civic authorities: not only did the pigs clean the streets, but also served to still the hunger of the populace, which ate the little rascals with the same relish as the porkers ate the city's filth. Alas, this inexpensive form of prophylactic ended when one of the cleaning crew ran amongst the legs of a horse carrying the royal heir to the throne, which caused the horse to stumble, the prince to fall and break his neck, and his father to ban pigs from the streets. However, he exempted the pigs belonging to the Saint-Antoine monks, who apparently lived in an urban monkery, but only if they, the pigs not the monks, wore bells around their necks. Privileged pigs, indeed. But the dogs, yes....

A recent newspaper report on dog-accessory stores notes no sales of pooperscoopers, so it is unlikely Paris streets will be any cleaner in the future; or, put another way, it is equally as likely that the streets will not be covered with dogpoop as the chance that the French will radically curtail smoking cigarettes because that despicable habit is killing them.

An even more recent article (*The New York Times*, November 5, 2001) provides an interesting update on the issue of "caninettes," the official name of the scoopers (the vox populi name is the more vulgar "motocrottes"). It seems that the motocrottes only such up about 20 percent of the 16 tons of daily dog poop contaminating Paris streets, cost around $5 million annually, *and* pollute the air with their gas powered engines! Thus city hall has decided to phase the things out of existence in 2002, and, in addition, will assign the 1000 parking ticket dispensers to also ticket dog owners who do not clean up after their pets. Fines will range from $180 to $420. I would say, "Don't hold your breath," but this would be inappropriate given the subject. Merde alors, indeed.

L'Académie Française. The French and Their Language with Some Useful Definitions. If you cannot tell the difference among the terms "bistro," "brasserie," and "restaurant," do not feel squirmy about it because few others can either, no matter what they claim to the contrary. Which is another way of saying, everyone can and does so claim, which is to say further that there are as many definitions as there are people interested in the question.

The names "café," "bistro," "brasserie," "restaurant," and others are often used interchangeably, except by the cognoscenti or those pretending to this status, and perhaps the august members of the Academie Française concerned with the relevant sections of the eternal, but ineluctable production of the official *Dictionnaire de la langue française,* currently at the letter J, or perhaps H.

The Institut de France, located at the foot of the Pont des Arts on the Quai de Conti next to the Hôtel des Monnaies and a block from the École Nationale des Beaux-Arts, contains various components including the Académie des Beaux-Arts, the Académie des Inscriptions et Belles Lettres, the Académie des Sciences, the Académie des Sciences Morales et Politiques, and the Académie Française. The latter, created by Cardinal Richelieu in 1635, is charged with the mission to maintain the purity of the French language, "to defend the integrity of the language threatened by negligence, ignorance, ephemeral neologisms, imported words, deviations of meaning..." The Members no doubt cringe at such importations as "le weekend," "le business" and the multitude of other examples of "Franglaise," but they no doubt approve of "l'ordinateur" ("computer").

Forty self-perpetuating "immortals," mainly writers, are elected by the Members, and approved by the head of state in a relatively complex, and, for the applicants, time-consuming and rather humiliating process, described with wit and sufficient skepticism by André Maurois, himself a Member, in his essay "The Forty Immortals" printed in Ludwig Bemelmans' collection, *Holiday in France* (1957). New Members must give a maiden speech praising the recently deceased Member whom he, recently also she because two women have actually been elected in the past decade, is succeeding. Occasionally, this tradition has led to some adroit speechwriting when the deceased and the new Member had been sworn public enemies.

One can imagine the tortuous, inversed, labyrinthine, wrestled-with prose some members found it necessary to construct in order to fulfill their contracts without totally compromising their integrity: for example, Jean Cocteau skimming over the "unsavory" aspects of his predecessor, Jérome Tharaud, a rightwing collabo who thrived during the German occupation. Cocteau himself did not come out of the occupation unscathed by circumstances, at least as he perceived them, that required him to snuggle up just a little too closely to the Germans and their French assistants. Indeed, only one Member, the frail novelist, François Mauriac, fully joined the Resistance. The Académie contained numerous reactionaries and conservatives who welcomed to one degree or another the advent of the Vichy government, if not the German military occupation. These included Pétain himself, the mean and vicious Charles

Maurras, the toadies Abel Bonnard (no relation to Pierre) and Abel Hermant, although it must be said that the institution did purge these four from the rolls *after* liberation. Of course, being an "immortal" has not saved the majority of the Members from total and well-deserved obscurity. Indeed, the list of those not elected to the Académie is quite impressive in the same way a similar list of those who did not receive the Nobel Prize for Literature is impressive (James Joyce, Lawrence Durrell, Marcel Proust, Jorge Luis Borges, et alia).

On the other hand, the Académy elected Henri Bergson to its hallowed precincts during the nazi occupation, and took in Paul Valéry when the literary establishment ignored him. He took the chair previously occupied by Anatole France and managed to give his entire maiden speech without once mentioning his predecessor by name!

Equally impressive is the sang-froid of the Members during May-June 1940 at the time the "drôle de guerre" became very unamusing. It is recorded that on May 16, the Members gathered in solemn conclave to deliberate the definition of the verb "aimer" (to love) whilst outside the stone walls of the venerable institution fear and panic drove Parisians to acts the nature of which later reddened their necks when they thought of them. With magisterial aplomb, which could also be defined as ignorant indifference, or perhaps "setting a good example," though the latter is unlikely, the Members occupied the morning exchanging learned opinions before settling the matter and, in the afternoon, moved cautiously forward to the next word, "aine" (groin). Or as Maurois explicates the issue, in 1939 when he left for military service, the Members had reached the word "agresseur"; when he returned after the war, they had moved forward to "ardeur." It takes approximately 70 years to bring out a new edition of the *Dictionnaire*. And that is as it should be. After all, as Ernst Renan put it, the Members "did in the course of three

15

centuries achieve at least one masterpiece, and that is the French language."

This, then, would be a logical place to say a few words about that language, particularly about the necessity for those who visit Paris to speak it with some virtuosity. Is a certain mastery of the language of France required to enjoy Paris? The answer depends upon the depth of one's interest in the city's agonies and pleasures. Frankly, one could spend months, if not years, in Paris without learning any French: dependence upon sign language and English (but no other non-French language) will allow one to exist; that is, eat and sleep and visit the usual tourist sites and socialize with those of one's own language who work or visit there. And a few Parisians will actually admit to knowing a language other than French under certain circumstances of brief duration. If one wishes to actually *live* in the city, even for a few days, rather than merely exist there, then at minimum a rudimentary fluency in the language of the natives is necessary. The old saw about catching more flies with honey than with vinegar is true if one substitutes French helpfulness for flies, the French language for honey, and all other languages (but especially English in American mouths) for vinegar. Why one would wish to catch flies, however, remains a mystery.

If you truly care about it, here are some personal definitions, tentative though they must be. If you don't really care about the matter, skip on to the 1st arrondissement.

Café. An essential French institution for dealing with vast areas of one's life, both rural and urban, usually containing two sections: rows of tables and chairs outside and two or three deep just within the building not covered with paper or cloth spreads at mealtimes; and, second section, further into the building, tables and often booths with such coverings. Drink and eat cold baguette sandwiches or hot croque monsieurs or croque madames or other "snacks" (this horrid word has entered the with-it French vocabulary, but one is grateful that it is not yet used as a verb) at the uncovered tables.

At those tables covered with paper or cloth, one can order a hot plât du jour. A café is often a fine place for omelettes, pommes frites, a baguette and cool, not cold, beer.

A croque madame is a croque monsieur with a fried egg on top; the Germans describe the egg addition as "à la Holstein" but this is about Paris, not Berlin. If you think of that portion of upper frontal human female anatomy much drooled over by the human male, you will know why this version of the melted cheese sandwich is called "madame"; the origin of the "monsieur" is rather more obscure.

The café is also the place to rest with a newspaper, notebook and coffee or a glass of lemonade. As Jean-Paul Sartre noted in his weighty tome of dense philosophical noodling, *Being and Nothingness* (1943), "The café is a fullness of being." And as everyone by now knows, one can sit for hours with glazed eyes staring into the middle distance feigning deep thought, all with the purchase of one café expresso. Or one can drink beer and write notes to oneself, to be later transformed into deathless prose. Or just spend 30 minutes reading the daily newspaper. Be forewarned, however, about the price of European newspapers vis à vis prices in the United States. In France, you will pay the franc equivalent of a dollar for what in the USA you pay 25 cents. Beer and coffee can also be unexpectedly harsh on your purse in famous and well-situated cafés.

Those who live in Paris more often than not use the cafés in a manner similar to the American use of the living room. This is the venue to meet friends, make new friends, conduct business, begin or end a love affair, receive the latest news and gossip, and pass on to others the same stuff; in short, given the traditional strict reservation of one's

17

home for the family, Europeans on the whole have tended to conduct their social lives in the cafés. Additionally, many Parisians live in extremely cramped quarters where there is simply no space to entertain. People who have been friends for years may never have been in each other's homes, and this is not viewed as anything but normal. Europeans, particularly the French, of my generation continue to use the formal form of addressing each other and, more often than not, continue to refer to each other as Monsieur This or Madame That, a reserve in social relations reinforced by the structure of the language, which requires a formal and informal form of "you," and which I find a relief from the invasive, relentless American informality which borders on the rude.

Consequently, choosing one's own café is an important matter, to be considered carefully after much weighing of empirical evidence gathered during many field trips. On the other hand, early and instant recognition has been known to happen: a few seconds in the place is often sufficient to evoke that sudden, warm flash, which tells you "this is it." And there is where one can be found, almost always, at certain times of the day or night.

J. Gerald Kennedy has found in the Hemingway papers at the John F. Kennedy Presidential Library at Dorchester (Boston) a piece perhaps written for but not included in *A Moveable Feast*, which categorizes cafés as those to which writers never invite anyone (where they write), the café in which they meet their mistresses, the café where they might invite others to meet their mistresses, and those at which writers sat to be admired by the public (in Montparnasse). This is a nice perspective from which to view the phenomenon.

Since we, alas, do not live in the city and are condemned to short, if regular visits, we have not chosen a café or a Stammtisch, but rather have tried out several in what we consider to be "our" quarter in order to experience the widest variety, ranging from the historic and expensive monuments such as the Café du Dôme and the Café de Flore to the small unnamed and much less expensive places on the corners by the métro stations, and the café-bar on the juncture of the Rue de Rennes and the Rue Cassette, whose name I've forgotten, in whose chairs we have enjoyed some fine hours of drink and people watching. The Café de la Mairie on the Place Saint Sulpice is another favorite, but this has become well-known and is thus always crowded. For an enjoyable discursive discussion on choosing a café, read the appropriate chapter in Claude Washburn and Lester Hornby's *Pages from the Book of Paris* (1910) and Richard Wright's essay, "There's Always Another Café."[4]

Things become somewhat confusing when you see establishments such as the Dôme referred to as a café. While the Dôme may have been a café, or more accurately a café-bar, for most of its existence, by the early 1980s it had evolved into an expensive restaurant specializing in fresh shell-fish (coquillage) with only a small front section remaining as a café. For several years Michelin awarded the kitchen a star, but revoked it four or five years ago.

Many cafés also sell tobacco products, which the French do not eschew to the same extent as the Americans, though they are slowly learning, and postal stamps, the retail prices for which, like the baguette, are government controlled.

Public Toilets and the Bidet. You should also be aware that the toilets and telephones in a café, usually located in the basement, may be used by anyone, at any time, whether you purchase anything in the café or not. This is one of the great French contributions to Civilized Life, helping to balance the destruction of those round iron Parisian pissoirs, which, of course, served only the Civilized Male. The French at times refer to these urinals as "vespasiennes." Emperor Vespasian in the first century of our era caused amphoras to be constructed for Romans to use as urinals, for male Romans of course, thus the name.

These pissotières date from around 1900 and numbered approximately 1300 in the city during the 1930s. They play a role in the work of Marcel Proust, and Henry Miller becomes positively misty-eyed and lyrical when he writes of them, which he often does. "There are some urinals that I go out of my way to visit, like the old dilapidated one in front of the school for deaf-mutes on the corner of the Rue Saint-Jacques and the Rue Abbé-de-l'Epée." Well, one can, I suppose, understand that, especially as an American who knows no tradition of accepted public peeing. Miller also wrote "[H]ow can a Frenchman know that one of the first things that strikes the eye of a newly arrived American, and which moves him and warms his guts, is the omnipresent urinal."

Aldous Huxley attributed a certain democratic quality to these Parisian comfort stations. "'Man,' the vespasiennes mutely proclaimed, 'man is merely the highest of animals. All pretensions abandon, ye who enter here!'"

Apparently the Paris city council ordered the pissoirs removed because they constituted an offense against "public morality:" homosexuals used them as contact locations.

Keep in mind, however, that now the café toilet may be unisex (an offensively ugly word), or indeed may be a Turk (a porcelain hole in the floor between two small raised platforms, or islands, for the feet, not the most comfortable or dignified method, but the apparatus is generally clean, if smelly, and remember to pull the flush chain after you've moved as far away as possible from the mechanism and *always* ensure you are supplied with some form of tissue, because chances are there is no toilet paper where and when you need it, or it consists of cardboard or neatly torn squares from yesterday's tabloid). Regardless of these considerations, do not hesitate to make use of this convenient tradition. The almost universal sign for these human necessities is "WC," for water closet, although the

Germans allowed themselves some smirks and chuckles with the name Winston Churchill in this regard.

The French have replaced the cast iron pissoirs with, yes, of course, *plastic* cabinets, which can be entered for a few francs, if one is not subject to claustrophobia, and used, if one is careful when flushing. Indeed, the mechanism flushes itself after one has left the cabinet. They are usually clean and not too foul-smelling. Certainly not as malodorous as in the past when, the English complained, "there are nuisances of [an] offensive kind which are hourly, indeed almost momentarily witnessed; and (which is more unfortunate still) which you cannot fail to witness as you pass along the principal streets of Paris." Thus James Grant in his 1844 book, *Paris and Its People.* Grant also exclaims that, while in England authorities exhort citizens through "perpetual inscriptions" not to commit the "indecencies," in Paris "so far are the civic or other authorities from putting down these offenses against all decency, that they actually, by small exposed constructions, invite passers-by to their commission. And this, too, in what Frenchmen tell us is the finest, the fairest, and most fashionable city in the world!"

Gaëtan Niépovi (Karol Frankowski) in 1840 warned women about acts of "bestial filth" in the nicest sections of the city. He found the American habit of spitting in public less disgusting than the perpetually pissing Parisians. (Curiously, no one writes about women urinating in public; this doesn't mean they didn't, just that no one writes about it.)

In this regard, you should also keep in mind that the attendants in public toilets expect and should be given a reasonable number of coins (say one franc's worth) regardless of whether or not you use the soap and the towels. If you do, the attendant will turn the water on and hold the towel for you. Pick up the soap yourself. The attendants in men's toilets are often women, known

21

vernacularly in some less-refined circles as "Madame-pipi."
Do not let this stop you: for them it is a job and they have
no interest in you beyond the franc or so you will leave on
the plate when you depart. A word to The International
Gender Equality Police: I have not heard of male attendants
("Monsieur-pipi"?) in women's toilets.

Which brings us, in what may be an oblique and warped
Viconian ricorso, that is to say by a commodius vicus of
recirculation, to The Ubiquitous Bidet.

FIRST PLUMBER: Now *how* is he going to present *that*
anachronism?

SECOND PLUMBER: Never mind *how*, what's he
going to *say* about this matter of privates?

FIRST PLUMBER: I'll watch the how and you watch
the what.

SECOND PLUMBER: And he'd better watch the words.

And so one shall, but there is no way around the issue.
After all, one can hardly avoid them in hotels and other
forms of overnight accommodations, as well as in many
private houses. Even the smallest hotel rooms provide
them on a wheeled mechanism that swings them out from
their storage spaces beneath the sink. As the Englishman
long resident in France, cited by Nicolas Freeling in *Lady
Macbeth* (1988), indignantly exclaimed: "Bidets, what do
they want with bidets, toothpaste is what they need."

In fact, there are two meanings to the word. In 1630
Ben Jonson is alleged to have written, "I will return to
myself, mount my bidet, in a dance, and curvet upon my
curtal," after which he no doubt visited his chiropractor, if
the Morality Police did not reach him first.

Actually, bidet in French means a small horse or pony;
that is the first definition. We, of course, know it means
something else as well, and the OED provides a concise if
quaint and incomplete second definition: "`A vessel on a

low narrow stand, which can be bestridden' (*Syd. Soc. Lex.*) for bathing purposes."[5]

The *Petit Robert* is only minimally more forthcoming for the non-equestrian meaning: "(1751). Cuvette oblongue et basse, sur pied, servant aux ablutions intimes." But this is not really helpful either, if one desires a stark, socially realistic definition, not of the proportions of the thing, which are generally similar to those of a toilet bowl, if narrower, but of the apparatus' function, beyond its use as a temporary storage bin for toiletries and etuis for which hotel bathrooms provide no other space. Even more interesting would be the answer, regardless of how speculative, to the question: "What kind of society would require a piece of equipment devoted solely to the washing of (mainly female) genitalia, and what does this indicate about the frequency of sexual activity vis à vis the frequency of bathing per se?" Since today there exist books and non-books, mostly profusely illustrated, on anything you can think of, you could with some diligence perhaps uncover one, which would afford you an answer. You will not find one here. This is, after all, a companion, n'est-çe pas, not a scatiosociological treatise.

Waiters. One tradition, alas not followed any longer in cafés and bistros, is that of keeping track of your tab according to the sizes of, or the prices marked on, the saucers upon which the waiter served your drinks and left in front of you for all to see how much you'd imbibed. One could build up quite a pile of saucers if one possessed a real and true thirst. Now you pay after every round or accumulate a tiny pile of small pieces of paper printed with the price of each item in such faded ink that only the waiter can read it. It has been our experience that the waiters, predominately men, always tally up correctly.

Americans have traditionally complained about the proverbial snarling, unhelpful French service staff, especially waiters. We have, on the whole, not found this

23

stereotype to be a truthful reflection of reality, at least no more so than anywhere else. In the USA, restaurant service positions are filled with amateurs, who are paid low wages and expect tips to make up for the lack of contracted income. Consequently, they fawn all over the customer in order to achieve a level of sympathetic understanding that will result in a 15% rather than 10% "gratuity."

In France, and the rest of Europe, these positions are usually filled with professionals, who are paid a living, regular wage, which comes from the 15% service charge which in general the waiter adds to your bill, the word for which in French is "l'addition," to which, when asking for it, always add "s'il vous plaît." When the charge is not already added, the bill or the menu itself will contain the phrase "service est non compris." If this is the case, leave 15% or 20% tip, or your departure from the premises might be somewhat uncomfortable. See the section below about the Brasserie Lipp for an example of such a departure.

French waiters will rarely spill tomato juice down your back, although that young woman did empty the plate of rougets down the back of our friend Gregory Masurovsky's shirt when she attempted too many plates in one hand. French waiters are, it is true, a more distanced breed than their amateur American colleagues: they are professionals. We have found them to be helpful and forthcoming, not obsequious and fawning. It is of great benefit if one speaks some French, of course, or is at the least willing to attempt to communicate in that language, and not conduct oneself like Lum or Abner. Think of the idiocy of a Frenchman attempting to order dinner in his own language in an American restaurant in a big American city.

Auguste Ricard, possibly related to the pastis manufacturing family, wrote, probably before the fin de siècle, a description of the archetypal Parisian café waiter; one who worked at the highest possible class establishment, it goes without saying.

Universally his shirt is of the finest linen; his patent leather shoes have been made to order by a bootmaker in the Rue Vivienne; he uses only the most perfumed soap, the smoothest almond paste; his dentist is Desirabode; his hairdresser, Michalon: he has taken lessons in the art of perpetual smiling from a retired opera mimic; he is patient, polite, obliging.

Perhaps Ricard mistook his butler for a waiter. We have, however, been served by waiters with at least some of these attributes, mainly in pricey restaurants. You would be unrealistic to expect such elegance and attention in the corner café or an eatery supplying sustenance to the mass tourist trade. (Almond paste?!)

Bar-Americain. You will see this phrase on signs hanging on the most diverse of establishments. Apparently, it signifies a place where mixed drinks - the dreaded dreadful cocktails - can be ordered by those foolish enough to do so. At least this seems to be the original definition. We know an establishment in Avignon with the name "Bar-Americain" where a request for an Old Fashioned would bring one a look of perfect bewilderment, and an order for a dry martini would elicit a small, un-iced glass of white vermouth. Best stick to that which comes directly out of the bottle, or a pastis, an anis flavored drink that turns milky when mixed with water, which is universally drunk in the South of France, certainly universally by the two of us and our friends in the Midi, the water for which one pours oneself from an angular Bauhaus-style carafe with the Ricard label if one is lucky. (Ricard is the brand name of a popular pastis.)

Some people say pastis only became popular after the government banned absinthe as dangerous to the health of the nation because it significantly increased the alacrity with which brain cells disintegrate. This is perhaps true, but it seems people in Provence have imbibed pastis since

Roman times. Drinking a pastis before dinner is not only healthier than drinking hard liquor, but also does not numb the taste buds as the latter is wont to do; indeed, the opposite is true: pastis evokes a desire to not only eat, but to taste one's meal. Too much of it, of course, will decompose your brain just as efficaciously as cheap whiskey.

Bar-tabac or **Café-tabac.** You will find this institution everywhere; however, in rural areas and in villages it will probably be the only public place to drink without being required, socially if not legally, to eat a meal. You may be grudgingly served a slice of ham or cheese on a half baguette or a glass of soda pop if you insist, but the true stocks-in-trade are alcohol, tobacco, stamps and conversation. Although a few ashtrays may be scattered about, if you are smoking at the bar in a bar-tabac tradition requires that you throw your buttend on the floor and crush the ember with your shoe. We do recommend you check the floor to ensure that others have followed this tradition earlier in the day before you participate in it yourself.

Salon-de-thé. The difference between this "tea room" sort of eatery and a restaurant lies in a generally limited menu with "healthy" items on it and an emphasis on a wide assortment of teas and pastries. In Paris, salons-de-thé can be quite elaborate and expensive, or so we've read, never actually having been in one in Paris, though we've eaten in one or two in Avignon. In salons-de-thé, the imbibing of wine, while not exactly frowned upon, is not exactly encouraged.

Bistro. This type of sit-down/stand-up, usually spatially small rather than large, usually family-owned and serviced meeting-and-eating institution may have begun as a bar where one tasted wine. The owners may have discovered that more wine is purchased and consumed if one feeds the customers. Be that as it may, the keynote has always been a certain informality, a limited menu from which one orders

26

until the items are exhausted. Bistros range widely in prices and decor, and are sometimes spelled "bistrot." But be forewarned, some starred restaurant chefs have taken to opening smaller, less expensive (but still very pricey) establishments and calling them bistros. Never fail to check the posted menus before sitting down. If the menu is not posted so you can read it outside the place, go in and ask for it.

Len Deighton has put together a fascinating, but deliberately idiosyncratic compilation of his delightful and often supportable, but sometimes inaccurate opinions in a book called *The ABC of French Food* (1989) in the guise of an encyclopedia of explanations on topics from "abricot" to "zabaglione," with a solid, but indiscriminate bibliography. There are a number of drawbacks to the book, including his use of the non-word "precooked," his recommendation that one blanch vegetables in water (*never* cook veg in water, they lose their texture, nutrition and taste), and his omission of an explanation of why the English, who owned the city of Bordeaux for 300 years, persist in calling red wines "clarets." These caveats to the contrary notwithstanding, read the book. Among other entertaining and useful things in the work, he notes that bistros were essentially cheap eating places with characteristic paper napkins and table coverings, carafe wine, often uncovered plastic table tops and simple plât du jour meals. Today, he opines, "inverted snobbery" causes owners to name their expensive eateries bistros. One can hardly argue with that opinion.

Those who know the Russian language might recognize the word. Legend has it that when, to the dismay and fright of the western Europeans, the Cossacks marched into Paris after Napoléon's defeat in 1814, they demanded wine and, always late for their next appointments, demanded the wine "Buistra! Buistra!" ("Quick! Quick!")

Brasserie. The brasserie began life in the mid-19th century as an appendage to the Alsatian beer industry; each brewery opened its own restaurant serving the traditional meals of Alsace or "country" food in general: luscious choucroute (sauerkraut, or Liberty Cabbage, as it was known in the United States during the 1914-1918 chapter of The Great 20th Century Catastrophe), smoked meats, buttered mashed potatoes into which the choucroute liquid silently seeps, Dijon or Düsseldorf mustard, deliciously oiled potato salad, mouthwater-evoking sausages, forms of cassoulet, all washed down with large containers (one can hardly call them glasses) of beer.

Beer seems to have become a major industry in Paris: the 1990s have seen the introduction and expansion of the micro-breweries and "brewpubs," which sell beers made in-house or by small manufactories in the city and elsewhere. Many of these sport British names (including, may the Deities save us, The James Joyce Pub!) and are made up to resemble a London local. I've never understood why someone visiting Paris would go to a saloon or restaurant advertising itself as being just like those in one's own country. Would I go to a burger joint in Paris? Do bears...? Nothing wrong with drinking good beer, mind, but let us not confuse our cultures.

It might be beneficial to distinguish between the size of the beer one orders. The general term for a draught beer is "une pression." You can also obtain a glass if beer by ordering "une bière." If you want a lager, ask for "une blonde;" if a stout or brown ale is desired ask for "une brune." If you qualify your order and ask for a "distingué," the waiter or barkeep will probably look somewhat bewildered: a couple of lost generations ago this term meant a liter-sized glass and half of this one called a "demi." See the chapter on hunger in Hemingway's *A Moveable Feast*. Nowadays, a liter of beer all at once is considered rather barbaric and a more civilized measure is ordered under the cute name "sérieux," which is about half a liter; the demi is smaller than that.

28

In some of the pubs mentioned in the paragraph above this one, you can order a yard of beer, and if you haven't already done this once, and you are with a crowd of acquaintances, and you are young and adventurous, and if you don't care that your blouse gets soused as the last couple of inches of beer splash over your face, then by all means give the thing a try. But nowhere else than an appropriate pub, that's the place for such adolescent experiments.

Whereas in a restaurant, one drinks wine with the meal in a sedate atmosphere of crepuscular comfort, in a brasserie one drinks beer, not by the yard, with food in a brightly-lit barn-like room filled with ornately framed mirrors and shouting colors, where, nonetheless, one can sit in a booth and form one's own pool of privacy and, if one wishes, one can drink wine with one's meal. As with other types of eating places, here and anywhere else, one should check the menu before entering to ensure one isn't fooled by the word brasserie being used for a rather expensive restaurant.

Restaurant. In addition to the differences noted above, the restaurant usually serves meals at standard times, lunch and dinner, and costs more than the bistro, but not necessarily more than a brasserie, or a restaurant claiming to be a bistro.

When dining anywhere in France it is useful to know that a "menu" is a fixed price meal and a "carte" is what Americans and the British refer to as a menu. French law requires that eating establishments provide a copy of their carte outside their premises so one can evaluate the fare before entering. A good standard is neatness and cleanliness. A smeared dirty carte does not bode well for a neat and clean kitchen one can trust.

Regardless of the carte's condition, all of these various types of eating places generally, but thank the Fates not always, have one horrendous factor in common: obtrusive music. Into the smallest snackbar and the most elegant restaurant off the Champs Élysées pours an offensively obnoxious roar of cacophonous sound, apparently ignored with ease by the French. No one except us ever asks to have the noise turned off or at least down, a request that has as often been ignored as granted. In one chic beanery near the Hôtel Georges V, the waiter informed us nothing could be done with the sound level because the system was controlled electronically elsewhere; he suggested we move to a different table. Instead we moved to a different restaurant. I wish I could remember the name of this expensive haven for the deaf so I could recommend no one go there. Perhaps there is some justice in the world and the place filed for bankruptcy. Would that this fate happen to all the others as well. Nothing can ruin a fine meal, or the prospect of one, faster than blaring noise pretending to be music. A softly-leveled string quintet as modulated background music is one thing, the raucous whine of pop musical illiteracy in an expensive restaurant is quite another.

One might point out that the French, like all other peoples, tend to congregate according to group tastes and interests. All of which is to say that in the 1950s one restaurant on the Boulevard Montparnasse nailed a sign to its facade proclaiming in large letters "Reservé aux Artistes & Intellectuels." See the book of Sanford Roth's quirky, marvelous and eccentric photographs called *Paris in the Fifties* (1988) for a picture of the place.

You might also keep the following information in mind. The usual post-meal coffee in France is a small cup of expresso. These days you can usually get decaffeinated (décaféiné), absolutely necessary for some of us. If you do wish expresso, remember to order it as such (or ask for "café bien serré," "tight coffee," which is an imaginative way of saying it) because if you ask simply for "un café" you are likely to get something not as "tight" as an expresso but "tighter" than American filter coffee. The Parisians tend to eat late and restaurants fill up after 8 PM, so appearing at 7 PM for dinner instead of 8.30 is recommended unless you have a reservation.

I hope these definitions, if not the opinions, will be of help, but hasten to note that, despite the possible confusion of nomenclature for both the novice and the oldhand, your own experience will give you enough of the "true gen" to operate successfully on the food front. Regarding the other Parisian fronts, you will no doubt also find your way.

What a place! In how many other cities, with New York as the usual exception, do the movers and shakers seriously discuss whether or not the graffiti on the subway station walls is art - at the Louvre stop no less?! Where else would the intensely with-it Minister of Culture so pander to knee-jerk avant gardeism as to glorify graffiti, rap and other "hip-hop" phenomena, whatever they may be, in an exhibition at the national museum of monuments, where after the scabby adolescent goons arrested for defacing public property could claim immunity because "We be fine arts"?!

Where else could the same minister, apparently unable to control his moronic staff who schedule his time and French national honors, find himself presenting official membership in the Order of Arts and Letters to the likes of S. Rambo Stallone, star of screen and *Paris-Match*? The contradictions are typically French, at least typically schizophrenic Parisian.

Frenchkiss. Have you ever wondered, oh you must have, which side of the head begins the extravagantly gestural social convention of kissing one's friends upon meeting and departing, so conscientiously practiced by the French and the denizens of the so-called Middle East? Despite what may be your political leanings, go to your right, then to your left (and sometimes back to your right depending upon the latest kissing mode). Thus, you will begin by kissing the left cheek of the person you are greeting. Of course, the same directions apply to that person as well. Remembering this will help you avoid those embarrassing and often painful thumps on the nose; you will be able to maintain both your dignity and your eyeglasses by following this rule.

Frenchletter. The French, of course, call it the "English sheath," but don't let that fool you, because the Germans, knowing from whence all sensual sin comes, call it the "Pariser"! In any language it means protection against various diseases transmitted via different types of pleasure and excitement. In the early 19th century, anonymous Parisian craftsmen, or women, made them out of fish bladders, and peddlers sold them in the city's streets. Today rationalized industry manufactures them out of synthesized chemicals en masse and they sell in supermarkets. They are no doubt of higher safety quality than the fish bladders, but who knows. Public opinion is currently paying a great deal of attention to this item, which in more innocent, and ignorant, times served as the object of so much self-depreciating, if not humiliating, humor.

1st ARRONDISEMENT

L'Hôtel Meurice, 33 – L'Hôtel Ritz, 34 – The Obelisk Press, 36 – Le Musée du Jeu de Paume, 37 – Le Musée de l'Orangerie, 37 – Henry James in Paris, 39 – The Former Les Halles, 42 – The Shucker and Redmeat, 44

Contrary to the opinion of some of our acquaintances with embedded graduate-student fiscal mentalities, one can indeed say something useful, if not profound, about the 1st arrondissement, which at first glance might appear to be both pretentious and very expensive. Of course it *is* both pretentious and very expensive (the least expensive single room at the Ritz is 3300 francs or about $445 (EUR 503) for the night, the most expensive suite is 4500 francs or about $608 (EUR 687), with breakfast going for 200 francs or about $27 (EUR 30), depending on the exchange rate, according to the 2000 red *Guide Michelin*), *but* one can organize several relatively cheap thrills and certainly eat well, if not *very* cheaply, in the 1st. (In France, when the context is clearly understood, one is not required to say, or write, "arrondissement"; the number is sufficiently expressive of one's meaning, e.g., "the first.")

To be honest, we remember an inexpensive lunch in a small, but busy café on the Rue de Rivoli across from the Musée du Jeu de Paume and a couple of blocks down from the W.H. Smith English-language bookstore. More to the point, perhaps, is the pharmacy with English-speaking pharmacists and English-language drugs and other curealls on the ground floor of the **Hôtel Meurice** (228, rue de Rivoli, but on the Rue de Castiglione side).

On the cold and rainy first day of January 1983, in Paris on a bargain package roundtrip from Avignon, we determined that we could really afford a coffee and a small amount of spirits in the Meurice bar, in typical European fashion actually a lounge with sinkintoable stuffed chairs and couches. The Meurice does not enjoy the same type of Hemingwayesque-Fitzgeraldian reputation as the Ritz just up the street, but Salvador and Gala (formerly Madame Paul Eluard) Dali lived there for several years and the facade looms with beige-gray elegance over the intersection. Perhaps this is what attracted the German military commandant of Greater Paris, who made the hotel his headquarters during the occupation 1940-1944.

In any case, the interior looked warm and comfy, so, weighed down with bags of books, scarves, and hats, we entered, divested overcoats, scarves and hats, sat and ordered. Steaming hot café-creme and lung-scorching, flavorbud bursting marc du pays (a brandy-like alcohol) provided solace from the stormy weather outside the hotel and the demons inside ourselves. Not inexpensive, but relaxing and a fine preparation for the trek to the subway and underground ride to our hotel overlooking the tracks of the Gare du Nord.

As Fortuna would have it, we would return to the Meurice the following August with our friends, Moira Egan and Jim Vore, to view some of the alleged works of the long since comatose Salvador Dali. Someone had arranged a sale of alleged Dali prints in the very suite of rooms he and Gala had occupied those many years past.

"Alleged" is the operative word here since it is fairly well known that unscrupulous hangers-on hectored the senile S.D. into signing several hundred blank sheets onto which the hangers-on then slopped some Dali-like images and, needless to say, found buyers thinking they were getting the "real thing."

We spent little time looking at the junk in the suite. Out on the hot street again, we thought to cool ourselves with an air conditioned drink in the bar of the **Hôtel Ritz**. So we strolled up the Rue de Castiglione to the stark Place Vendôme, its spacious minimalist vista reminiscent of the barren spaces in the early Antonioni movies, *L'avventura* and *La Notta*. Indeed, only the phallic obelisk, constructed of 1200 melted down Russian and Austrian cannons to commemorate Napoléon's 1805 victories, disturbs the bleak square; that structure about which André Breton experienced a vision in which a kneeling giant nude Negress fellated it, thus metaphorically at least providing for its detumescence, which in turn fit nicely into the Surrealists' vision of the city as essentially female, without erect monuments. (That the city is filled with erect monuments apparently is irrelevant to the Surrealist perception.)

Without a thought then about the rise and fall of monuments, commemorative or not, we made it safely across the square, but we never got up the front steps of the Ritz building. A uniformed apprentice teenage flunky dashed from the gates of the kingdom onto the sidewalk, arms out with palms up in the international sign-language meaning *Stop*. He had, even at a distance, weighed our sartorial accoutrements and had found them wanting. *Mene mene tekel u-pharrsin.* The little twerp, who no doubt regularly beat up his younger siblings, left no doubt that he, personally, found us unworthy of breathing the rarified and very expensive Ritz air, and, if he would in the future have his way, we would not be allowed into the place no matter what clothes covered our undoubtedly un-ritzian bodies.

It must be admitted that we conducted ourselves with the equanimity of aristocrats and, noses raised in the hot air, departed with dignity and grace; except Jim, who darkly muttered vengeful obscenities. On an earlier trip, Lynn-Marie and I had enjoyed an expensive scotch in what is now unfortunately called the Hemingway Bar, formerly the ladies bar, the smaller of the two Ritz bars. F. Scott Fitzgerald set a number of his stories at least in part in the Ritz bar, perhaps most effectively in "Babylon Revisited," which begins and ends in the bar. Next time we desire to spend a large sum of money for scotch whiskey, perhaps we shall try the bar at the Crillon down the street and around the corner on the Place de la Concorde.

The Englishman, Jack Kahane, looked daily into the interior courtyard at 16 Place Vendôme from the office of his publishing house, **The Obelisk Press**, which published Henry Miller, Lawrence Durrell, Anaïs Nin, Frank Harris, and a number of harmlessly "naughty" novels by Kahane himself written for the tourist trade during the 1930s. After the liberation, Kahane's son, Maurice Girodias, reopened the business under the name Olympia Press, which published Miller's more obscene stuff, but also *Lolita*, *Naked Lunch*, books by Samuel Beckett, Terry Southern, J.P. Donleavy, Jean Gênet, and a barrelful of forgettable attempts at "erotica," again for the titillation of the tourist crowds and the financial reward of the Kahane-Girodias family. Various factors forced him out of business in the 1970s. Maurice, whom I once met at the annual Frankfurt book fair, where he wore a nametag identifying him as "Girodias-Pornographe," wrote a cranky, meandering, and probably part fictional autobiography entitled *The Frog Prince* (1980).

I owe that brief meeting to my old friend, the late Karlheinz Schwaner, who during the early 1960s worked as the German sales representative for the Olympia Press and other publishers of what used to be considered risqué materials. I lived then in a coldwater room in the Heidelberg Altstadt (old city) and awoke one night to the tentative tapping on the wooden shutter and a young voice saying something like "Es ist ja ein Uhr früh, wir können das doch nicht machen" (It's one in the morning, we can't do this) and an older voice answering "Natürlich können wir, vielleicht ist er noch nicht zu Hause." (Of course we can, maybe he's not home yet.) The younger voice belonged to Karlheinz's oldest son, Teja, then 16 or so years old. A mutual friend, the late Hans-Manfred Rau, had insisted we meet before they left for home in the North. We sat up until dawn drinking mineral water, smoking furiously and talking intensely about Miller, Gênet, Lawrence Durrell, Günter Graß, the state of the English and German languages, and the sad lack of good German red wine. The last time I saw Karlheinz, he visited us in Tavel, near Avignon, where we lived in 1983, and took us for a hair-raising drive to Nîmes in his bright red Volvo two-seater. At 74 years of age he had no fear of other drivers, but his erratic driving put a certain amount of fear into us. A year or so later, his companion Renate informed us he had died in a Frankfurt hospital. We never did spend time in Paris together, a city he loved and often visited. Karlheinz, yes.

* * * *

French museum officialdom, a centralized administration inhabited by a cultural bureaucracy with all the unfortunate characteristics of its narrow-visioned species, ordered the renovation of the **Musée du Jeu de Paume**, located at the Place de la Concorde and Rue de Rivoli, after they removed all the lovely Cézannes and Degas and Fantin-Latours and Boudins and Manets and van Goghs and Gauguins and and and ... and hid them in the wings of the new Musée d'Orsay. The Jeu de Paume, remodelled, renovated, stark, angular, trés moderne and dead, they fill with changing exhibitions of shrill kitsch passing as post-1945 art, cramming it into a small space painted a dizzying off-white. There is also a cafeteria with close to Tour d'Argent prices. The best thing about the "new" Jeu de Paume is the view of the Eiffel Tower from one of the staircases. While meandering about the Jardin des Tuileries, walk around the structure and admire its architecture, but do not frivolously squander your money and time by entering.

You can definitely enter the **Musée de l'Orangerie**, the twin pavillion to the Jeu de Paume at the Place de la Concorde and Quai des Tuileries, which contains a fine Gauguin collection, along with the works of several other post-impressionists, and is manageable, which means good for the feet and generally pleasant to be in, despite the crowds.

Indeed, if you can put up with the crowds, the Jardin des Tuleries is a place of some interest to wander in, especially the sculptures and flowers should catch your eye, if it is not already satiated with form and color by then. Should it be so and should the weather be appropriate, you might briefly have a snooze on one of the greenswards which dot the gardens like Seurat's speckled daubs. There is a chance, however, that a uniformed female cop will harshly request you get off the grass.

Whilst you are enjoying the benefits of this relaxation think about the fact that just where you are now resting your tired eyes, on September 20, 1900, what has come to be known as The Not-So-Famous Mayors' Banquet took place, an event of such magnitude that nothing like it has been seen since, and previously only in ancient monarchies.

Imagine approximately 22,000 French mayors in their tight and heavy Sunday suits gathered to commemorate the 108 year-old Republic on a warm Indian Summer day at tables stretching from the Jeu de Paume to the river terraces, the freeway running between the Orangerie and the river bank mercifully not yet constructed, filled with food and drink. How else would the French commemorate anything other than with a banquet? One hundred fifty dozen Rouen ducklings, 2500 Bresse chickens, 4500 pounds of steak fillet, 2430 pheasants, 2500 liters of beans, potatoes and celery, 2200 pounds of grapes, and 10,000 peaches, served on six miles of table cloths, 250,000 china plates (not styrofoam!), 90,000 glasses (not paper cups!), cutlery (silverware, not plastic!) for 66,000 place settings, and 30,000 napkins (cloth, not paper!), served by 1215 headwaiters directing 20,000 waiters, dishwashers and cooks. Ouf!

The president of the Republic wisely decided to forego shaking the hands of all the mayors, which, calculated at one shake per second, or 3600 per hour, would have taken all day. No one complained about the quality of the food.

For those in need of English-language reading material, there are three bookstores in the immediate neighborhood of the Jeu de Paume: W.H. Smith at 248, rue de Rivoli; Galignani's shop ("The first English Bookshop Established on the Continent") further along the street at 224, which published its own autobiography modestly entitled *A Famous Bookstore* (1920); and Brentano's around the corner. Remember that imported books are very expensive in France, as indeed are French books. If you need to purchase a book in English, look for a British edition, which will be somewhat less expensive than an American publication, a fact whose origins no doubt lie in the cost-distance ratio.

* * * *

If you stand outside the northeastern end of the Musée du Jeu de Paume and look across the Rue de Rivoli, you will see straight up the Rue Cambon, formerly called the Rue de Luxembourg. Carefully negotiate your way across the overly trafficked street named by Napoléon I after one of his fields of victory in northern Italy, and slowly enter the Rue Cambon. Stop at number 29 and consider that, in November 1875, whilst still called Rue de Luxembourg, the street's cobblestones felt the footsteps of the 32-year old **Henry James**, a man of whom Oscar Wilde said that he "writes fiction as if it were a painful duty." James had, in fact, chosen his life's duty, painful or not, and at times so it would prove to be, and now, realizing that he would never be happy or at peace in the provincial mental climate of Boston and New York, he had come to Paris to experience a different form of social and intellectual intercourse, to test the Parisian waters to see if they might be agreeable and accommodating for a lengthy sojourn of unknown duration. His earlier stays in Paris had been in the nature of tourist visits during which he met mainly other Americans and waiters. Now he rented a sufficiently ample apartment on the third floor of number 29, and began his reconnaissance of literary Parisian society, which, in the final analysis, he would find not quite sufficiently accommodating of, nor agreeable with, his notion of how, and the environment in which, he wished to live. As the novelist, L. P. Hartley, sympathetically perceived, "... the Continent, in spite of its attraction for a sophisticated mind, did not fulfill his exacting moral requirements."

Whilst you are considering what the street must have looked like to Henry James, without automobiles and neon electric signs, also consider the cost to him of such an apartment in the heart of Paris. As Leon Edel describes it in the second volume of his definitively monumental biography of The Master (*The Conquest of London 1870-1881* [1962]), the flat consisted of "a parlor, two bedrooms, an antechamber which could serve as a dining room, and a kitchen filled with shining casseroles." The rooms rented for approximately $65 a month, the porter cost him $6.00 a month to run errands and take care of the fires in the heating stoves for which the wood cost him $5.00, and cleaning his linens less than $2.00 a month. The thought is almost unbearable to those today who would sacrifice much to live in Paris, but cannot afford to do so.

In any case, for a year Henry James valiantly made an increasingly dispiriting attempt to achieve a spiritual or mental affinity with those who he came to know as friends and colleagues. He met Ivan Turgenev, living in a menage with the singer Pauline Viardot, her husband, child and

various other relatives and friends, at 50, rue de Donai (9th).
Turgenev introduced James to Gustav Flaubert and
Georges Sand, Edmond de Goncourt, Guy de Maupassant,
Émile Zola, Alphonse Daudet, and, listening to their talk,
pungent, unfettered in comparison to the haute-bourgeois
society of genteel New England academics in which James
had grown up, rather rough around the edges despite the
elegance of the French language, and rather too often
referring to matters relating to, well, ahh ... the sensual
aspects of life (what exactly did Maupassant *mean* with that
story of the two Englishmen and the monkey?) - all of
which James found interesting, to be sure, but a little too
much for the protective carapace of the refined mentality
and repressed emotional state in which he believed he
could live a stable, comfortable and productive existence,
one which would be *undisturbed* by those frightening and
seamy matters of the flesh. He would always enjoy Paris,
but after a year in France, mainly in the city, he moved on
to London where he could live as he chose, in private and
safety, where so many writers were not infected with so
much venereal disease, and where they did not chose the
plebeian working poor as their subjects. After all, as he
wrote to his family in Cambridge, "There is nothing else for
me personally, on the horizon and it is rather ignoble to
stay in Paris simply for the restaurants," a sentiment with
which some would certainly not agree.

Perhaps Edel captures James' relation to the city best
when he writes that James "discovered the sense of Paris in
1876 ... without ever penetrating to the heart of Paris
itself." On the whole, he had found the exiled Russians
more accessible that the French. Indeed, James himself
wrote in his journal the most fundamental reason for his
departure from Paris for London: had he stayed, "I should
be an eternal outsider." This he would be regardless of his
geographic placement, but he did not know that then and,
with some exceptions, he would be more comfortable in

England than anywhere else. And he certainly did return to Paris often, among other reasons to eat in the restaurants.

* * * *

In an entirely different part of the 1st lie the ruins of **Les Halles**, formerly the gigantic marketplace in the belly of Paris that opened in 1857, famed in song, movies, book and on stage, as well as in the memories of countless people lucky enough to have visited it before "progress" ripped the old streets and buildings up at the root and tossed them onto the garbage heap of history. Oh, the markets still exist, of course; how could the city eat without les halles, but they are now located in the distant southern suburb of Rungis near Orly airport.

And with what did the intelligent visionaries, known as the "powers-that-be," replace the brawling, sprawling, pungently odorous food markets? A brawling, sprawling, pungently odorous glass-concrete conglomerate of underground levels, a métro station, stores for loose-lipped airheads, and a children's park made of concrete, the brawling and sprawling now accomplished by the booze and drug-addled dregs of urban society whose unwashed bodies and urination-defecation habits contribute to the pungent assault on one's olfactory senses. Our advice is to only use the place for the métro: get in and get out as quickly as possible. Architecturally sterile and cold, the new Les Halles stands out in a sore-thumb manner similar to its equally offensive neighbor, the Centre Pompidou.

Speaking of clochards, in the old Les Halles apparent chaos, loud and frenetic, ruled the night as a multitude of negotiations, carried on at the tops of the negotiators' voices, worked their way toward ensuring the city's restaurants and green grocers would be stocked with fresh food for the day. As in the stock exchanges, a bell ("cloche" in French) rang to signal the end of the night's trading, at which point gobs of scabby, ill-clothed creatures of all genders invaded the precincts to scarf up the residual produce lying unsold or discarded on the cobblestones. Thus the origin of the word "clochard."

If you want to see something of what Les Halles looked like before French officialdom destroyed the neighborhood, see Naomi Barry's article "Les Halles - A Last Look," in *Gourmet* (December, 1968), which contains several good photographs. Even better are Denise Colomb's photographs taken in the postwar epoch with the aim of capturing the crazy ambiance of the place. Several volumes of her work are available and can be had if one looks for them with sufficient perseverance. For the less attractive side, turn to the photographs of the place by Nico Jesse in *The Women of Paris* (1954), especially those of the scavengers arriving after the bell, bent over scrounging in the huge garbage bins, and that of the blankfaced, empty-eyed clochard about to pounce on a piece of discarded lettuce.

The poetry of the Paris cityscape shifts angles and curves from street to street, quarter to quarter, gently protected from ennui by sporadically placed swatches of green growths and gray-blue ponds of water until the eye slams against the stark occlusion of 20th century glass and steel, and the brain reels, staggered by the iniquity, the sheer stupid, short-sighted cupidity of the human race, so much of which values cynical destruction above imagination and respect for past accomplishment. The mind is dizzy, the body's equipoise shaken, until one yanks one's eyes away from that relentlessly aggressive ugliness to rest upon less wounding facades, which do not stab the brain and heart with such ferocity.

There exists the theory that landscape is the determinant of a people's character, recently outlined in Lawrence Durrell's book on Provence, *Caesar's Vast Ghost* (1990). If this does not exclude big cities and suburban shopping malls (the late 20th century debasement of the agora in ancient Greece), the human race is in deep trouble. When discussing anything but the beginning of a people's history, this theory has frightening implications for the future. *Mens sana in córpore sano.*

* * * *

To the west of what used to be Les Halles runs the Rue Coquillière, on which you will find a row of restaurants, several of which specialize in seafood. Seafood restaurants in Paris exhibit several common identifying characteristics, the two most obvious being the word "coquillage" emblazoned in a number of prominent places and a person, usually a man, dressed in workman's clothing covered by a greenish-gray rubber apron and shod with worn rubber knee-boots of no distinguishable color, looking something like Robert Newton as Long John Silver without the black eyepatch and ashen wooden crutch.

This person is **The Shucker**, a very important person directly related to your welfare and, possibly, to your happiness. He stands outside the building next to a massive container of chipped ice, into which he has stuffed an amazingly varied assortment of shellfish, over which he has casually tossed strands of seaweed (probably manufactured in Taiwan like the "straw" brooms the Paris street sweepers use since the city replaced the traditional natural twig implements with green plastic in 1985) and around which he has stylishly placed bright yellow lemons. None of this negates the taste of the coquillage, especially the oysters, which is uniformly good and very often a revelation, a transcendental, out-of-mind experience, the euphoria of which you will never forget.

Another characteristic of French seafood restaurants is the format in which the coquillage is served: platforms. A wire contraption, similar in appearance to those upon which

44

fondue pots perch over the canned heat flame, supports a tray loaded with chipped ice, seaweed, lemons and whatever shellfish you have ordered. Accompanying this magnificent repas is a pile of small sliced rounds of rye bread (the European, not the American variety), a small pot of unsalted butter, and small pot containing a vinegar mixture for which we have as yet found no function.

The best oysters we've ever eaten have been those consumed in Paris, better even than those enjoyed on the côte de la Méditerranée. The clear, briny, sunsparkling ocean soars through your mouth elevating your soul thrillingly upward until you reach a nirvana of voluptuous satisfaction, the radiance of which is known only rarely outside religious or controlled-substance ecstasy.

On the other hand, we ate the best langoustines on the terrace of La Colombe d'Or in Saint-Paul-de-Vence, another sunsplashed felicitous event, the very thought of which elicits tremors of delirium and intent. So much for the geography theory of food.

Speaking of **redmeat**, a word about ordering steak in Paris, or anywhere else in France, might be apropos here. As opposed to the Germans, who until recently thought a steak was not a steak unless it appeared uniformly gray throughout and as tasty as hot shoe soles, the French think about fresh blood when they consider steers. Consequently, if you must order steak, be sure to tell the waiter you want it "à point" (more or less medium) or "bien cuit" (well-cooked), otherwise you'll get it barely touched by the fire.

To be safe, you should not ever order redmeat in restaurants, unless you know what you are doing and can describe the cooking procedure you desire. However, one is, of course, aware of the iron-grip traditional American cuisine has on most American citizens. And we have all heard stories about, or experienced ourselves, the barbarians of all nations, abetted by cheap airline prices, who loudly infest one's favorite places and force us to the conclusion that in any rational society these creatures would be forbidden to leave their pens and would certainly not be allowed to vote or be given drivers' licenses. But then, French love these morons: they reinforce French social and cultural superiority, and bring into the country all those lovely greenbacks, pounds sterling, kroner, guilden, and marks.

So, you are on your own if you cannot eschew redmeat whilst traveling in France. We can be of little help to you. If you wish to be adventurous, try horsemeat.

You might, however, keep in mind Joyce's comment on the difference between red and white wine. When asked if he liked red burgundy, he replied, "Do you drink beefsteak?" He preferred white wine, which he thought of as possessing the quality of "electricity," which is how Leopold Bloom in *Ulysses* (1922) thinks of the nectar of the gods - but Bloom does order burgundy with his lunch, which gives him gas and serves him right for drinking beefsteak.

We can, however, offer you one bit of advice about ordering seafood, which may be of some value to you, based on personal experience of a mildly embarrassing nature. When we lived during an edenic period in that small village of Tavel not far from Avignon, we motored through the Camargue to the coastal village of Les Saintes-Maries-de-la-Mer, where, each October and May, Europe's Romanies gather for a party and the blessing of the sea. The bigger of the two events takes place in May and you should have a room reserved well in advance if you wish to be there then. The October event, however, given the usual rain and cold, is not as well attended, and this is the one we go to.

Ensconced in a warm window seat in the Brûleur de Loups restaurant overlooking the beach, comfortably away from the chilled wet autumn evening air, easing into a pastis to whet the appetite, I noticed the fresh lobster appeared to be very reasonably priced. The waiter stimulated my anticipation to a higher level of intensity by hauling the beast out from the aquarium to show me what I was in for, as it were.

There is no doubt in our minds that this was one of those existence-enhancing culinary experiences that occur all too rarely in one's life. But what price glory? The price I read on the menu reflected the cost of the lobster per 100 grams - the full animal weighed close to 600 grams! We barely had enough money to cover the cost of the trip, in those days before we could afford credit cards.

We lived through a similar experience in a snazzy western hotel restaurant in Istanbul, but this time the perceptive maître d' gently inquired if I really wished to spend $60 on such a minute amount of Beluga caviar as a first course. I decided to have a green salad. But that hotel did provide the dwarf who appears in the novel *Radovic's Dilemma*, which may some day see the light of print, and the salad was just fine.

Read menus with sufficient care.

2nd ARRONDISEMENT

L'Opéra de Paris (9th), 48 – Harry's New York Bar, 49 – La Bibliotèque Nationale, 50

Even if you do not care for opera as a form of entertainment or art, you should nonetheless walk around in the **Paris Opéra** at the northern end of the Avenue de l'Opéra, if not for the music and the singing, then to admire the architectural design and the murals. The opera museum is full of fascinating memorabilia and artifacts of past productions and the people who contributed to opera, especially French opera, during the last two or three centuries. Do not, however, expect to find anything relating to Virgil Thompson's operas, although he lived in Paris for close to 20 years and wrote them there, before moving to the Chelsea Hotel in New York City.

Doris Grumbach, in her book, *Coming into the End Zone* (1991), describes the building thusly: "Flying stone horses, ornate friezes, a copper cupola of Apollo holding a lyre above his head, Greek classical sculpture accompanied by baroque decoration, huge bowls of fresh flowers and thousands of well-placed lights and spotlights: the great wedding cake, block-square structure is...exciting and glamourous...." One can hardly improve on that as a brief description, so one will not try. However, you may find it useful at cocktail parties to know that the Opéra is built on an artificial body of water, whence the city's fire brigade gets its supply.

For those who need it, the Paris American Express facility is on the Rue Scribe across the street from the Opéra. We went there once or twice on our first visit to the city a decade and a half ago, but have found no use for it since. If you have an Amexco credit card you can have mail sent there, but with the common acceptance of American credit cards, the availability of French franc travelers checks (Euro checks by the time you read this) in many American financial institutions, and the ubiquity of Automated Teller Machines throughout the city, you probably will not need American Express facility on a short visit. Years ago one could avail oneself of various Amexco services, but now one must be a "card-holder" or be limited to cashing Amexco travelers' checks. So much for the expanding service industries in the post-industrial global village.

Actually, the Opéra is in the 9th arrondissement, but the object discussed in the next paragraph is only a couple of blocks away in the 2nd and why not describe them together since you can easily walk from one to the other?

After the Opéra, should you have a powerful thirst that only a beer in a shabby, would-be ivy league college bar can possibly quench (heaven forbid that you should suffer from this particular American affliction - after all, when in Rome...or Paris...), walk south down the Avenue de l'Opéra in the direction of the Place André Malraux (*something* had to be named in his honor) to the Rue Dannou and turn right. *Ecco!* **Harry's New York Bar**, at 5, rue Dannou, whose bartenders invented the Bloody Mary, the Sidecar and several other unspeakable concoctions, some to ensure the later presence of a headachy hangover, some to assist in the departure of same.

Originally called The New York Bar when it opened in 1911, this ginmill enjoys a long and oft-written, if not distinguished history, which informs one that in 1923, Harry McElhone added his name to the title and thus it remains today. George Gershwin is reputed to have composed some of *An American in Paris* on the piano in the cellar and the usual suspects all had a drink here at one time or another.

In 1927, a writer called Bruce Reynolds, who must have learned English in a particularly illiterate advertising

49

agency, published a "book" entitled *Paris with the Lid Lifted* in which he notes the following about Harry's Bar: "This, about as important an institution in Paris, as the French Chamber of Deputies.... [H]ere, is one of the breeziest, buzziest, bang-uppiest places on earth," apparently because it is the "fountain Head" of the "International Bar Flies." But, then, Reynolds also gives the definition "A gigolo is a male vamp," so not much can be expected from this quarter, amusing as it is today.

We did, however, have a couple of beers one day in Harry's and felt no particularly fascination: it is simply an aging American college bar. One does not go to Paris to be in Princeton or New Haven. One does, however, wonder what happened to the joint during the German occupation: did it become Heinrichs-München-Bar?

In the 2nd, behind the Jardin du Palais Royale, you will find **La Bibliotèque Nationale**, one of the world's great libraries, cobbled together over the centuries from pieces of this and that mansion, continuing to accession until, like most great libraries, it has run out of stack space. To solve this problem, the government approved the design and began construction of a hideously out-of-place structure along the Seine's left bank southeast of the Gare d'Austerlitz in the 13th, to be called La Bibliotèque de France. This is yet another affront to the sensibilities of those with both intelligence and an appreciation for the values of the past combined with the practicalities of the flush toilet. Other such blights include the Institut du Monde Arabe, the Montparnasse highrise, the Pompidou Center, and the giant sterility of La Défense. If you like this stuff, you'll love the design for the new library.

That aberration is yet another example of the social risk of a politician with pretensions to the status of "intellectual" attempting to make a visible mark of his passage in history by presiding over the construction of an edifice that should never leave the architect's drawing board, except perhaps to be shown as an example in an exhibition on "un-built presidential follies." By the time you read this, the barbarians will have done their work and Paris will suffer another eyesore. You can read about the background to this affair in articles by Patrice Higonnet in *The New York Review of Books* (August 15, 1991 and May 14, 1992).

In any case, the *old* Bibliotèque Nationale is a gorgeous, eclectic admixture of styles that melds into a coherent whole redolent of culture and books. As well it should since Mazarin had the palace constructed for his books, a library not only for himself but for the public as well - the first public library, a concept first formulated by Richelieu with, at this time, less application than during a period of universal literacy, such as that which we at the end of the 20th century are escaping from as fast as we can. The Scots banker, John Law, of the South Sea Bubble notoriety, resided and conducted his misguided speculations here.

I've also read that some of the galleries, especially the Mazarin, equal in splendor the main reading room of the Library of Congress in Washington. Yes, I read this in a book and yes, it is true: we've not been inside that part of the library. There are, in cities one regularly visits, certain places to which one does not readily go, but saves for the future, such as the massive Fort Saint André across the Rhône from Avignon and the Bibliotèque Nationale in Paris. And this despite the fact that so many of one's cultural heroes, such as Apollinaire and Walter Benjamin, worked there. As the great Walt Whitman wrote, "Do I contradict myself? Very well, I contradict myself."

One of the most fascinating departments of the library is hell, literally "enfer," which contains books that have been put on The Index by the Roman Catholic Church or banned by the government, mainly for reasons of alleged obscenity and/or pornography, but apparently, from time to time, also from political or religious motivations. One of the entries

51

under "l'enfer" in Pierre Larousse's *Grand Dictionnaire Universel du XIXième Siècle* (1870) notes the word is used to describe "the closed area of a library where books thought to be dangerous to read are kept." Many stories of various shades of veracity have circulated in the worlds of scholarship and journalism over the last century and a half regarding the origins and history of this repository. Several of them retold in an article originally published in *Le Monde* by Régis Guyotat and republished in the *Guardian Weekly* of June 28, 1992, as "A hell of a place for France's forbidden books," a title which, in some circles, might be considered amusing.

The head of the Library's reserve collection says that today there are 2,527 books specifically set aside in six polished wood Biedermaier cabinets as a part of the total number of books in the reserve collection. They are, of course, no longer sequestered and readers can read them after completing the appropriate application procedure. Imagine the illustrations to *Gamiani* or *La Nouvelle Justine* or *Les Adventures de Clitorix le Gaulois!* On the other hand, what can one expect as artificial titillation after skinflicks like *Deep Throat* and *Up Your Banana* at the local nickelodeon? A certain quality of richness and mystery leaves life when nothing is forbidden, when nothing is beyond the pale, as the Karamazov brothers and all subsequent existential characters discovered, to their and our detriment, when moral schizophrenia became the overwhelming spiritual disease of the 20th century.

One hopes that the security measures in place here are enforced with more rigor and attention than those at the national library of the USA (the Library of Congress), where the vandals handled thousands of books in a manner resulting in their disappearance, and handled razor-sharp knives in a manner resulting in the disappearance of thousands of engravings and other illustrations from old books. The barbarians are not at the gates, they swarm throughout the citadel.

3rd ARRONDISEMENT

Les Archives Nationales, 54 – Le Musée Picasso, 54 – Le Musée Carnavalet, 55 – La Bibliotèque historique de la ville de Paris, 57

On its southern limits, this arrondissement washes seamlessly into the 4th, which forms the section of town called Le Marais. Le Marais in the 3rd contains the Palais de Soubise, at 60, rue des Francs-Bourgeois, in which you will find the Musée de l'Histoire de France displaying various documents in facsimile important to the country's history, and the French **Archives Nationales**. If you are interested in the long road of French history from the Roman period to 1914, you will enjoy an hour or so in the museum.

In the former Hôtel Salé, at 5, rue de Thorigny, built in 1656 for a collector of salt taxes, the French government created the **Musée Picasso** to house the works his estate gave to the Nation in lieu of some form of taxes the very wealthy must pay if they die intestate. The Museum, much larger inside than appears to be possible from the outside, now holds a vast amount of Picasso's own works and works of others he collected. Be prepared to spend several hours here if you want to see everything on display. There are those who say that in order to see the really great Picassos one must go elsewhere, indeed quite a few different elsewheres scattered around the globe. This may be true, but you should unhesitatingly spend the thirty francs, or whatever it may be then, and stroll through this protean catchall of modern art.

Around the corner from the Picasso Museum, at 16, rue du Parc-Royal, one could formerly find a curious little store named Librarie Huitième Art, which specialized in American and British television series. The friendly owners sold posters, books, video tapes (in the PAL or SECAM, not the American gauge), and other paraphernalia related to such great shows as "Secret Agent" and "Star Trek: The Next Generation," as well as such not so great shows as "Dallas" and "Pink Vanilla Gadabouts." Unfortunately this store went out of business a couple of years ago, but I leave the reference here in order to be able to write the next sentence. The business card of this establishment tells you to preserve it carefully because "Elle ne s'autodétruira pas."

One of our favorite Parisian places is the **Musée Carnavalet**, the "artistic memory of Paris," at 23, rue de Sévigné, not far from the Place des Vosges and the Picasso Museum. The most well-known occupant of the Hôtel Carnavalet, which contains the museum, was Marie de Rambutin-Chantal, the Marquise de Sévigné, who wrote over the years 1677 to 1696 a series of perceptive and stylish letters about the foibles of the aristocracy in Paris and the events of the day to her daughter, Françoise Marguerite de Sévigné. Then wed to the much-married François de Castellane-Adhémar, a Provençal aristocrat described in a pamphlet as "in a way probably too brilliant because he ruined himself," the daughter lived in a château in Grignan (Drôme), which is also worth visiting if you're in the neighborhood. Down and around from the château there is a pleasant café where..., but these phenomena are part of our guide to Provence so they must wait until we get to it.

Madame Sévigné's letters are printed in various editions, which offer you both enjoyment and edification. A readily available selection to give you a taste of her style and the content of 17th century Parisian gossip in English is Frances Mossiker's *Madame de Sévigné. A Life and Letters* (1983), a volume which enjoys the additional advantage of being a pleasure to hold in one's hands, thanks to the traditional high quality of Alfred A. Knopf's book productions.

The museum exhibits memorabilia of the witty Marquise in her former apartments, and artifacts related to the history of Paris from the 16th to the Belle Époque in the early 20th centuries. Essentially a museum of the history of Paris, the artifacts and the temporary exhibitions on special Parisian themes make this a temple of learning that is also quite interesting. For instance, the storage rooms hold over 100,000 photographs ranging in date from the earliest days of photography to yesterday; that is to say the collection contains images from 150 years of Parisian history, all of which are fascinating, and some of which may be on display during your visit. The Museum bookstore contains what may be the largest selection of works about the city in the city - well worth a lengthy browse, but calculate the exchange rate carefully.

In reading Mme. de Sévigné's letters one is likely to come across several caustic references to one Ninon de l'Enclos, a woman noted for her literary salon and her love affairs, the last one of which she conducted when she reached the age of eighty! Ninon lived for many years in the Rue des Tournelles just east of the Place des Vosges, on the other side of the Place from Mme. de Sévigné. And what does all this have to do with anything? Before the great letter writer moved into the Hôtel Carnavalet, that is before her husband's death, that worthy gentleman, and their son, both, conducted love affairs with the charming, and amazing, Ninon. The husband squandered a great deal of his wife's money on his mistress, which endeared neither one to Madame, although those circles in those days did not consider such affairs quite as shocking as did those in later times. Nonetheless, n'est-çe pas....

Mme. de Sévigné could not disguise a certain admiration for her erstwhile rival. "In spite of her wit, which I will certainly admit is admirable, the thread of insolence that runs through Ninon's conversation is well nigh insufferable." Nicely put. An example of this wit is shown in the following story. For some reason Ninon at one point so scandalized the Queen Mother that the latter had a lettre de cachet issued ordering the former to withdraw to a religious order, but did not specify which one. Ninon is alleged to have said to the officer who delivered the letter: "Well, since the Queen has been so kind as to leave the choice of the order to me, please inform her that I will enter the monastery of the Franciscan monks in Paris." The Queen so appreciated humor of the response that she thereafter left Ninon to her own devices, which the charmer clearly manipulated to her own great advantage.

Although the **Bibliotèque historique de la Ville de Paris** (Historical Library of the City of Paris) is in the 4th, one can more appropriately discuss it in relation to the Carnavalet with which it has its subject matter in common. Indeed, the Hôtel de Lamoignon, which houses the Library, is across the street from the Carnavalet, but that street, Rue des Francs Bourgois, constitutes the border between the 3rd and the 4th. Viewed from a different point of geography, the Library is at the eastern end of the Rue des Rosiers where it abuts the Rue Mahler.

The Library's facade, bookstore and basement exhibition spaces appear to have been recently renovated, and the green *Guide Michelin* tells us that the painted ceiling in the reading room covers "one of the finest" such rooms in Paris. The monarchy founded the Library in 1763 and a republican city government installed it in the present location in 1968. We can tell you that the exhibitions are usually worth visiting; we saw a fine show of photographs by a Frenchman well into The Third Age who lives in the United States. We would have talked to him, since he was there for several days after the vernissage (the opening reception of an exhibition), but two well-dressed, self-possessed, very thin Americans dominated his attention with conversation about emulsion, angle of view and deepfocus lighting. Tant pis. We purchased a remaindered catalog of a photograph show from 1983 called "Paris 1950: Photographie par les Groupe des XV," which contains several memorable images of the city from that transitional time as the French advanced (despite Lionel Abel's kvetching) beyond the austerity of the immediate postwar years into a period of relative comfort. In any event, find out about the current temporary exhibition, and go to see the ceiling.

4th ARRONDISEMENT

There are several restaurants and cafés under the arcades around the edges of the **Place des Vosges,** a square that you should definitely visit. This is one of the most beautiful small urban parks in any city, *and* visiting the Place gives you the opportunity to wander around in the silverware store on Rue des Francs Bourgeois, which sells everything imaginable in silver and pewter, except, alas, the heavy elegant-handled knives for which we've searched for years.

The green *Guide Michelin* (1985) laconically notes about the Place des Vosges: "From 1800 it took the name of Place des Vosges after the Vosges department." One might wonder why. The 1990 green Michelin attempts to answer that question by suggesting the idea that the Vosges region paid its taxes to the central government before any other region, but when this is supposed to have occurred is unclear.

Guides in translation are often the source of unintentional amusement. The 1985 Michelin devotes a few lines to describing the Rue Saint-Antoine, a short block south of the Place des Vosges, as the focal point of celebrations and fêtes in the 16th century, noting that in 1559 during a joust on that street, the captain of the King's Scottish Guard, Gabriel de Lorges de Montgomery by name, accidentally delivered a "fatal blow" to Henri II's eye. Then, we are told, "Montgomery fled but was executed in 1574."

59

The fact is, as Victor Hugo so concisely put it, "C'est le coup de lance de Montgomery qui a crée la Place des Vosges." Indeed, the unfortunate captain did not wish to participate in the third joust of the day against the monarch, but Henri, having won the first two, demanded another match, during which Montgomery's lance unintentionally penetrated the royal cranium through the royal eye. The king required ten days of agony to die, during which time he apparently forgave his guard's captain for the accident, whereupon the cautious Montgomery slipped away to England and converted to Protestantism of some sort. Now, as Peter de Polnay notes in his entertaining book *Paris. An Urbane Guide to the City and its People* (1968), a Valois (Henri's family name) may forgive, but a Medici neither forgives nor forgets. The royal widow, Catherine de Medicis, waited for vengeance with the patience of an Italian dagger, and she got it. For reasons unknown to me, Montgomery lost his caution and returned to France after 15 years, whereupon Catherine's minions captured him and brought him to Paris. A royal court sentenced him to death, ordered him to be tortured, and, finally, carted in a tumbril to the Place de Grève and executed.

Henri's widow also had her son, Charles IX, destroy the royal palace of Tournelles located on the Rue Saint Antoine, although François I had moved the actual residence to the Louvre in 1527, and the neighborhood deteriorated gradually to the level of horse market cum rogues and other social misfits by the beginning of the 17th century.

Royal and plebian city governments alike have changed the character of the park over the centuries, but its nature as a haven from the hurly-burly of urban stress and speed has remained since 1605, when Henri IV commanded the construction of a "place Royale" for his capital city, which he wished to make the center of not only the young French nation, but the entire civilized world. Alas, as if often the case in human society, regardless of time in history, Henri did not live to see his idea expressed in the material world: a disgruntled fellow named Ravaillac assassinated the king two years before the completion of the square in 1612. If only Henri had paid more attention to plans for widening the city's streets, perhaps he would not have been caught in the early 17th century form of a traffic jam in the Rue de la Ferronnerie (near Les Halles), where his carriage slowed down sufficiently for the assassin to reach into the coach and plunge a stolen carving knife into the chest of the king, who sat engrossed in state papers, his mind elsewhere.

To be sure, if you listen intently enough under the arcades that border the Place des Vosges on its four sides, you may hear the faint clicking of steel against steel and the muffled grunts of the swordsmen seeking or giving absolution for an insult to one another's amour propre or size of the other's bank account. Gentlemen carried out their duels in defiance of Richelieu's ban on such aristocratic activities: did he believe the aristos to be killing each other off at such a rate that an inadequate number of them would remain to protect the royal family (and his as well)? In any case, with Henri IV dead, the young Louis XIII inaugurated the square which then became a true "place royale" and Louis' equestrian statue in the middle of the park testifies not only to the fact that the park opened during his reign, but also to its popularity as a center of entertainment, fine houses, and royal patronage. The Revolutionists called it Place de l'Indivisibilité during their brief and bloody years in power.

Indeed, what makes it so attractive to the educated and conservative eye today is its euphonic wholeness: the harmonious gradations in red brick and blue slate of the buildings quartering the square, each a mirror of its neighbor, leading to the perception, not of boredom, but of well-being, at-oneness with the universe, however briefly, before the racket-grinding of a diesel-motor delivery truck or the flare of a motorcar horn cracks the fragile shell of perception and allows another less pleasant reality to break into one's consciousness.

Many have wished to live here; a few have arranged to do so. In 1924, for example, Georges Simenon, then publicly known as Sim, and his wife, Tigy, moved into a two-room apartment on the ground floor of the hôtel particulier once owned by Richelieu, wherein the young couple indulged in various forms of social experimentation, many of which bourgeois society frowns upon. They gave up the apartment in 1931 in order to move to the countryside where the temptations would be narrower of scope if no less intense, given Georges' peculiarly constant sexual requirements.

Clearly, certain places lend themselves to the human experience of various forms of transcendence, like a dose of LSD assists in achieving a vision one would otherwise not be able to see, but no doubt less harmful to one's health. This square is one of them.

On the southwestern edge of the Place you will find the **Musée Victor Hugo**, variously listed at the Rue de Birague or 6 Place des Vosges, closed Mondays and jours des fêtes. When asked about the identity of the greatest French poet, André Gide, a great admirer of Simenon's literary works, answered, "Victor Hugo, hêlas."

It is not clear to me exactly why Gide uttered this so typically snotty French-intellectual's remark about Hugo. After all, he could have reasonably mentioned Valéry without the "hêlas" if he had to limit himself to considering "classic" French poets. Gide would hardly have mentioned Rimbaud, Mallarmé, Verlaine, or Baudelaire (too disgustingly decadent), Claudel (too Catholic and a personal enemy), Péguy (too obsessed with religion), Frédéric Mistral (too provincial, who can read Provençal?), but he might have thought of Eluard or Apollinaire (perhaps too "modern" and of the wrong political coloration), or René Char (though Char did his greatest work after 1945). Despite his public taste in poets, Gide has attributed to him one of the more lucid deathbed final statements: "If anyone asks me a question, make sure I am conscious before you let me reply." Certainly a more cogent expression than Dutch Schulz managed.

The French also treat certain writers after death, that is to say regarding burial rites, with the pomp and circumstances other countries reserve for their politicians and soldiers, few of who received funerals of the magnitude of those given to Hugo, Anatole France, or Jean-Paul Sartre. On the other hand, there are distinct similarities between the funereal falderal of Edith Piaf and Rudolph Valentino.

Death and theology, being ineluctable in human existence and discourse, inevitably obtrude into life and the admixture results in innumerable anecdotes, particularly when considering Parisians. On a cold February day in 1894, in a small hotel off the Boulevard Haussmann, the grande horizontale, Léonide Leblanc, former mistress of Louis Tiffany, the American designer of interior illumination devices, ended her life, alone except for the company of a nun, a ubiquitous character in this genre of story. The nun promptly reported a deathbed reconciliation between the celebrated whore and (presumably the Roman Catholic) god. Upon hearing this story, Gide, an open homosexual who sired a child not with his wife but with the daughter of a Belgian painter friend, is reported to have remarked: "Why not? God is a man." Which may tell us as much about Christianity as André Gide.

Speaking of les grandes horizontales, in the late 19th century some enterprising businessman, or businesswoman, published a book, so typically Parisian that it would hardly be printed anywhere else in the world except Hamburg in the 1920s or Bangkok anytime, entitled *Les Jolies Femmes de Paris*, a veritable directory of courtesans and whores with appropriately descriptive paragraphs devoted to each entry.

In any case, the Hugo Museum is really of interest only to confirmed Hugoistes or those profoundly curious about his visage and the alterations to it made by the aging process, his own drawings and paintings, and various artists' illustrations to his books *Les Miserables* and *Nôtre Dame de Paris* (known in English-language cultures as *The Hunchback of Notre Dame*). The apartment is large and consists of four floors, so do not venture there if your legs are tired.

Several other interesting people lived in various "hôtels particulières" around the square, including Marion de Lorme, Cardinal Richelieu's mistress (as you walk under the arcades evoke the image of the churchman wrapped tightly in his cloak stealthily slipping into Marion's doorway); the writer, Bishop Boussuet; and the old rascal Richelieu himself. On February 5, 1626, Marie de Rabutin-Chantal came into this world in the Hôtel de Coulange; we remember her today under her more familiar married name, de Sévigné.

The great tragédienne Rachel spent her final years at number thirteen: the daughter of a poor Jewish peddler, she sang with her sister in the streets of the city after they moved there from the provinces in the late 1820s. Seven years later she began acting at the Théâtre Français and entered theatrical history as the first real international star of the stage.

D'Artagnan paid visits to the sexy Joan Crawford of her time, Miladi, at number six. The Place is also the scene where d'Artagnan and his three pals meet again in a later book.[6] Alphonse Daudet and Théophile Gautier lived for a while at number eight. The de Goncourt brothers described the latter's apartment as "a jumble of odds and ends, like the rooms of an elderly retired actress who has only become possessed of pictures on the bankruptcy of her

Italian manager." Which, if nothing else, should pique one's curiosity to read the famous brothers' famous diary.

By the way, a "hôtel particulière" is not to be confused with a hotel where travelers stay for short period of time. When you see the word "Hôtel" engraved on the stone lintel of a large, old building, it means the edifice was at one time the family mansion of a well-to-do aristocrat or later a well-to-do bourgeois. If you think the French superciliously cruel to have one word with two relatively different meanings, think of how many things are described by the English word "trunk."

To the west of the Place des Vosges, the magnificent mayor's office called the Hôtel de Ville and the wide-open space before it is worth a walk. As the name of the quarter implies (le marais means the swamp), the official residence of the city's ruling mayor was built (1873-82) on what had once been a rather unstable foundation. It is not too far from the **Centre Georges Pompidou**, which, I suppose, you should see because the permanent collection of the Musée Nationale d'Art Moderne is worth viewing and, occasionally, there is a temporary exhibition of value and pleasure. The Gaullist politician Georges Pompidou had little to do with the erection of this aberration, which is also known as the Beaubourg from its location, and much has been written about it, the reason for which you will grasp when you see the thing.

According to this museum's collections, for some twisted, no doubt chauvinistic reason, American art begins with Jackson Pollock in the post-1944 period. The irony, and a reverse twist, is that with the advent of Pollock and his abstract expressionist associates and the 1939-1945 chapter of the Great 20th Century Atrocity, Paris lost its position as chief locus of the international art scene, which, powered by the amorphous and mysterious process similar to the shifting of a locust swarm, moved to New York City. But, then, the French think Jerry Lewis is a great film artist.

The bookstore in the Pompidou is good, but expensive unless there's a reduced-price sale, and the building complex does contain a library and other things of vague cultural interest to some, such as the Industrial Design Center, a film library, and the underground Institute for Acoustic and Musical Research. The architectural style called "Guts-Up-Front" started with the construction of this building, which has recently undergone an expensive restoration. The square in front of the Centre is jammed with tourists, and smelly colorful young people performing for, and smelly drunks of all ages begging from, the tourists.

Le Marais also contains a good part of the Jewish section of the city including the **Centre de Documentation Juive Contemporaine** which houses a library, an archive, a museum, and the Holocaust memorial (17, rue Geoffroy L'Asnier). Do not confuse this with the mildly elaborate memorial to the French deported during the period 1940-1944 on the eastern tip of the Ile de la Cité, which is not specifically Jewish, but memorializes all French deportees, without mentioning French officials' contribution to the deportations, of course.

The **Charcuterie Restaurant Goldenberg** (a.k.a. Goldenberg's deli) at 7, rue des Rosiers, the street known for hundreds of years as the Rue des Juifs (street of the Jews), is reputed to make the best cheesecake in the city and the best chopped chicken liver in the world. While I have not sampled the former, I can attest to the fact that the chopped chicken liver mixture is one of the best I've ever eaten. The menu contains at least one "ethnic" dish, Jewish or not, from all the eastern European countries as well as traditional Jewish food. It also contains a bar with numerous brands of vodka to be drunk cold and straight accompanied by fresh black bread, unsalted butter and, if you are flush, caviar. The wine list is more than adequate and you could meet a school friend from Hoboken you've not seen in 30 years sitting at the next table, which is to say practically in your lap.

The restaurant announces itself in the Paris yellow pages as "Delicatessen store lunch for kleine or groysse fresser," which is to say for small or large appetites or, more accurately translated, for small or large chowdowners. The verb "fressen" means to consume with vehemence, "fresser" is the noun denoting the one engaged in such fressen, but fresser also means mouth, which adds another layer of extrapolation possibilities to the discourse.

Mr. and Mrs. Goldenberg survived Buchenwald and migrated to Paris where they opened the original restaurant just across the street from the present establishment, which is now run by their son. There is an expressive photograph of Mr. Goldenberg senior standing in the doorway of the first restaurant in Sanford Roth's wonderful picture book, *Paris in the Fifties* (1988).

A few years ago, on August 9, 1982, to be exact, some misguided and undoubtedly insane terrorists, swollen with ignorance and hatred, shot up the restaurant, no doubt under the misapprehension that the world's leaders gather at Goldenberg to decide upon new methods to persecute the misbegotten killers' particular ethnic or religious cohorts. These fanatics did not shoot any world leaders, but did murder two customers, an assistant cook, and the longtime Polish cashier. Several of the bullet holes and shattered glass in the front window remain preserved as reminders of the stupidity of this kind of reaction to other kinds of human stupidity.

Use your green *Guide Michelin* and walk around the quarter; there are some amazing sites and a couple of richly stocked if cramped bookstores of various political persuasions. But food may be your main reason for ambling about. Indeed, the Rue des Rosiers is filled with food stores, now not only Jewish but vaguely middle eastern and North African as well, which specialize in

67

grilled meats on skewers. In 1980 we ate a thoroughly satisfactory couscous meal with a surprisingly light, palatable Tunisian red wine, served by a team of North African waiters who insisted on speaking German the moment they heard us speaking English. The small, crowded room then called itself Chez Léon, but by now it probably has a different name or has been transformed into a frozen food store.

Cross over the river to the Left Bank by way of the **Île Saint Louis**, which has its own history you can read about in any detailed city guide and well worth your while walking about on. If you can find a copy, and if you can read French, see Paul Guilly's fat tome, *Découverte de L'île Saint-Louis* (1955), which will provide you with 500 pages of information about the island.

We once stopped for a drink at a tiny corner bar on the island's main street, probably because one of us had to pee, and girded up the gumption to ask the bartender if we could buy the curiously angled water carafe with the Ricard label on it. He delved into his storage cabinet and presented us with a bottle of Ricard pastis. Mais non, monsieur, la bouteille d'eau avec le nom Ricard, pas une bouteille *de* Ricard. And so on. Actually, the whole issue became rather heated as some of the bar's other patrons joined in the fun of trying to figure out what these two obviously foreign goons wanted. Not that our French was all that bad, no. The crux of the matter was the incomprehensibility of our request! Finally, the frazzled bartender reached into his mini-dishwasher and pulled out a water carafe with the Ricard name on it and thrust it at us, free, gratis, pas d'argent, just leave me in peace. Now the story about how we obtained our two Ricard glasses to match our Ricard carafe took place not in Paris, but in Menton on the Riviera near the Italian border, so does not properly belong here.

Walk around the Quai d'Anjou, full of attractive old buildings you feel confident you could comfortably live in if only you could discover a way to make enough money to pay the rent, and stop at number 29. In October 1922, William Bird opened **Three Mountains Press** in the lower level former wine storage space. The Press, named after the three Paris hills of Montmartre, Mont Sainte-Geneviève and Montparnasse, published a number of small poetry and prose volumes by American and British authors, many totally unknown at the time, under Ezra Pound's erratic but brilliant editorial hand. Bird also printed several books put out by Robert McAlmon's Contact Publishing Company.

In 1928 Bird sold his huge Belgian Mathieu press to Nancy Cunard, who moved it to Réanville some 50 miles from Paris, where she published slim volumes under the Hour's Press imprint. In her sketches published under the title, *These Were the Hours. Memoirs of My Hours Press. Réanville and Paris 1928-1931* (1969), Miss Cunard writes well and interestingly about the books she published including Samuel Beckett's *Whoroscope* (1930), Henry Chowder's *Henry-Music* (1930), which set poems by Beckett, Richard Aldington, and others to syncopated scores, and the monumental anthology, *Negro* (1934), whose publication drove the Hours Press into bankruptcy.

Should you ever discover inexpensive copies of any volumes by these publishers, buy them for they are truly collectors' items. Ford Madox Ford edited the short-lived but important *Transatlantic Review* from a tiny gallery space in Bird's printing shop, copies of which also qualify as rare in the trade. Ford described the place as a "great wine vault on the banks of the Seine" and it is regretable that the building one sees there today is not the structure in which Bird, Ford and their colleagues worked and played. Apparently that edifice suffered a similar fate as all too many older places: some barbarian tore it down and replaced it with the present inoffensive and no doubt very expensive but rather bland apartment building.

On the corner of the Rue des Deux Ponts and the Quai d'Orléans at the foot, or head, of the Pont de la Tournelle, at 6, Quai d'Orléans to be exact, sits a flat-faced building of no particular character. Ah, but never judge a building by its facade, unless one is interested in architecture, of course. In this case, one is interested in the (European) second floor which houses the **Musée d'Adam Mickiewicz**, if one is interested in Adam Mickiewicz at all, he being the Polish national poet; that is, he would be if the Poles had a national poet, although there is some debate amongst Poles as to whether or not he should be the national poet, but this internecine wrangling need not concern us here. What might concern the interested Reader is the fact that Mickiewicz lived here in exile during a period in which Poland did not exist as a national entity, having been divided up like so much kielbasa sausage amongst the Prussian, Russian and Austrian monarchies, whose occupation bureaucrats found the poet's versified appeals to national sentiment to be subversive of their jobs, as indeed they were. So, if the Reader is, in fact, interested, let her be forewarned and be prepared to satisfy this interest on Thursday afternoons between 15 and 18 o'clock.

An American academic has figured out that, during Mickiewicz's time, between 1830 and 1848, the list of prominent "foreign intellectuals" in Paris included five Russians, two Italians, 16 Germans, three Americans, six Poles, two Englishmen, and one Hungarian, the latter being Franz Liszt!

A few doors down the Quai d'Orléans, at number 10, you will find the building in which the American writer James Jones, author of the classic *From Here to Eternity* (1951), and *The Thin Red Line* (1962), in addition to other more forgettable novels, and his family lived for more than a decade in the 1960s and early 1970s. The Jones'

70

generosity with their home, time and money is famous as are the parties they gave for friends and visiting cultural figures.

When you cross the Seine to the Left Bank from L'île Saint-Louis by way of the Pont de la Tournelle, you will undoubtedly note the numerous merchants called **bouquinistes** who sell books (not called bouquins, except informally, or as the Collins-Robert Dictionary informs us "in a relaxed situation") from small tin and wood bookstalls lining the riverside above the quais. The first bouquinistes set up shop in 1614 on the Pont Neuf, the oldest bridge in the city, at a time when inner-city bridges held kiosks and shops, much as the Ponto Vecchio (Florence) and the Ponto Rialto (Venice) still do.

In 1936, John Paynter noted the "the small stalls presided over for the most part by decrepit old ladies, and offering all sorts of wares from books, pictures and engravings to household wares and utensils. The most popular were the stalls selling old prints of early Parisian days, books and engravings, cellophane-wrapped paper novels of decidedly inflammable temperature." The "old ladies," decrepit or not, have generally disappeared, you cannot purchase eggbeaters and toasters in the stalls, and the perception of a publication's temperature changes from one generation to the next, but Mr. Paynter has got the essentials right.

Today, of course, motorcars, tourist buses and trucks infest the city's bridges. Nonetheless, take some time and peruse the stalls; one can still on occasion find a bargain, and some of the posters and postal cards are very funny and, if you are in luck, risqué (a passel of lovely round bottoms, some even meeting the Olympian standards of Romy Schneider and Rosanna Arquette; curiously, there never seem to be any male bottoms...). Indeed, not too long ago, we found an old German-language edition of *Ulysses* for 20 francs. The bouquinistes do, one must admit, stock a lot of expensive crap, but so what? You don't have to buy the junk, and the bookstalls are a traditional part of Paris, a very traditional city.

Alexandre Dumas père somewhere in his obiter dicta has an apropos paragraph for this subject. "Bibliomanic, evolved from book and mania, is a variety of the species man - species bipes et genus homo. This animal has two feet and is without features, and usually wanders about the quais and boulevards, stopping in front of every stall and fingering all the books. He is generally dressed in a coat, which is too long and trousers which are too short, his shoes are always down at the heel, and on his head is an misshapen hat. One of the signs by which he may be recognized is shown by the fact that he never washes his hands." Cleanliness may be next to godliness in some christian sects, but bibliomanes treasure their own set of deities for whom clean hands are irrelevant. Not that we worship dirty hands, as some of Sartre's more fanatical acolytes might, but bookdust comes with the territory, so to speak. You may be fairly sure you have a bibliomane in your eyesight when you see him plunge his nose into the crevice of an open old book and inhale deeply.

5th ARRONDISEMENT

Le Jardin Tino Rossi, 73 – George Whitman and the Reincarnated Shakespeare and Company, 73 – La Place de la Contrescarpe, 76 – L'Hôtel Grands Hommes, 77 – Le Panthéon, 78 – Le Musée Cluny, 80 – Les Pommes Frites, 84

Standing on the Pont de la Tournelle, if you look to the left down (or is it up?) the Seine, you will see the beginning of the **Jardin Tino Rossi** as it curves southeast along the river bank. Not many colorful plants (despite the park's name) or greenleaved trees bloom here (cross the Quai Saint Bernard to the Jardin des Plantes for plants and trees); rather this is the sparsely populated open air garden for angular, modern (or is it postmodern?) sculpture, which, I suppose, must have somewhere to stand in a city like Paris. What Tino Rossi has to do with avant-garde sculpture is anyone's guess. Generations of French from the 1920s to the 1940s made Rossi an extraordinarily popular singer, music hall performer and movie star, whose closeness to the Germans during the occupation caused him trouble after the liberation. Indeed, he served a short time in Fresnes prison, along with Albert Blaser (the headwaiter at Maxim's), Sacha Guitry, and other far more serious collaborators. The mixture of Rossi and abstract sculpture is incongruous, but typically Parisian.

Speaking of books, facing Nôtre Dame sits the latest incarnation of **Shakespeare and Company**, at 37, rue de la Bucherie, which you may want to see just to say you've seen it. After you reach the left bank from the Pont de la Tournelle, walk to the right along the river until you reach the most famous church in Paris. Look over your left shoulder and you will see the store, a shabby shadow of the famed Sylvia Beach establishment of the same name on

Rue de l'Odéon during the 1920s and 1930s. In the present store one can still find inexpensive English-language paperbacks among the more outrageously expensive stuff.

The American owner, George Whitman, who claims a familial bond with Walt and a spiritual bond with Miss Beach, was forced some years ago to obtain French citizenship in order to maintain his ownership of the store -- or so the story goes. Mr. Whitman arrived in France in 1946 to work as a volunteer in a resettlement camp for orphans; by the Spring of 1948, having desultorily attended GI-Bill-paid classes, he began a lending library in his room at the Hôtel de Suez at 3, boulevard St-Michel.[7]

By the Spring of 1949, with no space left for books, which Mr. Whitman bought cheap at the Sorbonne (I'm not sure what this means, but one of my sources insists it is so), he opened a shop in the Boulevard de Courselles at the Paris City Club (no, I don't know what this is either) called the Librarie Franco-Americaine. Unexpected success forced a move to larger quarters and, using an inheritance, he bought the current establishment in 1951. Before this it had the building housed an Arab grocery store.

Mr. Whitman originally called the store Librarie Mistral and, with the dynamic energy of a O'Neillian powerhouse, he forwarded the fortunes of expatriate English language writers in Paris through readings and book signings, and, of course, selling their works when they got them published.

In the mid-1950s and the decade that followed, this store and its upstairs couches served as a stopping-off point for a number of American writers often described as "beatniks" by such publications as *Time*, known to others of a different mentality as the "beats." Lawrence Durrell (by no means a "beatnik," but occasionally somewhat "beat") stopped in occasionally and at least once someone took his photograph on the premises with George Whitman. It was thumb tacked to the wall the last time we were there.

74

Indeed, the last time we were there a broken water pipe had caused the owner's youthful employees to dig a magnificent hole in the middle of the main downstairs salesroom over which customers and others had to crawl or stumble (or was this the famous "wishing well," out of which bubbles of some sort of gas would ascend and burst into flame during poetry readings?). And a year later, on July 18, 1990, to be exact, the upstairs library of precious books burned out, cause unspecified. Never a dull moment. In 1964, Mr. Whitman changed the name of the store to honor Sylvia Beach, who died in October 1962. (See below for more on Miss Beach and the original Shakespeare and Company.)

George Whitman, now beyond "a certain age" and having entered The Third Age, floats ethereally through the store, frail and thin, a whispery Mistral mustache and goatee now totally white (O, Buffalo Bill!), having apparently reached nirvana, a level of consciousness which allows one to face adversity with equanimity, but not indifference. All praise and glory to you, Mr. Whitman; I hope you stay with us long enough to read these lines, and beyond!

If you do not wish to see Mr. Whitman's store, keep walking straight off the bridge up the Rue du Cardinal Lemoine until you reach the Place de la Contrescarpe. Do not pass up this opportunity to buy a baguette ("when in doubt, buy a baguette," we always say) at the Lerch bakery (4, rue du Cardinal Lemoine); this is a classic baguette, nothing nouvelle or postmodern about it: crisp and flaky outside, airy inside. Any bread that can be described as "chewy" is not a real baguette, no matter who tells you otherwise. If you have gone to the store, walk south to the Place Maubert, then up the Rue Monge to the Rue du Cardinal Lemoine where you make a right turn and amble on to the Place de la Contrescarpe.

The two or three bistros on the **Place de la Contrescarpe** (names forgotten, if ever known, but one can't miss them) are fine locations to relax the feet and take a coffee or drink a beer in the afternoon. The Place is no longer that described by Hemingway and others; for one thing there are fewer clochards and circus animals performing for the tourists except during the high summer season. Indeed, the center of the square is now a small cement and grass combination effectively cutting off human use except as a walkaround.

On the front wall of the building on the square's west side, you may still be able to decipher the faded Au Negre Joyeux sign, the only indication that the structure housed a dancehall in times gone by, much like the one nearby in which Ford Madox Ford held his weekly tea-dances until they became so popular that things went awry, as did so much in Mr. Ford's life.

Just around the corner from the Place de la Contrescarpe, at 74, rue du Cardinal Lemoine, you stand before the building containing Hadley and Ernest Hemingway's first Paris apartment (fourth-floor walkup, no heat, malodorous toilet on the stairwell landing, and a noisy dance-bar on the ground floor), a fact blatantly proclaimed by a large wall plaque which, alas, repeats the misleading business about being poor and young but happy in Paris from *A Moveable Feast*. Further up the street at 71, you see the building in which Valéry Larbaud, whose work is sadly neglected today, had an apartment he lent for the summer of 1920 to the ever poverty-stricken James Joyce family recently arrived from Trieste, having spent the war years in Zürich.

The Rue Mouffetard south of the square is the scene of one of the more varied street markets in Paris, considered these days by "those-in-the-know" as tame and bourgeois; these folks prefer the street market in the 10th arrondissement along the Rue du Faubourg St. Denis, where they find a more intense, ahem, "ethnic flavor." Curiously, in the early 1970s, the Rue Mouffetard was known for the availability of information leaflets on contraception. Or perhaps not so curiously, given the residual effect of Madame de Gaulle's efforts to promote a higher birthrate for the country. Why, she even forced the closing of the legal brothels. Holy blue!

Just north of the Place de la Contrescarpe, at number 39, rue Descartes, is the house in which the poet Verlaine is alleged to have died, a small plaque on the wall attests to this, and on the top floor of which Hemingway alleges that he rented a small room with a view in which to write. Alas, this "fact" appears in his notoriously mendacious *A Moveable Feast* and no corroborative evidence has been located anywhere; it makes a good story though, like the one about catching pigeons in the Jardin du Luxembourg and, after wringing their necks, stuffing the warm corpses in Bumby's baby carriage to take home for dinner because they were so poor, but so happy in Paris, which is, after all, a circumnavigating repas! N'est-çe pas? To compound the fallacies, someone, perhaps the building's owner but certainly not city officials, has screwed an additional small plaque onto the facade stating in English "Ernest Hemingway lived in this building from 1921 to 1925." This is, of course, a flagrant abuse of the truth for commercial gain: the plaque is situated at the entrance to a restaurant on the building's ground floor.

In case you are somewhat confused geographically, the same street north of the Place de la Contrescarpe is called Rue Descartes, south of the Place it is named Rue Mouffetard. Actually, Descartes never lived on the Rue Descartes. He once lived briefly in the nearby Rue Rollin (at number 14, to be exact). So much for Cartesian logic.

In October 1985, when the franc stood to attention at ten to the dollar, we stayed in the top-floor suite of the **Hôtel Grands Hommes**, 17 Place du Panthéon, for $50 a night with a large color TV, on which to watch a lively if illogical Alain Delon adventure film whilst we enjoyed a varied dinner of ready-mades and wine purchased in the neighborhood charcuterie (a glorified deli selling already prepared foods and wine), a tiny balcony overlooking the Panthéon to stand on after dinner and very large bathing facilities.

Recently whoever is in charge of memorial wall plaques in the city added one to the facade of the hotel stating that André Breton and Philippe Soupault founded surrealism there in 1919-1920 during which time they wrote the automatic texts published as *Les Champs magnétiques* (The Magnetic Fields) in 1920. Since surrealism did not officially come into existence until 1924, the plaque-makers perhaps mean the dadist movement, though Tristan Tzara "founded" this in Zürich in 1917. Perhaps indeed they mean to say that the roots of surrealism are in part located in these lightly edited "automatic" writings, ideally created by jotting down whatever comes into the writer's head, which Breton and his colleagues believed thus expressed the unconscious mind without the mediating filter of the process of thought. Thus the human mind would construct not art, but a deeper reality. Contrary to its present splendid accommodations, when Breton lived there the hotel resembled a flophouse flea residence, though Breton kept his room squeaky clean and the name, of course, refers to those buried in the edifice across the street.

When you prefer to eat in your hotel room, but are tired of sandwiches, a charcuterie will supply all your needs except bread, for which you must visit a bakery (boulangerie), and eating utensils, which you must supply yourself. A relatively complex Swiss army knife is very useful to have with you on all occasions.

According to John Lemprière in his *Classical Dictionary* (1788), the **Panthéon** was a "celebrated temple at Rome, built by Agrippa, in the reign of Augustus and dedicated to all the gods. It was struck with lightning sometime after, and partly destroyed. Hadrian repaired it, and it still remains at Rome, converted into a Christian temple, the admiration of the curious." The Panthéon at Rome is a magnificent structure to this day; now a secular tourist attraction, its religious significance lost, it stands as a temple for tourist money and architecture fans.

The Paris version is also an impressive structure. The monarchy's officials laid the foundations in 1758, but financial problems obstructed the completion until 1789, when it opened briefly as a place of religious worship. Not an auspicious year for such projects. The Revolution changed it into a place of cultural worship and placed the bodies of those "who died for French liberty" in the building. During the 19th century various French governments switched the structure back and forth between sanctified and secular uses and it is now called a "lay temple," whatever that means, containing the tombs of Voltaire, Rousseau, Victor Hugo, Louis Braille (yes, he did invent it), Émile Zola, Jean Jaurès, André Malraux, and others, and a memorial to Antoine de Saint-Exupéry, the author of *Le petit Prince* and other books, whose small airplane disappeared over the southern French coast whilst on a mysterious mission during the war.

Some interesting murals by Puvis de Chavannes decorate the walls of the ground-level interior. Interestingly, Janet Flanner, in one of her 1927 Genêt *New Yorker* columns, collected in the compendium *Paris Was Yesterday 1925-1939* (1972), noted that there "is little danger that Zola's ashes will be transferred to the Panthéon...," which shows how dangerous it is to make judgments about cultural morality, that would-be eternally stable structure which changes with each generation's discovery of itself. This is also an example of what happens when a writer does not adequately check her facts: Zola's remains had been moved to the Panthéon on June 4,

79

1908. And *The New Yorker*, in those days, prided itself on its "fact-checking" procedures.

The official address of the **Musée Cluny** seems to be 6 Place Paul-Painlevé, but you will be better advised to look for it at the intersection of the Boulevard Saint Michel and the Boulevard St-Germain. When you are finished being edified in the Panthéon, walk west on Rue Soufflot (named after the man who designed the "lay temple" discussed above) to the Place Edmond Rostand (Cyrano's creator), which you cross and sit at a sidewalk café table for a coffee and a quiet read of *Libération* or the *International Herald Tribune* (affectionately known as the "Paris Trib" by those who can afford it).

This vantage point also allows you to observe the to-and-froing of pedestrian traffic in and out of the Jardin du Luxembourg, an activity requiring very little expenditure of energy and one that we highly recommend. A few steps down the street will place you in front of a store offering everything you could ever want relating to movies. If you are looking at the map, this puts you just off the Place on the Rue de Médicis.

One of the more transcendent moments in any city is that hiatus during which one experiences a rainy, windswept open square on a dark, lowering evening when the lights glisten brokenly on the puddled asphalt and no one crosses the square with or against the lonesome red traffic light, which in any case will change to green before you can raise your arm to warn the pedestrian not to attempt that dangerously skiddish crossing. This is a fine moment to remember Ezra Pound's brief imagist poem, "In a Station of the Métro":

> The apparition of these faces in the crowd;
> Petals on a wet, black bough.

Sitting at one of the window tables inside the glass walls of this café, observing the wet and winddriven inclement elements, affords a sense of warm comfort and security without which it is impossible to speculate on the possibility of enjoying life in this city or face the end of life with equanimity.

After you've completed your observations and coffee or menthe sûr glace, walk around the corner and down the Boulevard Saint Michel until you reach the Boulevard Saint Germain. A block before you reach the intersection, your attention will be attracted by an array of bookstands, some of which display sale products on the street to tempt the wary collector of "gut buks," as the rabid Norwegian bibliophile in Verona described them. In order to avoid a depleted purse and overweight luggage, cross the street, and finally arrive at the Musée Cluny.

And, finally, after years of promising to visit this small complex of buildings and gardens, in the autumn of 1991 we entered its precincts.

Apparently constructed as a huge bathhouse at the beginning of the 3rd century of our time, the "barbarians" plundered and burned it down at the end of that century. By the 14th century, the Abbots of Cluny lived on the grounds after rebuilding the structures, and they remained in possession until the Revolution confiscated and sold it. A procession of owners did various silly things to the place, including burying the baths under two meters of dirt and a veg garden, until 1844 when the French state purchased and opened it as a museum, which it has remained until this very day, and into which you may venture for a sum of money that increases each year.

In addition to the gardens, which are interesting if you like gardens, and if not too much construction is underway, you can see the museum's tapestries, the now uncovered baths, a chapel, and what are called "decorative arts" of the Middle Ages. Actually, the collection is quite good, but

81

under-lighted and scantily labeled, as is the case in many French museums. The Cloisters in New York City is closer for Americans and has similar collections. However, the architecture and the recent renovations of the Cluny Museum, which combine the modern and the medieval, are well worth the entrance fee if you are in the neighborhood.

Out on the Boulevard Saint-Michel again, cross the Boulevard St-Germain at the intersection, walk to the right for the space of one building, make a sharp left and enter the quarter of the Saint-Severin church, narrow twisting streets, rarely illuminated by the sun, in which the North African inhabitants' pigmentation fades into that of a Norwegian who has not been to Spain in two years. In these dark but hardly sinister streets you will find a plethora of couscous and similar restaurants amongst the pizzerias, several of which we have eaten in, Levantine in cuisine with an overabundance of grilled meats. Interestingly, many of these restaurants display samples of their wares in florid meat arrangements in windows facing the street - no secrets to conceal. Another unusual phenomenon here is the presence of the owners and/or waiters in the doorways hawking the glories of the food to be masticated within. They are often successful and invariably cheerful.

One problem does present itself to the unwary in that these places are inevitably small and the tables are situated in such close proximity to one another that one must be prepared to enjoy one's neighbor's meal and conversation as well as one's own. Privacy is not a consideration here. This is not necessarily negative should one have been trained to taste the varied pleasures of communal life, if only briefly. On occasion one has the good luck to find a table somewhat isolated from the rest - in our case in the window on a raised platform beside the entrance where we were the focal point of the action without being unduly disturbed by the hurly-burly. Indeed, we thoroughly enjoyed ourselves.

Whilst we sat for two hours in this Mediterranean oasis, where the staff shouted equally accented French and English, we did not suffer the neglect of assorted darkly mustached, whiteteethed waiters, and the owner/manager showered Lynn-Marie with his lascivious, but not leering attention. This individual appeared to be plagued by a gravitational problem somewhat akin to vertigo of the nose, the major symptom of which was its propensity to fall into Lynn-Marie's décolletage whenever he passed our table on his way to harangue potential customers from the doorway. The problem seemed to have reached an advanced stage because, given the height of our platform, he had to jump three feet into the air to achieve a decent view of the splendor.

This is perhaps indicative of the social results of societies, which repress their sexual inadequacies and displace them into genital-crunching trousers, combined with an inability to accept the human body as anything other than a receptacle for the bitter solace of solitary satisfaction, especially if the body in question belongs to a foreign devil of an inferior religious heritage. One is forced to the conclusion that Paris, City of Light and fine food, might be somewhat poorer in the latter if the former French colonies had not ejaculated so much of their citizenry into the heartland to open restaurants in which they could not only serve western women with tasty morsels for their digestive tracts, but also offer them the spectacle of adult men behaving in a manner more appropriate to horny camels after an extended period of desert celibacy. Their eyes continually masturbate before the diner's opaque indifference. Reinforcement of the stereotype by the stereotypee, a syndrome insufficiently analyzed by Edward Said in his lengthy and somewhat repetitive, but fascinating if quirky book, *Orientalism* (1979). If Mr. Kurtz were writing this, he might hoarsely cry out "The irony, the irony!" So, again, *caveat emptor*.

One virtue of the kitchen these restaurants share with other eating places in Paris is the preparation and serving of **pommes frites**, known in the USA as French fries and in the Britain as chips. I don't know about the Britain, but the best place in the USA to find fried potatoes closest to real French fries is MacDonalds fast food emporium. No, this is not a joke. Who jokes about something as gravity-weighted as pommes frites?

The art of deepfrying small slices of potato has reached its apogee in Paris. This is not to say that it is impossible to find in this city an occasional bistro that serves soppy or overfried frites, but it would be difficult to find another city in which so many bistros serve so many plates of so many perfectly done "French fries." Indeed, one could be excused for the act of stopping in such a bistro for a glass of beer and a plate of lightly salted but otherwise unadorned pommes frites.

In the Rue Marbeuf a few meters off the Avenue des Champs Élysées sits a tiny, unpretentious bistro with a few tables on the sidewalk and a typical bistro interior (pinball machine, zinc bar, two elderly men drinking pastis and smoking Broyards, toilets downstairs in a closet). On a Sunday morning before joining the massed crowds of Parisians and tourists gathered to witness the start of the May 1980 Paris marathon, one could relish a late breakfast consisting of an omlette jambon et fromage, cold but not iced Alsacian beer, and a towering portion of frites at half the cost of the same thing on the famous avenue a few meters away.

The pommes frites come piled high upon a large round plate that covers a third of the small table's surface. In the first few minutes after their arrival they should remain dangerous to touch, but soon the heat diminishes to a degree that allows one to place a few of them between the fingers and transport them to one's wildly salivating mouth. The agony of anticipation is about to end! The teeth slowly penetrate the slightly hardened golden surface to reach the soft startlingly white interior. By the time the salt has reached the taste buds the automatic pommes-frites-in-Paris method of consumption replaces the slow, appreciative delectation, which in any case is more appropriate for tasting wine at the bishop's club, and one begins to gobble the little devils at an incredible rate of speed. Satisfaction guaranteed.

6th ARRONDISEMENT

Jules Amédée François Maigret, 86 – Le Procope, 89 – Richard Wright, James Baldwin, and Chester Himes, 90 – Rimbaud and the Former Grand Hôtel des Étrangers, 97 – L' Hôtel Saint-Pierre, 98 – Le Café de la Mairie, 100 – La Place Saint-Sulpice, 102 – La Méditerranée and Orson Welles, 103 – Sylvia Beach and the Original Shakespeare and Company, 104 – Adrienne Monnier and La Maison des Amis des Livres, 105 – Gertrude Stein and Alice B. Toklas, 112 – Le Jardin du Luxembourg, 116 – Le Musée Zadkine, 124 – Le Musée du Luxembourg, 124 – Le Café de Tournon, 126 – The Rue de Tournon and the Hôtel Foyot, 128 – The Village Voice Bookshop, 133 – Saint-Germain des Prés and Postwar Enthusiasms, 134 – Dora Maar's Head and Guillaume Apollinaire, 138 – Aus Deus Magots, Le Café Flore and La Brasserie Lipp, 141 – Natalie Clifford Barney, 144 – Le Musée Eugène Delacroix, 146 – L'École des Beaux-Arts, 147

This section and that on the 14th are the largest in the book and you will understand why as you read through it. These two arrondissements form the heart of *our* Paris, the quarter we know best and feel most at home in. Indeed, a rather peckish illness once forced me to spend five days in a hotel without ever leaving the 6th except for a brief excursion to the Musée Picasso across the river.

Stretching the boundaries of the 6th and the 14th a bit to include parts of the 5th and the 7th arrondissements, everything one could desire is here. Why go elsewhere? Well, maybe to hear Serge Reggiani at the Olympia in the 10th, or see the Manet retrospective at the Grand Palais in the 8th, or visit the Montmartre cemetery in the 18th, or lunching with Margaret Corman and Irène de Caumont-La

Force in the 17th, or.... Well, the city's public transportation system is a wonderfully efficient one.

Should you be walking along the Seine on the Quai des Grands Augustins between the Pont Neuf and the Pont Saint Michel, stop and gaze across the river at the Palais de Justice on the Ile de la Cité. Without much effort you can see in one of the upper floor windows the bulky figure of Chief Inspector **Jules Amadée François Maigret** of the homicide squad, fiercely incinerating tobacco in his large-bowled pipe or chomping on sandwiches washed down by glasses of beer sent up from the Bistro Dauphine below on the Place Dauphine, and you know that the coppers will get the miscreant whatever his, or her, station in life.

The Bistro Dauphine is most probably based on the Restaurant Paul, or its predecessors, a very popular eatery once patronized by the Simone Signoret-Yves Montand ménage when they lived on the Place Dauphine. The Place also contains a fine boules court, a necessary appendage considering Mr. Montand's great attraction to the game. The well-known Surrealist personality, André Breton, called the Place "the sex of Paris," the magic triangle between the thighs of the Seine, the veritable delta of Venus, which is in fact how one might describe the Place if viewed from above. Various authors in addition to Georges Simenon have described the Place in their work, such as Gérard de Nerval in *La Main de gloire*, Anatole France in *Les Dieux ont soif* (1912), Jacques Prévert in *Histoires* (1946), and Breton in *Nadja* (1928), but you should also read the epilogue to Signoret's *Nostalgia Isn't What It Used to Be* (1976) for a personal evocative description of the square and its atmosphere.

You may wish to know that, as you might expect in this regard, Maigret ate exceedingly well of sumptuous meals prepared by Madame Maigret, and interestingly enough but hardly surprising, Robert J. Courtine has put together a book entitled *Madame Maigret's Recipes* (1975). For those who find life's pleasures enriched by a steady diet of Georges Simenon, it is disconcerting to discover that his "dear friend" Robert Jullian-Courtine was associated with the scabrous anti-Semitic publication, *Au Pilori*, the French imitation of the vile ignominious German sheet, *Der Stürmer*, and the he wrote disgraceful anti-Semitic articles for the equally scabrous newspaper, *Je suis partout*, during the occupation period. Henry Coston, an extreme rightwing hack journalist who also wrote for such publications during the occupation, confirms this in an interview published in David Pryce-Jones' *Paris in the Third Reich* (1988). Few in France escaped the corrosive pestilence of collaboration, including Simenon himself, but some embraced it like a flagellant embracing a leper.

Others ignored the matter. The French court convicted Courtine for his rabid collaboration and he served time in prison. From 1953 until 1993, Courtine wrote on gastronomic matters for *Le Monde*. Suddenly and without warning, he retired. His colleagues had, after 40 years, discovered his fascist activities. According to William Echikson, in his wonderful book, *Burgundy Stars* (1995), quoting the historian Pascal Ory, the newspaper's editors knew all about Courtine's despicable past, but hired and kept him on because he "only" wrote about food and eating.

The only American detective thus honored with a book about his eating habits is, as far as we know, Nero Wolfe, in Rex Stout, et alia, *The Nero Wolfe Cookbook* (1973). Some cookbooks take writers' names in vain, as some publishers are excessively venal: for instance, the concoction put together by Alison Armstrong called, excessively, *The Joyce of Cooking. Food and Drink from James Joyce's Dublin. An Irish Cookbook* (1986). That this piece was published in Barrytown, with a foreword by the ubiquitous A. Burgess, who can hardly have actually read it, only confirms the opinion of that place expressed by Steely Dan a number of years ago.

Some *New Yorker* readers suspect that Jane Kramer lives (or lived) on the Place Dauphine from which she and her Portuguese femme de ménage send out periodic reports on the state of the spiritual, economic and social health of the Hexagon (as the French at times refer to their country because of its shape) and other parts of Europe.

If you walk south from the river along the Rue Grands Augustins and turn right on Rue Saint André des Arts, you will quickly come to a narrow street called Rue de l'Ancienne Comédie. Should you turn left into this street and advance to the corner of the Boulevard Saint Germain, you will see, at number 13, **Le Procope**. This is the oldest still functioning "café" in the city. Legend has it that the Sicilian, Francesco Procopio dei Cotelli, who started his career as a minor clerk in the store of two Armenian coffee merchants in the Saint-Germain-des-Prés market, opened in 1686 a store in which Parisians could sample the still novel aromas and tastes of coffee in a jar while sitting down in small chairs at even smaller tables. A short time later, the Comédie Française moved into the building across the street and in no time at all, depending upon one's chronometry calculation methodology, the Sicilian's place became the focal point of the Paris intellectuals' social and cultural life, a function the café carried on through the occasionally cerebral philosophes of the Enlightenment, the fire-eaters of the Revolution to the mawkish poets of the Romantic period, and, in fact, into the first half of the 20th century. In the summer of 1790, the owners transformed the place into a necropolis for a wake honoring Benjamin Franklin draping its appointments in black crepe for the event. Now it is a restaurant where one can eat well, if not inexpensively, but nostalgia isn't what it used to be, as Simone Signoret noted in another context. On a bleak damp January evening in 1995, with our friends Manuela and Radu Ioanid we warmed, fed, and watered ourselves very well upstairs near the grand staircase. Good service, fine food, excellent wine.... Full participation in the meal cost about $85 per couple.

Voltaire, who took a coffee or two in the Procope, wrote in many genres and may arguably have invented an early form of advertising in the doggerel:

> Quand Piron, contre l'Olympie
> Avait bien vomi son fiel;
> Quand Rousseau le misanthrope
> Avait bien philosophé;
> Ça, Messieurs, disait Procope,
> Prenez donc votre café.

(When Piron enthusiastically vomited his bile against Olympia; when Rousseau the misanthrope joyfully philosophized; there, gentlemen, said Procope, you should take your coffee.) The references may be obscure today, but the point is fairly clear.

There are a sufficient number of other restaurants of various price ranges and qualities to satisfy everyone's tastes; you should have no trouble finding one or two to match yours.

Richard Wright, James Baldwin, and Chester Himes. At number 14, rue Monsieur-le-Prince you will find a large apartment building under loud and dusty renovation. On the third floor (it is unclear if this is the American third, counting the ground floor as the first, or the European third, not counting the ground floor at all) in 1948, Richard Wright, a sadly neglected American writer who moved to Paris in 1946 at least in part to escape the entrenched racism in the United States, rented a large apartment for his family and stayed there until just prior to his death in 1960, when he moved alone to a small apartment at 4, rue Régis, a tiny street west of the Jardin du Luxembourg. (Why alone? Private matters, no doubt, but also because the brave British refused him an entry visa after giving one to his wife and children; after all, a Negro anti-colonial writer of the Left, and the US State Department did, after all, ask a "favour.")

For many years the nondescript apartment building on Rue Monsieur-le-Prince boasted a plaque to the right of the entrance to the courtyard and staircase noting that the composer Camille Saint-Saens lived and worked there. Recently, the authorities in charge of such things allowed a second plaque to the left of the entrance, which reads

L'homme de lettres
noir Américain
Richard Wright
habita cet immeuble
de 1948 à 1959.

Do not expect a museum to be established in Wright's apartment. A plaque on the façade is one thing, making a profit on the interior is quite another.

The French are generally as racist as any nation, but they have traditionally welcomed American blacks, and even some African blacks, in small numbers, especially if they could be considered intellectuals or in any way creative or exotic (writers, painters, jazz and other musicians, and, of course, Joséphine Baker). Led by Jean-Paul Sartre and Simone de Beauvoir, Parisian intellectuals not only welcomed Wright as a black American, but also as the author of two vividly written, but as we now know, heavily censored, books on being a Negro in the United States: *Native Son* (fiction 1940) and *Black Boy* (autobiography 1945). At this point Wright had not publicly disassociated himself from the Communist Party of the USA so the French intellectual left met him more than half way.

Wright certainly suffered the slings and arrows of quotidian racism in France, but more so from his own countrymen. The State Department, the Central Intelligence

Agency, the Federal Bureau of Investigation and the US taxman all hounded Wright for alleged "unpatriotic activities," a disgraceful pattern of racially and politically motivated persecution of one of this century's most talented American writers.

These days Gertrude Stein receives more attention for having been a lesbian than for the aesthetic and other qualities of her writing, life apparently being more valuable than art in some circles. She should be recognized as well for the help she gave to Wright and her influence on his decision to move to Paris. She assisted him in overcoming the deliberate obstructionist behavior of the State Department by mobilizing French writers on his behalf, including Claude Lévi-Strauss, then French Consul in New York, who arranged to have the French government invite and fund Wright on a "goodwill" trip to Paris; suddenly the passport office found his application! Once Wright arrived in the city on this brief first visit, Miss Stein drove with him around the neighborhoods, pointing out sights she thought would interest him, but more importantly introducing him to various circles of American expatriates and French intellectual life. Miss Stein took him to Sylvia Beach's apartment, where the latter welcomed the newcomer with the same warmth with which she welcomed American writers to her bookshop two decades earlier.

Not only did the official white bureaucracy plague Wright whenever possible, but younger black writers played out the oedipal syndrome with Wright as the father-figure who must be destroyed so the son can have the mother to himself - in this case the mother being a metaphor for success as the leading Negro writer of the day.

As legend has it, James Baldwin turned to Wright for help when the younger man arrived in Paris, hurrying to the Café des Deux Magots directly from the train station to see Wright. How Baldwin knew Wright would be there remains a mystery. Baldwin had met Wright before this encounter when in 1944 the established writer helped the younger man obtain an award based on sixty or so pages of manuscript Baldwin had written. Wright also helped Baldwin receive a fellowship that paid his way to Paris.

Some months after the meeting at the Deux Magots, Baldwin published an essay entitled "Everybody's Protest Novel" in the English-language magazine, *Zero*, in which he savaged Wright for creating negative stereotypes on a par with Harriet Beecher Stowe in his works. The wounding quarrel occasionally broke out into shouting matches in various cafés and never completely healed.

John A. Williams, a fine and justifiably angry writer who deserves more attention, credit, prestige and royalties than he receives, has, with sensitivity and sadness, told the story of the years between 1934 and 1964 from a black American perspective, including a section on the black American artists in postwar Europe and the Wright-Baldwin rivalry in a roman à clef entitled *The Man Who Cried I Am* (1967). This book should also, indeed in the first place, be read because it is a novel of distinction and a major contribution to American literature. Baldwin's essay is in the various editions of the collection *Notes of a Native Son* (1972).[8]

Baldwin later claimed the "white establishment" had used him "against 'the king'." Whites "could only allow one token black. I was too young to realize how I was used." This justification, given 31 years after the essay's publication, is hardly convincing. The white establishment in 1948-49 hardly knew Baldwin existed, much less that he could be effectively used to attack Wright. One does wonder about the editors of *Zero*, but controversy is always good for circulation and sales, especially appreciated by small circulation "little magazines." Baldwin showed more honesty in another essay he wrote after Wright's death, "Alas, Poor Richard," in which he admits perceiving

Wright's work as "a roadblock in my road, a sphinx really, whose riddle I had to answer before I could become myself.... He had been an idol; and idols are created to be destroyed." Actually, as any theologian will tell you, idols are also created to be worshipped.

Baldwin wrote some beautiful prose, most of it in the 1940s and 1950s, some of it in Paris. There had been room for both of them after all. Baldwin died in St-Paul-de-Vence and is buried in New York; Wright died in Paris and is buried there in the Père Lachaise cemetery.

Since 1945 large numbers of black Americans have lived and worked in Paris for various lengths of time, though few permanently lived there. Wright came to stay, as did Chester Himes, who achieved solid success in France after the reading public in the USA ignored the books published before he left the country. At the request of Marcel Duhamel, the director of Gallimard's policier series, La Serie Noir, Himes wrote a number of stories about life in Harlem featuring two police detectives, with the eccentric but effective names Coffin Ed and Grave Digger, as continuing characters. The last of the series hints that the grave and the coffin are for racist America itself: *Blind Man with a Pistol* (1969). In 1970, Himes moved his white wife and his Jaguar to fascist Spain where he purchased a villa above a village on the Mediterranean Sea and devoted himself to writing his memoirs and complaining about his fate to any journalist who made the trip to listen. An example of the latter is the interview conducted by John A. Williams published in *Amistad I* (1970).

Himes' memoirs and his earlier novels written in the USA, such as *If He Hollers Let Him Go* (1945), *Lonely Crusade* (1947), and *Cast the First Stone* (1952), whose protagonist is white only because the book would not have been published with a black character, are worth reading, especially for white young people who simply cannot understand why black Americans carry on so. The

94

memoirs are *The Quality of Hurt* (1972) and *My Life of Absurdity* (1976). Several of Himes' novels have been made into movies of various levels of quality, the latest in 1991 being *A Rage in Harlem*, a book also known as *For the Love of Imabelle*.

Many other black American writers, musicians, and artists spent varying periods of time in Paris, though one would not learn about them in most guide books, except those few which are devoted to black people of various nations and cultures in Paris. The *Guide Litéraire de la France* volume on Paris, and its German version make no mention of any black American cultural figures. Morton's *Americans in Paris* is an exception, in which Baldwin, Wright, Joséphine Baker, Sidney Bechet, Bricktop (singer and owner of the nightclub called simply Bricktop's, probably situated at 1, rue Fontaine, down the street from Baker's short-lived club, or boîte, as the French called night locales), Langston Hughes, and several others appear. Arlen Hansen's *Expatriate Paris* (1990) also gives some space to the black American presence in the city, and Tyler Stovall's more recent *Paris Noir: African Americans in the City of Light* (1996) is devoted to the subject.

It might be expected that a few words about the inexhaustible Joséphine Baker would be found here, and that expectation is not altogether unjustified. However, in the past several years a number of books and articles about her have been published and at least one film biography is available at your local video rental emporium. Baker spent most of her life in France as a French citizen and lived for lengthy periods in Paris, where she performed most often. Alas, I have not found any addresses for her in the city, which is too bad. For the moment let it be said about this incredible woman that Alice Toklas created a desert in her honor called Custard Joséphine Baker, one the main ingredients of which is, of course, bananas, in addition to a certain Liqueur Raspail, for which, as Miss Toklas notes, "it will probably be necessary to substitute another." One does wonder why. Gertrude Stein wrote a short piece in her most eccentric, that is to say, hermeneutic, style called "Among Negroes," which she published in a book entitled *Useful Knowledge* (1928). The essay appears to be an homage of sorts to Miss Baker. After a series of nasty racial incidents during a trip to the USA, and to demonstrate her loyalty to France during the war when she worked in North Africa, she changed the lyrics of her theme song to sing, "J'ai deux amours, mon pays c'est Paris," replacing the original phrase "mon pays et Paris."

Two other volumes of interest are Ursula Broschke Davis, *Paris Without Regret* (1986), essentially a strung-together series of citations by and about Kenny Clarke, Baldwin, Himes, and Donald Byrd, all of whom lived in Paris at one time or another. Broschke Davis' book does not go much beyond journalism and there is little analysis of the city's influence on her protagonists. Bill Moody recently published a book called *The Jazz Exiles* (1993), but it is so badly written, organized and edited that one cannot recommend it except to masochists and fanatics.

(The lack of any substantial reference in the book in your hands to venues of musical performances, except the Olympia in the 9th, especially jazz clubs, requires a brief comment as to reason, given the author's well-known tastes in music. When we are in Paris we have time for food or music, rarely both. Music one can listen to at home; Paris restaurant food is not moveable. That is the reason. However, do see the chapter on the 9th arrondissement, below.)

A more solid and substantial work is by Michel Fabre entitled *From Harlem to Paris. Black American Writers in France 1840-1980* (1991), which is a scaled-down and translated version of his earlier *La Rive Noire: de Harlem à la Seine.* Fabre's book is well worth reading because it is the only such work available. Unfortunately, it is unfocused and makes no attempt to evaluate the artistic or aesthetic value of the art produced by the people he writes about, or the influence of the city on their art. Also, and this is a prime failure in a book by a Frenchman about Paris, Fabre never mentions food, except for one reference to the type of meals served at Leroy Haynes' "soul food" restaurant in the Rue Clauzel. Tiens, tiens! Haynes' place may still be there for those who like or wish to try southern American cooking using French ingredients.[9]

Rimbaud and the Former Grand Hôtel des Étrangers. The Grand Hôtel des Étrangers was until recently the name of a hostelry on the corner of Rue Racine and Rue l'École de Médecine, just up the Boulevard Saint-Michel from the Musée Cluny. (The Boul' Mich' divides the 5th and the 6th at this point.) The premises have an interesting history, and the changes to the place can stand as exemplary for what has happened to many a formerly cheap but clean hotel. The now-forgotten composer, Cabaner, in November 1871, allowed the hapless and homeless Arthur Rimbaud to sleep on the sofa in the composer's rooms in the hotel. The literary group called "Les Vilains Bonhommes" held their dinners in the hotel, to which the members incautiously invited the exuberantly scruffy Rimbaud and his absinthe-addicted pal, Paul Verlaine. Rimbaud delighted in hoisting the bourgeoisie on whatever petard he found handy, in most cases his own outrageous behavior. Thus he shouted the word "merde" at the end of each line of his poems during his reading at the gathering, and that assured that this first invitation remained the last. In the late 1920s the place was called the Hôtel des Facultés and served as an inexpensive home for young ladies of the night and day whilst they earned enough money for a dowry that would allow them to return to the provinces and marry the local pharmacist.

When we stayed there in the early 1980s, the rooms truly resembled matchboxes in size, with no TV, occasionally a small balcony just large enough for an intimate couple to lean out and look up and down the street, breakfast in the rooms because it enjoyed no salle de petit déjeuner, well located and cheap. A wonderful sign hung on the back of the doors which read: "En dehors des petites dejeuners il est interdit de manger dans les chambres" which someone with a sense of humor or a limited knowledge of English usage translated as "Except for breakfast interdiction to eat in the room."

Our friends, Martin and Kate Sullivan, with their six-month old daughter, Abigail, and Martin's eleven-year old niece, Erin, arrived by train in Paris on a cold February evening after visiting us in the South of France. On our recommendation they had reserved at the Grand Hôtel des Étrangers, but told the taxi driver to take them to the Grand Hôtel, rather a different type of hostelry! And in a very different part of town. They had quite an adventure straightening out the matter.

Alas, in 1991, new owners renovated and improved the hotel, now called Hôtel Belloy Saint-Germain, to the level of $100 and more a night, and we once again bid a nostalgic farewell to yet another piece of the past we had considered ours. We are constantly amazed, indeed *per*turbed, if not *dis*turbed, at the phenomenon of things we grow to value and enjoy disappearing just at the point of our depending on their being there.

However, the **Hôtel Saint-Pierre**, a few steps down the street at 4, rue de l'École de Médecine, which brother Dean Chamberlin reports is just fine if you are not inclined to claustrophobia, is reasonably priced and is the hotel in which Countee Cullen stayed during the academic summer holidays throughout the 1930s. Cullen, an avid Francophile with an MA from Harvard (1926), moved in with a French family on Rue Gay-Lussac (in the 5th, named after a French scientist) to improve his proficiency in the language. By all accounts this ploy succeeded and Cullen refined his

98

abilities each summer thereafter until The Great 20th Century Stupidity broke out again in September 1939. He planned to return to Paris in the summer of 1946, but he died that spring. Cullen's poetry is little read today outside black studies and American lit classes, which is unfortunate because his work is accessible and often beautiful, and clearly proclaims his love for the city. He played an important role in the development of black Francophone poetry through his meetings with black French-speaking poets and translations into French of his own poems.

The great eater and essayist, A. J. Liebling, lived here for a memorable year during 1926-27, during which time a Chinese restaurant that had dancing next door provided such a sufficient distraction that, thirty years later when he came to write about his life in Paris, he had to admit that the atmosphere was "not conducive to the serious study of medieval history, which was my avowed purpose in the Quarter." You can read about this in Liebling's book *Between Meals: A Appetite for Paris* (1962), which also appears in the omnibus collection *Liebling Abroad* (1981), and I strongly urge you to do so. Liebling's prose about France can be so beautiful that the only fully satisfactory response to it is weeping.

Across the street from the Hôtel Saint-Pierre, left of the entrance to number 5, is a plaque which notes this as the birthplace of Rosalie Bernard on October 22, 1844. She is better known under her nom de thêatre, Sarah Bernhardt, who died in 1923, before she could witness the spectacle of the French removing her name from her theater because of her Jewish biological heritage.

The novelist Georges Sand (Amantine Lucile Aurore Dupin, 1804-1876) at the end of her life lived at 3, rue Racine with her secretary-lover Manceau, where the de Goncourt brothers visited the old woman on March 30, 1862, and left this vivid description:

Mme. Sand looks like an automaton. She talks in a monotonous, unintelligible voice, which neither rises nor falls and never gets animated. Her attitude has something of the gravity, the placidity, the somnolence of a ruminant. Her movements are slow, unfriendly slow, almost like a somnambulist's, and they always lead to the same thing - always with the same methodical actions - to the lighting of a wax match and to a cigarette at her mouth.

Whereupon, the brothers write: "Mme. Sand has been very kind to us, and has praised us a good deal, but with a childishness of ideas, a flatness of expression, and a sombre good-nature which have made us feel as chilly as if we were in an unfurnished room." With friends like that.... On the other hand, a standard American reference work describes her as "French novelist, known for her numerous love affairs and her numerous emotional novels." The lady can't win. Who reads Georges Sand these days?

Several blocks to the west of the Rue de l'École de Médecine, the **Café de la Mairie**, on the Place Saint Sulpice is good for sandwiches and beer, an aperitif or coffee and a drink before returning to hotel in the evening if you can find a table outside. The French sit outside in the evenings until very late in the year so it can be somewhat chilly of a November night. We've also eaten a traditional Parisian breakfast there on occasion: croissant, café-au-lait, but no cigarettes, and the morning newspaper. This café is not simply an ordinary Parisian café, not simply, plumply, *there*: the Café de la Mairie plays a major geographic role in the second chapter of Djuna Barnes' formerly esoteric and slightly risqué novel *Nightwood* (1937) for which the Old Possum, Tom Eliot, provided a preface to indicate "an approach ... helpful to the new reader." O yes.

Furthermore, Deirdre Bair, an early biographer of Samuel Beckett, alleges that the men's Turk in the café constituted a device to separate the tourist from the cognoscenti in an "amusing" fashion, and that Beckett took advantage of this for various reasons during the 1930s. The Turk's large overhead water closet would create an instant Plumbing Victim if one pulled the chain without knowing one had to open the door before undertaking this seemingly innocent gesture (as opposed, I must say, to The Shanghai Gesture). With the door closed the water gushed torrentially down to drench The Hapless Victim. O, you can imagine the barrels of laughter resulting from this "trick." "Desmond, old cod, step in and have a pee before we dash off for dinner. I'll wait for you right here." Ah, the humorous Irish. The men's facility may still be a Turk and thus require some caution in its utilization, but the days of drenching are long gone. Apparently Paul Eluard sat regularly in the café to compose his poems and write letters, and, apparently, this is what first drew the young Beckett to the place.

This café was also a favorite of Man and Juliet Ray during the 1950s and 1960s, no doubt because it is down the street and across the square from his last studio at 2 bis, rue Ferou, which is across that narrow street from Hemingway and Pauline's first Paris apartment at 6, rue Ferou. (If you wish to observe the comparative luxury in the lap of which Ernest lived with Pauline during the Great Depression in Thirties, visit the Hemingway House at 907 Whitehead Street, Key West, Florida.) In March 1993, an announcement appeared in the real estate section of the *International Herald Tribune* noting that the Estate of Madame Man Ray would be willing to sell the late lady's apartment on the Rue de Rennes overlooking the Jardin du Luxembourg for a mere one million three hundred thousand yankee greenbacks, or the French franc equivalent thereof.)

At number 13, rue Ferou lived Henri Fantin-Latour, a painter of some note, whom James McNeill Whistler visited one cold day in 1858. Whistler made a drawing of his colleague as the former sat huddled in his overcoat as protection against the icy temperature in his unheated room. The drawing can now be seen in one of the rooms in the Louvre.

On the **Place Saint-Sulpice** itself, you will find a fountain in the middle of the square illuminated at night (when else?) and quite romantic, so that, if you are in luck and have someone you love, or even like very much, with you, you might lean against the fountain, embrace, listen to the falling water (unless you are leaning there after midnight), and thank the Fates that you are there. Indeed, you could do worse things with your life than make a tradition out of the leaning and embracing against the fountain, even in the deepest winter on the coldest night during a snowstorm. Allow yourself to live a little, have the taxi wait whilst the two of you dash into the square, laughing, gasps of cold breath puffing and streaming from your mouths as you ... kiss and laugh again and dash back to the warmth of the taxi. Moments of such tenderness are few enough in these inadequately civilized rough and tumble times. Embrace them when you can.

The Saint Sulpice church on the east side of the Place is well worth a visit. Delacroix painted two frescos here, which you can perhaps see if the electricity is working in the first chapel on the right as you enter. The massive organ, one of the largest in the world, is played regularly at recitals. Alas, one can no longer hear the great organist and composer, Charles Marie Widor, who in 1870 began a long duration of playing the organ at the 10 o'clock Sunday morning mass, during which recitals he commented on the music to admirers and acolytes in the gallery (sotto voce, no doubt). At least this is the story told in her memoirs of famous people she knew by that arch-culture vulture, Marie Scheikévitch, in which she is also highly laudatory about Widor's talents as an organist.

In this church, the young, handsome and short-lived Camille Desmoulins married his rich and beautiful girl friend with the spectral Robespierre acting as best man. History could ask for no more sombre spectacle.

On the west side of the Place the building housing the 6th arrondissement's mayor's offices and the local police precinct sits with stolid solemnity as benefits its inhabitants. While you are in the neighborhood, determine the subject of the current exhibition on the first (European) floor of the Mairie du 6eme in the Salon du Vieux Colombier. In the early autumn of 1993, we spent an hour dawdling through a fascinating exhibit on the life and career of Odette Joyeux, the actress and writer some Readers may remember. The exhibition rooms are open from 11 AM to 6 PM daily.

La Méditerranée and Orson Welles. The seafood restaurant La Méditerranée, on the Place de l'Odéon has a history that seems to have little relevance to the quality of its food, which is good. Jean Cocteau and his pal, Christian Bérard (a.k.a. Bébé), a genius of sorts and an opium addict who lived around the corner on the Rue Casimir Delavigne with the choreographer Boris Kochno, spent much time here during and just after the occupation, and Cocteau designed the logo on the menu. Our friend, Marc Masurovsky, whose school chum's father owned the place, reports seeing Orson Welles devour two dozen or so oysters with a bottle of white wine for each dozen, and then really begin the meal! On the other hand, Edmund Frost reports seeing Welles devour a complete roast baby lamb in a Madrid restaurant followed by the headwaiter's call for the ambulance to take him, Welles not Frost or the headwaiter, to the stomach-pumping facilities.

Orson Welles attracts gargantuan stories like blue serge attracts lint. French intellectuals admire and love Welles. They believe he should have been French so that he could have developed his immense talents as a filmmaker in a more congenial atmosphere than that offered by Hollywood, USA. One of the more poignant pieces of graffiti we have ever seen appeared on a wall in Paris the day after Welles died. In black spray paint it said, "Orson is died, don't forget." I cried openly when I saw it.

Across the square from the Théâtre de l'Odéon, the Mediterranée sits at the south end of the Rue de l'Odéon, a street re-known in the history of English and French literature. From the premises of 12, rue de l'Odéon, the long-time location of the original bookstore and lending library called **Shakespeare and Company**, the youthfully courageous, or foolish, American named **Sylvia Beach,** in 1922, published *Ulysses*, an event from which world literature has not yet, nor will ever, recover. Miss Beach never recovered from Joyce's consequent obsessive, often rather shameless dependence upon her and his callous refusal to allow her to obtain her financial rights when the Americans finally successfully risked publication of the book in 1933.

The equally as obsessive and shameless academic Joyce industry has produced a tome containing Joyce's various missives to Miss Beach, all demanding her time, or wheedling money, or both. The woman was a saint. If you must, see M. Banta and O. Silverman, *James Joyce's Letters to Sylvia Beach 1921-1940* (1987).

Actually, the first incarnation of the store appeared in November 1919 at 8, rue Dupuytren, from which Miss Beach moved it 18 months later, possibly at Joyce's or Adrienne Monnier's suggestion. The famous photograph of Miss Beach and Joyce in the doorway of her shop is often mislabeled as being the Rue de l'Odéon store; it is the first incarnation, not the second.

And speaking of incarnations, not only did Miss Beach have two Shakespeare and Company shops, and Mr. Whitman his of the same name, but in June 1996 a three-store chain called "Shakespeare and Company Booksellers" closed its West 81ˢᵗ Street branch after 15 years at that location in New York City (promising to keep the other two open and reopen the closed store at a new location), and a "Shakespeare and Company Bookshop" opened in the summer of 1994 in Avignon. How many others are there? A bed and breakfast business in California has a "Sylvia Beach Shakespeare and Company" bedroom. Where will it end? Will there be a chain franchise? Is there no sense of shame left?

After decades of indifferent neglect, Paris city officials finally allowed an organization with the initials JJSSF (which could, I suppose, stand for the "James Joyce Society of the Suffering Fools") to affix a small plaque on the front of the building, much too high to be easily seen much less readily read, stating:

En 1922
dans cette maison
Melle Sylvia Beach
publia "Ulysses"
de James Joyce.

This does not communicate much information compared to similar wall-plaques for other important cultural figures, such as Gertrude Stein, for more about see below, or Thomas Paine, who has a large plaque, dense with text, a few houses down the street from Miss Beach's.

Across the street, at 7, rue de l'Odéon, no plaque at all marks the location of Miss Beach's lover and lifelong friend, the writer and editor **Adrienne Monnier's** bookstore and publishing house, **La Maison des Amis des Livres**. However, in 1991 had you been walking up the left side of the street toward the theater, at the building marked number 9, and had you raised your eyes a bit, you would have seen a flat wrought iron shingle in the form of

Miss Monnier and Joyce strolling down that very street in 1938. Created after the well-known photograph made by Gisèle Freund, the painted-black image jutted out from the building to remind us that someone remembered the important things in life.

Curiously, we had not seen the sculpture before our 1991 visit. In the crepuscular air of early evening we stood still, astounded, necks craned back, and I seem to have uttered, "How the hell long has *that* been there?" Overhearing the question actually intended as rhetorical, a young woman entering the door less than a meter away halted and said, "Since I have lived here - eight years." Curious indeed, what one misses by not having one's eyes au-dessus de la mêlée. The sign hung outside a bookstore unsurprisingly named La Maison des Amis des Livres, in which the milieu naturally differed from the original shop but the contents of which you might nonetheless have found of interest.

Alas, you will never know about the second reincarnation of the store. In January 1995, the bookshop no longer existed there, and in November 1995, the sculpture no longer hung from the wall. The ineluctable irresistible possessive desire of a lunatic Joycean, that is to say: theft? The incomprehensible machinations of the city bureaucracy concerned with the aesthetics of street decor? A temporary sojourn at the restorers? Who knows? When I passed by one evening that November, the new bookstore at number 9 had closed for the day so I could not ask. Early the following morning I left the city. With any luck the sculpture will again grace the street, which once so many of the century's giants trod. However, in May 1996, the bookstore had become a salon de beauté, and in September 1999 the situation had not changed. So who knows?

Monnier published the standard French translation of *Ulysses* in 1929, the version Joyce personally supervised and approved. In her own writings (translated into English in *The Very Rich Hours of Adrienne Monnier* edited by Richard McDougall [1976]) named the quarter "Odéonia" to define it not only as a geographical, but also as an intellectual reality, a veritable state of mind cooking in the palimpsest of artistic ferment and good, well-watered meals. Indeed, to be invited to dinner by Miss Beach and Miss Monnier meant not only an evening of lively, exciting, intelligent conversation, but also a prodigious meal that one remembered for years afterward. Indeed, our acquaintance, William Gray, a nephew of Miss Beach, attests to the fine meals at his aunt's apartment in 1955!

It is true that more hagiography than objective reportage has been committed about Miss Beach since her death in 1962. One is hard put to find a negative word about her in the increasingly voluminous literature. And this is as it should be. Her contribution to 20th century English, and to a somewhat lesser extent French literature is enormous and incalculable. She is an exemplary feminist whose independence of spirit and intensity of purpose in living her life in a manner she chose should make her an unparalleled example for the next century. Yes, she did occasionally serve Mr. Joyce in what some have seen as a "traditional" (read "negative") female role, but she *chose* to be his publisher, banker, real estate agent, and general factotum, and when she grew exhausted from it, she stopped.

In her memoirs, *The Heart to Artemis* (1962), the English writer Bryher (Annie Winifred Ellerman Macpherson) writes of Miss Beach, "She loved France, she made us feel that it was a privilege to be in Paris, but the common modern mistake never occurred to her, she never tried to identify too closely with a foreign land whose childhood myths she had not shared." Wise words, indeed.

If she found it difficult to say no to Joyce, she found that response easier to make to the German officer who threatened her with unnamed "unpleasantness" if she continued to refuse to sell him her last and personal copy of *Finnegans Wake*. Overnight she shut down the store, painted out the signs on the facade, had a carpenter remove the shelves, and, with the help of Miss Monnier, her assistant Maurice Saillet, and the concierge, schlepped the stock, furniture and light fixtures to the fourth floor. There the stuff remained until liberation, thus ending the 22-year long functional history of Shakespeare and Company, as the Germans ended so much of European history and culture. With the exception of six months internment at Vittel in eastern France during the Winter of 1942-43, Miss Beach spent the rest of the occupation in Paris maintaining a "low profile," until Hemingway appeared with a motley gang of armed French youths and a couple of wayward GIs on August 26, 1944, to "liberate" Odéonia.

In fact, she moved into the Foyer des Étudiants at 93, boulevard Saint Michel, an American institution directed by Miss Sarah Watson, herself interned for a brief period before the rector of the University of Paris obtained her release, an accomplishment achieved because the Foyer was "attached" to the university and full of students. One wonders how many other non-French enemy alien residents of Paris remained there, or in other parts of Europe, during the war. Indeed, what about those American and British women who remained in Paris for one reason or another during the occupation? Additional Ph.D. dissertation topics.

Although I think Miss Beach, ever the good Presbyterian, made a fundamental error in judgment in deciding to be nice about everyone in her published memoirs (the drafts are much more candid and interesting), I have always admired this apparent paragon of patience and I wish I had met her on October 24, 1921, if only for a few hours in the shop. October in Paris is a good time of year, especially if the sun brightens the crisp Autumn air, and in 1921 one could still smell the roasting chestnuts on the street vendors' hot blackened metal plates without the noxious carbon monoxide fumes occluding the olfactory senses.

Not every one agreed that Miss Beach was a saint, of course. In 1925, Robert Forrest Wilson launched on the public a 356-page tome of chitchat, advice and general drivel entitled, imaginatively, *Paris on Parade*, a clear anticipation of *Wayne's World*. Anyone who can, deadpan, describe a bouillabaisse as "a seafood bisque" is an amateur standup comic aiming for slapstick heaven. Associating oneself with and defending, if obliquely, the Ku Klux Klan can be explained either as a result of the author's perception of the audience he intends to reach or his inability to lift himself out of the cesspool of his own background. Since he glories in his philistinism, it is no wonder he cannot but find Odéonia and its denizens incomprehensible, and the only reaction of which he is capable is a malicious burlesque in which his facts are as inaccurate as his mind is shallow. He calls Shakespeare and Company the "headquarters" for which the Young Intellectuals (his caps), who are never to be seen at the Dôme, where only those writers and painters gather who are serious about making money and not working "for the select few who matter."

Wilson's paragraph describing Miss Beach is worth citing in full to give the flavor of his lame ridicule and sophomoric contempt.

> Miss Beach herself is a comely young woman with poise, a quiet and attractive manner, a businesslike bobbed head, and a frequent cigarette. And of course she is intellectual. Long ago she despaired - or so she strikes one - of getting the message across to the less understanding and has thus arrived at a forbearing but unhoping and somewhat weary tolerance of the Philistine.

It is clear that, appropriately, Wilson considers himself as one. Perhaps Miss Beach, appropriately, snubbed him.

In any case, what exercises him is the fact that Miss Beach published *Ulysses*, and what really galls him, apparently, is the chutzpah of the "comely young woman" in charging sixty francs for the volume! And the volume is "a muddy slovenly job"! And the average French book retails for seven francs. Clearly this woman is out to soak the unwary tourist. And "if any filth hunter, however, thinks that in *Ulysses* he is getting a piece of light reading, the joke is on him." Our erstwhile guide to the city proceeds to describe Joyce, in the process getting his age, the gender of his children, the location of his residence, the time it took to write the book, the number of Joyce's residences during the writing, and the future publisher of his next work - all wrong.

He then goes on to belittle other expatriates in Paris who belong, with Miss Beach and Joyce, to the "interlocking directorate of the Continental advance movement in English letters," including William Bird, Robert McAlmon, Ezra Pound, George Antheil, Ford Madox Ford, and Ernest Hemingway. Interestingly, Antheil was a composer-pianist, Bird a newspaperman-printer, and Ford never wrote an avant-garde sentence in his life. All the Young Intellectuals, in capital letters of course. Curiously, no mention is made of Gertrude Stein, who really *was* avant-garde!

To be fair, some of the book is amusing in an archaic way. And some useful information may be dug out if one labors long enough. One might, for instance, in a gaudy chapter on "Apaches," discover the plot of one or two Maigrets, writ down years before Simenon began to write about the chief inspector. Or one might discover the plot of that incredible lovely, sad movie, *Casque d'Or* (1952), which somewhat romanticizes the contours of the story related by Brigadier Frédéric Berthin of the Police Judiciare Brigade Speciale, a "real life" model for Maigret. "Casque

110

d'Or" refers to the pile of blonde hair on the head of the lady in question - "golden helmet."

At the southern end of Rue de l'Odéon, on the eastern side of the theater, is the short Rue Corneille connecting the square with Rue Vaugirard. At number 5, the old Grand Hôtel Corneille stood for many years. Such hotels often have a history of being lived in by interesting people, and this one is no exception. The painter Whistler stayed here at the age of 21 when he first arrived in Paris during the summer of 1855; Mark Van Doren, famous Columbia University English lit prof, stayed here during the summer of 1919 whilst he worked on Dryden in the Bibliotèque Nationale, although why there on Dryden is a mystery.

On August 24, 1944, the hotel rather suddenly ceased to exist. During the exciting, if dangerous, days of the liberation of the city from the malefic clutches of the French fascist collabo thugs and evilly spiteful German occupation troops, the SS swine among the latter set fire to the old hotel along with their putatively invaluable paper records before scuttling off through the Luxembourg Gardens in retreat. Sylvia Beach, having lived with difficulty in Paris and environs during the occupation, krauthasselled at every turn, reports seeing the hotel go up in flames, an institution for which she had a particular fondness because her Irish soulmates, Yeats and Synge had stayed there in their youths. Even Joyce, whom Miss Beach may have considered to be a soulmate early in their relationship, stayed there while allegedly studying medicine at the Sorbonne in the winter of 1902-03.

Richard Ellmann calls the hotel "the favorite stopping place for British tourists without money." Thackery supports this idea in his *Paris Sketch-Book* published in 1840: "If you are a poor student come to study the humanities, or the pleasant art of amputation, cross the river forthwith and proceed to the Hotel Corneille, near the Odéon."

The Banque de France now owns the building, but one can still see the old reception desk and key racks in the doorway on the right, if one is lucky enough to be able to appreciate such things and knows where to look. And now you, at any rate, know where to look for this piece of Parisian history. Or at least where it should be: recent renovations of the building have removed much of the character of the structure and the last time we looked, we could not see the desk or the rack.

City officials long ago affixed to the front of 27, rue de Fleurus a plaque informing passersby that Leo and **Gertrude Stein and Alice Toklas** lived there for three decades.

Gertrude Stein
1874-1946
Écrivain Américain
Vécut ici avec son frère
Leo Stein puis avec Alice B. Toklas
elle y recut de nombreux
artistes et écrivains
de 1903 à 1938.

In 1938, Miss Stein and Miss Toklas moved with 130 canvases to 5, rue Christine in the 6th, victims of landlord philistinism. Leo, who had lived in the Rue de Fleurus apartment since he and his sister moved there in 1903, moved out in 1914 in something of a snit into an apartment at 203, Boulevard Raspail. The snit had either to do with Miss Toklas, who joined Miss Stein in 1910, or a dispute between brother and sister over the relative merits of Matisse (Leo) and Picasso (Gertrude).

Many have wondered what might have happened if Miss Stein had ever met James Joyce; what fantastic conversation might have resulted between the two apparently most radical experimenters writing in the English language, the veritable exemplars of modernism in literature, although Miss Stein insisted that Mr. Joyce wrote stuff not nearly as radical as it seemed, but that *her* stuff was truly radical - and she was right. Those who wonder about such a meeting are bound to be disappointed, regardless of the cast of characters. Geniuses generally speak, competitively to be sure, of banal things, such as their health and their royalties, when they meet at social occasions. In any case, Mr. Joyce and Miss Stein did meet. No one is quite sure of the exact date; "in the mid-30s" is the usual phrase, but Miss Beach gives it as late in 1930 and that is as good as any, since it does not really matter, certainly not here, where we Platonists are concerned mainly with the idea *of* it, rather than the gossip *about* it.

Jo Davidson and his wife hosted a party toward the end of the year 1930 in their Avenue du Maine apartment/studio. The room was large, light, airy, and full of people and Mr. Davidson's sculptures. In the mode of the times, many people carelessly smoked cigarettes, but few drank alcohol beyond a glass of wine on this occasion. In one corner sat the almost blind Mr. Joyce, who could not rightly tell if it was night or day, so those of his fan club hovering tightly around him delightedly described the party crowd and the surroundings in a manner pleasing to him.

In another corner, Miss Stein warily eyed the crowd, murmuring occasionally to Miss Toklas and to those standing tightly around her avidly listening to her comments on the intelligence or sartorial taste of those individuals who briefly attracted her attention.

Miss Beach, aware and fearful of the historic occasion, decided to throw caution to the winds of chance and, with Mr. Joyce's vague permission, approached Miss Stein behind *her* screen of fans. With the natural reticence of a naturally shy person in the age before Powdermilk Biscuits, she said,

- Miss Stein, would you care to meet Mr. Joyce?

- O, I think not, Miss Stein answered casually, he seems to be fully occupied.

- I believe he would not take it at all amiss, said Miss Beach politely.

- O, *he* might not at all, Miss Stein replied haughtily, but in all these years he has not ever once or any time called on me on Saturday or any other day, so *I* might take it all somewhat amiss, don't you think.

- I do not believe he meant to give offense, Miss Stein, said Miss Beach somewhat defensively, by no means, but he has been so very busy and he can barely see the light, so I must take you to him, you see.

- I certainly know what it is like to be very busy, don't I, and I work only at night.

Miss Beach drew into her lungs a deep, slow bushel of smoky hot air, smiled tightly, and softly said,

- Well, then, the hell with it.

- O, Miss Stein quickly said, but after all we are known as the two most important writers in this century, he writing in the Persian style and I in the modern. At least many think he belongs in that category with me. So, Miss Beach, perhaps, it might be well, don't you think, if we did meet after all.

With that, Miss Stein began slowly to sail stately through the room with Miss Beach tugging along beside her. Miss Toklas remained behind to guard the Stein corner and fans.

- Miss Stein, Miss Beach said hopefully, this is Mr. Joyce.

- After all these years, said Miss Stein squinting slightly.

- Yes, said Mr. Joyce affecting a mild bewilderment, our names are always linked together.

- We live in the same arrondissement, I think, said Miss Stein helpfully.

Mr. Joyce retreated into his blindness and made no response.

114

Miss Stein flushed slightly, turned around, and sailed back to her corner, from which she tugged Miss Toklas out the door and home to the Rue de Fleurus. Miss Stein and Mr. Joyce never saw each other again.

Is this story true? Some version of it appears in a number of memoirs and biographies. (Richard Ellmann, unusually for him, has it wrong in his standard Joyce biography). The spirit of the story as related above is accurate and the two writers never did meet again thereafter. In any case, all the versions agree on the basics, which is more than can be said about the various versions of the meeting between Mr. Joyce and Marcel Proust. And, when Miss Toklas came to complete her book of recipes and memoirs, available in various editions as *The Alice B. Toklas Cookbook* (1954), she did not hesitate to include instructions on how to make "Dublin Coffee James Joyce," which he most probably never tippled himself.

Miss Stein earlier met another English-speaking resident of Paris, a fellow American, Mary Cassatt (1844-1926), the Philadelphia railroad heiress and arguably the best American impressionist painter. Having no eye or taste for post-impressionist styles and concepts, Miss Cassatt visited the Stein apartment in 1908. After a few minutes spent looking at the Picassos, Cézannes and Matisses, she had has enough. She wrote shortly thereafter, "I have *never* in my life seen so many dreadful paintings in one place! I have never seen so many *dreadful* people gathered together." And she wanted to be taken home immediately. And so she was, to her large modern and comfortable apartment at 10, rue de Marignan (8th) off the Champs Élysées just up from the Rond Point, where she lived from 1877 until her death, when she was not in residence at her 45-acre estate north of the city, Château de Beauxfresne.

Her response to the Steins and their art collecting parallels her response to the paintings they collected. Keep in mind that the Steins required no expert to broker their

115

choices for them, they hired no mentors to guide their way as Isabella Stewart Gardner had Bernard Berenson and the Henry Havemayers had Mary Cassatt, who wrote about the Steins to a friend in 1910 "[T]hey are Jews and clever, they saw they had no chance unless they could astonish, having not enough money to buy good things so they set up as apostles of Matisse and pose as the only ones who know, and it has succeeded! ... It is very amusing but cannot last long.... Those who have the money buy Manets." Miss Cassatt had the money.[10]

There is some mild, post-facto satisfaction in knowing that both Miss Cassatt and Miss Stein bawled their first infant critiques in Allegheny, Pennsylvania, and lived most of their lives in Paris, France. While their common birthplace is misspelled on Miss Stein's tombstone in the Père Lachaise cemetery, Miss Cassatt's family vault at Mesnil-Theribus cemetery makes no mention of it at all, stating merely:

Sépulture de la Familie Cassatt
Native de Pennsylvanie
États-Unis de l'Amerique.

Miss Stein died in 1946: Miss Toklas lived on alone until 1967. I will never forgive myself for not seeing her during my first visit to Paris in 1964. But all Miss Toklas wished during those 21 years alone was to rejoin Miss Stein. This, finally, she achieved. They lie together in the Père Lachaise cemetery. Miss Toklas' name is carved on the back of the tombstone, an irony few appreciate, although the grave has become a shrine to many.

The Stein-Toklas residence is but a short stroll from the **Jardin du Luxembourg**. To adequately describe this park would require many pages and would still not give you a full sense of its wonders. Walk into the park from the eastern end of the Rue de Fleurus and enter a world apart, a world no less urban than the rest of the city (the modish styles of clothing could not be mistaken for the countryside or suburbia), but simply apart, more urbane, less hectic, less impatient, less tintinabulatory in the ear and eye.

The present day assault on one's hearing faculty is not new, of course. Frances Trollope in 1836 described the noise of Parisian thoroughfares in almost satanic terms: "The exceeding noise of Paris, proceeding either from the uneven structure of the pavement or from the defective construction of wheels and springs, is so violent and incessant as to appear like the effect of one continuous cause - a sort of demon torment, which it must require great length of use to enable one to endure without suffering."

The park was not always so peaceful, of course. Today's quiet park may have been yesterday's arena of clashing armies and bloody political upheaval. To be fair, there are spots where destruction wrecked its savageries in the past and continues to do so now; the stones of the Place de la Concorde, despite its name, absorbed the blood of royalty and revolutionaries during the Terror of 1793-95 as Dr. Guillotin's rationalized, industrial-strength axe (or as he preferred to think of it "a philanthropic engine:" "a puff of air on the neck and all is done") indifferently severed head after head from aristocratic and plebian bodies alike. Now gasoline-engine powered motor vehicles in their thousands and tens of thousands sever mind from head with unbearable pandemonium, and threaten bodily injury, if not death, to any pedestrian foolish enough to attempt invading their turf. Paris, a city built for people on foot, for horses and for carriages, is now infested by asphyxiating motorcars, trucks, and tourists.

But the Luxembourg Garden is one leopard that changed its spots while leaping forward from one era to another, in fact from the Roman occupation of the region to the very day you are reading this, pouncing from period to period like a demented cat bounding down history's highway, a road potted with hidden traps and snake-filled pits anxious to skin the beast in many ways.

After the Gallo-Romans abandoned the area, its flora and buildings, such as they were, fell to ruin, "became a desert," as the 1990 green Michelin neatly states. Apparently a medieval gangster named Vauvert, who may or may not have actually existed, used the ruins as a headquarters from which he and his band of cutthroats and cutpurses forayed out to spread terror and bloodshed, presumably to the financial enrichment of the gang members. The Carthusians, who, according to the Oxford English Dictionary, belonged to a monks' order founded in 1086 by St. Bruno in the Dauphiné "remarkable for the severity of their rule," in 1257 appealed to the king (the venerable Saint Louis) to be allowed to rid the neighborhood of this pest. The order's motivation may not have been purely altruistic: after the successful surgical operation to remove the unwanted wart from the city's jowl, the Carthusians constructed a large monastery in the neighborhood. Exactly where this complex sat is not entirely clear, but approximately 300 years after the disappearance of Vauvert from recorded history (what *did* happen to him?), "a wealthy nobleman" (have you ever seen one not so described in the popular literature, except as perhaps a "down-on-his-luck" nobleman?) built a mansion amidst the gardens on the site of the Palais du Luxembourg, which he owned. Upon his death in 1564, his widow sold the property to François de Luxembourg, of an old family from Lorraine, who expanded the grounds and gardens through purchase and lent his name to the location.

In 1612, the garden so captivated the eye of Marie de Médicis, widow of Henri IV, that she arranged to buy the land and the mansion from the Duc de Luxembourg. What Marie de Médicis wanted, she usually, but not always, got, one way or another. Queen Marie then commissioned Jacques de Brosse (a.k.a. Salomon de Brosse) to tear down the buildings and construct a more spacious, elaborate villa, better suited to a queen with very definite Italianate tastes, and no wonder. De Brosse modeled the structure on the Pitti Palace in Florence, and completed construction in 1620, after which Marie attempted to have it called the Palais Médicis, but as Harold Clunn notes in his book, *The Face of Paris* (1933), "the previous appellation eventually persisted," which is a nice way of saying that the French would only take so much from the ostentatiously Italian Marie.

Indeed, pauvre Marie did not long enjoy living in her grand palace with her 24 specifically created large Rubens paintings tracing the events of her life, allegorically of course. She made the mistake of crossing Cardinal Richelieu: on November 10, 1630, probably first thing in the morning, but one is not sure of the exact hour, she extracted a promise from her son, Louis XIII, to dismiss the Cardinal. Within 24 hours, Louis, weak or smart depending upon one's point of view, retracted the promise and Marie, fuming with rage, found herself on her way to exile in Cologne, where in 1642 she died "penniless," as they say.

Despite the caveats and cavils of such small minds as Sidney Dark (in *Paris* [1926]), who described Marie as "an unattractive, unpleasant and unhappy lady" and "immensely fat, immensely stupid, and immensely lazy," we prefer a different vision: certain things one remembers, certain images one retains, certain sounds one always hears...

> Marie, the dawn is breaking
> Marie, your heart is aching
> ...
> And tears will fall as you recall
> The words "will you surrender"
> ...
> Until the dawn when you'll be gone...

One must know the music to fully appreciate the song's effect; even better is to remember the sound of it: not the silly chunk-a-chunk Tommy Dorsey version, but that of a vocal group in the early Fifties whose name I have, to my dismay, forgotten. "The fat she-banker," indeed. (If one requires any further evidence that lyrics and music must be heard together to be fully appreciated, one need only remember the sound of Steve Allen reciting the words to the song "Bebopalulu" without the music. Would the lyrics to "Like a Rolling Stone" be as effective and affecting without the Band's melodic and harmonic richness to carry them forward? Indeed, would the soundtrack to *High Noon* have the same emotional impact without Tex Ritter crooning the words to the title song?)

Marie left the garden and the buildings to her second son, Gaston d'Orléans, in 1642, but "he eventually grew tired of it," having the attention span of a flea and the character of a Yokum. The property moved down the great hall of history through a number of hands including those of Mademoiselle de Montpensier, and the Duchesse de Guise, second daughter of Gaston d'Orléans, and in 1694, for some reason the ruling house took possession and Louis XIV gave it to the Duke of Orléans, no doubt as a quid pro quo for some favor. Presumably the place remained in the hands of the Orléans family until the Revolution, when the bureaucrats of terror converted the buildings into a prison for both the aristocracy and the plebeians, all jumbled together in the same smelly primitive conditions, most of whom died at the guillotine, separately to be sure, but from the same swift sharp blade edge.

The Revolutionary Terror imprisoned not only Frenchwomen and men, but also the occasional luckless American who strayed from The Straight and Narrow. The one American no one would have thought of as bait for this jail was the radical democrat, Thomas Paine. The fact that four departments in France elected him to the Convention (he actually served from the Pas-de-Calais) and that he had been given French citizenship did not help him when the Committee of Public Safety incarcerated his tush in the Palais de Luxembourg after arresting him on the night of December 27, 1793, on suspicion of one thing or another, perhaps that he aided the British, with whom the French were then at war. The unsavory but elegant Gouverneur Morris, having succeeded Thomas Jefferson as American Minister-Plenipotentiary, refused to intervene in his official capacity, thus thwarting the efforts of others, such as Joel Barlow, to obtain the old Quixote's release. Finally, James Monroe, who in turn succeeded the intransigent Morris, arranged Paine's freedom. The garrulous pamphleteer never regained his mental and physical equipoise and died an unpleasant death in the USA comforted only by the tender attentions of his Paris printer's widow who sailed to America with him in 1802.[11]

Napoléon and his government used the building for state affairs and the Restoration used it as a high court seat until the Revolution of 1848 put an abrupt stop to the rule of the house of Orléans. After the upstart Louis Bonaparte's coup d'état in 1852 the Imperial Senate resided there until 1871 when, as a result of the depredations of the Commune, the Paris City Council occupied the premises whilst authorities rebuilt city hall. In 1879, the French Senate moved into the building and the Senators are there to this very day.

In the latter part of the 19th century, the painter Carolus-Duran received a commission to paint the ceilings of the palace. In the habit of using his students, especially his American students (perhap because they did not protest as loudly), as models for his work, he cajoled several of the latter, including the young John Singer Sargent, into posing for him, and their heads consequently appeared on the great ceiling. But Sargent's visage is no longer there. Apparently, Sargent's hands drew Duran's attention like blue serge attracts lint and the older artist painted the younger's paws on numerous occasions. At some point Sargent began his own career and refused to leap every time Duran said, "jump." This had the not surprising effect of annoying the older painter, who, it is said, reached such a level of spite that he stomped into the palace, climbed up a sufficiently tall ladder and painted out the ingrate's head. When asked about his relationship with Sargent, Duran replied "c'est fini" and so it was.

To the west of the palace is the Petit Luxembourg, built in 1629 for Marie de Médicis and currently the residence of the Senate President. Next to this structure on the western side is the Musée du Luxembourg, whose former permanent collection is now in the Musée d'Orsay by way of the Musée du Jeu de Paume.

Parks and gardens are used for a variety of purposes, not all of them intended by their creators: in 1940 during the mass flight south by a torrent of refugees fleeing the lines of battle, farmers scurrying to what so many misperceived as safety repressed their hysteria long enough to graze their cows in the still green and French grass of the Luxembourg Garden.

Remember, you are entering the gardens from the Rue de Fleurus. To your left as you enter, in the tennis courts, young well-muscled youths teach adolescent girls in expensive short white outfits to play at a level of the game that will not shame them in the next physical education class at school. All about you, little mini-parks have been laid out with benches upon which to rest and sculptured busts on pedestals to engage your curiosity as to identity and, on occasion pleasingly grotesque, appearance.

Further down the sandy allée you espy a small collection of dwarf ponies on which even smaller children are placed by medium-sized adults to ride slowly up and down the path. The pony turds, or horse apples, are swiftly swept into plastic bags or, on busy days, simply ignored by one and all, except you and me and some of the less well-bred little people who giggle and point at them. In any case, it is better to smell natural horseshit than to die of equally malodorous, but unnatural, automobile engine exhaust pollutants. The happy quasi-hysterical cacophony of the children is diffused in the air and in the vegetation, which seems to absorb their limitless enthusiasms; no boombox affronts one's solitude. The joggers' earphones flit by too fast to become annoying.

Continuing ahead you pass a group of six people of varied ages engaged in oriental mystic exercises, moving with slow contorted grace in unison and in silence in the shade of the massive chestnut trees; in an alliance of ancient arcane wisdom-seeking and contemporary insecurity, the figures attain a grave beauty as they perform their rituals of hope and transcendence.

And then, suddenly, you are out of the shade and standing on a terrace at the top of the steps leading to the vast wide open plaza containing a round pond bordered by lavishly flowering bushes and statues of French queens, or rather queens of France, along the terrace. Around the pond are scattered municipality-provisioned green iron chairs in which people of all ages sit and enjoy the sun, actually read books, observe the lovers entwined in a kiss, or the children sailing their small craft under the watchful eyes of their nannies. To your left sits the seat of the French Senate in the Palais. And you realize you have only been through twenty percent of the park! And if you live in North America, you are startled in the realization that the chairs are not chained up or nailed down! The park does close at dark.

The Greeks may say "happiness is just a little scented pig," but for a city dweller buffeted about by the intrusions and offenses of late 20th century civilization, the Luxembourg Garden and other similar urban parks throughout the city, allow happiness to exist along with the more negative aspects of life, so one can maintain a modicum of sanity in an fundamentally insane world. D. H. Lawrence once opined that ours is an essentially tragic age, but that we refuse to perceive it as such. Most intelligent people would admit, however, that the society we live in, regardless of its nationality, is insane. Thus we require locales such as this magic park.

If you are at the southern end of the park, walk south along the Avenue de l'Observatoire for a block, turn right into Rue Michelet, and continue to the Rue d'Assas where, at 100 bis, you will find one of the more interesting museums in Paris: the **Musée Zadkine**. The Russian born sculptor, Ossip Zadkine (1890-1967), lived here from 1928 until he died. His unsold works are scattered throughout the garden, studio and apartment. If you desire a bit of quiet after the circus of the larger museums, you will find it here: silence and art simultaneously, a phenomenon not to be lightly dispensed with.

For years Zadkine's spectral bust of Van Gogh sat on a plinth in a wall niche on the garden path at the old Saint-Paul-de-Mansole monastery, currently called a "convalescent home," in Saint-Remy-de-Provence. When Vincent stayed there in 1889-90, everyone knew it as a discrete loony bin. In 1989, no doubt aware of the chronological symmetry, vandals stole the bust. However, Zadkine created a life-sized statue of the Dutchman for the small park near the Chambre de Commerce in Auvers-sur-Oise, where Van Gogh spent the last months of his life. A smaller plaster version of this can be seen at the Zadkine museum, which charges no entrance fee on Sundays.

After you've walked around and sat sufficiently in the Jardin du Luxembourg, step into the **Musée du Luxembourg**, 19, rue de Vaugirard, if an exhibition is currently being mounted; if not, enjoy the exterior design of the building. Before the 1939-45 chapter of the Great 20th Century Inanity, this museum housed the late 19th and early

20th century French paintings that French museum officials moved to the Jeu de Paume, where you can no longer see them because the same officials moved them into the Musée d'Orsay. Indeed, the same type of officials refused at first to accept the bequest of paintings donated by Caillebotte, which formed the nucleus of the collection: too modern, especially those strange blotches of paint by that uncouth creature from Aix-en-Provence! ("O, why can't they just paint those nice landscapes of trees and bushes and sheep like they used to?!")

If you are a fan of the Annenberg Project/CPB telecourse, *French in Action*, the heroine, Mireille, lives just down the Rue de Vaugirard across from the Senate. Indeed, if you cannot get to the city and wish to see what the shouting is all about, or if you've been already and loved it and wish to return but circumstances preclude this, or if you wish to learn French following Pierre Capretz's idiosyncratic, interesting, and successful methodology, by all means slip the tape cassettes into your VCR and vicariously saunter with Mireille and Robert and their families and friends through the Jardin du Luxembourg, the Sorbonne, and practically all the rest of Paris where the lessons were filmed. You will be edified, enlightened, and amused.

"Sorbonne" is the vernacular for the University of Paris, now a sprawling collection of buildings and campuses spread all over the city and its suburbs. In 1257 Robert de Sorbon created a college for poor theology students, and somewhat later the entire university faculty became known as the Sorbonne, and still later the entire university took on that name in the vox populi. Today one refers to the various parts of the university structure by their mundane numbers, as in "Paris VIII." There is very little sense of the Romantic or the past in the tunnel minds of bureaucrats, academic bureaucrats not excepted.

Just across the Rue de Vaugirard from the main entrance to the Palais du Luxembourg, one will find a useful and friendly postal office on the corner of Rue de Tournon. A few steps up this street the **Café de Tournon** allegedly still contains the pinball machine Richard Wright played during one of his frequent visits to the favored café which he shared with his rival for the role of prémier écrivain noir américain in Paris, William Gardner Smith.

The Café de Tournon also served as the unofficial editorial office of literary journal, *The Paris Review* (for more about which, see below). The firm which published the French journal, *La Table Ronde*, at 8, rue Garancière, parallel to the Rue de Tournon, loaned a small room to the young editors of the *Review*, but insisted that the building be locked at six in the evening, which curtailed the enthusiastic activities of the Americans, who made the café the meeting place in which their bumptious and often raucous energies suffered less restraint, until the owner closed the place at two in the morning. Someone took a photograph of the *Paris Review* crowd in front of the Café de Tournon in 1954, in which William Gardner Smith and Muffy Wainhouse, but, hélas, not Harold Humes, appear.[12]

Joseph Roth lived in this building, in the late 1930s called the Hôtel et Café de la Poste, after his regular Paris residence, the Hôtel Foyot across the street, was demolished in 1938 in a demented attempt to do something else with the fine old building.

After January 1933, the New Order in Germany forced the Austrian Jewish writer, Joseph Roth, into exile from his main locus of income, and after the Austrians welcomed the Germans into their country in March 1938, he could no longer return to the place of his birth, as a plaque high up on the building's facade tells you. His continual presence in the café at his Stammtisch made it a center for exiled Austrians of all political, aesthetic and religious colorations.

On an August Sunday in 1929, Roth visited Lotte Israel, a friend of Ernst Toller, at her country house in Stölpchensee near Berlin, where he met the beautiful Andrea Manga Bell and for the next six years the alcoholic writer and the mulatto magazine editor remained entangled in an intense erotic and intellectual relationship during which time they lived, with her two children from an earlier marriage, at the Hôtel Foyot. Born in 1900 in Hamburg, the daughter of a Cuban Negro father (a student of Franz Liszt and a composer and pianist) and a white woman of Huguenot bourgeois heritage, she married a prince of the royal blood from the former German colony Cameroon, Alexandre N'doumb'a Douala Manga Bell, with whom she had two children during the years they lived in Versailles. When the prince returned to Cameroon after 1919, she remained in Europe with the children, moving to Berlin in 1925 where she worked as an editor for the art magazine, *Gebrauchsgraphik*. In September 1931, Manga Bell and Roth moved to Paris. After the war, Andrea Manga Bell lived in Paris; I do not yet know what happened to her during the last years of peace, after she and Roth separated, and during the war itself, but she was still in Paris in 1945. Did any of these black and white Anglo-Saxons know anything about Andrea Manga Bell, or Joseph Roth, when they chose the Café de Tournon as their local? Unlikely, but, as John Lewis, Milt Jackson, Percy Heath and Connie Kay once collectively stated, "Sait-on jamais."

After many years of finding the café closed for one reason or another, on a cold, damp March night we stepped briskly along down the Rue de Vaugirard on our way to dinner past the miniscule Square Francis Poulenc formerly the site of the Hôtel Foyot with its even more famous eponymous restaurant. And, lo, we beheld lights, and the inn had room, and we installed ourselves at a table in the window to drink a pre-prandial beer. The café was warm and pleasant to sit in, but we did not hear the flattened drawls of the darktimbered voices of the past's ghosts. We did, however, think about them and for a short while perhaps we believed they had either just left or had not yet arrived for their aperitifs.

By the way, Richard Wright's other favorite café, in which he gave audiences to interviewers and acolytes alike, is not far from his apartment building, but it is doubtful that he would recognize it today. The Café Monaco, formerly Monaco Bar, on the Carrefour de l'Odéon is now an exemplar of the influence of the plastics industry and the necessity for feeding tourists as fast and as efficiently as possible. (In October 1994, the owner began to tear the place apart in order to rebuild it and the old Monaco is no more and hasn't been for many years, and now, in any case, is not called Monaco.)

The Rue de Tournon and the Hôtel Foyot. At 19, rue de Tournon you can read a plaque on the wall that reads

"I have not yet begun to fight."
JOHN PAUL JONES
Capitaine de Vaisseau
de la Marine des États-Unis
Chevalier de l'Ordre
du Merité Militaire
et
L'un des heros de la Guerre
de l'Independence Americaine
est mort dans cette Maison
le 18 juillet 1792.

When the American minister-plenipotentiary, the charming but devious Gouverneur Morris, ordered the least expensive funeral for the then penniless sailor, the outraged French took the helm, so to speak, and lavished a full national burial with all honors and cortège to the Protestant cemetery. The French also buried him in alcohol in a lead-lined coffin, believing that some day the Americans would

wish to bring home one of the heroes of their War for
National Independence.

The author of that great elegy to the civilizing of the
American frontier and its destruction by the gasoline-
powered motorcar, *The Magnificent Ambersons*, Booth
Tarkington, lived from 1905 to 1908 at 30, rue de Tournon,
where he wrote *The Guest of Quesnay* (1908) and dined at
Foyot. Many years later, he wrote "Ah! the Rue de
Tournon! I still haunt the neighborhood in my thoughts of
Paris..."

In *The Guest of Quesnay*, Tarkington touches on a
sensitive subject for many Americans who have lived and
are living on a relatively permanent basis in Paris, or
anywhere else outside the borders of the USA for that
matter. The narrator at one point says, "I am no 'expatriate.'
I know there is a feeling at home against us who remain
over here to do our work, but in most instances it is a
prejudice which springs from a misunderstanding. I think
the quality of patriotism in those of us who 'didn't go home
in time' is almost pathetically deep and real." On the other
hand, some of us who have lived for long stretches of time
abroad find the term "expatriate" to be irrelevant.

In 1941-42, Orson Welles created a film based on the
story of the Ambersons. This may have been his greatest
movie, though it is truly difficult to imagine anything
greater than *Chimes at Midnight* (1966), but we will never
know because, under pressure from studio administrators,
in Welles' absence, some of his colleagues savagely
mutilated the film leaving it the tortured and despairing
wreck that is currently available on the television and on
videotape.

Nina Hamnett claimed that one got the best food in Paris
at Foyot's; not only was it good, but rather expensive as
well, which does not come as a surprise. Many Parisian
cultural luminaries ate here including the organist Charles
Marie Widor, Anatole France (when he served as librarian

of the Senate across the street), François Coppée, Alexander Dumas fils, Carolus-Duran, Leconte de Lisle, et alia. The list of people who stayed at the hotel until 1938, when for some unholy reason the place was torn down, contains what might be termed some of the "usual suspects:" Louis Aragon, Robert McAlmon, the poet H.D., Bryher, Rainer Maria Rilke, George Moore, Mary Butts, Tommy Earp (an English essayist, no relation to Wyatt that I know of), the poet Elizabeth Bishop, John Barrymore, Dorothy Parker, Raymond Radiquet (whose legend notes that Jean Cocteau locked his then 20 year old lover in his room at the hotel to force him to finish his precocious novel, *Le Diable au corps* [*Devil in the Flesh*], published in 1923, the year the author died of typhoid), Virginia Pfeiffer (Pauline Hemingway's sister), Stefan Zweig, the prima donna Jeritza (according to Arlen Hansen, who provides no further identification), and Michael and Sarah Stein with their son Allan in 1904 before they moved into the apartment at 58, rue Madame.

In 1894, a bomb thrown by a classic anarchist assassin severely wounded the poet Laurent Tailhade as he left the restaurant. It is not clear whether or not the assassin meant to rid the world of the poet, but it is likely that the unlucky Tailhade suffered what was in fact an Accident of Fate.

And speaking of anarchists, as it were, in his novel about a German exile from Nazi Germany, *Die Wenigen und die Vielen. Roman einer Zeit* (1959), Hans Sahl describes as "an anarchist type" a rare book dealer in Paris who says, "Wenn ich unglücklich bin, gehe ich ins Hotel Foyot und trinke zwei Flaschen Vouvret, Jahrgang 1929." (When I am unhappy I go to the Hotel Foyot and drink two bottles of Vouvret, vintage 1929.) The narrator remarks that the dealer appears to be often unhappy. The wine probably was Vouvray, which sounds the same as "Vouvret," but isn't.

130

Joseph Roth lived in the Foyot for sixteen years before the happy demolitionists obliterated that cultural monument. He claims to have invited the two of them, the younger respectfully calling his older colleague "The King of the Demolitionists," to have a drink with him in the café after they finished their work. Thereafter he sat in the café across the street from the empty space and listened as the hours ran out. "Man verliert eine Heimat nach den anderen," he thought to himself.[13]

On May 27, 1939, Roth died of alcohol, malnutrition and exile, in abject poverty in the Necker hospital for the poor in the Rue de Sèvres.

A bit further north up the street, Gérard Philippe, the cosmically talented actor, moved into number 17 in the spring of 1955 and remained there with his family until his all-too-early death from inoperable cancer in November 1959. That summer he had finished his last two films, *Les Liaisons dangereuses 1960* for Roger Vadim and *La fièvre monte á El Pao* for Luis Buñuel.

Indeed, ghosts of the past permeate the Rue de Tournon: Balzac lived for two years (1824-26) on the fifth (European) floor of number 2; the New Zealand writer, the unfortunately tubercular and shortlived Katherine Mansfield, unfortunately married to the longlived John Middleton Murray, lived for a brief period at number 31; Alphonse Daudet, father of the vicious little fascist Léon, but more importantly author of numerous novels and stories, many of them about his native Provence including the well-known *Letters from My Windmill*, lived with his brother in poor circumstances in the attic at number 7 until he began to publish poems and stories which allowed them to move to more comfortable quarters elsewhere in the city; as a child André Gide lived on the second (European) floor on corner of Rue Saint-Sulpice and Rue de Tournon from 1874 to 1880 when the death of his father forced the family to move to a less expensive apartment; and numerous

131

others graced with their presence at various times this single block-long street that is worth a slow walk up and down to view the architecture, dip into the bookstores, and think about the ghosts.

According to Sidney Dark, M. Tussieu, a barber who had a shop in the Rue de Tournon for an incredibly long time, boasted that he had cut the hair of Hugo, Daudet, and countless other luminaries of French culture. He also hung a plaque outside thes shop that read:

> Ici Monsieur Tussieu barbier
> Rase le Sénat,
> Accommode la Sorbonne,
> Frise l'Académie.

To which, after August 1914, he added:

> Bulgares de malheur
> Turques, Austro-Hongrois, Boches,
> Ne comptez sur Tussieu
> Pour tondre vos caboches.

The street is in name very short, becoming the Rue de Seine at the Rue Saint-Sulpice.

At the eastern end of the Palais du Luxembourg on the Rue de Vaugirard, at four and a half kilometers the longest street in Paris, is a small square named after Paul Claudel. It is merely a piece of urban landscape, but as much as one cannot admire the Catholic poet and playwright who locked up his sister Camille in the Montdevergues loony bin in Montfavet near Avignon for thirty years and who wrote an ode to the glory of Marshal Pétain during the occupation ("Ode au Maréchal"), one must admire the French for naming public places for the creators of high culture. Not far away, as we have seen, on the eastern corner of the Rue de Tournon and the Rue de Vaugirard juncture, is an even tinier square called Square Francis Poulenc in honor of the composer (1899-1963) who set texts by Apollinaire and Eluard and wrote operas based on plays by Cocteau, Georges Bernanos' *Les Dialogues des Carmélites*, as well as great choral works such as *Sabat Mater* (1951). Is there a Eugene O'Neill square or a Leonard Bernstein square in a major American city? Dare one hope that some day there will be a Charles Brockton Brown Street in Washington DC? Not likely.

Some years ago, if you had walked up the Rue de Seine to number 74, you could and should have entered the Galarie des Femmes, a brightly lit feminist bookshop with a wide spectrum of literature by and about women, including taped readings of books and plays, and an occasional small exhibition of works by women artists and photographers. In the autumn of 1984, we saw a small but moving exhibition of Imogen Cunningham's photographs here, and we have always found one or more books or tapes here that we simply could not do without. If it's not one thing, it's another, and in the winter of 1994-95 it was a magnetic, trés chèr coffee-table volume on Jeanne Moreau, with whom I have been in love since 1960. Lynn-Marie, for whom I was waiting in the bookstore while she purchased elsewhere a baguette for dinner, later commented, "That's the most expensive baguette we've ever bought!" Well worth it, too. Alas, in early 1999 the store disappeared to be replaced by a boutique selling the latest style expensive accouterments for toddlers.

From this former bookshop, make your way to Rue Princess a few streets to the west, where you will find Odile Hellier's **Village Voice Bookshop** at number 6, which is of interest for English language reading material. We visit this comfortable emporium whenever we are in the city. The shop sponsors readings and book signings, and carries several literary journals and general critical publications such as *The New York Review of Books* and the *Village Voice Literature Supplement* (naturally). The range of subjects offered by the store is astonishing. The staff speaks English and we've always found them ready and willing to be of help, even if this means recommending another bookshop!

Again, be forewarned that books, especially imported books, are not inexpensive in France. But how can one pass up the British edition of Ian MacNiven's collection of the Henry Miller-Lawrence Durrell correspondence, so much nicer to handle than the American edition? And with a less expurgated cover photograph! For those who have been wondering, in November 1990 some of Lawrence Durrell's ashes were indeed buried in the cemetery at Sommières, where in the summer of 1998 a totally inappropriate cross still blasphemously marked his otherwise unidentified grave. I hope by the time you are reading this that the ludicrous situation has been changed.

From the Village Voice shop, walk up to the Rue du Four, turn left and stroll two blocks to the Rue Bonaparte where you make a right turn and have before you the juncture of Boulevard St. Germain, Rue de Rennes, and the Rue Bonaparte, called the Place du Québec south of and Place Saint-Germain des Prés north of the boulevard. This is the core of the quarter known as **Saint-Germain des Prés**, which lived its halcyon days in the postwar era of dark rollneck-sweatered, bluejeaned existentialists gulping down presumably expensive whisky and listening to a multitude of Juliette Grécos in damp ill-lighted antediluvian cellars. The restaurants and cafés are still inhabited by those involved in the French publishing business when they can find a seat amidst the masses of teeming tourists. But the "caves" are long since gone.

They formed part of the Parisian pattern of the postwar era. Liberated from the oppression of the occupation, though not its lack of food and other shortages, youngsters rebelled against the past and the present of their elders, and, not believing in the future, easy enough for a twenty-year old, they took their lifestyles to what they thought to be extremes. The "scene" did not last long; once the photographs began appearing in *Paris-Match* and *Life*, the authenticity drained away and the stark black and white scene bleached into a monochrome public relations syndrome for the tourist trade. But while it lasted, it kicked up a storm, allowed several young men and women their moment in the spotlight, and made at least two longer-lived careers, those of Juliette Gréco and Boris Vian, though his was much shorter than hers and few remember them today.

Legend has it that the girls wore their hair long because they could not afford to have it cut, wore dark rollneck sweaters because they are warm and the dirt doesn't show as clearly as if they wore pastels, wore jeans and dark men's trousers because they could not afford to buy stockings; one supposes that the boys harbored similar reasons for their attire. One does wonder, however, about the hair: wouldn't it have been much easier if kept very short? It doesn't pay to investigate myths too closely, unless they are far enough removed in time and space so the results of the investigation do not destroy any illusions.

In any case, legend also has it that one night Juliette Gréco, a young underemployed actress, accidentally dropped her coat down the cellar staircase at the Tabou, a small bistro in the Rue Dauphine, a couple of blocks from the Odéon métro station near the Seine. Upon descending the stairs to retrieve the coat, she discovered a dark, damp and rather smelly room, a place which immediately appealed to her pals as being appropriate to their lives, and where it would be warm in the winter. Consequently, by some mysterious process not even understood by nightclub owners, the Tabou flourished as an all-night spot where one could drink relatively cheap whiskey and dance the jitterbug to the quasi-American jazz music provided by the small group put together by the trumpeter, novelist and poet, Boris Vian. Word continued to spread, as it does in its mysterious fashion, and soon the American GIs appeared eager to spend their dollars, and the pace picked up, to be quickened yet again when the American Negro jazz musicians discovered the musical and social advantages of being jazz musicians and black in 1947 in Saint Germain des Prés in Paris, France. The Tabou was only the best known of such places, which proliferated like mushrooms after the rain.

Indeed, the Tabou and Miss Gréco became so famous that, as legend has it, the Right Bank (and thus more affluent) cabaret called Le Boeuf sur le Toit, formerly associated with Cocteau and the composers known as Les Six, hired her, but to do what? Sing songs. But only if they were serious stuff written by serious men such as poets! Ah well, but what about the music. Jean-Paul Sartre to the rescue. Not only did he, allegedly, write a lyric or two for her, but he also sent Miss Gréco to Josef Kosma, a brilliant bit of matchmaking. Kosma composed music that not only fit the words of the poems, but also appropriately surrounded Miss Gréco's particular husky voice quality with appropriate music. Miss Gréco is still around, but performs rarely; you can listen to her lovely performances on records, and I recommend you do so. Boris Vian is dead, but his ghost is undergoing something of a revival in Paris, where two lengthy books and a lavishly illustrated magazine cover story appeared in mid-1993. His songs and music are also available on records and will repay listening. On the other hand, Barbara Laage (who Sartre chose to play the whore in the film version of his play, *La Putain Respectueuse*), Anne-Marie Cazalis, Agnes Capri ... who today knows about these very creative then very young women, whose stars shot so brightly into the sky?

If you wish to see a fictional and slightly warped approximation of what the chic aspects of the existentialism period (circa 1944-1959) looked like, Roger Vadim's film, *Les Liaisons Dangereuses 1960* (1959), with Gérard

Philippe and Jeanne Moreau, and music by Thelonious Monk and Art Blakey's Jazz Messengers, would be of interest. The film caused something of a scandal when the French government refused to give it an export license on the grounds that it defamed France and the French. This, of course, is hogwash; the only people it defames are those responsible for its production. Simone de Beauvoir's roman à clef, *The Mandarins* (1956), also tells the story, if at tiresome length; at least her fictional characters clearly resemble their actual counterparts, such as Albert Camus, Arthur Koestler, Nelson Algren (who claimed to be incensed at her be- and por-trayal of their love affair, whose American edition she, curiously, dedicated to him), Sartre, herself, et alia.

If you look into the photographs by Nico Jesse in *The Women of Paris* (with text by André Maurois, 1954), you will find several existentially expressive of the nightlife in the Saint Germain des Prés caves (Jazz! Uninhibited dancing! Whiskey! Cigarettes! Sex! Arrggghhhh!), and photographs of the young and plaintively beautiful Anouk Aimée, Juliette Gréco, and the now forgotten Barbara Laage.

You will also see a photograph of a young woman, the perfect expression of the era during which youthful optimism (We've won the war, haven't we? Haven't we?) carelessly mixed with the skepticism of the intellectuals (existentialism, after all, posited a universe without meaning in which the individual nonetheless had to make moral choices, although the youngsters jitterbugging in the Tabou hardly knew anything about the philosophy and never pretended to). This to us anonymous young woman I imagine to be a not so innocent twenty years of age with one lengthy, severely-felt and two brief, less painful affairs in her short past. Cigarette smoke cascades from her nostrils across lips that verge on being thick, to which only vague traces of lipstick vainly stick. Her unlined face is bereft of makeup, her unplucked eyebrows arch over her pale blue eyes (or are they hazel?), she is weary, but still alive to the night, glancing to her left out of the frame, hope not completely abandoned, but wary of the future, shoulder-length brown hair enclosed her face, a gray rollneck pullover absorbs the boogie-woogie sweat at her neck, she holds a black blazer tightly to her body.... What is she saying? "I am capable of many things including greatness however you care to define it; my intelligence is sharp; my ambitions still know no limit; but I am also capable of loving you beyond your ability to conceive of human love, if you are lucky ... If I smiled at you, your eyes would ignite into incandescence and you would envision divine rapture ... but I will always remain out of reach ... I am the image you chase in your dreams ... I am your unrealized epiphany ..." She is also the most beautiful woman I have ever seen.

* * * *

Bordering the west side of the Place Saint Germain, the church of St. Germain des Prés is worth a visit, and be sure to see Picasso's giant muscular bronze **Head of Dora Maar** which has been placed in the churchyard as a memorial to the French-Polish poet **Guillaume Apollinaire**, a great friend of Picasso's during the period before 1918, but who never met Dora Maar. Dora Maar herself met Pablo Picasso in the mid-1930s at the Café des Deux Magots across the square from her head. Only Picasso knew the connection between the Head and the Friend.

On November 9, 1918, two days before the armistice, Guillaume Apollinaire died at the age of 38 as a result of war wounds and the influenza epidemic, which killed 21 million people worldwide that winter. The poet lived with his wife of six months, Jacqueline Kolb, in an apartment at 202, boulevard Saint-Germain. There is a photograph of the two of them on the tiny roof terrace of the building in Francis Steegmuller's *Apollinaire: Poet Among the Painters* (1963). As he lies dying, headwounded and trepanned, this brilliant poet and mediocre art critic, an "unnaturalized Italian of Polish descent and French education," as Roger Shattuck describes him, drifts up from the depths of his dying to the bare edge of consciousness. On the boulevard below the victorious and vengeful French crowd surges joyously up and down chanting at the top of their voices "À bas Guillaume! À bas Guillaume!" In his delirium, Guillaume Apollinaire grasps only that all his fears, as a foreigner, a stranger never quite at home anywhere, all his anxiety phantoms had been, finally, real. His fellow humans wished him dead. The screaming crowds of course meant Emperor William, the hated Kaiser Wilhelm II, Archboche, not the dying poet, of whom they had never heard.

But wait, shall we. This story is probably apocryphal, because he died on the 9th and the belligerents signed the document on the 11th, and this is the cause of the crowds' presence. Indeed, Paul Léautaud, who sat with the corpse in the apartment on the 11th, confirms that the crowds yelled and swarmed on that date; so while this may have been, as Shattuck speculates, "the kind of wake Apollinaire would have wished," Picasso's great Friend died a less paranoid death that the romance would have it. In any case, you now know the location of his apartment.

In 1951, the Paris city government renamed the short block between the Place Saint-Germain des Prés and the Rue Saint-Benoit "Rue Guillaume Apollinaire," which is no doubt why Dora Maar's Head is placed in the churchyard across the square from the street named after the Friend Picasso was supposed to honor with a Work of Art. Madame Maar lived to see her Head thus placed, but in the depths of old age she could perhaps no longer visit her Head. She died in July 1997 at the age of eighty-nine.

139

Those interested in sometimes witty, often snide, always titillating gossip about Madame Maar, Señor Picasso and James Lord, should see the latter's book *Picasso and Dora* (1993), which perhaps should be called "Me and the Others."

In what can be viewed as the last gasp of the surrealist movement, André Breton, well into The Third Age but undaunted, led a band of younger generations to protest the installation of Madame Maar's Head as a tribute to Apollinaire. Typically, the reasons for the protest are not clear. (Perhaps the ghosts of Breton and his acolytes were responsible for the head disappearing from its plinth in 1999. By the time you read this it may be back in its place.)

Guillaume Apollinaire wrote "modern" poetry before 1914, which is to say that he treated the form of poetry in a new way vis à vis the layout of the words on the page, and used language differently than hitherto, often choosing words more for their sounds than for their contextual meanings. Gertrude Stein wrote what many consider to be gibberish passed on as "modern" prose, in which, as anyone can ascertain with the expenditure of a certain amount of mental effort, the sounds of words are often the determinant of their choice, which leads fairly straightaway to the four line poem by Miss Stein, written in 1913, entitled "Guillaume Apollinaire."

> Give known or pin ware.
> Fancy teethe, gas strips.
> Elbow elect, sour stout pore, pore caesar,
> Leave eye lessons I. Leave I. Lessons. I.

Imagine Miss Stein, an American whose favorite song was "The Trail of the Lonesome Pine," sitting at her writing table in the depths of the blue-black Paris night creating a sound portrait in English of a Polish poet who wrote in French. The possibilities for the imaginatively fecund manipulation of language are incalculable, as are the chances of incomprehension.

On the west side of the Rue de Rennes next to Le Drugstore, just south of the Boulevard Saint-Germain, you will find a very useful French equivalent of the American five-and-dime store called Monoprix. The location of these chain stores is useful to know because one can find sundry items regularly required to make life livable at reasonable prices. And you do not have to speak French since no one will wait on you: gather your goods and head for the cashier, where you can read the tariff on the register.

Aux Deux Magots, Le Café de Flore, and La Brasserie Lipp. Across the Boulevard Saint-Germain from Le Drugstore on the west side of the Place Saint-Germain des Prés, you become aware of the two famous cafés: Café des Deux Magots (technically Aux Deux Magots, at 170, Boulevard St-Germain) and the Café de Flore (174, Boulevard St-Germain) at whose tables *every*body has sat at various times, including us. On a cold, wet November night in 1988, while taking a postprandial drink at the Flore, we sat next to Gerald Durrell and a shifty-eyed person described by one waiter as "a famous Egyptian novelist" (possibly Naquib Mahfouz?). We regret to this day that we didn't say hello and tell Durrell how much we enjoy his books about animals and other friends and family. We would even have made a contribution to his zoo. Now it is too late to tell him anything: Gerald Durrell died at the age of 70 on January 30, 1995, on the Channel Island of Jersey, where he had lived and worked since 1958.

In the summer evening hours and into the night, street performers ply their trade to entertain the cafes' patrons and pass the hat. Be forewarned, however, that anything except coffee in these high-volume tourist attractions is going to be expensive, and the coffee will not be cheap.

141

In the Café de Flore, at any rate, you can determine the price of your drink beforehand by checking the menu, the cover of which is printed in red and black ink to simulate the famous covers of the Gallimard publisher's NRF series. The back cover discusses the range of personalities who have imbibed at the Flore's tables. The list is interesting, especially for those interested in lists, because those on it do not fall into one category, but stretch across the entire rum spectrum of public life from politicians (Trotsky) to fashion types (Paco Rabanne) to those intellectuals whose names are perhaps more familiar to us (Camus, de Beauvoir, Sartre, Juliette Gréco, Roger Vadim, Léo Malet, Jacques Prévert, Léger, Lawrence Durrell, Brigitte Bardot, Alain Delon, Picasso, Jean Vilar, Gérard Philipe, Jean-Paul Belmondo, Joseph Losey, Simone Signoret, and yes, of course, Hemingway). All the usual suspects. In the autumn of 1989, a small beer cost 17 francs, a small coffee 13 francs, and a Ricard 20 francs. In January 1995, the same small beer cost 38 francs, the small coffee 21 francs, and a glass of plum schnapps (mirabelle) 65 francs. Add a five percent increase for each subsequent year and you will arrive at the approximate current price.

Although somehow the Deux Magots (no, not maggots, but treasures) became more famous, we've always preferred the Flore. De Beauvoir explains the value of the place during the occupation when she notes the importance of the stove in the winter of 1942-43 when (almost) all Paris, except the Germans, froze. An entire community of intellectuals, including many of those named above, spent the winter at the Flore creating a club-like milieu (advantageous to Members, not so to non-members, thus Everyone wanted Membership) with the relaxing warmth of the stove, a close-by métro station and few, if any, Germans.

Across the street from the two cafés is the famous Brasserie Lipp, noted for its Alsacian food and beers and as being the meeting place for various Parisian elites. If you do not wish to eat there (the prices are moderately expensive, whatever that means), take a coffee in the narrow café section facing the street. If you do wish to eat there, check the prices beforehand and, if they are acceptable, make a reservation, without which you will hardly be allowed to cross the threshold.

To avoid becoming a German, the Alsacian young man called Lippmann left his home after the Franco-German War of 1870-71 and moved to Paris where he opened his eatery at 151, boulevard Saint-Germain. The place originally no doubt shared the characteristics common to brasseries in the city, namely to be owned or operated by Alsacians, funded by breweries, exist in large open spaces, serve sauerkraut and various kinds of sausages and pigsfeet in a happy atmosphere awash with light and beer. Needless to say, things have changed somewhat since then, and the Lipp has not escaped the alterations, usually known, inappropriately and inaccurately, as progress. I suggest you read the relevant chapter of Hemingway's novel, *A Moveable Feast*, to savor the texture and tastes of what it was like to eat at the Lipp before it became so chichi.

We ate there, finally, after many years of considering the matter, in October 1991, thanks to Gregory Masurovsky and Grethe Knudson. The smoked meats accompanying the sauerkraut tasted so good, the smoke flavor caught in the nose, we wanted to take the chef home; the bland, almost tasteless sauerkraut (apparently a tradition here) convinced us the chef might just as well remain in Paris - we shall cook the meal ourselves. If you are seated upstairs, you are not famous and you do not know anyone with the right type of influence. Tant pis, actually, but you can eat a better meal for the same price in less hierarchically-inclined, less class-conscious restaurants. En bref, one does not come here for the food.

143

The waiters in the Lipp (pronounced Leep as in jeep) are mildly snotty, but efficient and professional as they scurry about their tasks. However, should you absentmindedly neglect to tip the guard robe lady sufficiently well, she will let you know about it in no uncertain, though polite, terms, in a manner so weighty with condescension that you will, of course, vehemently overtip her and feel uncomfortable about the issue for an hour afterward. Thereafter, with sufficient distance from the experience, the whole thing develops into an amusing anecdote, no doubt, but back in the far reaches of one's mind lurks the thought that one had committed an unforgettable faux pas. You can read more about the Lipp in Jean Diwo's *Chez Lipp* (1981) and Waverley Root, "Brasserie Lipp - Rendezvous for le tout Paris" in *Holiday*, 46 (October, 1969), but we suggest you go yourself and see if you get a seat downstairs. You might also see a celebrity or two. Michèle Morgan, as lovely as ever, graced the place with her presence during our dinner there.

At the northern end of the Place Saint-Germain des Prés begins the Rue Bonaparte. Walk past the Rue Guillaume Apollinaire into the Rue Bonaparte and make a right into Rue Jacob (not named after the saintly Max, alas); continue until you reach number 20 on the left. With luck, if the gate is open, you may be able to see into the walled garden where a small Temple à l'Amitié, one of a series built during the Revolution to replace churches, sits in a state of some disarray. The incredible **Natalie Clifford Barney** (1876-1972), poet, intriguer, dubbed l'Amazone by one of the Goncourt brothers, lover of the painter Romaine Brooks (whose mysterious paintings are in the National Museum of American Art in Washington), Liane de Pongy, Renée Vivian and sundry other young, talented, beautiful women, lived here for five decades.

Her gender-restricted dance parties in the garden around the temple became as well-known as her gender-mixed and more sedate salon evenings on Fridays from five to eight. Although Gertrude Stein appeared occasionally at Miss Barney's salon, they competed as social hostesses. Despite the earlier competition, Miss Barney did write a foreword to the posthumous publication of Miss Stein's *As Fine As Melanctha* (1954). Miss Stein remained cool to Ezra Pound, who she once referred to as a "village explainer, excellent if you were a village, but if you were not, not," so Pound's circle, including T.S. Eliot, when his health allowed him to be in Paris, and occasionally James Joyce, tended to congregate at 20, rue Jacob, where the shy Erik Satie from time to time played one of his piano pieces, rather than 27, rue de Fleurus, where no music was allowed to detract from the conversation, or Miss Stein's monologues or her brother Leo's lectures. Miss Stein, however, did have Matisse, Max Jacob, Picasso, Hemingway, Juan Gris, Francis Rose, Bernard Fäy, Pavel Tchelitchev, et alia, until one after the other, they either offended or died.

For some reason, Miss Barney is buried in the Passy cemetery across the street from the Palais de Chaillot in the 16th, perhaps because René Vivian rests there. Miss Barney's grave is not yet a shrine. She remains one of the century's most fascinating, beautiful and interesting people, and she deserves a full-blown serious biography that combines succulent gossip with sociology and literary criticism. Until someone writes such a book, we will have to do with the shallow *Portrait of a Seductress* (1979) by Jean Chalon, who knew her during the last decade of her life, and *The Amazon of Letters* (1977) by George Wickes. Shari Benstock has a perceptive and sympathetic, if rather academic, chapter on Miss Barney in *Women of the Left Bank: Paris 1900-1940* (1986), which also contains a good chapter on Miss Stein and Miss Toklas and the validity of the notion of lesbian literature.

145

Meryle Secrest, *Between Me and Life: A Biography of Romaine Brooks* (1974), prints a photograph of young Natalie lying barenaked on her back in a forest glade so achingly lovely and sensually magnetic that it would shiver anyone's timbers.

Too bad one cannot enter Miss Barney's Rue Jacob garden any longer.

Down the street toward the Rue de Seine from Miss Barney's former residence a very short block called Rue de Fürstemberg is interrupted briefly by a small quiet square called Place de Fürstemberg much admired by Henry Miller for its peaceful aura of wellbeing. Just off the western side of the square you will see a small wall-sign informing the public that within the walls of that building is the **Musée Eugène Delacroix**, the house in which the great Romantic painter lived out his final years and which now serves as a memorial to his life and work. His most important paintings are all in museums around the world, and many of the pieces on the walls here are facsimiles from reproductions of notebooks he kept during his fecundating trips to North Africa. If you have any interest in the painter and the history of 19th century European art, do not pass up this museum. Julian Green describes the studio as an "oasis in our century that is so wretchedly devoid of poetry." And George Elliot Clarke has noted "At the Musée Delacroix, the well of impressionism, shimmering pastels spark blazing colors. Haunted by Africans, Delacroix limns a black character in each of his Hamlet drawings."

A bit further to the east, somewhere near the Rue Saint-André des Arts, around 11 o'clock at night, we passed a bakery shop still open in whose front window a raspberry-custard tarte jumped up and down and carried on so at the sight of us that Lynn-Marie and Dean, without further ado, strode into the shop and purchased the little devil. At the sidewalk tables across the intersection we sat to eat the tarte and drink a glass of white wine. Dean attempted to order a Guinness stout, openly advertised in the window behind us, but could not make the waiter understand the word Guinness so finally settled for a demi of Kronenbourg. The tarte tasted so good we ate another before wending our way to the hotel and raspberry sweet dreams. We have not been able to find that bakery since then.

This is the quarter of **L'École des Beaux-Arts**, and you can see the courtyard and some "monuments" at 14, rue Bonaparte, unless you know someone on the faculty or one of the students, then perhaps you can see more. To wet your dry curiosity, here is a citation about the School of Fine Arts buildings from the green *Guide Michelin*, as unexplained here as it is there:

> A monastery dedicated to the Patriarch Jacob was
> founded in 1608 by Marguerite of Valois, Henri
> IV's first wife, when she regained her freedom,
> and was occupied by the Augustine order.

For a brief, but amusing lesson on one possible method of enrolling in the École des Beaux-Arts, and how to quickly disenroll from the school, see the relevant passage of the sculptor Jo Davidson's autobiography, *Between Sittings* (1951), in the section on his life in Paris as a young man in 1910-12.

Raoul Dufy spent several years at the École des Beaux-Arts refining his technical skills, where he trained his right hand to such heights of dexterity that he became frightened and began using his left hand; he rarely thereafter painted with his right hand. The school was known over the years as being very conservative in its methods and philosophy; it is unlikely to have changed, for which we can be grateful: at least the students learn the rudiments of the trade, whether they forget them later or not. Too many of our so-called major painters cannot even draw, but are very good

147

at slapping paint and other matter on flat surfaces and calling it "Art."

7th ARRONDISEMENT

L' Hôtel des Invalides and Le Musée de l'Histoire Contemporaine, 149 – Le Musée Rodin, 150 – Aristide Maillol, the Germans in Paris, and Arletty in *The Children of the Paradise*, 152 – Le Musée d'Orsay, 169

The **Hôtel des Invalides**, and its immediate surroundings is a curious place, and possibly the most visited tourist attraction in the city, so caveat emptor. The Invalides contains a famous church; an army museum; a museum of plans and relief maps; the Musée de l'Ordre de la Liberation, which has an interesting history; Napoléon Bonaparte's tomb, which is quite colorful, but rather a joke in its surroundings; and the **Musée de l'Histoire Contemporaine** (formerly the Musée des Deux Guerres Mondiales) may have a worthwhile exhibition during your visit.

Should you happen to be in Paris on July 14, and should you not happen to be among those invited to sit at one of the levels of the Eiffel Tower to observe the musically accompanied fireworks extravaganza, let me make the following suggestions. Stay in your hotel room and watch the show on the telly. Much more comfortable and safe from amateur detonation experts who light explosives and throw them into the crowds for amusement.

If you must, and you should after all do it *once*, take the métro to the Latour-Maubourg stop at the Place de Santiago du Chile on the west side of the Place des Invalides. Walk westerly on the Rue de Grenelle, one of the longest streets in Paris, as we well know, having walked its length twice one very hot and humid July evening, toward the Champ de Mars. When you reach the Place de l'Union on the corner of the Boulevard Bosquet, stop in the small bistro-café and eat something light with a drinkable rosé to fortify yourself

149

and enjoy observing the types in the ever-thickening parade of people trudging with deliberate stride westward ho. Then, as the clock ticks closer to 22.30 hours, join the crowds, the pace now quickened with anxious anticipation, until at last you sweep into the now tightly-packed, dusty, hot Champ de Mars, turn to your right to face the blackiron tower, maneuver to find a standing place, and await the piecemeal darkening of the famously useless erection which signals the start of the display. At this point you will see the exploding colors through the black grillwork of the tower. If you want a clearer view, take your life in your hands and shove your way forward as far as you can go before the massed humanity refuses to budge another body. If you have ever tried to leave a sports stadium after attending a sold-out game, you have some idea of the nature of the situation when the 45 minutes or so of fireworks are over and everyone wishes to be home first.

The fireworks themselves are set off over the Palais de Chaillot and the Jardins du Trocadéro on the other side of the river. If you like fireworks, and can appreciate the attempt to orchestrate them to music, then you should not miss this annual event.

Over the years we have returned on a number of occasions to the **Musée Rodin**, Hôtel Biron, 77, rue de Varenne, not only for the aesthetic thrill of seeing his marvelous sculpture, but to sit in the garden and watch the small, intensely cute baby ducklings waddle around the grounds or paddle around in the small pond at the garden's center. In the cute category as well are the rather numerous stone Pimmels available for chortling over or for a brief caress for the benefit of a slightly warped Mensch with a camera.

While the building is off the usual tourist trails, if anything can be so described today, and it does possess the capacity to absorb a fair amount of insipid gawkers, the garden is the main attraction. Some art sculpture (as opposed to decorative sculpture) cannot be contained in buildings and should be presented in meadows, gardens and forests, not in museum rooms. The works of David Smith, for example, come immediately to mind because they lose much of their effectiveness when seen inside a man-made structure. (More obvious examples would be Calder's attempts at gargantuan immortality and the silly pieces of Robert Caro, which not even the Gobi desert, where they might be more appropriately placed, could absorb the oceanic egos they represent.) Much of Rodin's work falls into the David Smith category and we can be grateful that the arrogant old bastard made such a good deal with the French government to house his pieces.

While the museum is not saved from being inundated by tourists and art lovers quacking louder than the ducks, and not nearly so cute, as they "do" yet another site they can later say they "saw," it does have the unique distinction among museums of serving as the locus of The Nannies' Social Hour. This daily event takes place in the afternoon when the governesses of the quarter bundle their little charges into the garden to sleep more or less peacefully at nap while the "adults" sit in the sun and chat and read and eat small portions of cheese and bread simultaneously. The fact that the works of one of the great sculptors of modern times in silent majesty surround their quotidian conclaves intrudes not as bit upon their placid indifference. On the other hand, they in turn do not disturb the serious visitor's contemplation of the art that is massively, and simply, there.

Here is one of those places of quiet and green in the city where one can relax and breathe normally. Indeed, years ago as we attempted to set up the camera with an automatic timer so we could both be in the same photograph, a nanny quietly took the apparatus from us and made a fine image. The photograph is still on the wall of the house near Avignon, which does not yet belong to us.

One cannot help comparing the studio-home atmosphere of this museum and the Rodin Museum in Philadelphia, its small cold and rather sterile marble rooms jammed with the sculptures without context. Still, better the Philadelphia mausoleum than no Rodin at all. One does wonder, though, how much of that work should be attributed to the tragically abused Camille Claudel.

The German poet, Rainer Maria Rilke, served from September 1908 to the end of the peace in 1914 as Rodin's secretary and, as such, lived in the building in the ground floor room that is now the gift-bookshop. Another poet, Jean Cocteau, also rented a small apartment in a side wing of the villa in 1908 in order from time to time to get away from his mother, with whom he lived in the very social Avenue Raymond-Poincaré. He gave it up in 1909, and he describes it, typically with the wrong date, in his autobiographical notes "Démarche d'un poête" (1953).

Aristide Maillol, the Germans in Paris, and Arletty in *The Children of the Paradise*. Aristide Maillol's last model, Dina Vierny, announced in 1990 that she would open the Musée Maillol, 59, rue de Grenelle, the following year to display 400 or so of his works the sculptor apparently left to her. The building is a short walk away from the Musée Rodin. The 1990 edition of the Michelin green guide to Paris mentions the museum in passing, but provides no details about such things as opening hours. We discovered the reason for this on the evening of Bastille Day 1992 whilst trekking to the Eiffel Tower to observe the fireworks: the massive building complex seemed to be a construction site, at least that part of it one could see behind the appropriately massive wooden gate and stone wall; the rest was surmise. One hoped the museum would open before one grew too aged to appreciate Maillol's works. If one had enough luck to live nearly as long as the artist himself, and maintain as avid an interest in the sexual nature of the opposite gender, that would not occur for many years to come. In the end, one did not have to wait so long. In February 1995, *Paris Match*, that reliable source of high cultural information, announced in the society news section that Madame Vierny, in the presence of "cinq cents privilégiés," including the president of the Republic, opened the Musée Maillol/Fondation Dina Vierny the previous month at 59-61, rue de Grenelle.

The new museum not only houses some of the most elegant toilets in a public institution, but also a considerable collection of artworks of varying quality. Maillol is naturally well represented, but the three floors also exhibit a large number of works by the great and near-great of the modern movement that the sculptor, Madame Vierny and her foundation collected over the years. Many of these have a single factor in common: they all portray Madame Vierny as a young woman in various stages of undress. The museum is a shrine not only to Maillol but to Dina Vierny as well; and why not? She created the institution by persevering over the decades and over the diverse hurdles a swollen overblown state bureaucracy stacks up in the path of such projects. She has earned her monument.

In any case, Maillol created some of his most astonishing, very erotic, work during the last decade of his life, inspired no doubt by his young, sexy muse-model. See for yourself; a visit to Maillol's art is always worthwhile, and here you also can lavish upon your eyes the work of Tsugouharu Foujita, Degas, Gauguin, Rodin, Duchamp, Matisse, Dufy, Kandinsky, Picasso, and many others not so well-known, in addition to whatever temporary exhibition happens to be up during your visit.

(A bit down the Rue Grenelle from this intersection, the ground floor room at number 15, the Hôtel de Bérulle, served for several months as the location of the Bureau of Surrealist Research [also known as the Surrealist Central], where the group held exhibitions and the members served as reference resources, on a strictly scheduled time plan, for the tides of curious to purchase books and artworks and the potential applicants they expected. Only drips and driblet's of either category appeared and, after the grandly expectant opening on October 10, 1924, the Surrealist leaders closed the place in the spring of 1925.)

Maillol died as a result of an automobile accident at the age of 82 in September 1944, while returning from a visit to his son jailed in Perpignon for membership in the vicious fascist French milice, and on his way to see Raoul Dufy in a nearby village. His car went out of control and smashed into a tree, hereafter some of his collaborationist friends claimed the Resistance murdered him, a claim never substantiated. Unfortunately, David Pryce-Jones and others, including Arno Breker, repeat the claim as fact. Gerhard Heller denies the claim, saying that a "reliable source," the art dealer Louis Carré, assured him the story is not true. While such an act by the Resistance would appear to make little sense, curious things did happen during the occupation and immediately thereafter during the epoch de l'epuration (purge) which clearly defy reason. We may never know for sure, but an accident seems most likely.

Maillol seems to have had an uncomfortably eerie connection with automobiles and death. In July 1939, one of the 20th century's most well-positioned art dealers, Ambroise Vollard, dozed in the back seat of his chauffeur-driven black Talbot convertible about 40 kilometers from Paris on the road to Pontchartrain en route to his country house at Tremblay-sur-Mauldre. For some reason the chauffeur lost control and the car crashed into an immoveable object. A small Maillol bronze on the shelf beneath the rear window tumbled onto Vollard's neck rupturing his cervical vertebrae. Vollard died a few hours later in a Versailles hospital, his last words being "a lawyer, a lawyer," which lack the weighty cultural significance of Dutch Schulz's last words, but represent the attitude of a significant percentage of the western world's population these days.

Vollard's famous shop was located at 6, rue Laffitte (9th), known as the Rue des Tableaux because of the number of dealers with shops there until the early 1920s when the art market migrated to the Rue de la Boétie (8th). Vollard's memoirs, *Recollections of a Picture Dealer* (1978), similar in style to Sylvia Beach's reminiscences, are nevertheless of interest because he knew everyone from the impressionists through the cubists (Renior, Rouault, Bonnard, Cézanne, and Picasso, who painted his portrait in the cubist manner), and for the vast chunks of dialogue he made up to lend a touch of veracity to his stories.

Louis Carré considered the term "art dealer" to be vulgar and preferred to think of himself as a "publisher of artworks." Trained as a lawyer and author of two books on gold and silver collecting, he is a one of those fascinating characters known only to those who know a great deal about the history of art buying and selling in Paris in the 20th century, but unknown to the general cultured reading public. Viewing an exhibition of Toulouse-Lautrec's paintings in 1933 apparently brought on a transcendental epiphany revealing to him his destiny as being intimately bound up with modern art. He thereupon plunged into that world, establishing his own gallery on the Avenue de Messine, through which he began to cultivate the American market, a sensible move given the severe depression in the European art market. Carré's behavior during the occupation may not have been pristine, but the investigation committee after the liberation gave him a Persilschein (clean bill of health, as it were). Picasso sold through him in the immediate postwar period, playing him off against the artist's old friend and long-term dealer, Daniel-Henry Kahnweiler. In many ways, Picasso was something of a swine.

Gerhard Heller seriously took up his work as an active supporter of a German-French cultural rapprochement when he served in Paris as the German censor of French literature during the occupation. In his old age, he wrote his memoirs (with Jean Grand) entitled *Un Allemande a Paris* (1981), called in the German edition *In einem besetzten Land. Leutnant Heller und die Zensur in Frankreich 1940-1944* (1982), a more descriptive if mundane title.

A certain amount of healthy skepticism vis à vis the memoirs of Germans who worked in Paris during the war is required. Less vehicles of atonement, these volumes are more justifications and claims to anti-nazi positions. Thus caution is advised when reading Heller (though one does want to believe him somehow), Ernst Jünger's diaries, Ernst von Salomon's *Der Fragebogen*, and similar excuses.

The case of Jünger is particularly instructive as an example of an extreme nationalist antisemite who hated the nazis as primitive, uncultured guttersnipes responsible for losing the war. In his 100th year, Jünger continued to give interviews to historically ignorant journalists in which, of course, he makes no mention of his naming antisemitism as a "foundation pillar" of the national movement and other, now embarrassing statements about there being no room for Jews in a truly German nation. He also reworked the diaries before publishing them. He died in 1999.

It is clear that Heller committed acts of resistance against his own nation's authorities while he lived in Paris, such as allowing student demonstrators and certain writers and their relatives to escape arrest. He deliberately did not force himself into a close association with many writers he admired, such as François Mauriac, Albert Camus and Jean-Paul Sartre, because he did not wish them to be too much identified with the German occupiers. He justified his close relationship with Jean Paulhan and others because he had to officially work with them. On the other hand, he came to know such collaborators and fascist fellow-travelers as Pierre Drieu La Rochelle, Marcel Arland and Marcel Jouhandeau fairly closely.

This story, however, I believe one can credit: Maillol at the age of 80 possessed a fine wit. In the spring of 1942, Arno Breker arranged an exhibition of his massive sculptures in the Orangerie and wanted his former teacher, Maillol, to attend the vernissage. The old man, a political fool who, out of a truly frightening indifference or an equally frightening act of will, behaved as though the Germans were in France as guests of the state, responded positively to the invitation. Thus, Maillol continued his relations with Germans much as he had done before 1940: he hadn't changed, circumstances had. According to James Lord, in the winter of 1944-45 Picasso raged against the recently deceased sculptor's "turpitude," accusing him of using Breker to benefit his own existence. How Picasso knew this to be so, if indeed it was so, remains a matter for speculation.

That Maillol presented himself as a naïf is unquestionable. In July 1905, André Gide noted in his diary "Maillol talks with animation, graciousness, and innocence. He looks like an Assyrian from Toulouse. If only Mirbeau does not force him to 'think'." (Octave Mirbeau was an outspoken satirical writer.) Gide also reports Maillol as having said in "a strong southern accent," later that year, "A model! A model; what the hell would I do with a model? When I need to verify something, I go and find my wife in the kitchen; I lift up her chemise; and I have the marble." But as Clotilde, to give her her name, aged he turned more and more to young maids and models, the last of the long line being Dina. Mme. Maillol grew plump, old, bitter and graceless - and grew to hate her husband as well as his young girls. As John Rewald, who knew Maillol in the 1930s, notes, the sculptor did not make matters any easier for either of them when he tried to placate her by saying "But you can still pose for me ... from the back!" Gide also commented on a large Maillol woman: "Elle est belle, elle ne signifie rien, c'est une oeuvre silencieuse." And one can hardly argue with that. Now, Breker and his work were and are controversial. I think of him as an unscrupulous opportunist, possibly with a modicum of talent, who created gigantic kitsch figures which so pleased that exemplar of petit bourgeois taste, Adolf Hitler, that many then and now view Breker as the unofficial Nazi "State Sculptor." On the other hand, he had lived in Montparnasse, admired both Rodin and Antoine Bourdelle, and quite possibly loved French culture. Perhaps he, too, was a true naïf, but this is unlikely; he rose too far too quickly to be classified as an "artist-fool," such as his compatriot, the actor-singer Hans Albers, was reputed to have been. Breker also famously claimed to have saved Dina Vierny, a Russian Jew, from arrest and deportation and to have been responsible for protecting Picasso from the depredations of the Gestapo.

Hitler, or someone in his entourage, chose Breker to guide the failed artist/architect become politician through the city on the Führer's three-hour visit on June 23, 1940, the city that could then be spared because it would be irrelevant in the future, but the city that in August 1944 elicited Hitler's insane telegram to the German military commander of Paris: "Brennt Paris?"

But we were considering Maillol's wit at 80 and the accepted invitation to attend the vernissage of Breker's exhibition, allegedly held in aid of Wehrmacht charities. The old man lived in the Pyrénées Orientales in Banyuls-sur-Mer near the Spanish-French border, and had to be driven from Vichy France into the occupied zone, a task Heller arranged to do himself. Maillol agreed to make the trip, but evaded committing himself to an opinion about his former student's latest works by slyly answering Heller's question with the statement   "On m'a dit que c'est trés grand." ("Yes, I'm told they are very big.") Mumbled into his great gray beard, no doubt.

And so they are. They stand at least larger than life, idealizations of the ("Aryan" of course) human figure, mainly male, meant by Breker to be "heroic" through his use of magnitude and classical proportions including small but perfectly shaped uncircumcised Pimmels for boys, large jutting breasts and hairless pudenda for girls. Tout-Paris, that is to say, the art world of collaborationist Paris, showed off its finery at the Orangerie vernissage on May 1, 1942, including Cocteau, Derain and Vlaminck (the latter two received one-year "sanctions" banning them from exhibiting their works at liberation), Arletty (arrested at liberation), leading German occupation officials, and several important political collaborationist French porks such as Pierre Laval and Fernand de Brinon (both executed after liberation), Abel Bonnard (no relation to Pierre, sentenced to death in abstentia after liberation), and Jacques Benoist-Méchin (imprisoned after liberation). Apparently no one commented publicly on the absurdity of the event.

One is compelled here to write a few words about Arletty. While the rest listed above, and countless others, are guilty of crimes ranging from treason to stupidity, not to say cupidity and optimism, Arletty, I am convinced, is guilty of little more than ignorance, ambition and perhaps a modicum of naïveté. That she indulged in what wits at the time termed "collaboration horizontale" with a German Luftwaffe officer with whom she lived at the Ritz, is beyond doubt. That she deserved to be arrested and suffer her head to be shaved and serve a brief incarceration in Fresnes prison (from which she was allowed out, in a wig no doubt, to appear in last minute retakes for *Les enfants du paradise*) is possible, but that was sufficient. Ironically, one of her lines in the film reads, "I am the victim of a miscarriage of justice."

Her German lover worked on the staff of the Luftwaffe commander in France, General Hanesse, who confiscated the Rothschild Avenue de Marigny residence for his own use, where he organized a series of parties for high-ranking Germans and their French collaborators. According to Antony Beevor and Artemis Cooper in their book on the post-Liberation period, the following conversation took place between Baron Elie de Rothschild, just returned from a prison camp, and the stalwart family butler, Félix. The Baron suggested that life must have been rather quiet during the German general's stay.

"On the contrary, Monsieur Elie. There were receptions every evening."

"But ... who came?"

"The same people, Monsieur Elie. The same as before the war."

Which seems to be a fairly accurate summing up of the period: one made accommodations and carried on as before. Not everyone, of course, but most.

Moving through the rough-and-tumble world of the demimondaine, guided by her first Pygmalion, Paul Guillaume, whose magnificent collection of impressionists and post-impressionists is in the Orangerie, and his successor as "guardian," Paul Poiret, the great clothing designer and director of the Capuchines Theater, Arletty achieved successive successes in both careers: mannequin et comédienne. On the way, it seems all Montparnasse painted her, usually in the nude: Moïse Kisling, Kees Van Dongen, Marie Laurencin, Braque, Matisse, et alia. Whether or not she was an intellectual hardly matters, she reigned in all environments. After all, she did, allegedly, make the statement "Fermer les maisons closes, c'est plus qu'un crime, c'est un pléonasme." Alors!

Very quotable, Arletty. When a reporter pretending to be a member of the intelligentsia asked her why she had never received the medal of the Legion of Honor, although

Elizabeth Taylor, Brigitte Bardot and Marlene Dietrich had, she answered, "Au départ, on vous la donnait. Puis on a ajouté un article au Code Napoléon où l'on indiquait qu'il fallait la demander. Comme Marcel Aymé, j'ai oublié d'écrire..."

In 1962, Arletty, known to her friends by her preferred name, Arlette, absentmindedly reversed her strongly medicated eye drops, putting those for the right in the left eye and vice versa; in doing so, she destroyed most of her sight. Two months later she struggled through the making of her last, alas mediocre, film, *Le Voyage à Biarritz*. She had the misfortune to die in Paris at the age of 94 during the 1992 Olympic Games in Barcelona, thus missing la grande publicité, though *Paris-Match* gave her a cover story entitled "Nôtre grande Arletty," including such revelations as "ses dernières confidences sur l'amour, Dieu, la drogue..." and, of course, "douze ans de passion pour un inconnu."

Type-cast at first as une femme légère, a veritable horizontal vamp, Marcel Carné offered her the chance to break the mold by casting her against Jean Gabin in the archetypal film noir, *Le jour se lève* (1939), written by Jacques Prévert and designed by Alexandre Trauner. If you have seen the version without the mysteriously radiant nude shower scene in which Arletty, with chilled nipples in the unheated studio, seems to be standing, sponge in strategically placed hand, in a shallow bowl of milk, you have not seen the film at all. (There is a photograph from this scene in several books on French cinema and also in the printed material included in the CD of her songs entitled "Arletty.") And if you have ever wondered about the origins of the work of directors such as Nicholas Ray and Jacques Tourneur, and Josef von Sternberg's forgotten *The Shanghai Gesture* (1941) and *Macao* (1948), look to Carné in this film, and his *Hôtel du Nord (1938), Les visiteurs du soir (1943)*, both with Arletty, and *Quai des brumes* (1938).

The Arletty film most Americans are likely to see is Carné's *Les enfants du paradis* (1945), a lengthy "historical drama" about the Parisian demi-monde of the early 19th century theater, with a vibrant if occasionally obscure anti-fascist subtext. Made under the occupation in 1943-44, but released after the liberation, this film creates a historically identified hermetic world, which nonetheless is said to be a metaphor for the Parisian situation under the nazis and their French collaborators. Ignore the subtext and you still experience the transcendent performances of Arletty as Garance, Jean-Louis Barrault as the mime, Pierre Brasseur as Frederick Lamâitre, the mysterious Maria Casarès as Natalie, Marcel Herrand as Lecenaire, and, for those who appreciate odd careers, Gaston Modot as the blind beggar.

The title is usually, but incorrectly, translated into English as *Children of Paradise*. As some of us, including Peter Hartsock, have pointed out over the years to deaf and blind audiences, the correct translation is "Children of *the* Paradise" since the "paradise," in context, is not some vague edenic locus of realized dreams, but that section of the theater Americans once referred to as "seventh heaven," the "second balcony," and other, unprintable, designations. In short, the cheapest seats in the house.

Jacques Prévert, the fantastic poet and photograph model for Parisian street scenes, wrote the script and the dialog. As he often noted, a number of people worked on the film who were, in effect, ghosts: as Jews, Joseph Kosma, the composer, and Alexandre Trauner, the set designer, could not exist - if they did it could, paradoxically, mean their deaths, so they did not exist. But the film opened after the liberation of Paris and by then they could exist again, and so received credit for their work. The company shot the film between August 16 and November 9, 1943, much of it in Nice, with an interruption of two months in September and October when the Allies landed in southern Italy. The Gestapo regularly visited the sets in Nice and Paris because informants said Jews and other suspicious types worked on the film. The Gestapo caught none of them, as far as I know, and that brings us back to Breker, who never had to worry about the Gestapo, and Maillol, who as far as one can tell simply did not.

Breker's monumental, bombastic pieces could hardly have appealed to a strong, sensitive southern soul like Maillol, who at the age of 80 saw the young girls dressed in their summer clothes and said, "Look at those legs. What weight they'll carry!" There is, indeed, strength in his works, but hardly the bombast of the Breker variety. A representative sample of the work of each is found in Michèlle Cone's Artists Under Vichy: A Case of Prejudice and Persecution (1992). You can see some of Maillol's works in the garden of New York's Museum of Modern Art, the New York Guggenheim Museum, and in the Hirshhorn Museum and Sculpture Garden in Washington, D.C.

In his diary, Harry Graf Kessler tells the sadly comic story of the then 69 year-old Maillol's attempts to escape his shrewish wife's "scènes perpétuelles," by visiting Kessler in Weimar, taking with him his current not-quite-twenty-one-year-old model, with whom he apparently cuddled on occasion. But, also apparently, not on a sufficient number of occasions, for once they settled in near Kessler's house, the situation became painfully clear to their host as the young woman moped about, frustrated in body if not in mind, to the old man's embarrassment. "We have here the old tragicomedy of the aging man and the hot-blooded girl, the very stuff of the most ancient comedy. Mme. Maillol is avenged!"

Well, she may have been for a while. Her creaking, but randy husband nonetheless appreciated the German propensity to publicly remove their clothes in clement weather. "Maillol was in raptures about the unabashed nudity." Having spent some time myself on a Baltic Sea beach with hundreds of nude Germans, I can rather understand his enthusiasm. But, to paraphrase Kessler on the subject of architecture, this German nudism "cannot be understood unless it is visualized as part of an entirely new Weltanschauung." Part of this new Weltanschauung forced Kessler to flee across the German-French border in March 1933, barely escaping arrest and detention in "protective custody." Kessler died in France at the age of 69 in December 1937, spared the horrors his countrymen perpetrated after September 1939. His diaries make fascinating reading and are relevant here because he spent so much time in Paris. They are published in English under the inaccurate title *In the Twenties: The Diaries of Harry Kessler* (1971).[14]

Kessler was not the first, nor the last of the countless Germans who have escaped from their own xenophobic, nationalist cultural traditions to appreciate and admire the French, or at least the Parisian alternative. Even more countless numbers of them have visited Paris at one time or another, some willingly, some not. Karl Marx, during his first exile, is reputed to have first met the modern (i.e., mid-19th century) proletariat in Paris, but in truth he met under-employed German artisans and craftsmen in exile for political or nascent trade-union activities.

Another large group of Germans, not on the best of terms with the swinish regime in Berlin that came to power in January 1933, fled legally or illegally across the border into France in order to save their lives or their souls. This migration continued until the war practically put an end to it and the French imprisoned most of those in France as enemy aliens! The British did the same for a time and the Americans only put a few, such as Carl Zuckmayer, under house arrest for several months, whilst allowing others to carry on their activities without any hindrance whatsoever.

One up for the USA, indeed, but alas the same country put the west coast Japanese-Americans in concentration camps, which says something about the country's racism as well as its security consciousness.

As conditions worsened and it became clear that the nazis would in fact enter Paris as typically arrogant victors, the anti-fascist and Jewish exiles perforce moved on again, south, away from their persecutors. Many of them did not complete the journey to safety. This was not France's most glorious hour. Nor were the four years of occupation that followed, despite the all-pervasive and generally inaccurate myths about the Resistance.

One German who twice successfully fled is Josef Breitenbach (1869-1984), a photographer, who visited Paris during the 1920s in search of inspiration and learning. In 1933, after the Gestapo "interviewed" him in his home city of Munich, he moved to Paris permanently, where he continued his work in the genre of portraiture (James Joyce, Bertolt Brecht, Wassily Kandinsky, Max Ernst, et alia) and expanded his subject matter to include landscapes filmed in color with which he experimented in the darkroom. The objects in some of his pictures seem to glow with an unusual intensity. In the autumn of 1939, the French interned him. Somehow he survived the camps in France and succeeded in reaching New York in 1942, where he continued his work, and taught at the New School and Cooper Union - one story among countless others of people who looked to Paris for salvation and to earn a living.[15]

The great poet Heinrich Heine is buried in the Montmartre cemetery, having spent so many years in exile in Paris. Rainer Maria Rilke, Max Ernst, Ernst Jünger, Heller, and even Friedrich Sieburg, whose behavior in occupied Paris was hardly exemplary, but whose book *Gott in Frankreich?* (1929) is a classic expression of, in this case somewhat ambiguous but clearly nationalistic, German delight things French, are among those Germans whose often sympathetic appreciation for French moeurs they clearly expressed in various ways.

Sieburg, the "evangelist of the Third Empire," as he described himself in his tract, *Germany: My Country* (1933), published in London, is an interesting case. After working for years as the *Frankfurter Zeitung* correspondent in France, where after January 1933 he became the enemy of the German refugee intellectuals, he arranged a position in the Foreign Affairs Ministry for himself and went to Paris via Brussels in the baggage of the Wehrmacht to serve the occupation government in some not clearly defined position because of his reputation as an expert on France and things French. This is all the more bizarre because at various times during his stay in Paris he publicly allowed as how the Germans had to take over France because the French were incapable of governing the country. He said his experiences in France had made him into a National Socialist. This state of affairs apparently stunned several of those who had known him for a long time and they had no choice but to mark it off as opportunism of the crassest sort. Pouring salt in the wounds, he became insufferably snobbish and condescending to everyone he deemed beneath his social and official position, without exempting fellow nazis. One would much like to see his denazification file, if he had one.

Sieburg appears as the character Wiesener in Lion Feuchtwanger's book *Exil* (1940), published in the USA as *Paris Gazette* (1940), an interesting, if somewhat turgid fictional account of the lives of German writers and newspaper journalists in exile. Sieburg reappears in postwar Germany and achieved a solid reputation as a cultural critic.

Not all Germans went to France with this cerebral and equivocal attitude, of course. Hundreds of thousands spent time in France during 1914-1918 and 1940-1944 with not only no appreciation at all, but with a knack for destruction they only surpassed on the Eastern Front. This lack of cross-cultural understanding is vividly shown in such sources as Jean Eparvier's book published shortly after the liberation of the city, *A Paris. Sous la botte des Nazis* (1944), which has a concise text with many black and white photographs of daily life in Paris during those years taken by Roger Schall, and Serge Klarsfeld, *Memorial to the Jews Deported from France* (1983). You might also look into Henri Michel's *Paris Allemand* (1981), a solid but not boring narrative of this fascinatingly perverse period of French and European history.

The German occupation, then, represents a time of ambiguity, confusion and terror for most Parisians. George Kennan, then an American Embassy official in Berlin, visited Paris on business on July 2, 1940, and, in a book of remembrances entitled *Sketches from a Life* (1989), captured the mood of the city. He thought it resembled a vast tomb: a few policemen on corners found no traffic to direct, the square before the Opéra lay void of life or movement. But six German officers sat alone on the terrace of the Café de la Paix, attempting to appear normal, with the café empty behind them and the streets empty in front of them, the terrace deserted except for themselves, the victors sat, the conquerors with no one to admire them or hate them, with "no one but themselves to witness their triumph." In time, of course, they taught the French to hate them; for this they possessed a great talent.

Perhaps the most romantic, and thus inaccurate, image of the German occupation of the city is that of the German leader landing on June 23, 1940, early in the morning, spending a few hours speeding about the empty boulevards and streets accompanied by a few aids and the Offical State Sculptor, Arno Breker. No crowds cheering, no one knew he had arrived. And what did he see? The usual tourist sites and sights: Eiffel tower, Napoléon's tomb, the Place de la Opéra. Bouf!

But he saw few Frenchmen. The emptiness of the city has been much commented on, and this phenomenon is easily explained and has nothing to do with resisting the Germans even passively: more than two million Parisians hastily fled the city as the German troops closed in on it. Most soon returned to take up their lives and work, and tried to make the best of the situation

While Parisians ignored the Germans when possible, the inhabitants of the city did have a number of words to describe their oppressors, two of the more printable being "les Épinards" because of their spinach green uniforms, and the simple "Fritz." One of the less printable was "Gestapette," which referred to fraternizing males formed by the punning combination of "Gestapo" and "tapette," French argot for "faggot."

After the war, certain Germans came to Paris for the same reasons all "cultural workers" have always come to Paris. Günter Graß lived at 111, avenue d'Italie (13th) in a small, two-room apartment from 1956 to 1960, during which time he wrote much of *Die Blechtrommel (The Tin Drum)* and fathered twins. Volker Schlöndorff, the film director apprenticed with Louis Malle among others and directed the film versions of Graß' novel, Max Frisch's *Homo Faber*, and Marcel Proust's *Du Côté de Chez Swann*. And, of course, the ever lovely and delicious Romy Schneider, who made her best films in France, although she actually was an Austrian, who does not require an active verb, effervescing sufficiently on her own.

For those interested in the subject, a tour of the places of the anti-nazi German exiles would fascinate, but directions for such will have to await a different sort of guide. In the meantime, if you happen to be in the northwestern sector of the 13th arrondissement, stop at the artists' complex called Cité Fleurie at 65, boulevard Arago with its wall plaque noting this is a repository of books by anti-nazi writers from the period 1934-1940. Rooms here also served as offices for various anti-fascist organizations devoted to propaganda against the nazis, and to a lesser extent the Italian Fascisti.

Not only painters and sculptors lived, and continue to live, and work in this lively arrangement of studios and living quarters; a certain number of writers inhabited rooms here as well, such as Ford Madox Ford in 1923 when he began editing *The Transatlantic Review* at this address before he moved the editorial desk to William Bird's Three Mountains Press printery on the Quai d'Anjou.

* * * *

The **Musée d'Orsay**, Quai d'Orsay, situated on the banks of the Seine in the former Gare d'Orsay, hardly expresses French glory either, but for entirely different reasons. Unfortunately it is on the list of places one simply must see because all the lovely pictures formerly in the Jeu de Paume are now hung here, if you can find them around, behind, above, below the architectural bric-a-brac that chokes the interior and disrupts any attempt at contemplation or even the simple act of seeing. And the pictures *are* lovely, when you can see them in adequate light. Alas, this is not always possible in the present museum arrangement. One's disappointment is compounded by the fact that the pictures are some of the most beautiful man-made objects in this ugly, mean little world, even if often created by mean little humans. You do not have to know, or to care, that Cézanne treated his wife badly, or that Picasso treated all women badly, to be stunned by the manifold loveliness and multitudinous meanings of their paintings. But you must be able to see them.

After all, Cézanne did say "The artist is only the dog of his work, and when the master whistles, he must come - even on Sundays." One wonders if this constituted a sly dig at Henri Rousseau. Pure speculation, of course, since I can find no evidence whatsoever that the former knew of the latter's existence.

Jed Perl has described this museum as the place "where 19th century art is now treated as mere cultural archeology and great painters are put on the same plane as artisans and technicians." Is this accurate appraisal based on an elitist attitude? You bet it is. High culture is not democratic; when art is made for the masses it generally becomes kitsch; when it is presented to and for the masses it becomes, for the duration of the exhibition, unviewable for anyone who deeply and seriously comprehends and appreciates it. Alas, the Musée d'Orsay, in its presentation for the hordes of culturally illiterate but ravenous for notches in their art pistols, panders to the extent that the art disappears in the excrescences of the building and the "folk craft" meant to please the tourists from Düsseldorf, Dubuque and Dijon.

Ideally, one should visit this museum, when it is located in a different venue in one's fantasy, at some time of year when not more than a dozen or so visitors are present. Since the ideal time cannot be found, one suffers the mobs of tourists and gaggles of high school students being herded against their better judgment past the greatness of 19th century French art, giggling moronically, while their harried teachers unsuccessfully attempt to point out the grandeur of the paintings on the walls. All this, in addition to the awkward interior design, makes concentration impossible, but one can let one's eyes travel over the surface of the canvas, absorbing the forms and colors, which perhaps trigger memories of other paintings and other circumstances. On the other hand, there is a fine

170

bookstore/museum shop, which can be visited for fun and edification.

During the interregnum between its use as a railroad station and its misuse as a museum, the building served as a set for Orson Welles' unreasonably underrated film of Franz Kafka's novel, *The Trial*.

8th ARRONDISEMENT

The Keystone Kops in Paris, 172 – Le Restaurant Garnier – Yves Montand, 172 – Caillebotte and the Rainswept Square, 174 – The Ambiguous Florence Gould, 176

What would it take, you may well ask, to move us beyond the boundaries of the 4th, 5th, 6th and 14th, our regular stomping ground? We had, in fact, spent time in the 8th in 1980 when, on our first visit to Paris together, we stayed for five days at the Hôtel Madeleine on the Place de la Madeleine, in the middle of which sits the ugliest church in Paris named for the Place, or vice versa. Luckily our window overlooked the Rue Tronchet, thus sparing us the view of that holy shrine to bad taste.

The Keystone Kops in Paris. That particular room and that particular window having, willy-nilly, been assigned to us led immediately to our first unusual experience in Paris, although brother Dean apparently underwent something similar some years earlier. The bleating sound of the Paris police van can be heard at all hours of the day and night as these underpaid, often harried officials scurry about the city enforcing the law or hurrying off to lunch. As we washed some of the travel grime down the drain, that unique sound, having replaced the siren after 1945 because of its association with bombs and death from the sky, klaxoned its way up the walls and into our window with increasing volume.

Curiosity only itches so long before one must scratch it. From the window we observed the van jolt to a sudden halt across the Rue Tronchet. Six or seven flics fled the confines of the vehicle as if they had just been informed it contained a bomb about to explode. As quickly as they alighted, equally as slowly in reverse did they mill about on the sidewalk as if embarrassed by their own alacrity in abandoning their transportation, which never did blast a hole in the Paris street.

Eventually, after some further milling about, things began to happen at a speed midway between the disembarkation from the van and the sidewalk confabulations. From a second story window (by American count) an old couple gestured toward another window on their floor further down the side of the building. A young man carrying a ring of European keys came out of the gate to the edifice's courtyard and discussed matters with the police. A crowd gathered. Various people stretched their arms pointing to the end of the building. An evidently lunch-hungry cop finally made a decision: call the fire department. It must be admitted that the old couple on the second floor did not appear to be unduly disturbed by the possibility of their demise in a conflagration.

Some minutes later a small truck whipped around the corner of the Rue Tronchet from the Place de la Madeleine and yanked itself to a full stop behind the police van. As if entwined in a fine net of strong cobwebs, two young firemen eventually made their way out of the truck and conferred laboriously with their police department colleagues. The original crowd, bored by inactivity on the part of Paris officialdom, had gone off in various directions. Now, with the prospect of something, anything, about to happen, a new crowd gathered hoping for some mild excitement to enrich their day.

Once the conference between the two departments of public safety and welfare resolved itself, one of the stalwart members of the fire brigade began to climb a ladder, conveniently placed against the facade of the building by his colleague, to the second floor; just that floor which the entire dither apparently concerned. Having achieved the height of the old couple's apartment, the young man cautiously inched his way along a small ledge to the last window of the building and began to bash at it with an axe. The axe had a long handle and resembled an American fireman's axe, which for some reason surprised me. Having bashed enough of the glass and wood to allow an arm through it, he opened the window and climbed into the room beyond. With this act several civilians and a goodly number of the assembled uniformed police rushed pell-mell into the courtyard and disappeared from our view.

This episode might be entitled "A Unsatisfactory End to a Vague Paris Story." The truth of the matter is that readers in this age of the thirty-second attention span do not possess the patience to profoundly savor the fullness of a tale longtold, but with a bit of mystery to it. Today's readers, bloody barbarians, require everything to happen hard, fast, clearly and above all simply. (Exemplifying Willard Motley's phrase describing the philosophy of those once called "juvenile delinquents" in Denver: "Live fast, die young and have a good-looking corpse.") Never mind the commas and the beautifully dithyrambic Jamesian phrases, which only lead to irrelevant subordinate clauses. Get to the redmeat of it - schnell! What a perversion of P.O.P.'s (Poor Old Papa) lucid ideal!

Having forsaken the window for other pleasures, we eventually made our way downstairs and crossed the Rue Tronchet, probably with some culinary goal in mind. As we reached the far side of the street two of the policemen disinterestedly trundled an empty body sack from the van into the building. We walked to a sidewalk café where our conversation desultorily probed the possibilities. Suicide? Old age? Overdose? Ennui? A case for Maigret? We never discovered the answer, if there was one.

But to answer the question at the head of this chapter, two things so motivated us in the autumn of 1991 and again in the following year north to this quarter where we've barely spent any time at all: oysters and Caillebotte, not a

174

terribly uncommon combination of physical and spiritual succor, one would think.

Le Restaurant Garnier and Yves Montand. Our friends, Margaret and André Corman, then living in Paris, recommended to us the Restaurant Garnier, 111, rue St-Lazare on the Place du Havre across the street from the Gare Saint Lazare. They praised its high quality seafood, especially the oysters, which, we are thoroughly convinced, are best eaten in Paris anyway. Since this couple, whose seafood addiction equaled ours in discrimination and gusto, we readily agreed to leave our traditional venue and subway north.

The restaurant per se may indeed serve excellent seafood meals, at prices not very different from any other well-known Parisian eateries, but we cannot tell you about them. Just to the left of the large glass door through which one enters the main dining area, a narrow glass passageway leads to a horseshoe-shaped bar of no particular design or appointments distinction called Bar Dégustation. We zipped unhesitatingly through the passage and plonked ourselves down in the personless room. Chilly October air moved gently but persistently through the small opening through which passed the shucked shellfish to those of us fortunate enough to be there to receive this manna, veritable food for the gods. The Shucker, needless to say, stood in his rubber boots just outside on the sidewalk.

The menu contains seven items: six different types of oysters and a line of text informing one that the bartender would serve a vin du jour. Nothing else. This is a true oyster bar. If you arrive after the lunch-hour rush, say around 14 o'clock, you may find a customer having a late repas. You will certainly find several older matrons of the city, clearly widowed, not poor, and very willing to discuss the merits of the wine, the various types of oysters, and the desirability of living in California, or all of the above and much more besides, should you even slightly hint that you might be ready for conversation, in French of course, though one or another of these wonderful regulars may have some English.

The vin du jour was a Riesling, somewhat lacking a sense of character, but still fine enough to accompany the oysters. We could carry on here about the wine's qualities vis à vis the oysters, such as metaphorically throwing up our hands at the very thought of drinking a rosé with fish, but we are too ignorant. We don't read much about wine because most "corksniffers," as Frank Prial calls them, do not seem to be able to write anything but boring pretentious hyperbole. There are, of course, exceptions, such as Kermit Lynch and Robert Parker. We will read A. J. Liebling any time because he believed, with George Orwell, in plain English. Alas, one has not the time necessary to really learn about the nectar of the gods, but perhaps some day....

To balance this paean to the mighty mollusk, one might remember General Andache Junot who, legend has it, regularly consumed 300 oysters as a starter, but who, as Patricia Wells puts it, "died insane in 1813." However, since none of us would, even ever so briefly, contemplate anything approaching this level of conspicuous consumption, we can ignore the cautionary element of the tale and consider it as a mildly amusing anecdote of vague provenance and veracity.

In the autumn of 1993 we did not eat oysters in the Garnier restaurant, we ate the restaurant's oysters in Mrs. Corman's apartment, where we enjoyed them even more intensely than previously. We consumed the fruits of the winedark sea at a pitch of pleasure almost embarrassing to admit to, and rose to a plateau of existence known only to those fortunate enough to be able to eat oysters in Paris, even if they cannot be graced by the presence of Mrs. Corman and Dean to increase the pleasure of the table. Thank you, Margaret.

When one crosses the street from the Garnier to the Gare Saint-Lazare, one cannot avoid seeing the five-meter high advertising kiosk standing at the edge of the station's terrace. In October 1991, we stopped to admire on it the larger than life representation of Yves Montand, slim and limber as ever at 70, hat cocked over one eye in a typical Montand music hall pose. Under the photograph the sadly unfulfilled words

MONTAND
à BERCY
A PARTIR DU 29 MAI 92

Ivo Livi, known as Yves Montand, died in November 1991.

* * * *

Caillebotte and the Rainswept Square. Now, about Caillebotte, Gustave (1848-1894). A well-respected late 19th century "post-impressionist" painter, he made, among other marvelous paintings, a very large oil on canvas portraying a few pedestrians with umbrellas amiably strolling about in the rain at the intersection of the Rue de Turin and the Rue de Moscou in 1877, entitled appropriately enough, "Rue de Paris, temps de pluie" and in English, "Paris, A Rainy Day (Intersection of the Rue de Turin and Rue de Moscou)," mislabeled "The Place de l'Europe, Rainy Day" in John Milner's *The Studios of Paris* (1988), where Milner mistakes the intersection for the Place de l'Europe, which is actually southeast down the Rue de Léningrad. Caillebotte did paint two works entitled "Le Pont de l'Europe," but it doesn't rain in either of these.

Having been fascinated by the painting's haunting qualities, we naturally wished to see what ravages Progress had wrecked upon the original cityscape. We found the intersection by walking up the hill from the Gare Saint-

177

Lazare; that is, we found more than a corner, indeed we found several corners of fine old buildings abutting on an area not quite a square, but a large intersection into which eight or ten streets enter and out of which an equal number leave. By some odd twist of fate, our camera happened to be functioning according to the quirky directions provided by the oriental manufacturer, and we documented the intersection for comparison. Progress in the shape of automobiles, telephone wires, streetlights, motorcycles, and a barrage of large trees all conspire to obscure that which once was a rather austere if lovely urban scene. Nonetheless one can see it all. Caillebotte had a good eye; it did not fail him, nor does it fail us. In the end, one has the art, of course, in this case hanging prominently in The Art Institute of Chicago. A much smaller study for the work is in the Musée Marmottan in Paris.

The perspective in the painting is so perfected that, on looking closely at the canvas, one is surprised to find it a flat surface. Caillebotte's studies for this and other paintings point clearly to the arduous and often profound process a painter goes through to reach the heights of technical mastery without losing the spontaneity necessary to raise technique to the level of art. In 1994-95, on the one hundredth anniversary of his death, French and American curators organized a major Caillebotte retrospective, which appeared in the Grand Palais in Paris and in The Art Institute of Chicago. This resulted in a widened popularity and knowledge of the painters work, in addition to the vastly increased sale of postal cards and t-shirts. When he heard about the painter's death, Pissarro wrote to his son, Lucien: "En voilá un que nous pouvons pleurer, il a été bon et génereux, et, ce qui negâte rien, un peintre de talent." Surely a good and generous man, but more, I think, than merely a talented painter.

Sit in the Primrose Café at the southern corner of the intersection and take a coffee or drink a glass of wine or eat ice cream, while you contemplate at least one part of the city which remains and reminds of a less anxious, less polluted, perhaps even free-er past, when one could carry on a conversation without the use of obscenities and could make one's point without one's interlocutor jabbing his eyes at the nearest timepiece. But, of course, they didn't have the medicines we do now and, yes, sure, of course....

In the southern reaches of the 8th, along the river the Avenue Winston Churchill divides the Grand Palais and the Petit Palais, which contain exhibitions of art and other cultural artifacts of the centuries of human aspirations toward humanity. The Grand Palais, as its name suggests, houses the blockbuster shows of major retrospectives such as those of Manet, Seurat, Gericault, et alia. Check in *Pariscope* to see if something you should see is on during your visit.

* * * *

The Ambiguous Florence Gould. For many years after the war, no one, except the Germans, mentioned Flo Gould. Why? Was she too déclassé? Too tarred with the brush of collaboration with the Germans? Too much the social climber, having married Frank Jay Gould and the Gould fortune? All of the above? None? Who knows? But some of us, if we do not exactly care, are at least interested, nicht wahr? She did hold a "salon" during the years 1940-44 to which came the more cultured of the Germans in uniform, the few in Paris at the time, such as Heller and Jünger (the 1920s antisemite who later became a universal humanitarian, and reputed by some to have been her lover), and the unnamed military engineer she also allegedly took as a lover, or so it is said, whilst Frank Jay carried on in the unoccupied zone, in his elaborate villa in Juan-les-Pins to be exact, with side trips to officially neutral Monaco for banking and wagering.

179

Flo held forth Thursdays at the Hôtel Bristol, 112, rue Faubourg Saint-Honoré (8th) until April 1942, when she moved into a grand apartment in the Avenue Malakoff (16th) near the Bois de Boulogne ("on déjeune à Malakoff"). Thursdays, because this was Marcel Jouhandeau's only free day - he taught in a Catholic private school. He also wrote large amount of prose, among other things a pamphlet called *The Jewish Peril* (*Le Peril juif* - 1939) that contains the essay "How I Became an Antisemite." Fine company, indeed. She served fine wines, including excellent champagne, food not generally seen on French tables during the war, and, a rarity at the time, real coffee. The presence of Germans such as Heller and Jünger and other alleged non-nazis, and her engineer lover, may have helped keep the larder full, but her position as Frank Jay Gould's wife probably had more to do with the issue. The Gould's connections extended in many directions both political and economic, including into the Abwehr (German military intelligence).

George Kennan stayed briefly in the hotel during his trip to Paris in early July 1940, when the building had been appropriated to house the official Americans who remained when the German Army and the Gestapo entered the city. The hotel offered makeshift accommodations and little service since most of the staff had scurried away from the city with hundreds of thousands of other Parisians, but the Americans enjoyed the fact that they had been able to keep the Germans out of the hotel, at least temporarily. By the time Madame Gould moved in, the Germans had already done so and the Americans had left.

Frank Jay had participated in the founding of the Maisons-Laffitte department store; Jünger and Heller made up a story about his wine cellar in an obscure corner of the store's underground storage rooms containing over 100,000 bottles - enough to sell to the German police, *and* the Americans and British when they arrived.

Madame Gould experienced a little trouble during the purging in 1944-45. According to Jean Galtier-Boissière, shortly after the liberation of Paris, she had a few friends to lunch, a lengthy and traditionally enjoyable event chez Gould. At one point, the butler slipped into the room and murmured briefly into Madame's pearly ear, after which she excused herself. The lunch continued in her absence, but at 5 o'clock the butler finally gave in and told the gathering: "I think, ladies and gentlemen, that it would be better not to wait any longer. Madame has been arrested."

But the Gould story has never been told in the fullness it deserves. What role did Frank Jay really play in the German planning for hiding away assets to be used after the war? Perhaps Herbert Lottman will get to it; he should, since he never mentions them in his book on the postwar purge. Perhaps Marc Masurovsky will uncover the details since he is already on their trail, so to speak. After liberation, Flo continued her salon, with members of the new social, political and economic elite, replacing the collabos and their German masters, to mix with the older French friends of the house. Resilient is the word. A Florence Gould Foundation currently funds museum exhibitions in France and the USA.

9th ARRONDISEMENT

J'suis l'pornographe
Du phonographe,
Le polisson
De la chanson.
— Georges Brassens

L'Olympia and an Interlude about Music, 182 – The Surrealists on the Rue Fontaine, 191

Most of the world's best popular entertainers with, and without, musical talent have performed on the boards of **L'Olympia**, the Carnegie Hall of French popular culture, which opened on April 12, 1893, at 28, boulevard des Capucines, including groups such as The Beatles, Téléfon and The Rolling Stones. Though it is no longer possible to see and hear Edith Piaf, Jacques Brel, Marie Dubas, Maurice Chevalier, Mistinguett, Georges Brassens, Serge Gainsborough, or Yves Montand at the Olympia, you should seriously consider spending an evening at this shrine to musical wit and imagination, especially if someone on the same level of talent as Charles Aznavour or Serge Reggiani, may they be with us for many years to come, are performing.

Late in the autumn of 1984, the Fates smiled and arranged to have us in Paris during Reggiani's stint at the Olympia. Backed by a four or five man ensemble, he stood loosely before the microphone, his cheeks broken out in a white beardstubble, in a shabby but well cut black suit, opennecked white dress shirt, cigarette in hand, the minimalist of motion exhibited a maximum of straightforward emotion within a limited range of vocal color, and mesmerized the audience, most of whom knew every word to every song.

Only a few other French singers, perhaps "performers" would be more accurate, had the presence and talent equal to Reggiani, and they are all dead or no longer singing except for Aznavour. No one else could render "L'Italien," Apollinaire's "Sous le pont Mirabeau," "Ma Liberté," Rimbaud's "Prélude: le Dormeur du val," or Boris Vian and Harold Berg's "Le Deserteur" with the same effect on an audience.

Léo Ferré would go over the emotional edge into hysterical pathos (ah, but he does do a solid job on "Poètes, vos papiers!"), others would depend upon the orchestration to carry them through. Reggiani sings, or recites to music. The latter is important, given the French popular music tradition of Sprechstimme, which may have originated, not in a non-existent French proclivity toward Arnold Schönberg's musical theories, but in the lack of singing ability of movie stars whose managers felt compelled to force them to record songs. This unfortunate propensity perfectly exemplifies the statement made to Arlo Guthrie by a seedy 13-year old asking for his autograph in *Alice's Restaurant*: "someday you might be an album," as the singing careers of Brigitte Bardot, Jane Birkin, and Jean Marais suggest. Even Romy Schneider and Princess Stephanie made records, mon.

Jeanne Moreau is, as always, a special case. She recorded her first (78 rpm) disk of two songs from the play *L'Heure éblouissante* (The Dazzling Hour) in which she played a leading role in 1953 after working in the Comédie-Française and with Jean Vilar's theater group at the start of an extraordinary career as an actress. Thereafter she made a number of records, including one LP with her own lyrics (*Jeanne chante Jeanne* 1970), but the most unforgettable example of her thin, softly metallic singing voice is her rendition of the late Georges Delarue and Cyrus Bassiak's "Le Tourbillon" (The Whirlwind) in François Truffaut's elegiac film *Jules et Jim* (1962).

Chacun pour soi est reparti
Dans le tourbillon de la vie
Je l'ai revue un soir à là là
Elle est retombée dans mes bras
Elle est retombée dans mes bras

Jean-Paul Belmondo in his younger years appeared in a what many took to be a musical comedy, but since Jean-Luc Godard made the film, *Une femme est une femme* (1961), it is more an homage to Hollywood musicals than an imitation, and Belmondo doesn't sing, which may be a blessing, though he may have danced a bit of the old soft-shoe with Anna Karina and Jean-Claude Brialy, who also do not sing in the film. As Godard himself said, "...the film is not a musical. It's the idea of a musical." It is also bursting with color, charm and the enthusiastic embrace of cinema's technical possibilities combined with some very funny silent slapstick movie tricks. And, it being a Godard film, there are moments of didactic stasis to remind the audience that this is, after all, a movie, but these are not as disruptive as one might expect.

On the other hand, Belmondo's most direct predecessor in the French cinema, Jean Gabin, started his career on the stage in singing roles, which he continued in his early film roles, and, yes, he also made records. Some of the songs are still available on audio-cassettes and compact disks. In 1928, he recorded with Mistinguett and sang in films until 1936, including the 1935 *Zouzou* with Joséphine Baker, after which he segued into dramatic roles.

If you cannot twist the tail of Fate sufficiently to allow you a visit to Reggiani's performance at the Olympia, listen to the recording of it taped in 1983 entitled *En Public à l'Olympia* on the Polydor label: over an hour of music you will not soon forget. And you can see him in a number of movies including the wrenchingly beautiful *Le Casque d'or* with the youthfully beautiful Simone Signoret. The film portrays a poor working-class Parisian fin de siècle milieu, long since disappeared from the city, and complexities of emotions and behavior long since beaten out of most human beings.

There is an interesting difference in the pop music cultures of France and the USA, which Ned Rorem almost gets a handle on in his essay, "The More Things Change. Notes on French Popular Song" to be found in his collection of occasional pieces *Settling the Score: Essays on Music* (1988). In the United States popular entertainers roughly equivalent to Montand or Aznavour would be Frank Sinatra or Tony Bennett, who have never sung a political song or even one with radical subject matter, nor exposed themselves to the raw emotional nature of songs traditionally performed by French singers with minimal instrumental accompaniment or support. For similar American types, one must turn to the blues and gospel genres, which cannot be defined as pop culture without stretching the limits of the term beyond usefulness, or groups such as the Doors.

Pop singers are magnetized by movies and appear in them as often as possible. There are exceptions, of course, such as Tony Bennett, Johnny Mathis and Johnnie Ray in the USA, but in France as well as America the trend is clear when one thinks of Yves Montand; Serge Reggiani; Jacques Brel in at least ten movies; Charles Aznavour most notably in *Shoot the Piano Player* (1961, Truffaut again), but also in a number of forgotten adventure films and at least one short film about sin with Claire Bloom; and Georges Brassens made *Porte des Lilas* for René Clair, without much success. On the other side of the Atlantic consider Barbra Streisand, who has also become a director of some power; Sinatra in *From Here to Eternity*, *Suddenly* (which has not been seen in a movie theater since November 1963, but which is available in the videocassette format), *The Manchurian Candidate* and dozens of others, most of which are forgettable; Nat Cole in an obscure film about the French chapter of the Indo-China War; Willy Nelson; Kris Kristoferson; and of course all those horrid Dean Martin movies. Singers such as Lena Horne, Nat Cole, Johnny Ace, Billy Eckstein, and Pearl Bailey would have starred in many more movies had they been born white.

It is interesting to contemplate the question of singing and such American movie actors as, for example, Rod Cameron, Bob Steele, Mari Blanchard, Rhonda Fleming, Forrest Tucker and Joanne Dru - if they had been able to warble or croon with some competence and in tune, would they now be remembered stars instead of forgotten second bananas? Think of Katy Jurado in *High Noon* and *One-Eyed Jacks*: she should have married a king because she is a true queen! On the other hand, we have the case of John Payne warbling and hoofing in all those Alice Faye movies. While no Mario Lanza, or even Gordon MacRae, not to speak of Vaughan Monroe, he did croon in such non-classics as *Tin Pan Alley* (1940), *Weekend in Havana* (1941) and *Hello, Frisco, Hello* (1943). Of course, in some circles he is remembered more for his roles in westerns and an occasional gangster movie. One might also mull over a different career for Robert Mitchum, had someone with Power and Influence been impressed with his singing of "Londonderry Air" in Raoul Walsh's great dark western *Pursuit* (1948); the actor possessed a fine if slight medium tenor, which with a bit of training and practice.... You can hear samples of his singing in a recent CD, which includes songs he taped at home for his family's pleasure.

American audiences, at least white American audiences over 30 years of age, apparently prefer their pop singers (as opposed to pop performers whose reputations and popularity depend upon extra-musical talents and factors) to be cooler, distanced by large orchestral environments

186

and generally more detached from the responses generated by their performances, and certainly not political in their song content.

As Janet Flanner has astutely remarked in a 1949 article on Yves Montand, "Paris has no bobby-soxers." Parisians, she thought, would only put up with a more adult concept of love in life without all the "crooning and mooning" of American pop songs. (*Paris Journal 1944-1965* [1965].) Fly me to the moon, indeed, but autumn leaves are les feuilles mortes, and young Parisians bellowed and screamed their lungs out for the Beatles, but this is not what Flanner meant, n'est-çe pas?

There are exceptions, to be sure, such as Bob Dylan, after he became popular (that is, no longer a cult figure), or Leonard Cohen, both of whom can be situated with their French equivalent, Georges Brassens. Brassens, however, never relied upon electricity to support his voice, though he did once or twice record with a number of jazz musicians, at least one of whom played a few tunes on the electric piano.

There are those who would prefer Johnny Hallyday as the French singer similar to Dylan and Cohen, but Hallyday, not his birthname needless to say, for all his undoubted talent, is not very adventurous in choice of songs or arrangements, and has rarely ventured into political commentary or controversial subject matter.

Brassens, one of the cleverest and productive song writers in recent French history, also sang at the Olympia, but is more closely associated with the club in Montparnasse called Le Bobino, which is still open, but rarely now books acts on the Brassens level. As an indication of how the French venerate their maverick cultural figures, Brassens had a room of his own in the Musée Paul Valéry in the Mediterranean coast town of Sête, their common birthplace. He now has his own "multi-media" museum on the outskirts of town. Brassens

187

and Valéry are also buried there, but not in the same cemetery. Valéry and the great theater actor-director Jean Vilar lie above the town on a hill overlooking the sea. We may detect a certain irony in the fact that Brassens lies closer to the sea than Valéry, one of whose most well-known poems is called "Le cimetière marin." There is also a park in the southern reaches of Paris named after Brassens and we've seen schools in isolated regions of southern France named L'Ecole Georges Brassens. I have not yet discovered a greensward in the United States named Pete Seeger Park. An Atlantic City hospital wing is named after Sinatra, but he bought the honor with a large donation.

Writing of the big names and stars who came to see Montand perform in his first one-man show in the Spring of 1951, his biographers Hervé Hamon and Patrick Rotman have the following sentence: "Of course, he was flattered at the recognition, touched that his friends had taken the trouble to come: he was moved to see Edith Piaf in the third row between Eddie Constantine and Charles Aznavour." I do not know if Eddie Constantine (born in Los Angeles an American citizen in 1917 - died a French citizen in Wiesbaden, Germany, in 1993) ever sang in the Olympia. Eddie Constantine was a star in Europe. The heading of his obituary in *The New York Times* reads "Eddie Constantine, A Movie Tough Guy and Singer, 75, Dies." You probably never saw him in the role of the FBI agent, Lemmy Caution, which he played in a number of French films, though you might have seen Jean-Luc Godard's *Alphaville* (1965) in which Lemmy is more Godard's than FBI's, but still completely Eddie Constantine.

Just before Constantine died, Godard made what might by a wild stretch of the imagination be called a sequel to *Alphaville* called *Allemagne Neuf-Zéro* (1991). Lemmy Caution, the agèd Cold War spy in hiding in East Germany wants to come in from the cold, and does so reciting French and German poetry and philosophy in French and German,

188

as he stumbles from one horrid experience in the sterile materialism of the West to the next, wondering if he shouldn't go back to sleep in the East. Or at least one thinks this is what happens. With Godard one is never sure.

After he mustered out of the American army in France, Eddie Constantine served his singing apprenticeship as a protégé of Edith Piaf, following in the voicesteps, so to speak, of Montand and Aznavour. He had, it is true, studied music at the Vienna Conservatory and in New York City. How well he actually sang may be debated, but his film career can be safely graded as mildly successful, even though some of those "tough guy" films are truly atrocious. It would be well worth your time to listen to him, if you can locate his records, and to see him, if you can locate his movies. He is part of Parisian, if not French, culture of the postwar period that extends into the early 1970s. Eddie Constantine also allegedly wrote and published at least one novel, *Le Propriétaire* (1975). Perhaps one should not be so cynical, perhaps one should omit the word "allegedly," especially in view of the fact that a number of actors, who may or may not have made recordings on which they sang, did actually write novels and memoirs, such as Dirk Bogarde, Lili Palmer, David Niven, Tom Tryon, Marie-France Pisier, and Hildegard Knef (though she also sang rather in the Milva-Marlene Dietrich tradition). About the plot and stylistic qualities of the novel I admit to knowing nothing, except that racehorses play a major role, not surprising when one knows that Eddie Constantine raised racehorses in France for 20 years.[16]

Indeed, here is a theme for an adventurous musicologist: an examination of American pop singers and musicians who lived and worked in Europe after 1945, usually after serving in the army there.

In the year of the Olympia's 100th anniversary, the French government has initiated a process to declare the

189

establishment of a historic monument to protect it from a threat from what the French Embassy in Washington describes as "a real estate renovation project."

* * * *

For those who wish a bit more musical sustenance relating to the city, one could do worse than consulting Irving Schwerké, the music critic for the *Chicago Tribune* (Paris Edition) from 1921 to 1934. At some point, he compiled the following data about music in Paris during his residence there. Regarding musical performances, he discovered that in the 1925-26 season, New York City had 1,156, but Paris had 3,394; during the 1926-27 season the statistics read: New York 1,218, Paris 2,978. Schwerké further notes that during the period 1921 to 1934 Paris experienced the performances of 86 full-sized ballets, 255 operas and operettas, and hundreds of new plays, while countless salons, societies, soirés, groups of various tendencies, individually and collectively, presented new works or old ones in new formats in theaters, music halls, ballrooms, and living rooms in private residences. Open-air concerts, however, except for military bands and marching music, were not as yet performed.

So. Now you know something about music in Paris. For further information and delight, I recommend you read the works of Virgil Thompson, Ned Rorem, George Antheil's memoirs (which are at least partly fiction), Schwerké's columns (all too few of which have been reprinted in Hugh Ford's compilation *The Left Bank Revisted: Selections from the Paris Tribune 1917-1934* [1972]), and Elaine Brody's *Paris: The Musical Kaleidoscope 1870-1925* (1987).

* * * *

While you are in the 9th, you might walk over to the Rue Fontaine, which is a bit of a hike so you may wish to take the métro to Place Blanche. This is the heart of what the American soldiers on leave used to call Pig Alley, a notorious den of iniquity where they expected whores, dope and whiskey; the French arranged for them to find these without difficulty. What the GIs and their civilian counterparts did not discover so readily, if at all, was the apartment of André Breton, which served additionally a the headquarters of the **Surrealists, at 42, rue Fontaine**. Breton moved into a two-room apartment there in 1922 and remained in the building, albeit in a different flat, until his death in 1966, with the exception of the period between 1940 and 1946, which he spent in the USA in exile.

According to Mark Polizzotti, in his massive 1995 biography of Breton and the Surrealist movement, the apartment remains exactly as it was on the day Breton died, a dusty, static memorial to a man and an ideology of constant flux and shifts of position. The irony is almost too much to bear. But you need not concern yourself with this paradox, which Breton himself might have appreciated. Stand for a moment before the plain facade (the Breton flat is not open to the public) and stretch your imagination simultaneously backward in time and into the living room in front of you.

Envision the nightly gatherings of the faithful to debate the correctness of excluding yet another deviant member or the possible inclusion of a new acolyte, amidst the clouds of gray cigarette smoke and the dark wet voices hoarsened with critical passion and staid conviction. On the walls hang early works of Picasso (though only a part-time Surrealist), Braque (though never enough of a Surrealist to be excommunicated), André Masson (barely a Surrealist, but excommunicated anyway), the metaphysical turned classicist Italian Giorgio de Chirico (also excommunicated), primitive African masks, photographs of tactile but vague images and portraits of the group's members and predecessors by Man Ray and others, all of which seem indifferent to the roiling volume of zealous fabulation crowding the space of the small room. There they sit, on the edge of the seats, loins tight with euphoria, drinks clutched in their fists, their minds swooping from radiant delirium to apocalyptic derangement (a much sought-after condition, often chemically initiated), as they changed the world and partners in a voluptuous round of enthralling verbal and physical action. Sexual energy flies about the room in quantum packets combining with the cosmic flights of language and mental strain to create a condition bordering on hysteria about to explode. And sometimes it did.

10th ARRONDISEMENT

The Métro to Stalingrad and Le Pneumatique

With the best of wills I cannot tell you much about the 10th. It does contain a street named Chabrol, but I think this does not refer to the erratically brilliant film director Claude since he is still alive and, one hopes, well. We stayed for a couple of days one turn of the year in a hotel overlooking the Gare du Nord, but I've long since forgotten the name and would not recommend it for location in any case.

However, we recently spent a few hours in the 10th examining the Saint Martin canal, an effort which at one time and in summer may have repaid the energy required to hike the length of the thing in a general north to south direction. Urban ugliness, alas, blights the course of the canal, the scene for a number of Maigret mysteries and many of those "barging into France" movie travelogues. There are some things of interest if you have a sufficient amount of time in the city to squander a bit of it on a low priority site. Several of the buildings along the waterway offer various architectural curiosities and three or four mini-parks mark the course, along which you may see a barge or two being shifted liquidly from lock to lock.

Take the métro to Stalingrad (and that is certainly the title of a Krimi set in Paris, or a geographically perverse political thriller larded with cognative dissonance-inducing drugs) and cautiously make your way through the dangerously carefree traffic to the head of the canal. Walk down the western edge and you will immediately see three black barges tied to marine stauncheons, or whatever they are called, unless two of them are off plying the watery byways of the continent with their cargoes of culture and entertainment. They are, in fact, two of them, theaters of a sort, namely one an opera and one a musical theater. I have not the foggiest notion as to what function the third barge fulfills. We would have gone to a performance of Weill-Brecht songs in one of the boats, but the box office had not yet opened.

Because the 10th is so far removed from our usual quartier, if we had friends there in the days before the general distribution of the telephone, we would have communicated urgent news via **Le Pneumatique**. Like the iron-grilled pissiors, but not as malodorous, the pneu is no longer with us, the one having been replaced by a plastic-metal unisex contraption, not unique to Paris, that costs two francs to open, out of which one fears one will never emerge, and the other by the obstinantly intrusive telephone, an appliance appreciated by those for whom time is more important than a well-written, not to speak of a thoroughly-contemplated, response to the vicissitudes of making money as swiftly as possible.

When one had an urgent message for someone across the city, but was prevented from making the trip oneself, one hastened to the nearest post office to write the message on the blue flimsy (thus the other name for the missive: petit bleu), folded it, paid the bill, and a civil servant sent it rattling through the pressed air system underground to the post office nearest to the addressee, whence another civil servant delivered it. Those readers old enough to remember department stores in the 1950s may recall seeing their money disappearing into the mouth of a system of pipes on its way to the cashier hidden away on another floor. Some minutes later the tube returned with a cancelled receipt and change. The sales floor contained no cash and thus remained secure from robbery, unless the thief made off with merchandise, of course. In Paris, the city inaugurated the pneumatique system around 1885 as the first such system in the world. Other major European cities followed suit, but the arrangement lasted longest in Paris, closing down in the late 1960s. Another piece of civilized urban life fragmented into the dustbin of history. Only the Library of Congress in Washington, to my knowledge, continues to use this type of communication device via miles of pressed air piping to transmit book requests from the reading rooms to the stacks, but by the time you read this, the LC system may also have disappeared into the insatiable maw of electronic computerdom.

Indeed, in the early decades of the 20th century, one could mail a letter in Paris to a Paris address before noon and expect it to reach its destination later that afternoon. In the early 1960s I recall German postal officials accurately boasting that a first-class letter mailed from a German post office to a German address could be read by its recipient no later than the next day. That was the West German post office, natürlich. By the end of this century, with the rapid advancement in post-modern technology, we have reached the stage in which a letter now requires a minimum of five working days to reach a destination four blocks distant from the post office from which it is mailed, and a letter from Washington to Baltimore, some 40 miles to the north, takes ten days. In the 1920s, a letter mailed from Paris to New York City averaged six to seven days by sea. Today, one is lucky to have one's letters travel the same route by air in less than ten days.

14th ARRONDISEMENT

Geography and Some Denizens. Arbitrary geography be
damned! Or at least ignored. The dyspeptic cartographers
who blindthly drew a line down the length of the Boulevard
de Montparnasse, dividing the 6th from the 14th
arrondissements, could not have known (or were the rascals
prescient?) the trouble they would cause writers writing
about the quarter of the city emotionally centered at the
intersection of that thoroughfare and the Boulevard Raspail.
For some arcane reason, the sight-disadvantaged
cartographers named this crossroads the Carrefour Vavin.
The contingent places in question here cannot be divided
by arrondissement, or any other recondite mental construct;
rather, we must represent them as they exist in an ambient,
non-geographic reality; that is, an area the boundaries of
which have been determined by the protean ebb and flow of
human society in its and multifarious forms of rational and

irrational intercourse. In short, this is one case wherein a force other than mere geography and the bureaucracy's capriciousness must be the determinant, namely convenience and history. This is the quarter referred to generically as Montparnasse and known to the 1920s expatriate generation as "The Quarter," as they and their critics called themselves "The Quarterites."

In 1930, Robert Sage wrote the following sentences about this now mythical place.

> The more I have lived in Paris the less certain I have been as to the exact definition of that mysterious and derogatory word Montparnasse. It may mean the cafés in the vicinity of the Carrefour Raspail [sic], or it may mean the Montparnasse quarter (which comprises probably a thousand times as many humble French working people as it does artists, near-artists or pseudo-artists), or it may mean a more or less definite social atmosphere of affectation, drunkenness, freakishness, unmorality, perversity (or perversion, if you prefer) and degeneration.

Which is not to say all those adjectives apply to that quarter today, or in fact ever did, except maybe between 1921 and 1929 during which time American and British newspaper and magazine articles wrote a great deal of trash about the large number of English-language expatriates and their antics in Paris to titillate the homefolks, who had no chance to join in the fun. And it is true that thousands of these expats and would-be expats lived, however briefly in Paris, each and every one of them writing a novel or painting a picture. The serious expats, of course, despised the unserious expats as much as they detested the journalists who parodied them all as the same bunch.

An overly nostalgic, but still sentient littérateur would desire a few words about such culturally important locales as the Hôtel des Écoles, built in 1900 and now called the Lenox, at 15, rue Delambre, which housed many artists throughout the 20th century (for instance, the Swiss painter Irène Zurkinden 1929, Man Ray 1921-22, André Breton 1921 [although the Hôtel Delambre at number 35 currently claims this distinction on a wall plaque], Tristan Tzara 1922-24, Isaac Grünewald 1908, Einar Jolin 1908, Fried. Ahlers-Hestermann 1907-08, and Jules Pascin 1905-08).

Now Pascin, Breton, Man Ray (somehow the last name alone simply doesn't sound right), and Tzara are familiar names to most of this book's readers, but what of Zurkinden, Grünewald and Jolin? A short identificatory excursus here would be in order.

We begin with the person one knows most about, Isaac Grünewald: born in 1889 at Stockholm, lived in Paris from 1908 to 1911 when he returned to Stockholm to work at the opera designing scenery. During those halcyon days in Paris, when he lived in a shabby studio at 3, rue Vercingétorix to the southwest of the Montparnasse cemetery, he spent much of his time in cafés, mostly the Café du Dôme, where he earned small amounts of money acting as a good luck charm for the poker players. A student at the Académie Matisse after falling completely for the Frenchman's radical use of color, Grünewald lived in poverty for several years, dancing all night to keep warm and sleeping on the billiard tables in the Café de Versailles for a few hours before hurrying off to the Matisse school. As was not unusual in those days, and in these, his cheap studio had no functioning heating system, which may be one of the reasons he occasionally drank to excess with Per Krohg and Pascin, the latter of whom painted his portrait.

He married the painter and fellow Matisse academy student Sigrid Hjertén in 1911 and when they returned to Paris in 1920, they moved into the top floor studio at 86, rue Nôtre-Dame-des-Champs. During 1932-1942 he taught at Stockholm art academy. He died in airplane accident in 1946 somewhere in the waters off Oslo. Hjertén suffered the fate of many female artists married to other artists (the names Dorothea Tanning, Lee Krasner, Elaine de Kooning, and Dorothy Dehner, curiously all Americans, come to mind): subordination of her career to the imperatives of his and the demands of a family, and being relatively ignored by the art establishment. In Hjertén's case the unbearable tensions these antonymous demands made on her resulted in mental imbalance and a botched lobotomy operation, which killed her in 1948. In 1998 the Swedish Cultural Center in Paris mounted a small exhibition of some of her best work, and during the winter of 1999-2000 she had a long overdue and much welcomed retrospective of her vividly colored works at the Berlin Käthe Kollwitz Museum.

Their photographs appear in Billy Klüver and Julie Martin's misleadingly titled but extraordinarily rich and indispensable book, *Kiki's Paris. Artists and Lovers 1900-1930* (1989), as do those of Einar Jolin, another member of the Café du Dôme circle, and Irène Zurkinden. Jolin arrived in Paris with Grünewald in September 1908, where after both enrolled at the Matisse school and shared the Rue Vercingétorix studio until Jolin moved out because of the cold during the winter. Klüver and Martin note that by the spring of 1910, he had rented a more comfortable studio in the Rue Jeanne, but there is no Rue Jeanne on my Plan Guide Blay nor in Jacques Hillairet's comprehensive work on the streets of Paris. Perhaps the name changed. There is a Rue Jeanne d'Arc in the 13th, but that is rather far from Montparnasse.

When she arrived in the city in 1929, Irène Zurkinden became enthralled with the long-since disappeared Paris of Toulouse-Lautrec and styled her hair and dress accordingly. She moved directly into the life of the Dôme, where, as she told Klüver and Martin in 1979, "almost immediately I was in the swing of things." She remained in Paris into the 1930s, but the rest is silence for I know nothing more of her life and career.

Then there is the Dingo Bar at 10, rue Delambre, where F. Scott Fitzgerald and various personages who appear under different names in *The Sun Also Rises* (including the sad Duff Twysden who, notoriously, appears as Brett) gathered to drink themselves silly and merry, if possible at someone else's expense. The Dingo Bar was for years called L'Auberge du Centre, but is currently named L'Auberge de Venise, and we have not yet put our elbows on the bar there, which is alleged to be the same one that all the expatriates put their own sodden elbows on.

The **Rue de la Grande Chaumière** is choked with history. Walk into this brief street and linger for a moment, thinking of those who lived and studied here: Stephen Vincent Benét, Manuel Ortiz de Zarate, Paul Gauguin, Nathanael West (in the Hôtel Libéria at number 9 during the Winter of 1926-1927, now called Hôtel Villa des Artistes with a plaque on the facade stating that Samuel Beckett and other artists and writers lived there), Alphonse Mucha, Amedeo Modigliani and his unfortunate, but ethereal love, Jeanne Hébuterne, Jules Pascin, Nina Hamnett, August Strindberg (at number 12 where he experimented in alchemy), and Rudolf Levy (who took over the direction of Henri Matisse's Académie when the painter found the students too exhausting), all lived in the street at some point.

At number 10 you stand before the deservedly famous Académie Colarossi, where so many known and unknown artists taught and studied that a list of them would fill a hefty volume. In 1870, a former artists' model, Colarossi, took over the Académie Suisse, the oldest (opened in 1815) such institution in Paris, and moved it under his name to the Rue de la Grande Chaumière, where it prospered.

Now mull over in your mind some of the names associated with the school: Anna Diriks (wife of the Norwegian painter, Edvard), Helene Schjerfbeck (an unfortunately not too well-known Finnish modernist painter), Pascin, Kuroda Seiki (who studied here in the 1880s before he became a teacher at the Tokyo Art School), Jeanne Héburtene, Thora Dardel (sometime sculpture student who posed for one of Modigliani's last paintings and who worked as a journalist in Paris for Swedish newspapers and magazines during the 1920s), Antoine Bourdelle (teacher of sculpture, who must have suffered many jibes at his name), Robert W. Service (known, no doubt to his chagrin, as "The Canadian Kipling"), the American "regionalist" Thomas Hart Benton and Gauguin (who briefly taught there). And, then, the incredible Norwegian Krohg family: the free-spirited, not to say promiscuous Oda; her husband, Christian, pater familias and teacher at the Académie; and Per, the son, who studied with his father at the school.

Per Krohg also studied at the Matisse Academy, where in the spring of 1910, Cecile Vidil, known as Lucy, posed for the students. In the autumn of 1910, Lucy and Jules Pascin engaged in a brief affair when she posed for him at his Montmartre studio. In December 1910 or January 1911, Lucy began to pose for Per in his studio at 9, rue Campagne Première in Montparnasse. Legend has it that they fell in love at the Bal Bullier, one of the best of the elaborate and vast dancehalls in Paris, formerly at 33, avenue de l'Observatoire across the intersection from the Closerie des Lilas. (Hansen has it at number 39. In August 1914, the government turned it into a military quartermaster clothing depot, but in December 1921 it once again became a dancehall, retaining over the entrance its grotesque, but lively ceramic arch advertising the adventures to be had within, until its demolition in the 1930s.)

The story of the incredible intersecting lives and loves of Per, Lucy and Jules and their friends who became lovers, wives, husbands, and friends again, would, alas, consume too much space here. The complex dance of their lives (at one point during the First Chapter of the Great World

Assininity, Per and Lucy became the Tango King and Queen of Scandinavia) continued on and off the dance floor for more than twenty years with Paris as its main locus. Klüver and Martin have a photograph of the nude Lucy standing in the doorway of the Rue Campagne Première studio in 1911 or 1912, her hair in a short bob she wore a decade before it became de rigueur, a tortoise crawling slowly across the floor of the seemingly empty studio ... she stares with sad but unflinching eyes at the camera, at the observer-voyeur, as if she already saw the bloody end of Jules Pascin, who would write on June 2, 1930 in a suicide note to her on the back of an invitation to an opening at the Berlin Flechtheim Gallery, "Lucy, don't blame me for what I am doing. Thank you for the packages. You are too good, I must leave so that you can be happy! Adieu! Adieu!" and who would scrawl on his door in his own blood "Adieu Lucy." But surely something else caused the sadness then. Or perhaps it is not sadness at all, perhaps that is only what I see in this evocative, contradictory image of raw sensuality and preternatural knowledge.[17]

* * * *

At number 14, rue de la Grande Chaumière, the Académie de la Grande Chaumière opened in 1906 and served as a school for Augusta Savage (for more about whom, see below), William Gordon Huff (about whom one knows at the moment nothing beyond his name), Berenice Abbott (a strikingly talented photographer who learned her trade working with Man Ray), Abraham Rattner (a sadly neglected American painter), Caresse Crosby (at least she claimed to have studied here), Alexander Calder (whose work, like that of Henry Moore, has become all too ubiquitous),Anaïs Nin (promiscuous lover of the male body and author of what may be the longest 20th century novel, *The Diaries of Anaïs Nin*), Isamu Noguchi (a sculptor who

202

also studied with Brancusi and who designed the sculpture garden of the Israel Museum of Art in Jerusalem as well as his own museum in Long Island City), Pierre Matisse (yes, it is his son), Alberto Giacometti (about whom his fellow students prophesized: "he will either go very far or go mad" and whom they called "the crazy genius" due to his solemnity and actual *seriousness* about being an artist and creating high art), the very talented and tragic Flora Lewis Mayo (a fellow student of Giacometti's, who influenced his work but could not entice his love; he sculpted a flattened head of her in 1927), Laura Wheeling Waring (an altogether too-little known Negro painter), Paolo (actually Paul Müller), a Swiss who gave up a career as a watchmaker (what else?!) to study painting on a stipendium 1936-39 under Franz Masereel, who taught there in the 1930s, the French-American writer Julien Green, the lovely Meret Oppenheim, and hundreds of others.

Some considered the Grande Chaumière better than the Colarossi, perhaps because Antoine Bourdelle and Fernand Léger occasionally taught there. Bourdelle, who also taught at the Colarossi, querrelled with his student Giacometti; how could it have been otherwise given their diametrically opposed visions of what sculpture actually *is*. James Lord reports Bourdelle telling the young Alberto: "One can do things like that at home, but one doesn't show them." But where are Bourdelle's pieces today? If one looks hard and long enough one may find some (such as his interestingly curious head of Beethoven in the Jardin du Luxembourg west of the Musée du Luxembourg and the 1898 "Great Warrior of Montauban" in the garden of the Hirshhorn Museum in Washington). And, of course, in his own museum, in the street of his name (where his obsession with Beethoven is clearly in evidence). But Giacometti's, are prominently displayed in the great museums of the world, especially prominently at the Fondation Maeght in Saint-Paul-de-Vence. This does not mean everything since much crap is thusly displayed in "great museums," but nonetheless I believe Alberto Giacometti to be one of the greatest modern sculptors of the 20th century. Perhaps *the* greatest? Therefore it is Bourdelle's total misunderstanding of Giacometti's genius that offends one's senses. Other than that, one might actually enjoy some of the Frenchman's better works.

The school is still open, should you, Dear Reader, wish to join the list of those who sat in the uncomfortable studios and tried to give their lives meaning by creating something eternal.

If you come back out to the Boulevard du Montparnasse and turn to the right, you will walk past Rodin's statue of Balzac on the island in the middle of the Boulevard Raspail. Balzac, it should be noted, was not noted for hanging about in Montparnasse, probably because, like Dickens and Zola, he spent his time writing reams of copy to pay the rent, during which he drank uncountable liters of strong, black coffee to maintain his pace. Rodin apparently believed all this expenditure of energy did not sufficiently deplete Balzac's reservoir of such: there is credible evidence to indicate that the statue's hand underneath the cloak is clearly in possession of his erect penis.

Across the street you will see the **Café du Dôme**, at 108, boulevard du Montparnasse (14th). This historic establishment is both a café and a restaurant, the latter being expensive, but worth at least one full lunch or dinner (for two with a good wine ca. $120) so you can enjoy the quiet plush of maroon velvet and shining polished goldgilded newel posts and railings, in addition to one of the most elegant set of restrooms and telephone booths anywhere. We ate the best fresh oysters ever here. In the café section on the street, glass-enclosed in cold weather, one can sit for a while over a cup of coffee and watch the people, always worthwhile in Paris.

Le Dôme is "famous" as a gathering place for the 1920s expatriates from the USA and Great Britain, and elsewhere, but the French literary set has also collected here from time to time. And somewhere, someone, probably a White Russian or at least a retrograde tsarist agent, says Ilya Ehrenburg spent some bolshevik rubles here after the Rotonde across the street became too americanized for him in the early Twenties.

Ehrenburg allegedly composed the ditty:

> Read all about us and marvel!
> You did not live in our time - regret it!

which sums it up pretty nicely, though the original Russian probably scans better. (What if he wrote this doggerel in English?!)

One source tells us the Dôme is the oldest of the Montparnasse cafés (the word used loosely) starting out in 1897 as a laborers' saloon with a billiard table and no customers even pretending to high culture. The tale about the workers' bar, however, probably refers to the much smaller bar of the Rotonde across the street, which did begin as a standup coffee and marc drinkerie, although some memoirs note that coachmen and other laboring men stood at the Dôme bar enjoying an apéritif and discussing whatever coachmen discuss at bars. Lenin, Trotsky and some of their revolutionary colleagues allegedly met in the Dôme on occasion before 1914 and photographs from the antebellum era show only a few tables and chairs in front of the establishment. Klüver and Martin's big book has the photographs.

In fact, Klüver and Martin give the opening date as 1898, and 1902 as the date of the installation of the two billiard tables in the backroom. It seems that a group of American painters from the schools and studios in the Rue de la Grande Chaumière and the surrounding neighborhood immediately acquired squatters' rights in the backroom by running a game of poker, which lasted for a decade or more. However, one source says the Americans played billiards forever and the Germans played poker in the front rooms. Take your pick.

The results of the Franco-German Belligerency of 1870-71, in which the Germans soundly defeated the French in what may have been the last "gentleman's war" in history, cut France out of the German tour schedule for many years. But by the turn of the century memories had dimmed somewhat and, in 1903, Rudolf Levy moved to Paris from Munich where he had been one of the main figures in a loose grouping of young German-speaking painters from Central and Eastern Europe. He and Walter Bondy, a painter from Prague who had also studied in Munich, began meeting in the Dôme, thus establishing a Stammlokal in the café's front space. So, if we believe all the sources, we have the Americans in the backroom playing poker and/or billiards, the coachmen at the bar drinking coachman cocktails, the bourgeoisie in the banquets with their aperitifs and newspapers, and the Germans at the tables in the front space playing poker and smoking cigars, with the terrace as the only common meeting ground. Even if reality did not exactly mirror this arrangement, it is pleasant to think it did.

Levy and Bondy did not make a secret of their happiness at finding the café, and soon artists such as Albert Weisgerber, Hans Purrmann, Wil Howard, Richard Goetz and Friedrich Ahlers-Hestermann; the art dealers, Wilhelm Uhde, Henri Bing and Alfred Flechtheim; and writers such as Erich Mühsam, began to think of the Dôme as their second Parisian home, or at least as their living room, since their sleeping quarters usually did not include sufficient space or comfort for socializing in groups numbering more than two. By 1908, the Germans had absorbed a number of other nationalities all of who spoke

German: artists, dealers, and writers from Eastern Europe, Scandanavia, the Balkan states - collectively they became known as les Dômiers. The Germans called the café "the cathedral," logically enough, since "der Dom" in German means "cathedral."

Alfred Flechtheim, born in 1878 in Münster into a family proud of its Jewish-Spanish heritage, began his adult life as a grain merchant in Düsseldorf, where in 1904 he rescued Carla Mann, an unsuccessful actress and the sister of Heinrich and Thomas Mann, from a life of perpetual carnival, "things one should better not experience," as she expressed it at the time), after which they carried on an intense, brief, but apparently "pure aesthetic" affair, which Heinrich immediately turned to use as the basis of a novella, *Die Schauspielerin* (1904). One wonders what Fred, as Carla called him, thought about the book. In 1912-13, Daniel-Henry Kahnweiler, the grand impresario of early 20th century modern European art, reinforced in Flechtheim, the businessman who loved modern art and enjoyed the company of painters, the notion of becoming a dealer as a fulltime profession. This, after some searching of his soul and securing of start-up capital, he did indeed do.

In December, 1913, he opened a contemporary art gallery in Düsseldorf and after 1918 moved to Berlin, where he opened another gallery and also published and edited the influential periodical *Der Querschnitt* until the Ullstein publishing house purchased it and changed its style and content into something more "popular." Flechtheim became the most important "spreader of propaganda for contemporary French art in Germany" who also had galleries in Frankfurt and Cologne. On being asked by Christian Zervos in 1927 which artist had the greatest impact on Germany in the 20th century, he unhesitatingly replied "Schmeling, the boxer." Of course, during his days as a habitué of the Dôme before 1914, he was much younger and less brash than later during that interview.

In 1925, Hemingway wrote to John Dos Passos that he and Flechtheim planned to do a book on bullfighting (a book he finally wrote alone in the early 1930s), describing Flechtheim as a "swell Spanish Jew 25 years an aficionado," a mark of distinction to be respected in the American's universe. Klüver and Martin have a series of photographs the journalist Thora Dardel took in Pascin's studio of Flechtheim and the painter in torero costumes on the day that Pascin, another "Spanish Jew," painted the dealer's portrait. The Musée d'art moderne in the Centre Pompidou now owns the painting. *Der Querschnitt* published a number of Hemingway's poems and several short stories in the second half of the 1920s. In 1933, the Spanish Jew Flechtheim fled his homeland into exile, making his way through Switzerland to London, where he died in 1937.

One thing the German Cathedralites retained in common with their fellow countrymen across the Rhine: they did not generally welcome women to their tables; at least this is the legend that has come down to us the garden paths of time. They made an exception, however, for Hermine David, whose mother claimed she, Hermine, not her mother, had been sired by a Hapsburg prince during a brief visit to Paris (his, not hers), but the reason for the exception was surely her talent as a painter rather than her dubious paternity. Though on occasion they brought their wives or mistresses with them, rarely at the same time, Hermine David was the only female "regular." The fact that she became the lover of Jules Pascin, a male "regular," in addition to her talent and ability not to be bored when they spoke German all night, of which she understood not a word, also contributed to her exceptional status in this circle.

In any event, the Germans thus added themselves to the polyglot stew simmering and occasionally boiling over in

Paris during the brief ante bellum period in the early 20th century. This milieu has often been described and narrated and analyzed by the talented and the untalented, the experts and the amateurs. Adolphe Basler published a book entitled *La peinture, religion nouvelle* in 1926, in which he describes some of the stew's ingredients: "... expressionists from Smolensk, who came much later [a reference to Chagall?], followed by the dadists from Moldo-Valachia [definitely Tristan Tzara], the constructivists from Leningrad [Archipenko? Lissitzky?], the neo-romantics from Baluchistan, who were all there, and not just to drink vermouth-cassis." That last sounds vaguely threatening, and occasional violence did punctuate the evenings at the Dôme -- no longer, of course, now that the place is a high priced restaurant. And Basler eventually found himself defending certain "foreigners" (that is, Jews from Eastern Europe) because they worked within the "French tradition" and not defending, but not actually attacking, those "foreigners" who could not fit within that "tradition." Two years after writing about the "new religion," Basler had soured on the whole development within the School of Paris and published another book entitled *Le Cafard après la fête* (1929), which seems to sum up his disappointment. Basler's works are all out of print, but the works of the painters he discusses are in museums all over the civilized (and parts of the not so civilized) world.

The war, of course, changed everything. In August 1914, the Germans disappeared from Paris along with many Frenchmen and others, if for different reasons, as the Germans had vanished in 1870, and would vanish again, if for a much shorter period, in 1939. In June 1940, they returned to France and again occupied the tables at the Dôme, though for the most part these were different Germans entirely, and the study of high art and culture did not constitute a fundamental part of the reason for their presence.

Most dramatically a change at the Dôme occurred during the Winter of 1922-23: by Spring, in time for the infestation by American and British carbon units (as tourists are known in certain circles), what had almost been a neighborhood local had become a café four times its previous size with rows of tables and chairs on the sidewalk. The Dôme immediately became chic and a must if one wished to be seen by other tourists or artistes. This is the incarnation most well known to those who ride the hobbyhorse known as the "roaring twenties in gay Paree."

Jo Davidson has left us a concise description of the Dôme during the period before the opening of the Great 20th Century Slaughterhouse in 1914. "At the Dôme, one was certain to meet artists, poets, derelicts and other kindred spirits. It was open till two in the morning and you could go there for girls, chess, poker, billiards or conversation." But do not look for derelicts or billiards or poker now: the Dôme has transcended its origins.

If you can find a copy of Elliot Paul's *The Mysterious Mickey Finn; or, Murder at the Café du Dôme: an International Mystery* (1939) or its sequel *Huggermugger at the Louvre* (1940), and if you read them, you will have something of the feel of the place, the time and the quarter, and afford yourself a few hours of amusement because they are very funny. Elliot Paul, an editor on the Paris edition of the *Chicago Tribune*, assisted Eugene Jolas, a city editor of the *Chicago Tribune*, in editing *transition*, a literary periodical published in Paris during the 1930s, perhaps the most well-known of such "little magazines" for having printed many sections of Joyce's *Finnegans Wake*, then called "Work in Progress." Paul's active private life precluded his giving sufficient attention to his editorial duties, so in 1928 Robert Sage, also on the *Chicago Tribune* staff, became co-editor. Sage described Paul as "rotund and bewhiskered and as mischievous as a Katzenjammer Kid," which is probably close to the truth.

You can read examples of the work the journal published in a volume entitled *In* transition: *A Paris Anthology* (1990), which apparently a book-packaging company in London put together; there is no editor listed, but Noël Riley Fitch has written a brief historical introduction. You can see the spot where the Hôtel de la Gare des Invalides (now destroyed) housed *transition*'s editorial cubicle at 40, rue Fabert (7th). The street runs along the western edge of the Esplanade des Invalides. The cramped room on the fourth floor had a magnificent view, but the plumbing equaled a Turk.

Elliot Paul also wrote two books about the life on Rue de la Huchette (5th), where he lived for several years during the Thirties, called *The Last Time I Saw Paris* (1942), and *Springtime in Paris* (1950), a sequel taking up the story upon his return after the war. Do not confuse Elliot Paul's book with the horrid 1954 Hollywood movie called "The Last Time I Saw Paris," which is actually, very loosely, based on an F. Scott Fitzgerald's story "Babylon Revisited"!

"Wacky" is not too an extreme adjective for life at the Paris *Chicago Tribune* and we are fortunate that Waverley Root, a constant critic of *transition*, wrote about his years as a reporter for the paper: *The Paris Edition: The Autobiography of Waverley Root 1927-1934* (1987), which you should read.

You might also read the short piece entitled "The Nineteen Twenties: An Interior" by Nathan Asch, taken from his unpublished novel, "Paris Was Home." Asch describes a night at the Dôme in great detail, including the restrooms, which were extremely primitive compared to the present facilities; in point of fact, then a veritable Turk. Asch's story can be found in George Plimpton's compilation of pieces from *The Paris Review,* unsurprisingly entitled *The Paris Review Anthology* (1990).

One would very much like to read the rest of Asch's book, wherever it might be.

Asch, the son of the writer, mostly in Yiddish, Sholem Asch, was born in Warsaw in 1902, lived in Germany and Switzerland before attending school in Paris from 1910 to 1913, and emigrated with his family to the United States in 1915. During The Interregnum he spent two years on Wall Street doing things that made him ashamed, after which he moved to Europe to redeem himself and ended up in Paris in early 1924. In 1925 he published a novel called *The Office* and over the years wrote a pile of manuscripts most of which remained in the desk drawer. Asch is an exemplar of that traditional marginal figure, the underpublished writer who possessed an unfortunately unrealized amount of talent. That Asch admired Hemingway, who helped him revise a section from the novel for publication in the *Transatlantic Review*, did not stop Hemingway from perceiving him as a stiff competitor, especially since Asch's novel appeared a year before *The Sun Also Rises*. One night, probably in 1924, on the way to the Dôme for coffee after dinner, the two well-watered young men argued which of them possessed more talent, a discussion that later required serious dental work for Asch and drove Hemingway, who always felt terrible guilt after knocking another man's teeth out, to appear at Asch's room in the Rue Campagne-Première late that night to apologize and to admit that Asch possessed "more of everything than any of us," at least according to one source.

Hemingway's own version, written at the time to McAlmon, employs The Substitution Subterfuge: Asch and the sometime poet Evan Shipman, apparently arguing over money the latter had lent the former to purchase some false teeth, spent thirty minutes harmlessly swinging at each other, leaving not a mark on either. Hemingway said that Shipman's girl had left him because he lent Asch the money and that Asch had hit Shipman out of "kike gratitude."

Commentators on Hemingway, similar to those on T. S. Eliot, expend a great deal of energy and space explaining how the writers' antisemitism was not lethal but part of the general climate of opinion and the specific milieux in which they grew up. Sure.[18]

Hemingway does tell an amusing story about Asch in another letter to McAlmon from 1924. Apparently Asch at one point in November of that year believed he had contracted the syphilis and felt so badly about it that he publicly berated himself for his lack of morals, noting that if the test showed he actually had "the syph" he would return to America to rob a bank and live like a hermit on the proceeds. Hemingway told him that if he was so immoral he'd better return the books he'd borrowed. It turned out that Asch only had a case of the crabs, thus was not required to enter a life of bankrobbery or hermitry.

Asch did say after Hemingway's death that "I hated the son-of-a-bitch and I loved him." Klaus Mann and Fritz Landshoff published Asch's story "Sammy" in the January 1934 issue of their exile journal, *Die Sammlung*. Asch died in 1964 in Mill Valley (California) three years after his former Paris comrade killed himself. None of Asch's work is in print, except the story about the Dôme noted above.

As long as you are reading about the Dôme, see if you can find the October 1925 issue of *American Mercury* in which Sinclair Lewis, the first American writer to win the Nobel Prize for Literature, tasted his revenge against the younger crowd of American expatriate would-be writers in Paris who had insulted him. According to the story, Lewis showed up at the Dôme not quite sober and feeling sorry for himself one night, believing himself, no doubt correctly, to be ignored by the herd of the "crowd." He began bragging about his sales and boasted that his writing was equal to that of Flaubert, at which point someone bellowed across the terrace "Sit down! You're nothing but a bestseller!" A few months later, in his article, Lewis singled out the Dôme as the headquarters of shallow, ignorant, drunk, untalented American jerkdom. A nasty, and to some extent justifiable, diatribe, which still did not make him a more than mediocre but lucky craftsman.

Since 1945, the Dôme has become a superior, and expensive, restaurant. The red *Guide Michelin* awarded it a star for many years, but this marking has disappeared from the 1993 edition. Nonetheless, we recommend it highly, if you're flush, for lunch or dinner. Make a reservation. (Recently the management has opened a small room across the Rue Delambre from the Café du Dôme, called the Bistrot du Dôme, with a limited selection and lower prices.)

One cold gray early morning in October 1991, we found the Dôme a supremely relaxing haven when, drooping from a seven-hour airplane trip, we gratefully sighed into the café chairs at 8 AM, hotel room far from ready at this hour, to read the papers, drink nourishing and warming bowls of café-au-lait and taste the ineffable flavor of freshly baked flaky croissants. A fine way to return to Paris, exhausted but happy and in one's own quarter again. Of course, there are far less expensive cafés in the neighborhood where one can read the papers and drink coffee, if one wishes.

* * * *

The late, lamented, English-language Paris monthly called *Passion* publicly stated that **Le Select** (6th), obliquely across the street from the Dôme, serves the best croque monsieur in Paris; we can substantiate the richness of the cheese and recommend one drink copious quantities of Kronenbourg beer to help digest this masterpiece of fast, if heavy, food. Otherwise, the café-bistro has long served as a gathering place for literary and artist types of various nationalities, especially Americans in the 1920s. Be reminded again that prices in such well-known places tend to be rather higher than similar cafés located on side streets with no reputation.

A few doors down the Boulevard du Montparnasse from the Select and directly across the street from the Dôme, sits the equally well-known (and for the same reasons) **La Rotonde** (6th), which doesn't enjoy the croque monsieur recommendation, but is similar to the Select except that the Rotonde inside is more of a traditional restaurant. We have not eaten there, but have lolled about the outside tables for an apèritif or a nightcap on various occasions. The Rotonde you drink and eat in today is not the Rotonde of literary and art history of an earlier 20th century epoch. Opened in 1911 at 105, boulevard du Montparnasse, the owners took over the Café du Parnasse at 103 in 1924 and doubled the size of the place. In the summer of 1959, a developer razed the old Café Rotonde and plunked down the Rotonde Cinéma in its place. In the early 1960s the movie house showed foreign films of quality with earphones for French translations and permitted cigarette smoking. You can imagine an entire theater filled with Gauloise smoke and thin, intense, young French intellectuals desperately seeking sub-textual meaning in Howard Hawks' westerns. Now the rather small house shows the same current movies you can see anywhere else in the city. The "new" Rotonde is two doors down on the Boulevard Raspail corner across from Balzac's penetrating stare.

La Coupole (14th), a few doors down from the Dôme, across the street from the Select and the Rotonde, forms the fourth of the quartet of café-restaurants situated in the Montparnasse-Raspail (Vavin) neighborhood, all of which appear in all the memoirs and biographies of all the creative (and some not so) people who have moved through the milieux d'art in Paris.

Opened with great brouhaha in December 1927, the place swiftly became one of the chic spots to be in, whether to eat, drink or be seen. Judging by the photographs of it in the 1930s the neon signs illuminated the Paris night as the drinks and the atmosphere lit up the customers. Noël Riley Fitch, in her recent biography of Anaïs Nin's erotic life, notes that Lawrence Durrell, Henry Miller and Nin dubbed themselves the "Three Musketeers of La Coupole" during the late Thirties. One would love to have witnessed *those* shenanigans! Unfortunately, all most people are concerned about knowing these days relates to sexual peccadilloes, the more obsessively perverse the better, not what Sonny Rollins once called "real matters."

In his curious biographical book about Sartre, John Gerassi calls La Coupole "an amazing institution ... it was a restaurant mostly for exhibitionists and voyeurs." Be that as it may, Gerassi's subject and Simone de Beauvoir apparently ate quite often on the right "aristocratic" side, where the staff kept the masses at bay, so to speak. Indeed, Gerassi has a wonderfully apropos story of a lunch with Sartre and Herbert Marcuse during the latter's halcyon days as guru to the rebellious youth of the late 1960s. Since Sartre had never read anything by Marcuse, he asked Gerassi to come along to help him out with the encounter. As Gerassi tells it, the lunch at La Coupole, of course, did not require such intervention because Sartre played Marcuse so well the latter thought the former possessed a thorough grounding in his works. Two aging gurus, with attendant, at La Coupole eating cassoulet, the plat du jour on Thursdays, diligently cleaning their plates and feeding their egos.

A few years ago, the owners completely renovated the inside and, according to those who know best, ruined a historic monument, the only one of the four in which one could dance to a real dance band. There is still afternoon tea dancing in the basement, but I can't remember whether a band or a machine plays the music. In any case, from outside the place appears to be a great well-lighted barn or a railroad station waiting room with tables. For a vicarious look at what it may have been like before the barbarians got their grubby paws on it, see Françoise Planiol, *La Coupole: 60 ans de Montparnasse* (1986), which quotes our friend Gregory Masurovsky frequently, but misspells his name. Mr. Masurovsky, who has lived and worked not far from the carrefour Vavin since the mid-1950s, has written (1991) a short, informal explanation of the "new Coupole."

René Lafon, the original owner, *sold* the Coupole to a Monsieur Bucher who directs the restaurant group "Flo," a group of brasseries in Paris characterized by their often "authentic" turn-of-the-century type décor, real or renovated. They are in the middle to lower-high price range. When Mr. Bucher bought La Coupole, he had it gutted so the present office building could be built on the site. He reproduced "his Coupole" afterwards, which has little in common with the original, but the cooking is good. It's just that the ambiance and the life-style that made for the charm of the place have been eradicated. One ought to call it, as someone mentioned, "La Coupole II." It is very successful and very noisy.

Clearly, we are not the only people who suffer depression when thinking about unnecessary and detrimental change. The famous phrase "plus ça change, plus c'est la même chose" does not apply to the wanton destruction of cultural artifacts, the process of which also transgresses the ancient proverb "If it aint broke, don't fix it." Mr. Masurovsky's opinion is that of a Stammgast during the period 1954-80 and this opinion carries weight, but judging by the photographs of the "old" Coupole, I can't see any radical difference in the basic structure. We have nonetheless enjoyed an apéritif with friends late in the afternoon in the café-bar section, and have eaten quite decent meals in the restaurant. But be aware that you may not find a seat for coffee and tart on Sunday afternoons, when The Third Age and others are pursuing their weekly outings. Mr. Lafon died on the anniversary of Armistice Day 1998 at the age of 101.

Someone says somewhere in someone's obiter dicta that French intellectuals moved from the cafés at the Carrefour Vavin to those in Saint-Germain des Prés in 1940 after the Germans occupied the Dôme and its neighbors allegedly bringing their own coffee with them -- insult to injury, but which is not surprising since they confiscated everything tasty or useful and left the French to drink a hot liquid made from chestnuts and tree bark. Nowadays, the Germans are indistinguishable from other European tourists in Paris, and the coffee is both real and delicious, and you can sit for an hour for the price of one cup without waiter-pressure to order more or leave.

* * * *

The **Closerie des Lilas** (6th), several blocks down the street from the Dôme and the Select, at the corner of Boulevard du Montparnasse and Rue Nôtre-Dame-des-Champs, is another former tavern that is now a good, but very expensive restaurant. Sit in the garden and have a drink, observe the statue of Marshal Michel Ney, sword raised as if to ward off the demons that may harm you. The sword did not help him when the restorers of the Bourbons executed him on this very spot, on December 7, 1815, for supporting the return of Napoléon and commanding troops at Waterloo. Now contemplate the long literary history of the place. The section on the Closerie for the early 1920s in *A Moveable Feast* is apparently accurate and brings vividly to life how the author remembers his youth in the city where he matured as a writer if not as a human being.

Keep in mind, however, that the Closerie Hemingway described disappeared to a disheartening extent in the modernization the owner undertook in December 1925. If a

218

waiter there tells you he remembers Monsieur 'Emingway, as one did to some naive tourists one night whilst we drank an apéritif, he's lying. If he tells you there is a nameplate in the bar marking the very spot where Monsieur 'Emingway drank, he is, alas, not lying. Nameplates also mark some of the very tables and spots at the bar where some of the famous cultural figures of by-gone eras allegedly spread their rearends and flatfeet.

The shattering of the dadist avant-garde has complicated origins and did not occur all at once, but by the end of February 1922 the split between André Breton and Tristan Tzara and their respective followers became irreversible. Into the post-bellum spiritual and intellectual malaise of metaphysical uncertainty and broken faith Breton injected plans for a "International Congress for the Determination and Defense of the Modern Spirit," or "Congress of Paris" as it became known. The Congress would examine the state of culture in crisis and attempt to resolve "the current confusion." One of the questions meant to assist the participants in their deliberations read "Among objects considered modern, is a top hat more or less modern than a locomotive?"

Although very serious about the state of affairs he organized the Congress to address, Breton carried another agenda in his dadapocket: to relegate Tzara, and indeed Tzara's forms of dada per se, to the graveyard where isms are interred. When this agenda became public, a scandal of sorts broke out with supporters of both men enthusiastically taking sides in print and on the streets. A number of those to be involved in the Congress withdrew their support and called for a meeting to discuss Breton's apparently paranoiac behavior and his "unfortunate circumlocution" in the phrase describing Tzara as "the promoter of a 'movement' that comes from Zurich," thus playing into the hands of the conservative, anti-modern right wing xenophobes. In brief, while many agreed with Breton's other points, the "Breton trial" at the Closerie on February 17, 1922, tumultuously ended in a vote of no-confidence in Breton by the hundred or so writers, artists and intellectuals there assembled. With plans for the Congress in shambles, the future "Pope of Surrealism" found himself free to move on toward yet another organizing task, which, with the participation of his loyal friends and colleagues, resulted in the creation of the surrealist movement.

Shortly before the "modernization" in 1925, the Closerie witnessed what may have been the last of the big banquets for literary figures organized by colleagues rather than agents or publishers with profits in mind. The poet thus honored few, alas, remember today: Pol Roux, known as Saint-Pol-Roux-le-Magnifique, according to Michel Leiris, one of the most brilliant, and last, members of the symbolist generation. However, the occasion brought out the worst (or the best) in Breton and his surrealist chums, who the organizers should have known better than to invite. The group marched into the upstairs banquet room with the firm intention of disrupting the event and garnering as much publicity as possible. They succeeded. After skirmishing throughout the greater part of the meal, Breton brought the affair to an explosive standstill.

Claiming that his friend Max Ernst had been insulted by an anti-German remark made by the 65-year old Rachilde (née Margurite Eymery), a conservative, nationalist "man of letters" as her calling card stated, Breton protested in such a manner as to provoke a melée of food-throwing, chair-hurling, fist-punching, oath-tossing, and insult-thrashing in which his fellow surrealist, Philippe Soupault, careened about hanging from a chandelier kicking everything animate and inanimate in his arced path. The sight of several of France's cultural figures, avant-garde or not, being led away in the panier à salade (Black Maria) and ambulances amazed the fascinated bourgeois pedestrians who gathered outside to discover what dire and loud event was taking place. Interestingly, years later Breton excommunicated Ernst from the Church of Surrealism because the Dadamax refused to renounce his deep and lasting friendship with the previously excommunicated poet Paul Eluard, and because he had the temerity to accept a prize for painting at the Venice Biennale.

* * * *

The ubiquitous 'Emingway (at number 113, original building torn down and replaced), Ezra Pound (at 70 bis) and innumerable French people lived on **La Rue Nôtre-Dame-des-Champs**, conveniently around the corner from the Closerie. The strange poet and opium eater, Ralph Cheever Dunning, lived in a tiny room at 70 from 1905 until he died of exhaustion and debilitation in 1930. Hemingway wrote that Dunning forgot to eat and wrote poems in "terza riruce" when smoking opium and drinking liters of milk. Yes, well, some people have clear minds under the most baffling circumstances. Alice Toklas, before she moved in with Gertrude Stein in 1910, lived at number 75, Ford Madox Ford at 84, Fernand Léger at 86 (in his book *The Artist in His Studio* [1988], Alexander Lieberman has a marvelous photograph of Léger looking out the window down to the street from this studio, and, yes, there are two women represented in the book despite its, in certain circles, currently politically incorrect title), the sculptress Malvina Hoffman at 72, John Singer Sargent at 73 bis, Augustus St. Gaudens at 49, James McNeill Whistler at 86, Friedrich Ahlers-Hestermann at 117, and, briefly, Robert McAlmon stayed at number 59.

From 1934 to 1936 Katherine Anne Porter lived in the Pounds' former apartment. Ten years earlier, when the Pounds moved to Rapallo, Italy, Janet Scudder moved into their flat. The once-famous American Impressionist,

Alexander Harrison, lived for a while after 1888 in the building, as did Jean-Léon Gerôme (in 1861) and F. U. Wrangel (1888-89) when he was not gambling away the Queen of Sweden's money at Monte Carlo. The now almost forgotten American cross-dressing painter, one of the few who learned the lessons of cubism, Morgan Russell, began his career in 1908 in a small studio on this street. Russell would remain in France through both parts of The Great World Misery, returning to the USA only in 1946 to die near Philadelphia in 1953.

Rudolph Klément, born in Hamburg in 1910, worked for a number of years during the 1930s as Trotsky's secretary, until his arrest for driving without sufficient headlight illumination led to his employer's deportation from France in June 1935. Klément remained in Paris in fear and in hiding: NKVD assassins moved about the hemispheres at Stalin's behest conducting liquidations of Trotsky's followers. Klément hid in a small room in the Rue Nôtre-Dame-des-Champs and in another in the Passage de Vanves (where Léo Malet, the anarchist mystery writer, protected him) until August 1938, when the police fished his headless corpse out of the Seine. No one knows for sure who murdered Klément, but the presence of "Jacques Mornard" in the city at that time leads to certain conclusions, especially since three years later, under the name "Ramon Mercader," Mornard appeared in Mexico City with an ice pick in his luggage and eeled his way into the Trotsky household. Before too long he found the opportunity to plunge the ice pick into the exiled Russian's skull, thus completing his mission for his NKVD masters and ridding Stalin of his last real competition for the leadership of the communist world.

This story has an interesting postscript, which reflects the ironies inherent in 20th century ideological commitments. The Cuban writer, Guillermo Cabera Infante, discovered that after 1960 the new revolutionary

Cuban government replaced the young, attractive receptionist at its Embassy in Paris with an elderly, rancid Spanish female. The irony lies in the fact that the German and other Trotskists collecting their visas for the new anti-imperialist, socialist homeland had the door opened for them, so to speak, by Caridad Mercader, the mother of their ideological mentor's murderer. Mercader lived out his existence in Cuba after release from a Mexican prison.

Just walking hurriedly through this street with another destination in mind will not do if one is to appreciate the thoroughfare's thick history. A list of those painters, sculptors and writers who lived and worked in this street's ateliers and apartments over several generations is astounding in its length. For example, in addition to those already mentioned above: Camille Claudel; George du Maurier (writer and general dilettante); Émile-Auguste Carolus-Duran; Rosa Bonheur (partial source of Marcel Duchamps' cross-dressed nom de peintre "Rrose Selavy"?); Augustin-Jean Moreau-Vauthier; Jean-Léon Gérome and his oddly trained monkey, Jacques; Jules Breton; Jean-Paul Laurens; François Bonvin; Henri Chapu; the English sculptors Frederick William Pomeroy and Sir George Frampton; William-Adolphe Bouguereau whose giant genre paintings of Greek and Roman mythology scenes sold in the mid-19th century for so much money that he allegedly remarked, "I lose five francs every time I piss"; Charles Cottet; Manès Sperber; Henri Le Fauconnier; but why go on? The point is made.

Look up at the buildings. Notice, for instance, the cute little stone-mullioned doorway built into the glass facade of the top floor studio at 57-59, or the facade at 86 where Whistler kept his studio, or the more mundane present construction at 113 and 73 bis. For further details about the street's past, see John Milner's "lavishly illustrated" *The Studios of Paris* (1988).

Victor Hugo lived at 11 during the years 1827-1830, where he sired the unfortunate Adèle and her brother François, and wrote his plays *Hernani* and *Marion de Lorme*. In his apartment (number 11 is now 27 and the original building no longer exists), Hugo held openhouse for fellow militant Romantics, including Balzac, Alexandre Dumas, Prosper Mérimée, Sainte-Beuve (who moved with his mother into number 19 in 1828 and began his relationship with Hugo's wife, also named Adèle), Gérard de Nerval, Théophile Gautier, and Alfred de Vigny, and here they planned the famous *Hernani* battle. Indeed, after the premier of the play and the tremendous scandal it caused, the owner of the building cancelled Hugo's lease in March 1830, forcing him to move his family to the Rue Jean-Gonjon.

Of what, some may justifiably wonder, does the "famous *Hernani* battle" consist, and why should one know anything about it? One could read about it at some length in Malcolm Easton's handy little volume, *Artists and Writers in Paris* (1964), or in any biography of Hugo. However, the jist of the matter is that Hugo wrote his play as a deliberate provocation to the predominant school of art and literature of the Bourbon restoration period, namely Classicism. Hugo and a group of fellow Romantics, the other end of the polarity (think of it as The Old Apollonian-Dionysian Duality), mounted an uproarious public relations program to ensure the succée de scandale they desired in what they viewed as the decisive battle with the previous generations' rigid and restrictive artistic methods, styles and subject matter, and the current State censorship of the written word.

According to plan they turned the opening night, February 25, 1830, into a circus. Groups of young Romantics and Art Students converged on the Comédie-Française at mid-afternoon, armed with food and drink, and locked themselves in the theater for four hours during which time they ate and drank with abandon and giggles, one would like to think. Actually, the intensity of their youthful commitment to The Cause probably precluded them from any real enjoyment of the event: no doubt they all remained stoically sober. The respectable theater-goers who arrived at seven o'clock for the performance reeled with shock at the sight of the theater as a public restaurant. Garlic sausages and red wine, indeed! As the play went on, it became clear that the actors did not agree with its revolutionary message and scuffles between antagonists in the audience broke out throughout the performance.

And what an audience! Hugo's fan club dressed in outlandish costumes (scarlet satin waistcoats, 16th century Venetian doge outfits, oddly formed mustaches and beards, shoulder-length hair, and so on) rubbed and joggled elbows with the conservatively clad haute-bourgeoisie and residual aristocracy. The play ran for 45 performances and the Romantics considered themselves victorious.

No, the poet Gérard de Nerval did not walk his lobster on a rhinestone leash down the theater aisle on this occasion. He accomplished that later on a fashionable Parisian thoroughfare. At the end of the 20th century, one finds it difficult to determine the "revolutionary" nature of the play's plot. In any case, Verdi's *Ernani* (1844) is based on Hugo's drama.

Robert W. Chambers lived in Paris from 1886 to 1893, and wrote hundreds of pages in books and short stories about the environs of the Left Bank. In one of the latter, entitled "The Street of Our Lady of the Fields," he describes the Rue Nôtre-Dame-des-Champs thusly: "It is a pariah among streets -- a street without a Quarter. It is generally understood to lie outside the pale of aristocratic Avenue de l'Observatoire. The students of the Montparnasse Quarter consider it swell and will have none of it. The Latin Quarter, from the Luxembourg, its northern frontier, sneers at its respectability and regards with disfavor the correctly costumed students who haunt it." Clearly a man writing before true knowledge had unskinned his eyes and lucid comprehension had illuminated his brain. This street has been many things, but a pariah has never been one of them.

A Camille Claudel Chronology. One of the artists who lived on this street late in the 19th century was the sculptor Camille Claudel, who could be added to the list of wives who suffered neglect because of their husbands' overwhelming career demands. But Rodin never married Claudel and in the end she spent 30 years in an asylum for the insane. The following sad chronology outlines the contours of her wrenching life.

1864 - born in Fère-en-Tardenois (Aisne).

1881 - at age 17, moves to Paris with mother and siblings to 135, boulevard du Montparnasse; Claudel shares a studio at 117, rue Nôtre-Dame-des-Champs with three English girls; the well-known sculptor, Alfred Boucher, who had guided her efforts in Nogent-sur-Seine before she moved to Paris, stops by each Friday to correct their work; begins to study at the Académie Colarossi.

1882 - not 1883, as many sources have it, Boucher moves to Rome to take the prestigious Prix de Rome at the French Academy there and asks his friend Rodin to take over tutoring the girls; within a very short time the 43 year-old Rodin falls passionately in love with the 17 year-old student, whom he calls in a letter written during a painful break in their relationship "my ferocious love" and "malevolent goddess"; while there can be no doubting the depth and honesty of Rodin's feelings for, and dependence on, the younger woman, there are those who insist that on the balance, the negative weight of the affair fell on Claudel, who ended insane; it is clear that she tormented him, but depended upon him in various ways.

1884 - with her close friend, Jessie Lipscomb, one of the English girls at the Rue Nôtre-Dame-des-Champs studio, works as an assistant in Rodin's studio at 182, rue de l'Université.

1886 - Claudel family moves to a new apartment at 31, boulevard de Port-Royal; she continues to work in Rodin's studio and their erratic affair continues to bring them both satisfaction and despair, with the latter increasingly dominating their lives.

1888 - in January, Rodin rents work and living space for her, in a building called La Folie Neubourg (Ruth Butler's 1993 biography of Rodin has this called "La Folie Payen, and has the number as 113), a ruin of an 18th century villa at 113, boulevard d'Italie (now Boulevard Auguste-Blanqui), allegedly so they could "work" together, though many Claudel adherents claim that the move made it easier for him to steal her work and plunder her sexually as well, away from the   watchful eye of his longtime companion, Rose Beuret, who he would marry in the end; (according to J.A. Schmoll gen. Eisenwerth's 1994 book on the two artists, Claudel rented a small apartment down the street from the studio).

1892 - breaks away from Rodin for various reasons, but certainly because he refuses to give up Rose Beuret Eisenwerth has her moving out of the studio, but Ruth Butler has her remaining there until

1896 - when she moves into a studio at 63, rue de Tureen, near the Place des Vosges.

1897 - last correspondence exchanged between them on the subject of Rodin's statue of Balzac, which Claudel unstintingly praises, as Rodin had and continued to praise and use his influence to obtain commissions and recognition for her work.

1899 - she moves to her final workspace, 19, quai de Bourbon on the Ile Saint-Louis, by which time her mind has begun to crack and her body deteriorate; paranoia increasingly dominates her life: she becomes convinced that Rodin wishes to kill her because he fears her talent and competition; as the 20th century begins, she begins to destroy her own work, while at the same time sporadically creating new pieces.

1908 - Eugène Blot shows her work in the last exhibition during her lifetime; her mental and physical condition deteriorates further until

1913 - when her brother Paul determines that she should be interred in a mental institution as suffering from "dementia"; transferred at end of August 1914 to Montdevergues asylum in Montfavet near Avignon where, thanks to her brother's apparent indifference, she remains until

1943 - when, at the age of 79, she dies, after 30 years incarceration, and is she is buried in the anonymous public plot in the section of the Montfavet cemetery reserved for inmates of the asylum.

1951 - the Musée Rodin holds the first posthumous retrospective; Paul Claudel writes the introduction to the catalog.

Adrienne Monnier sent Paul Claudel, then Ambassador in Washington, a free copy of the French version of *Ulysses*, which she published in 1929. He returned the book to her declaring, "I once wasted a few hours reading *Portrait of the Artist as a Young Man* by the same author, and that was enough for me.... [Both books are] full of the filthiest blasphemies, in which one feels all the hatred of a renegade - afflicted, moreover, by a really diabolical absence of talent." This about a book in which even the most despicable characters are portrayed with a certain love and tenderness. No wonder he never understood his sister.

It is interesting that after the end of their relationship (ca. 1885), Rodin created no new sculpture and devoted himself to reproductions of his best pieces done while they worked together. Rodin, *the* modern sculptor, thief and wretch, brillant and genius.

See the darkly wrenching, somewhat overwrought film entitled *Camille Claudel* (1990) for a passionate reenactment of their years together, with the perfect Isabelle Adjani as Claudel and the ubiquitous Gérard Depardieu as Rodin, the artistically gifted brute.

* * * *

Back on the Boulevard du Montparnasse, between the Rotonde and the Closerie there is a secondhand bookstore you should not pass by without going through the volumes on the sidewalk tables. We've discovered some nice bargains here, but one must be willing to spend the time to look closely. A selection of English language books is occasionally available, often in prewar Continental editions at very reasonable prices. Since a number of bookstores matching this description have sprouted in this stretch of the boulevard, you might wish to note that the one in question here is called **Les Nourritures Terrestres** and the address is 129, boulevard du Montparnasse. It may still be there when you read this.

The building that houses the branch of the Batifol chain at 127, boulevard du Montparnasse, a door away from the bookstore, has an interesting history. From 1925 to 1927 the building's ground floor contained Monaco American Bar, about which little is known, and from 1927 until the early 1930s a nightclub called **The Jungle**, which catered to American tourists and some of the less discriminating writers and painters, watered its drinks to make money from the tourists and the slumming bourgeois women who came late in the evening for the sweaty thrill of rubbing their bodies rhythmically against another person to the cacophonous blare of the thundering herd of an orchestra imported from some Carpathian village. As André Thirion described it during his own musical rubadubdub nights there: "extreme tensions of love and desire ... achieved by the tune 'I Can't Give You Anything But Love'." Henri, the former manager of The Jockey across the boulevard, owned it and Hilaire Hiler, who designed the decor of The Jockey, created the decor here as well. The obscene song singing dwarf called Chiffon provided part of the entertainment, not only by her questionable abilities as a singer, but with her popular trick of kicking up her skirts at regular intervals to reveal her small parts to the applause of the titillated audience.

> Jotta, jotta
> Jink, jink
> Jing.

The Jockey existed from 1923 to 1930 at 146, boulevard du Montparnasse at the corner of the Rue

Campagne Première. The clientele considered it to be a spiffy nightclub, but despite its being managed as well as decorated in a mock cowboy and Indian motif by Hiler, a true American cultural polymath, today one might have a somewhat different opinion. Both American and French writers, artists, and hangers-on, including Kiki who sang filthy songs and danced there, patronized the place and, according to Robert McAlmon, "almost any body of the writing, painting, musical, gigoloing, whoring, pimping or drinking world was apt to turn up at the Jockey." This boîte is not to be confused with the Jockey Club, the home-away-from-home of the rich and aristocratic French in a very different neighborhood.

* * * *

If you walk south on the Boulevard Raspail from the Carrefour Vavin, the second street you will see on your left is the **Rue Campagne Première**, which, while not so permeated with European cultural history as the Rue Nôtre-Dame-des-Champs, is nonetheless studded with gems of past social and cultural glories if one has the imagination and time to call them up out of that vast storage bin we call history. On your right, as you walk up the street toward the Boulevard du Montparnasse, you will see the venerable Hôtel Istria at number 29. The facade has recently been renovated so it does not appear to be venerable, and if one's notion of venerable dates things from the 18th century then the place is probably not venerable, but if one can accept as venerable a building with a history and importance dating from the year 1919, then the Hôtel Istria is indeed venerable.

A plaque on the hotel facade will tell you about its and the street's place in Parisian cultural history by simply listing the names of some of those who lived and worked on the street, a list which includes Man Ray, Rainer Maria

Rilke, Louis Aragon, Elsa Triolet, Kiki, Francis Picabia, Marcel Duchamp, Moïse Kisling, Eric Satie, Tristan Tzara, and Vladimir Mayakovsky. The remainder of the plaque is taken up with a fragment of a poem called "Il ne m'est Paris que d'Elsa" by Aragon, the Stalinist poet and French Communist Party cultural functionary, whose self-degradation before the Party's quicksilver policy changes was so base and servile that one might perversely see it as almost heroic.

Ne s'éteint que ce qui brilla ...
Lorsque tu descendais de l'hôtel Istria,
Tout était different Rue Campagne Première,
En mil neuf cent vingt neuf, ver l'heure de
midi ...

(Only what once sparkled fades.../when you would come down from the Hotel Istria,/everything was different Rue Campagne Première/in nineteen twenty nine, around noon....)

Indeed, Aragon and his life companion, Triolet, who danced even more closely to the erratic rhythms of the Party's shifting music, lived next to the hotel at number 31 in 1929. Of course, nothing is as simple as that; although it is the truth, it is only a part of a larger truth, an exploration of which would offer a context for understanding their abject and deplorable behavior. The Calvin (Elsa) and Hobbes (Louis) of 20th century French literature, though in the end, after Elsa's death, Louis made his homosexuality public. Hêlas, this is not yet the place for such an investigation.

Mayakovsky's verse about the city is worth citing and is retrospectively particularly sad given his suicide in Moscow.

I would like

232

to live

        and die in Paris,
  if there weren't
  such a land

        as Moscow.

But we are not quite finished with the Hôtel Istria. The wall plaque does not tell you that Duchamp moved into the hotel in December 1923, most probably not with Thérèse Treize, as Hansen has it; she was a well-known model, teacher of gymnastics, and companion of painters at the time, whose name should have its place in a public site. Robert McAlmon lived here during the summer of 1927 and found a room in the hotel for William Carlos Williams, the poet and physician, and his wife, Flossie, when they sorely needed a place to stay during that summer of the American Legion Decentennial, which during those months raged like the plague, infesting most of the hotel rooms in the city and countryside alike.

In 1922, that clever elf, the Surrealist painter and photographer Man Ray, rented a studio at number 31-31bis, having outgrown his earlier studio apartment after shifting his creative emphasis from painting to photography. He always considered himself foremost a painter, a matter that constituted a painful irony for him given his world-re-known as a photographer. The double numbers reflect the fact that the building has two entrances. This unusual building (its facade stands out quite impressively from the rather more traditional facades on the street), constructed in 1911, contained not just studios, but living space as well. Man Ray's quarters stood just to the left of the 31bis entrance on the ground floor. A narrow staircase at the back of the studio led to a 10 by 29 foot loft containing a toilet and sink, which Ray and Kiki used as a bedroom. If you really want to know, the studio measured 15 by 25 feet. Man Ray sent a postal card with a photograph of the street and the building to his parents in July 1922 noting, "Here's where I live, $25 a month - a swell place!"

In 1923, Man Ray hired Berenice Abbott as his assistant, saving her from "mourant de faim," and she began here her apprenticeship as a photographer. Three years later she began an independent and highly successful career with her own studio. In December 1923, Man Ray could afford to move into the Istria, and a number of sources say he did so at this time. One assumes Kiki moved in with him, at least at one point she had her own room there. In the late 1920s, Man Ray rented a small studio at 8, rue Val-de-Grâce in the 5th arrondissement in order to paint undisturbed. He maintained this studio at 31bis, rue Campagne Première until 1937, when he moved into a combined studio and living quarters at 40, rue Denfert-Rochereau (now Rue Henri-Barbusse), where he lived until he left France in July 1940. Henri Hayden (1913-1914) and Thérèse Treize (c.1925-1930) also lived at the Rue Denfert-Rochereau address.

As you look at the building, think about the following: in the autumn of 1924, Francis Picabia and Erik Satie struggled to create the ballet *Relâche*. Picabia also wrote the scenario for the short film, *Entr'acte*, which René Clair directed to be shown during the ballet's intermission following its premiere on December 4. Picabia, Satie, Man Ray and Marcel Duchamp all appear in the film; all four of them lived at the time in the Istria. A furious fount of fecundity, that hotel. Satie returned to the hotel in January 1925, when Man Ray got him a room one night because he was too ill to return to his house in the shabby suburb Arceuil; shortly thereafter Satie went into the Saint Joseph Hospital in the Rue Pierre-Larousse where he remained until he died early that summer.

Continue on up the Rue Campagne Première until you come to 17bis. Here in a bare apartment on the fifth floor from 1899 until his death in 1927 lived the photographer

Eugène Atget and his life companion Valentine Delafosse Compagnon. Once practically unknown and during the later years of his life poverty-stricken, Atget is now "world-famous" and requires no further description here. However, it should be recalled that, in a heroic gesture of cultural prescience, Berenice Abbott saved Atget's glass plate negatives from the garbage pail after he died, and thus committed an altruistic act that allowed the old man's work to later become so "world-famous" and the subject of many exhibitions and large-format books. Atget's photographs are quiet, filled with beauty (which often denies the squalid reality of the cityscape he is photographing), and should be known to anyone who has pretensions to being kulturnyi.

The next number (17) on that side of the street is a wide alley with studios on both sides. This mews-like thoroughfare may always have been an alley, but might have been a building at some passed time, but which, in any case, housed the studios of Per and Lucy Krohg, Martin Kaelin, Walter Pach and Léopold Gottlieb.

Number 9 is a building on a courtyard containing studios of varying sizes, mostly small to judge by the facades, built from metal and wood from the demolition of the 1889 World Exposition. Mina Loy and her two lovely daughters (one of whom married the art dealer Julien Levy), Modigliani, Whistler, Rainer Marie Rilke, Mathilde Vollmöller, Malvina Hoffman, Stanley Hayter all lived and worked in this building. Hansen has Loy, as well as the Irish poet James Stephens, living at number 11, and Brian Morton has Loy at number 15, but number 9 is probably the correct address. The German painter, Hans Purrmann, lived at number 5 in 1907.

Further up the street at number 3 is the site of the well-loved eatery called Chez Rosalie, after its owner, cook and mother hen to impecunious artists, models, laborers, and writers who frequented the place during its halcyon days 1906 - 1926.

Turn right on the Boulevard du Montparnasse, stroll for a block and turn right into the **Rue Boissonnade**, which runs parallel to the Rue Campagne Première. Elie Nadelman, an East European sculptor lived at number 15 (1912-1914), as did the American sculptor, Mariette Mills (1920s); Amédée Ozenfant, the "cubist" painter and lover of Germaine Bongard, Paul Poiret's sister and art dealer, lived at number 16 (1911); Conrad Kickert, the Netherlandish painter (1925-1936), Edvard and Anna Diriks (1903-1923), painters from Norway and Sweden respectively, and Stella Bowen, for many years Ford Madox Ford's companion and mother of his daughter, Julia (b. 1927), all lived and worked at number 18. On the left as you look toward the building at number 19, gaze over the wall into a lovely park-like garden and wonder at the price of the apartments with such a view in the middle of the city. Then look up at number 19 and see if this art deco facade, from a certain angle, doesn't remind you of the Flatiron Building in New York City, except this one is round! A plaque on the facade of number 33 notes that Conrad Kickert lived and worked in that building from 1937 until his death in 1965, which makes him the longest living non-Frenchman on that street that I know of. Umberto Brunellschi, the art nouveau illustrator and stage-costume designer, lived in Paris from 1900 to 1949, but so far as I know at number 22 on this street only in 1912. The Symbolist poet and editor of the journal *Vers et Prose,* Paul Fort, lived during the decade preceding 1914 at number 24, not far from his dear friends, the Diriks.

Look into the end of the 17, rue Campagne Première alley of studios and see if the spraypainted graffito reading "Elvis tu est mort!" still decorates the white wall.

At the end of the street, turn left and continue down the Boulevard Raspail past the cemetery to the Place Denfert-Rochereau and look to the southeast, you will see the broad Boulevard Saint-Jacques. In 1891, after studying with

Thomas Eakins at the Pennsylvania Academy of Fine Arts, the young painter, **Henry Ossawa Tanner** left Philadelphia for Paris to refine his technique and live in what he hoped would be a more liberated, less racist society. Whether or not he obtained the latter may be questionable, but he certainly achieved the former before he died in the city in 1937, beginning with winning a medal at the 1897 Paris Salon for "The Raising of Lazarus." His work deserves to be better known: several of his paintings are in the permanent collections of the Philadelphia Museum of Art and the National Museum of American Art in Washington DC, including works resulting from his trips to North Africa and Palestine, and a very curiously posed Salomé from around 1900 done in various shades of blue and white, simultaneously threatening and erotically magnetic, a perfect Oscar Wilde-Richard Strauss emasculating vamp.

For most of his 46 years in Paris, a duration rarely equaled by non-French Parisians (for example, Gertrude Stein lived here for 42 and Alice Toklas for 57 years, and their friend Picasso lived there for approximately 50 years before moving permanently to the South, while the ever-eccentric Raymond Duncan spent more than 50 years in the city), Tanner had a studio at 51, boulevard Saint-Jacques, just across the street from the elaborate art deco métro station. From 1906 to 1912 he also had a studio at 70bis, rue Nôtre-Dame-des-Champs. He deserves a plaque on the wall of the Boulevard Saint-Jacques building, the facade of which surely has been remodeled since Tanner lived there.

Tanner's painting, "The Raising of Lazarus," attracted the attention of whichever official government Frenchman administered the painting budget and the government purchased it in 1897 for the Musée du Luxembourg, an act that lent tremendous prestige to Tanner, and, one hopes, gave him deep satisfaction. Booker T. Washington, himself, in 1899, visited Tanner and published an appreciation of the artist that may have been more politically oriented than aesthetically motivated. Nonetheless, Washington seems to have grasped that, as much as he repressed its darker meaning, this recognition of a Negro painter could not have occurred in the USA. He wrote, "Here in France no one judges a man by his color," which is, of course, not true, then or now, especially now. By 1904, "The Raising of Lazarus" had marched into the Louvre, but apparently marched back to his studio again because, apparently, it hung there in 1925 and 1929. I must admit I am not sure where it is now, but in 1969 it apparently belonged "to the Musée d'Art Moderne and has been stored at Compiègne." In 1906, the French government purchased another of Tanner's works, "The Disciples at Emmaus," which they lost at some point during the 1939-1945 Era of Evil Tidings.

In 1928, Countee Cullen rented an apartment on the Avenue du Parc Montsouris for his new wife and himself in order to be near his friend Tanner. Cullen made annual trips to Paris and he continued to visit Tanner until the latter's death. One would much like to know that about which they talked! Perhaps not so curiously, Tanner's name appears in none of the memoirs of the "expatriate 1920s." Perhaps, indeed, his mentalité and his art were too conservative for the young, white avant-garde. Even Nancy Cunard had nothing to say about him. However, in 1969, the University of Chicago Press published Marcia Mathews' biography entitled *Henry Ossawa Tanner, American Artist*; Dewey Mosby published a longer biography in 1991, and there have been several exhibitions of his work in the last twenty years or so.

Tanner died at peace in his sleep on May 25, 1937, in his apartment at 43, rue de Fleurus, and is buried beside his beloved wife, Jessie, in the cemetery at Sceaux, a Parisian suburb where they owned a summer house.

The French government awarded three black Americans the Legion of Honor, Henry O. Tanner (1923), Joséphine

Baker (1961), and James Baldwin (1986), all of them so honored before the award became debased in the 1990s.

Matters have recently moved forward, which is satisfying to those who still believe in The Idea of Progress, that much battered and tattered notion of the development of human history. To wit, on October 26, 1996, the White House announced the purchase of Tanner's "Sand Dunes at Sunset, Atlantic City," painted circa 1885, which is to hang on what one hopes is permanent display in the Green Room, the first painting by a Negro American artist to be so honored. Hillary Rodham Clinton is reported to have said on this occasion, "The works of Henry Ossawa Tanner remind us that talent has the power to transcend prejudice." While this may or may not be the case, the fact that the White House Endowment Fund paid $100,000 to a member of the Tanner family for the painting is a cause for some celebration.

Of course there have been other American artists of color who studied, worked and exhibited in Paris. These include, for example, Palmer Hayden (1890-1973), whose extreme images of urban Negro life caused controversy then and now, and William Henry Johnson (1901-1970), who also lived for many years in Denmark with his Danish ceramist wife and whose deliberately primitively styled images, a large collection of which are in the National Museum of American Art in Washington, unfortunately continue to raise questions about his talent.

Loïs Mailou Jones (1905-1998), probably the only American Negro woman painter to achieve success and fame abroad during the 1930s and 1940s, studied at the Académie Julian during 1937-1938, living in a studio at 23, rue Campagne Première, during which time she produced an amazing number of beautiful works drawing on the post-impressionist and cubist traditions in an original and stimulating manner, and exhibited at several of the salons. In 1952 a book containing 100 of her paintings done in

239

France appeared, appropriately enough, in France. Ms Jones spent 47 years (1930-1977) teaching at Howard University in Washington DC. The Corcoran Gallery of Art in Washington housed a retrospective of her work in honor of her 89th birthday in 1994, and a large-format book devoted to her life and art appeared in the same year.

Beauford Delaney (1901-1977), a "spiritual father" to James Baldwin and the subject of an essay by his friend Henry Miller, who met him in the early 1940s in Greenwich Village ("The Amazing and Invariable Beauford Delaney" [1944]), began exhibiting in New York City in 1930 and moved permanently to Paris in 1953, where he continued to develop as a painter, alternating between relatively representational portraits and brilliant, glowing rhapsodies on the color yellow, and to encourage young black artists in their work, while in constant need of encouragement himself. Mental illness, which threatened his equilibrium throughout his life, clouded his last years during which he ceased painting entirely. His life and work, though increasingly better known since his death, deserve a comprehensive study. David Leeming has made a sympathetic, useful and informative beginning with his 1998 biography of the artist entitled *Amazing Grace*.

Archibald John Motley, Jr. (1891-1981) spent the 1929-1930 year studying in Paris on a Guggenheim Fellowship, which he received after winning the 1928 Harmon Foundation gold medal for fine arts. At least one of his Paris paintings is in the Schomberg Center collection in New York City. He painted scenes of city life as he saw it, especially interiors of The Jockey and the Bal Nègre.

William Edouard Scott (1884-1964) trained in the classical techniques of oil painting at the Art Institute of Chicago and then spent the years 1909 to 1911 in Paris studying with French teachers and with Henry O. Tanner. In 1918, he returned to France with an apparently official commission to make drawings of Negro soldiers in action,

240

several of which subsequently appeared on the cover of *The Crisis*, a journal edited by W.E.B. DuBois.

Laura Wheeler Waring (1887-1948) traveled in Europe and North Africa on a scholarship in 1914 and stopped in Paris before the diplomats, newspapers and military officials extinguished the lamps of Europe at the end of August. In 1924, she returned to Paris to study for a year at the Académie de la Grand Chaumière. Hale Aspacio Woodruff (1900-1980) studied at the Académie Scandinave and the Académie Moderne during 1927-28 and remained in France until 1931 when he returned to the USA to teach at Atlanta University.

Albert Alexander Smith (1896-1940) presents an intriguing situation: according to the entry in *Against All Odds: African American Artists and the Harmon Foundation* (1989), after studying at the Ethical Culture Art School and the National Academy of Design in New York City, where after he became quite well-known and respected for his prints, he moved to France in 1928 to work as an entertainer in the cabarets and to continue to pursue his printmaking and engraving. The entry is illustrated by three examples of his work, one of which, an etching entitled "Market, Nice" is dated 1925, which makes one wonder if he imagined the scene or if the date of his arrival in France is wrong. (Unfortunately this is not the only such anomaly in the book.) Smith died in Paris in 1940. What occupied his time and talents during those years? Where in Paris did he live? What was the nature of his relationship with Tanner, of whom he made a portrait? With whom did he pal around in Paris? What was his life like in the city, especially as war approached? Under what circumstances and in what month did he die? Before or after the Germans occupied the city?

* * * *

The Unknown Ladies: Augusta Savage, Janet Scudder, Malvina Hoffman, Meta Warrick Fuller, and Elizabeth Prophet. The sculptor Augusta Savage (1900-1962) lived and worked for some time in Paris. She not only possessed a remarkable name, but also considerable talent. If what remains of her sculptures is any indication, one of the great mishaps of the century is the loss, due to indifference and destruction, of the bulk of her work. In the New York Public Library's Schomberg Center for Research in Black Culture, her ironically titled piece "Gamin" (1930) sits, according to one source, unseen by those who might most benefit from exposure to this disturbing portrait of a young black boy, whose future might possibly be bright and successful, but the skepticism of his visage seriously considers his chances less than favorable. White liberals will experience wrenching guilt when they look upon the six-inch darkened plaster; black Americans today may be forgiven for wondering, when they see the statue, when, not if, the boy went out into the street with fire in his eyes and a gun in his hand. A nine-inch high bronze of "Gamin" dated 1929 is in the permanent collection of Howard University's Gallery of Art in Washington, D.C., as is the bronze "La Citadelle - Freedom." Photographs of these pieces, as well as the painful "Green Apples" (1928), appear in *Against All Odds* and photograph of "Gamin" appears in *Harlem Renaissance: Art of Black America* (1987). A photograph of "Green Apples" also appears in the catalog to the exhibition *The Figure in American Sculpture: A Question of Modernity* (1995). C. S. Rubenstein's reference book, *American Women Artists from Early Indian Times to the Present* (1982), devotes a few paragraphs to Miss Savage in addition to a photograph of one of the magnificent, but destroyed sculptures she made for the 1939 New York World's Fair. No money could be found to cast the plaster in bronze.

242

One does not know much about Augusta Savage in Paris. Her name appears from time to time in Michel Fabre's book, *From Harlem to Paris* (1991), wherein she is praised for her work, but none of it is illustrated in the photographs. For several years in the 1930s she kept a studio on the Rue de Chatillon, or the Avenue de Chatillon as Fabre indicates, in the southern reaches of the 14th arrondissement. It is possible that what is now Avenue Jean Moulin was Avenue de Chatillon before 1945. In any case, both are southeast of the Place Victor Basch and the Alésia métro station.

Augusta Savage applied to become a student at the Palais de Fontainebleau summer art school in 1923. School officials rejected her application, evidently thinking that white parents would not send their daughters to a class with a black girl as a classmate. Miss Savage fought with bitter determination to have the rejection overturned; with the support of public personalities, such as W.E.B. DuBois, she pursued the issue in the major newspapers and weekly magazines. It is not clear from the sources I've read whether she succeeded or not, but the hostility the campaign engendered in the white, male museum and art dealer world made it impossible for her to earn a living from her sculptures, and she worked for years in factories and laundries to pay the rent and eat. In 1929, or 1930 depending on the source, the Julius Rosenwald Foundation and the Carnegie Foundation gave her a series of fellowships to study with Félix Bueneteaux at the Académie de la Grande Chaumière.

She returned to New York in 1931, or 1932 depending on the source, where she became deeply involved with administering school programs for young Harlem artists; indeed her own work suffered from lack of attention as she concentrated on assisting others. Indeed, she gave so much of her time and energy to others that she hardly had anything left for herself. William Rose Benét includes a brief reference to her in his *The Reader's Encyclopedia* (1948), which notes that she is "best known for her studies of Negro heads. One of the four women sculptors commissioned to do work for the World's Fair in New York (1939)."

Her last major exhibition occurred in 1939 at the Augusta Savage Studios in Harlem, where after she apparently withdrew for the final 20 years of her life to a small upstate town. It is not surprising, but nonetheless intensely sad to read that, "few of her works from the 1920s and 1930s have been located."

Janet Scudder (1869-1940), who also received the Legion of Honor award, belongs to an earlier generation of American women who struggled against male spite and resistance to their work. General information on this sculptor is easier to come by than that about Miss Savage, if only because Miss Scudder and the Misses Gertrude Stein and Alice Toklas developed a lasting friendship while they all lived in Paris before and after the 1914-1918 phase of the Great 20th Century Idiocy. Consequently, Miss Scudder appears flittingly in the various Stein-Toklas biographies. She published a book of memoirs called *Modeling My Life* in 1925, but this is out of print and difficult to locate.

In Chicago as a young but stongwilled girl, Scudder saw the Frederick William MacMonnies fountain in the court of honor at the World Columbian Exposition in 1893 and decided then and there that she would study with him and become a sculptor. The next year she began work as his assistant in his Paris studio at 16, rue Antoine Bourdelle, then called Impasse du Maine. She lived then at the American University Women's Paris Club, now Reid Hall, at 4, rue de Chevreuse (6th). The house and gardens may be visited, but not at all times, so be prepared for disappointment if you wish to follow Scudder's life in Paris. (MacMonnies, a handsome young man, taught at the

Académie Vitti, at 49, boulevard du Montparnasse during the 1890s, a school for young ladies only.)

You can at least walk by Scutter's former residence at 70 bis, rue Nôtre-Dame-des-Champs into which she moved in December 1924 after Ezra Pound and Dorothy Shakespear transferred their activities to Rapallo. Scudder thereafter moved to 24, rue de Verneuil (7th), which runs parallel to the Rue Jacob and the Seine north of the Boulevard Saint-Germain, where she continued to work in Paris and sell her pieces in New York City. She must have had a studio elsewhere during the period she spent in Pound's former apartment, which was barely large enough to hold the Pounds much less a sculptor's studio. That she continued to turn out her work is not in doubt: in the summer of 1932, at the age of 62, she participated in a Paris exhibition entitled "American Women's Show." In her *New Yorker* letter of June 22, 1932, Janet Flanner wrote that the works exhibited "showed an amazonian quality of strength that did not surprise or fail to please." Not quite a rave review, but sympathetic and appreciative nonetheless. Flanner's standards were rigorous, stringent and difficult to meet. The word "Amazon" served during the period before 1939 as a codeword for lesbian.

According to James Mellow's *Charmed Circle: Gertrude Stein and Company* (1974), Scudder's "forte was pleasant and inoffensive garden statuary - prancing fauns, nubile girls, boys on dolphins." Veritable lawn toys. No wonder one of her principal buyers was Stanford White, the unfortunate architect, who commissioned her to make such things for estates he built on Long Island.

Miss Stein named her the "doughboy" because "there were only two perfectly solemn things on earth, the doughboy and Janet Scudder." According to Miss Stein, Miss Scudder had "all the subtlety of the doughboy and all his nice ways and all his lonesomeness." Miss Stein approved less of Miss Scudder's "real pioneer's passion for buying useless real estate," but this is all gossip, required from time to time to loosen the ties that tend to bind, but tedious in the long run. Miss Scudder and her companion, Mrs. Camille Lane, did not buy a house in Grasse, but did take one in Aix-en-Provence, which did not work out, as Miss Stein had previously warned, and they returned to Paris.

Miss Scudder's work can be seen in private collections as well as those of the Metropolitan Museum of Art ("Frog Fountain"), the Peabody Institute in Baltimore ("Tortoise Fountain"), and the Art Institute of Chicago ("Fighting Boy Fountain," which brings to mind Alan Ladd standing on a box to reach Sophia Loren's height in *Boy on a Dolphin*, the movie in which Miss Loren rises from the sea soaked in a thin blue dress in one of the most innocently erotic scenes on the American screen in the 1950s, the image of which became a popular poster in the mid-1960s).

Prior to August 1914, Miss Scudder held Saturday "afternoons" (not to conflict with Miss Stein's Saturday "evenings") in her studio at 1, rue de la Grande Chaumière (6th), where, it is said, Gordon Craig and Henry Adams might appear. Miss Scudder did not meet Malvina Hoffman (1887-1966) when the latter young lady moved with her mother briefly into a pension at 77, rue Nôtre-Dame-des-Champs in 1910. Miss Hoffman had met Miss Scudder earlier that year in Florence at Mabel Dodge's villa under unusual circumstances having to do with Miss Scudder's belief in ghosts. The interested reader is referred to Miss Hoffman's memoirs, *Yesterday is Tomorrow* (1965), for further details of the meeting. The younger woman called on the other, worked briefly as the latter's studio helper mixing clay and whatnot, and one Saturday found herself saying hello to Miss Gertrude Stein amidst the Picassos, Cézannes and Matisses. All this in 1910, the year when, according to Virginia Woolf, everything changed.

The 23 year-old Hoffman then rented a small studio at 72, rue Nôtre-Dame-des-Champs, her first with a northern exposure, presumably to be near the two academies of art, Académie de la Grande-Chaumière and the Académie Colorossi. Later that year, having pressured Rodin into reluctantly allowing her to be his assistant, a job she held on and off when in Paris until his death in 1917, she moved into a studio-apartment at 17, rue Campagne Première. The artist, William Stanley Hayter, lived at the same address in the 1930s, before the international crime syndicate called The Great Powers went to war again in 1939 and forced him to move to New York City with his etching business called, not surprisingly, "Atelier 17."

The French added Miss Hoffman's work "Russian Bacchanale" to the permanent collection in the Jardin du Luxembourg, but do not look for it now. The Germans melted down the bronze in 1941 to make artillery shells. Her first commission in Paris was for a bust of the American Ambassador to France, Robert Bacon, in 1910.

In 1927, Miss Hoffman purchased a plot of land at 25 Villa Santos-Dumont (15th), described as a "19th century alleyway," designed a three-story house with large windows cut into the roof over her studio, oversaw its construction and moved into it the next summer. During the next ten years she worked with the same demonic strength of will she showed in forcing Rodin to recognize her as a serious artist. One of her pieces, "Bill Working," the French accessioned into the Jeu de Paume; it is presumably now in the Musée d'Orsay collection. She spent the war years in the United States and returned to Paris in 1948 to find her house dusty, but in perfect condition except for the garden which had grown rampant and wild.

Shortly after her return she sculpted a bust of Teilhard de Chardin, which the Ministry of Fine Arts purchased and, one assumes, added to the collections in the Musée

National d'Art Moderne in the Centre Pompidou. She also sculpted the memorial for the United States military cemetery in Épinal in the Vosges. In 1961, at the age of 74, she sold the house. Browsing through her autobiography, *Heads and Tails* (1936), in addition to an earlier book mostly about her travels in the Near and Far East and Africa, is well worth the time for it is full of anecdotes, now amusing though perhaps less so when they occurred, such as how her tenacious persistence gained her the position as Rodin's assistant.

One cannot escape his presence if one considers sculpture during and surrounding the Belle Epoch in Paris. He encouraged the work of Meta Vaux Warrick Fuller (1877-1968) and accepted her as a student, which gave her immense prestige among those who thought of themselves as cognoscenti. Fuller needed both the encouragement and the association with Rodin, not because she lacked talent, quite the opposite in fact, but because she was an American black woman, and thus carried built-in disadvantages that had nothing to do with her abilities as an artist. In 1899, after graduating from the Pennsylvania School of Industrial Art, she won a scholarship to study in Paris, and searched for a room at the American Girls Club. The management refused, though she was both American and a girl; her problem of course lay in her color. No room at that inn, but Tanner, a fellow Philadelphian, found for her a small, and one hopes well-heated, room in a residential hotel in the Latin Quarter.

On the advice of Augustus Saint-Gaudens and Tanner, in 1899 she enrolled in the École des Beaux-Arts where she had a scholarship and studied drawing for three years with Raphael Collin, in addition to studying at the Académie Colarossi with Injalbert and Rollard. In 1902 she exhibited some pieces and met Rodin at the Salon de l'Art Nouveau, the gallery owned by Siegfried Bing, who also published the influential review *Le Japon Artistique* (1888-91). This show took some courage for Bing to put on at the time, not only because Fuller was female and black, but also because her pieces represented symbolically the anguish of Negro life, indeed one American critic described her, inaccurately, as the "sculptor of horrors." Bing himself bought two of her works from the show, and the encouragement she received in Paris better enabled her to carry on the struggle for recognition in the USA. In the following year, she exhibited "The Wretched" and "The Impenitent Thief" at the Paris Salon, and returned to Philadelphia to enroll in the Pennsylvania Academy of Fine Arts. In 1939 she exhibited at the Augusta Savage Studios in New York.

Fuller was the first black American artist to make consistent use of American Negro and African motifs and forms, long before the Harlem Renaissance brought these to public notice. (However, Alain Locke credits the sculptor May Howard Johnson in the late 19th century with being the first to move into "frank and deliberate racialism" in Negro art.) Until Fuller began her professional career as a sculptor, only a few scattered images that could be described as African or American Negro existed in American high art. Tanner, who normally worked in the white European mainstream both stylistically and in terms of content, painted two of these works ("Banjo Lesson" 1893 and "The Thankful Poor" 1894). Fuller created what is perhaps her most well-known piece, "Ethiopia Awakening" (now at the Schomberg Center in the 135th Street branch of the New York Public Library), in 1914, a pan-African work tying together black nationalism, a perceived if not historically accurate black Egyptian heritage, the emotions of motherhood and the idea of renaissance. Yes, I know this sounds pompous if not impossible, but I suggest you see the sculpture itself or at least the photograph of it (along with other Fuller work) in *Harlem Renaissance: Art of Black America*. You might also see the Danforth Museum of Art catalog, *An*

Independent Woman: Life and Art of Meta Warrick Fuller (1985). It is said that most of her work has disappeared, which is truly unfortunate and a bloody outrage, if not surprising.

Of the sculptress Nancy Elizabeth Prophet (1890-1960), even less is generally known than of the others discussed above. In the summer of 1929, Miss Prophet exhibited her work in Paris and had tea on July 2 with Countee Cullen and other black Americans to celebrate the occasion. On August 2, 1929, the newspaper *Afro-American* published a gossipy article entitled "Beth Prophet Hailed as Artist in Paris."

And that paragraph contains all I knew at first, this sparse information found in a brief textual reference and a source note in, again, Fabre's book. All well and good for a throwaway reference in a short paragraph, but who was she? Why was she in Paris? Where had she come from and what became of her after Paris? And if I knew all this, would it be relevant to this book? Well yes, it would; so gradually and sporadically, when other pressures allowed, I began in 1991 to look for her life.

The exhibition catalog *Against All Odds*, contains the bare bones of information about her life, leaving one even more curious than previously. Then, thanks to the good offices of Susan Vander Closter of the Rhode Island School of Design, photocopies of a 1987 article by Blossom S. Kirschenbaum published in *Sage*, Prophet's diaries printed in *The Rhode Island Magazine* (July, 1994), Countee Cullen's article about her work in Paris from *Opportunity* (July, 1930), and other materials gradually accumulated on my desk; bits and pieces of a life to be woven together into a narrative, however brief, that coalesced into some knowable story: her life would seem to be the stuff of melodrama, a particularly sad, American melodrama.

Born in Providence or Warwick or the village of Artic Center (depending on the source), Rhode Island, in 1890, child of a Narragansett Indian father and a mother described as "mixed Negro," which gave her the opportunity later in life to bitterly claim descent from her Indian side and deny her Negro side. Against the advice of her family, she enrolled in 1914 at the Rhode Island School of Design from which she graduated in 1918, the only woman of color in that class. In 1915, she married a former Brown University student, Francis Ford, a black man with whom she seems to have had an erratic relationship from the beginning. Ford had been the only black student in the Providence Hope High School classical study course in 1900.

She moved to France in 1922 when she was 32, having worked herself sick at unspecified but humiliating jobs to save the $380 she took to Paris, accompanied only by a fierce determination to succeed as a sculptor. Accepted by the École des Beaux Arts, she attended classes there but did most of her work in cheap, drab, and unheated studios, her health further undermined by too little sleep, too little food, and that obsessive drive to learn her art and create a body of work of unparalleled quality for which she would achieve public recognition sufficient to give her the economic base from which to continue her work. One of her early diary entries reads: "I worked away on my first piece with a dogged determination to conquer ... with a calm assurance and savage pleasure of revenge." Lonely and dejected, she wrote her husband to come to Paris, "a stupid mistake" she realized soon after because, although a good man, he possessed no ambition and could not adjust to living there.

Thus during the early years in Paris she moved from one small studio to another, sometimes sharing the quarters with another woman sculptor, whose dog's food she ate in desperation, but always working even when she could no longer stand up because of malnutrition and general debilitation which sent her to the American hospital for three weeks.

Eventually she exhibited in the Salons d'Automne, the August Salons and the Salon of the Societé des Artistes Français to positive and encouraging reviews. Indeed, despite her poverty, for many years she achieved a series of what must be considered successes, even if they brought her no permanent economic relief. In the summer of 1926, she finally moved into a real studio in Montparnasse and, although continually plagued by poverty (several of her journal entries read simply "Starvation."), she works on occasionally selling a piece, remaining reclusive and withdrawn ("O delicious and adorable Solitude how you soothe and calm the soul." November 30, 1930), finally sending her husband home in 1929. Despite her deliberate isolation, she came to know W.E.B. DuBois, Henry Tanner, and Countee Cullen, while she lived in Paris. DuBois introduced her to Augusta Savage when the latter arrived in the city and Prophet may indeed have influenced some of Savage's work at the time.

During her residence in Paris, Prophet exhibited at the Rhode Island School of Design, the Boston Society of Independent Artists and the Harmon Foundation at Tanner's suggestion, the latter of which awarded her the 1929 Otto H. Kahn exhibition prize. In the summer of 1932, she returned briefly to Providence and Newport to attend the opening of a successful exhibition of her work. She returned permanently to the USA in 1934 where she taught at Atlanta University and Spelman College in Atlanta, Georgia, until 1944 when she moved to Providence and held a final exhibition of her work in the public library there in 1945, after which she disappears into a life of poverty and obscurity. Miss Prophet died in 1960 at the age of 70. Her poverty necessitated that a funeral fund be raised to preclude the authorities from burying her in potter's field. Raised by whom? What did she do during the last sixteen years of her life? Why indeed did she leave Atlanta? All we know is that she may have had a mental breakdown, that she probably worked as a housemaid for part of the time, and that Mr. Andrew Bell, Jr., gave her a fine burial from his funeral home in Providence, from which he arranged the burial of much of black society in that city for fifty years.

Where did Miss Prophet have tea with Cullen in July 1929? At what cafés did she drink an apéritif and heatedly discuss the questions of form and content, money and space to work, the eternal questions argued about by all artists at all times? Where were her studios located? What motivated her to withdraw into herself so deeply? Her poverty? Did the lightness of her skin color trouble her? Did she have a boyfriend, or a girlfriend? On what Parisian streets did she pace back and forth agitated by those particular problems that confront the artist regardless of geographical locus, skin color or race? Why did she destroy so much of her work?

Clearly a biography of Nancy Elizabeth Prophet is overdue. Her works, especially the powerful *Congolais* (1931, Whitney Museum of American Art), is being shown with increasing frequency in group exhibitions such as "The Figure in American Sculpture" which toured to several museums around the country including the National Academy of Design (1995-96). Kirschenbaum's article on the sculptor constitutes a good start and the publication of Prophet's diaries adds important information to our knowledge. She deserves a full-blown retrospective and a comprehensive volume devoted to her life and work. The exhibition would not require much space since apparently less than ten of her sculptures have survived the vicissitudes of her peripatetic existence.

* * * *

253

The sculptor Antoine Bourdelle (1861-1929) created an extraordinary number of public pieces during his lifetime, some of which somehow were never placed in public places. These and many of his maquettes are to be seen in the **Musée Bourdelle**, at 16, rue Antoine Bourdelle, a block northwest of the Gare Montparnasse. If he was alive, one could send his mail to him "dans sa rue," surely a very nice way to receive one's mail, a rare occurrence when one is alive. Augustus Saint Gaudens, an American sculptor despite his name, had in 1878 a studio in this street, then named Impasse du Maine.

Jo Davidson, creator of the stolid Gertrude Stein stone image, among countless other busts, had a stonecutting shop in the street during the 1920s, from which he visited Bourdelle's atelier from time to time. The Stein bust is prominently displayed in the National Portrait Gallery in Washington, which also holds many of Davidson's bread and butter bust portraits of politicians, industrialists and soldiers. In 1931, Davidson's monumental 16 feet (just over five meters) tall stone doughboy, originally intended for one of the American cemeteries in France, had to be demolished when the city enlarged the Impasse du Maine to create what is now the Rue Antoine-Bourdelle, necessitating the destruction of his studio and with it the huge figure: Davidson could not pay the cost of moving such a monolith.

In his memoirs, Davidson tells the possibly apocryphal story about walking to his studio in the Impasse du Maine with Maillol and passing Bourdelle, who ignored -- or snubbed -- them. According to Maillol's explanation of this unusual behavior, the two French artists had been friends since their youths when Maillol painted, before he began to sculpt. One day while waiting in Bourdelle's studio, Maillol started to model his own hand with some clay to pass the time. Bourdelle finally arrived and, furious at what he saw, yelled: "Il ne faut pas faire de la sculpture!"

And they rarely spoke again, at least according to Maillol. Bourdelle had reason to fear Maillol's transferring his talents to sculpture.

Alas, that gigantic erection to the worst of modern man's seemingly unquenchable thirst for power over the natural and human environment, the mean and terrifically ugly **Montparnasse highrise**, literally overshadows Bourdelle's museum and everything else in the neighborhood. Its 55 stories in dark glass and gray concrete are a tribute to the worst, the basest of mankind's destructive acquisitive instincts. Here the 1985 green *Guide Michelin* to Paris suffers a rare lapse in discrimination: the drivel written about the Tour-Maine-Montparnasse, to give this inexcusable excrement its proper name, is on the level of Jackie Collins. In his ninth decade, Julian Green, member of the Académie, whom I have read with some admiration up to this point, has something seemingly positive to say about this ruthless act of barbarism in his recent collection of texts and photographs called *Paris* (1991). Perhaps Mr. Green loves too much of Paris too much. On the other hand, the passage in question is about a "refraction phenomenon" and "fiery windows" and "blazing pink," so the positive aspect of it might, perhaps, be interpreted in another way. Indeed, elsewhere in his slim volume, he writes of the "strange abomination" of the School of Medicine on the corner of Rue des Saints-Pères and Rue Jacob, whose "hideousness" constitutes an "outrage" in a city as beautiful as Paris. In deep bitterness Green suggests a paraphrase of an old Roman jibe against the Barberini family as an inscription over the School's portal: "What the Barbarians left undone, Parisians have finished." Green is obviously on the side of the angels in the end.

Franz Kafka's one-page story, "The City Coat-of-Arms," attributes to the unnamed, no doubt emblematic city a closed fist as the coat-of-arms. "All the legends and songs that come to birth in that city are filled with longing for a

255

prophesied day when the city would be destroyed by five successive blows from a gigantic fist." The Centre Pompidou, La Défense, Euro-Disney, and the Montparnasse highrise are harbingers of that day. In fear and trembling we await the Moloch-developers' final blow in the realization of Kafka's nightmare when Paris becomes, not *Alphaville*'s sterile wasteland of the spiritually mor(t)ibund (the egregious Bibliothèque de France will ensure this), but the setting for *Blade Runner*'s stinking, acid-rained metropolis of the replicant living dead.

The American painter, Marsden Hartley, subleased a studio at 18, rue Moulin de Beurre, a street that is no longer there because the devil-opers obliterated it to erect the Gare Montparnasse office complex connected with the tower. But in 1912, Hartley moved into a working class neighborhood far enough from the cafes and bars so that he could feel productively isolated and get his own work done. He appreciated the colorful attire of the workmen of the quarter in their "baggy corduroy trousers of light blue, dark brown and some wonderful rose color -- and wide sash belts of fiery red -- big shoes -- often sabots -- and caps or hats." He also appreciated the workmen themselves, finding "some very handsome," as his biographer puts it. He seems to have done a considerable amount of work here, but the studio and its building are dust and ashes.

The Dutch painter, Piet Mondrian, came to Paris in 1911 and visited a fellow Dutch artist, Conrad Kickert, in his studio at 26, rue du Départ. Kickert left the city for a while and lent the place to Mondrian, who stayed there and in another studio in the building for a number of years. He returned briefly in 1919, and in 1921 moved in for a stay of 15 years, where after he left Europe for New York. Mondrian, as one might expect from his geometric paintings with the vernacular titles ("Boogie-Woogie"), spent little time in the cafés due to an obsession with his work, the style of which reflected his living quarters, described by an unknown visitor cited by Arlen Hansen: the apartment showed "an order that was balanced and cunningly calculated beyond perfection, a few squares of yellow and red and blue against vast stretches of white. The gramophone was red, so was the table. The wardrobe was blue. The plates yellow. The curtains red...." A street with the same name is still there, but do not look for a building with studios at number 26: the Montparnasse tower brutally dominates the entire block in all its fascist machoisme.

Sic transit gloria mundi.

Actually, the hideous tower, called "la grande vilaine" (the big eyesore) by the neighbors, is in the 15th arrondissement, but it looms implacably, inescapably, ominously, over a large part of the 14th, which is our concern here. One feels positively compelled to hurry along to the Montparnasse cemetery where one can pretend the despicable monster doesn't exist, if one doesn't look up to the west.

(One might, I suppose, in fairness mention that the French had a theme park outside Paris prior to the infestation of Disney's Americanized fairytales. In 1989, the Parc Astérix opened for business and the 20-acre park played host in 1994 to 1.5 million visitors; not quite on the scale of the 10 million at Euro-Disney, but a respectable showing for the much smaller enterprise. Those who do not yet know Astérix can look forward to a modicum of pleasure, especially if they appreciate comic strips and French nationalism: Astérix and his associates are sort of anti-hero Gauls who put up various, mostly hilarious forms of resistance to the Roman occupation of their homeland. The French named their first space satellite Astérix, and several animated films have been made about the characters antics in turning the army of Julius Caesar into Roman stumblebums. The very expensive recent movie with

Gérard Depardieu as Astérix might be of interest to any 12-year olds you know.)

The **Cimetière de Montparnasse**, officially named the Cimetière du Sud, is located south of the Boulevard Montparnasse and a short walk from the Dôme. The concierge maintains in his hut at the Boulevard Edgar Quinet entrance, an "Index Sommaire des Célébrités," which is now sufficiently up to date to list Man and Juliet Ray and will have references to the designer of the Statue of Liberty (a smaller version of which can be seen below the Trocadero on the Seine), Friedrich August Bartholdi, as well as Baudelaire, Guy de Maupassant, Jules Pascin, Jean Seberg, Alfred Dreyfus, Brancusi, Tristan Tzara, Sartre and de Beauvoir, Ossip Zadkine, Léon-Paul Fargue, Eugène Ionescu, et alia. The Index will not tell you that the American painter and diarist, Shirley Goldfarb, is buried here, but she is, as she wished to be, nor that Manès Sperber (1905-1984) lies next to Emma Sperber (1979-1991), nor that Joris Ivens (1898-1989) is here and not in the Netherlands or China, nor that the great patroness of the arts, Marie-Laure de Noailles, lies in the largely Jewish 28th division under her maiden name, Bischoffsheim, not in the non-Jewish crypt of her husband's family, wherever that may be. All in all, we think we, too, would rather be buried here than in Père Lachaise; in Montparnasse death is less visited, if not quieter.

The Paris Review, **H. L. Humes and *The Underground City*.** At the outermost edge of the southwestern quadrant of the cemetery, walk into the mouth of the Rue de l'Ouest for one block and turn right into the tiny Rue de Perceval just off the Rue Vercingétorix (what a name! reminds me of a comic book), and stop in front of number 14. You will be looking at the building in which, on a bright warm afternoon in the Spring of 1952, a small group of young American writers and friends made plans to launch one of the most important English-language literary journals of the latter half of the 20th century, *The Paris Review.* (You might also stop in front of what at one time was number 53 and think about the fine American Negro painter, Beauford Delaney, who had a studio apartment here from 1961 until 1975. Shortly thereafter city authorities destroyed the building as part of the ubiquitous and rebarbative urban "renewal" program.)

This coterie acted in a tradition that includes hundreds of known and obscure "little magazines" published in various forms for hundreds of years and, in the 20th century, many of them in English in Paris. Elsewhere in this book I have written a bit about *transition*, but there are dozens of others that could be mentioned such as *Zéro, Broom, Points, Contact*, Pound's *The Exile, The Little Review* (banned in New York for publishing parts of *Ulysses* in 1919), *The Booster* later called *Delta* (Henry Miller, Alfred Perlès and Lawrence Durrell), *This Quarter, The Transatlantic Review, The New Review, Tambour, Gargoyle, Succession, Larus, The Boulevardier, Janus, Olympia, Frank, Merlin*, and so on. Some lasted only two or three issues, some lasted years. Two or three English language literary journals continue to be published in Paris today, but *The Paris Review* is not one of them; since 1973, it has been published in New York City. The editors had, in the beginning, the aim of publishing creative work by young writers rather than acrid academic theorizing and ratiocinative criticism full of sticky cobwebs and the odor of drains. This standard the journal has continued to uphold, albeit the Paris linkage has long since ceased to be meaningful in terms of authors and content.

The apartment belonged to Peter Matthiessen and Patsy Southgate, whose guests that afternoon included John Train, Thomas Guinzburg, William Pène du Bois, George Plimpton, William Styron and Harold L. Humes. Mattiessen and Humes, who had met at Le Dôme in early 1951, wanted to publish a real literary journal to print the work of writers too good for Humes' current rag called *The Paris News-Post*, a curiously hybrid magazine containing gossip and recommendations for places to eat and other crepuscular activities. It has been speculated that these young men may have been less than interested in this wild-eyed project than in simply being in the same room with Southgate, an incredibly lovely example of the type usually described as "American beauty rose." Her then husband, Matthiessen, describes Humes as "burly and curly... with a deep laugh... aggressive, warm-hearted, curious, yet with convictions on every subject... all of which made him impossible." In short, the kind of young man who amuses and challenges you in a saloon, but who you would not necessarily think of taking to your parents' house for dinner.

So by the spring of 1952, they gathered a number of friends together with the young Plimpton, whom Matthiessen brought in from England to be editor-in-chief when it became clear that Humes, who originally appointed himself to that position, could not possibly deal with other people in a manner necessary to the successful management of a literary journal. On that sunny spring day, energized by Plimpton's two bottles of absinthe, the group accepted the name of the magazine suggested by one of them and declared their readiness to surge forward into the world of publishing. But a name does not a publication make and the journal's founders rollercoasted through many months before the first issue saw the light of booksellers' windows and kiosk stands. The group made Humes managing editor because of his previous experience publishing *The Paris News-Post*, and actually expected him to manage the business, a responsibility he apparently found himself unable to fulfill due to the pressures of other matters demanding his attention.

Indeed, in "The Paris Review Sketchbook" (*The Paris Review* 79), Plimpton tells the story of Humes' reaction to being demoted on the masthead from managing editor to advertising and circulation manager. Not only did he not find the time to carry out his managing duties in Paris, being too occupied with reading *Huckleberry Finn* at the Rotonde and working on the novel which would become *The Underground City*, one of the great unknown American masterpieces of the latter half of the 20th century, but he moved to New York City before the first issue appeared! When the copies of the inaugural issue reached the docks of New York and Humes discovered his demotion, he immediately acted to write the wrong. A letter of complaint to his fellow editors, however elegantly written, would not do, it could be ignored. Humes purchased a rubber stamp engraved with his name and his more prestigious original title, and a red ink pad. Racing to the wharf, he tore into the crates containing the magazine and, wildly wielding both items, stamped the masthead page of 500 or so issues "before his arm got tired."

Perhaps Humes was simply difficult to get along with? *The Underground City* shows a twisting, labyrinthine mind that cannot stop making connections (far beyond Morgan Forster's desperate command), but in the end there is a diamond-like lucidity that is both charming and honest, demanding space and time to narrate the unnarratable without exhortation or vulgar psychoanalysis.

According to Barnaby Conrad III in his book, *Absinthe: History in a Bottle* (1988), the French government banned the wormwood-based drink on March 16, 1915, and the Swiss in 1907 made it illegal to distill, sell or transport the stuff, but not to drink it! In Spain, absinthe manufacture is still legal and perhaps that is the source of Plimpton's, or it might have been bootlegged, or may have even been pastis -- who knows, and it does not really matter: we shall continue to think of it as absinthe. And in any case, Mr. Plimpton has stated that the two bottles story is apocryphal![19]

One curious matter has engaged my attention for some time without being resolved: Richard Wright was the preeminent American writer living in Paris during the early years of *The Paris Review*'s existence, yet none of his writings ever appeared in the journal, and the editors never included him in their deservedly well-known interview series "The Art of Fiction." One wonders why not. Mr. Plimpton notes that Wright should have been interviewed, but was not, and that he never submitted anything to the *Review* for publication, and that the editors were more interested in the writings of their own generation.[20]

Everyone who reads American literature knows William Styron; many who know anything about paper lions or watch American television commercials or, indeed, read *The Paris Review* know George Plimpton; this is as it should be. But which of you knows H. L. Humes, author of *The Underground City* (1958) and *Men Die* (1960)? I no longer remember the source of the money, savings perhaps, though I possessed little enough of that living in a Greenwich Village tenement in 1959, but I clearly remember buying the 755 page *Underground City*, the title referring in one sense to Paris, in another to the depths of men's minds and spirits where loyalty and betrayal are, often unconsciously, formulated, tested and reformulated. I clearly remember rushing back to the fourth floor flat a few blocks south of Washington Square in the American underground city.

I also clearly remember reading for days until I finished it, not quite getting it all, but reeling under the impression it made. It begins and ends in the rain in Paris after the war; the bulk of the action takes place in the south of France during the 1943-44 period of German occupation in which the American OSS agent named Stone confronts a complexity of life for which he is not fully prepared. A Jamesian situation acted out, not in the drawing rooms and gardens of the haute-bourgeoisie, but in the moral and spiritual miasma of war and sudden death. For some reason I did not read the second and last novel, or I no longer remember it. This is sadly appropriate since the first is really about memory and how one remembers chosen fragments and must learn to remember the others under terms of intense pressure and disgrace. The book also shows how politics can wreck decent men and women who fought the complex underground war of resistance and collaboration, sacrificing them in the power struggle, according to the exigencies of the time, when behavior and ideas supported and reinforced during the war were made to seem as exemplars of betrayal and criminality after the war. It is not an easy book, and no doubt it is too long, but the cumulative effect of its narrative drive and character delineation breaks through the lines of critical defense to take the high ground of the art of fiction: the extremes of human behavior contained in a massive epiphany encompassing the variety of human experience.

The jacket cover is basically blue, shading upward from almost black at the bottom to almost skyblue at the top; the Eiffel tower rises out of the primeval darkness toward the light, assuring reader-identification with the correct city and foretelling the essentially masculine tone of the book. A third of the way down a thin red line runs horizontally across the cover, the spine, and the back, which mirrors the front. I think of the red line as the American agent's conscience, dignity and loyalty to his comrades and the truth as he knew it. A long book, a heavy book, with its epigrams from *Ulysses* (Stephen Dedalus on history and God) and Cristóbal Colón, Grand Admiral of the Ocean Seas ("There live the happiest people, who only die of weariness of living"); a book which, somewhere in my peregrinations about the western world, I mislaid.

With some certainty I can say that I did not think of Humes or the book for over 20 years. The gods who guide our destinies may know what triggered the memory several years ago when I began to think of the book again, but I no longer recall those origins. Perhaps I wondered if it actually had to do with Paris and France, or if my memory misled me, and the underground city was, in fact, Odessa. I started looking for the distinctive cover, which I did remember, in second hand bookstores, those idiosyncratic establishments that ineluctably draw me on almost as intensely as das ewige Weibliche. Some time later, in a Washington suburb known for its country clubs (restricted) and its "actual" 1940s diner (unrestricted, open all night), blessed with the good luck-charm presence of brother Dean, I found an almost mint copy and my heart soared simultaneously back to New York City in 1959 and forward to Key West where Lynn-Marie and I would soon spend a warm, sunny week of rest during which time I could again devour the book, testing my memory, and scratching the itch of curiosity.

The book knocked me out again, if this time for somewhat different reasons, coming to it now so much older if not so much wiser, perhaps looking for different things in the nuances of narrative, political ideology and poetic voice. I had not remembered the amazing amount of stuff Humes crammed into the book, most of which fit, some of which stuck out awkwardly. It is a young man's book, but a young man oddly middle aged with too much knowledge of certain things and more than his share of cynicism. The war and its disappointing aftermath did that to some of the best creative minds.

At the end of September 1992, I pondered how I could reasonably inject into the book you are now reading a few paragraphs of appreciation of Humes. Then Dean sent me a clipping from the *New York Times* obituary section, the headline of which said "Harold Louis Humes, 66, Novelist And a Paris Review Co-Founder." Immobilized for several moments, I finally read the text and discovered certain things I had not known about this man who had exercised my mind for such a long period of time. Why, for instance, had he not published anything of note after 1960? Apparently he told his family that "mental illness" had caused him not to finish his third novel. The obituary is tantalizingly incomplete: in 1973 Humes moved to Boston and Cambridge (where had he been since 1952?); he played chess in Harvard Square (perhaps he had what are known as "private means"?); he participated in "unorthodox activities" including founding a community service organization called Unidentified Flying Idea. He was survived by five daughters and one son, Malcolm Einaudi of Turin, Italy.

What had he done all those years besides siring children? What was the nature of the "mental illness" that blocked the work of what was clearly one of the major writers of his generation? Did he work as a plumber over those long years since Paris and Harvard (class of 1954), a watchmaker, a teacher of Latin in a prep school? Why is his son's name Einaudi? (Is that any of our business? Perhaps not, but the seductive temptress Curiosity is difficult to resist.)

With some research in the Library of Congress down the street, a few letters to Styron and Plimpton and others, perhaps one could answer these intrusive questions. But why now? Twenty years and more passed before I found *The Underground City* again. I have some hope that I will not require that amount of time to find *Men Die*. One of these days I will discover some of the answers about the enigma of Harold Humes, but the quest does not have to be pursued with a young man's intense enthusiasm and relentless energy. It is no longer a matter of patience, for I am not a patient man, but rather one of exhaustion and the acceptance of delayed satisfaction.

To some stories there apparently are no endings. On November 7, 1997, while packing up parts of my library to go into the storage bin to make room for new acquisitions, I found a copy of the spring 1962 issue of Jonas Mekas' *Film Culture (America's Independent Motion Picture Magazine)*. Leafing through it I discovered to my delight a full page grainy black and white photograph of a burly, curly-haired young man in a trench coat, white shirt, tie and suit being hustled unceremoniously out of the south end of Washington Square Park in Manhattan by three of New York City's Finest. The caption reads "The New American Cinema Director, Harold Humes ('Don Peyote'), Casts His Second Film." This leads of course to even further speculation and curiosity.

Should you walk past 14, rue de Perceval, stop for just a moment, raise your eyes to the third floor and briefly think of that group of young men, sure of themselves and their ability to make a difference to literature, to achieve their ends without compromising their standards, and wonder for a fleeting few seconds whether Harold Humes drank his absinthe with carbonated or non-carbonated water, or neat, strained through a sugar cube.

Le Sphinx: The Egyptian and the Modern. The Boulevard Edgar Quinet obliquely borders the cemetery on its northern edge. If you stand in front of number 31 you will see a nondescript building devoted to the arts of medicinal cures. This was the first building in France to have air-conditioning; how French that it was a whorehouse! (Interestingly, the first locale in Shanghai to be air-conditioned in the 1930s was a nightclub called Ciro.) Named Le Sphinx, the only brothel in Montparnasse opened with a bang, so to speak, in the late 1920s (or 1930, depending upon the source) under the efficient management of Marthe "Martoune" Lemestre, matronly and always dressed in black, who sent out invitations to the inaugural night that included wives and companions (or "mistresses," as we formerly called them). Half the artists and writers in the quarter, real and would-be, received the notices, and apparently all of them showed up to guzzle the free champagne, if not nuzzle the unfree service, and view the rooms upstairs, which housed a wide range of implements and styles to satisfy the broadest spectrum of tastes and desires. Wambly Bald, that tireless chronicler of the goings-on in Montparnasse for the *Chicago Tribune* (Paris Edition), noted that on opening night everything was free except for the girls, who charged double because it *was* opening night, and that's "French thrift for you!"

It might be noted that, at least according to Erwin Blumenfeld, the well-known German émigré photographer who lived around the corner from the place in the mid-thirties, the French minister of the interior, Albert Sarraut, and his brother owned a piece of the action. This may only be a rumor, of course, but Alfred Kantorowicz, a generally reliable source on matters unconnected with his activities as a communist in the 1933-1940 period, bitterly relates Sarraut's corrosive contribution to the murderous fate of the Czech and Polish anti-nazi exiles in France during the early months of the war when French xenophobic paranoia reached one of its most vicious heights (or depths). On the other hand, Sarraut was a great collector of modern art, and the Germans deported him in 1944. He survived.

In any case, the downstairs decor became famous and rivaled that of La Coupole, until then the most brilliant chromium and glass art deco lounge-bar interior in Paris. While the upstairs workrooms contained rather less decoration (Samuel Putnam said "[T]here was a connotation of Grand Rapids rather than the new functionalism -- although the inevitable bidet was functional enough," but he's an American and what do they know about bordellos, or bidets for that matter), the bar americain and salon on the ground floor attracted, and the house encouraged, even those who wished only to have a drink, chat with friends, and ogle the bare breasted girls, to whom the management gave annual paid vacations. Having broken with the traditional heavy plush fabric decor de la

267

maison close, the Sphinx allowed men to bring their wives and children to the public rooms: a café is a café even if it is in a whorehouse.

Alberto Giacometti said, "It was for me a place more marvelous than any other." Signor Giacometti also said, "Whores are the most honest girls. They present the bill right away. The others hang on and never let you go." Some might not find that so oppressive.

The gregarious Henry Miller claims to have written some of the publicity texts for the opening in return for "a little rake-off," which he defines as "a bottle of champagne and a free fuck in one of the Egyptian rooms." Since Miller wrote what is known in some circles as an "autobiographical novel," he felt no compunction to be faithful to factual exactitude, but the story has the feel of truth to it. He also tells the story of taking his friend, the journalist Van Norden, to the Sphinx hoping for his little rake-off for this agreed upon bit of pimping; when the manager discovered Van Norden's profession, she refused to charge him for the services of the house, knowing full-well the value of publicity, especially in an English-language newspaper. This act of self-interest, of course, cost Miller his rake-off.

Living on Corfu, the young Lawrence Durrell read *Tropic of Cancer* soon after its publication, christened his sailboat "Van Norden" and wrote Miller a glorious fan letter. The rest is literary history. Miller patterned the Van Norden character after the writer Wambly Bald, who worked on the Paris Edition of the *Chicago Tribune* as a proofreader and wrote a regular column, already referred to, about the huffing and puffing of the Quarterites entitled "La Vie de Bohème," sections of which Benjamin Franklin V. edited in the book *On the Left Bank* (1987). Wambly Bald is not to be confused with the writer Waverley Root, also mentioned earlier, who also served on the *Tribune* staff, and who wrote about the era, noting that Wambly

Bald did not particularly like his Miller-created Doppelgänger. Miller, too, worked briefly as a proofreader on the *Tribune*, before someone made him an offer he could not find the willpower to refuse: a free, if short, trip to Belgium. Putnam, who attended the opening with his wife, called Le Sphinx "nothing if not respectable," and after the liberation, in April 1946, perhaps under the pecksniff morality of Mme. de Gaulle, the National Assembly in a paroxysm of faux virtu passed a law closing the bordellos and the building became a dormitory for students at the Sorbonne. The writer Pierre MacOrlan noted in this regard, "It's the foundation of a thousand-year-old civilization which is collapsing." Klüver and Martin's book has a photograph of the salon and several of the staff, which will give you some idea of the "Egyptian" motif of the decor.

Somewhere on this street, during the same time period, an intimate bar called Le Monocle existed as a where lesbians could feel at ease and enjoy themselves without being on show, reputed to have been as famous in its day as Le Sphinx. This too is gone, but Brassaï's book, *The Secret Paris of the 1930s*, has several photographs of the place and its clientele, and there is an interesting picture of an event in the late thirties printed in Carol Mann's *Paris Between the Wars* (1996), where it is described as a "notorious lesbian club in Montparnasse which ran from 1935 to 1940.". In April 1996, a night spot called Le Monocle, at 60, boulevard Edgar Quinet, advertised itself as a "bar, cabaret féminin ... strip tease ... " with drinks starting at 100 francs. Someone clearly did some historical research.

269

16th ARRONDISEMENT

Le Palais de Tokyo and Le Musée d'art moderne de la ville de Paris, 270 – Le Palais de Chaillot and Le Musée du Cinéma Henri Langlois, 272 – Jean Villar and the Théâtre National Populaire, 273 – La Maison de Balzac, 274 – Le Musée Marmottan, 276

Constructed for the World Exposition in 1937, the **Palais de Tokyo**, 11 Avenue Président Wilson, houses the **Musée d'art moderne de la ville de Paris**, and several other museums. The modern art museum has a solid permanent collection of 20th century art, but expends most of its space on temporary exhibitions that are always worth seeing. On one of our visits several years ago we saw a "major retrospective" of the works of El Lissitzky from which we learned much, including the intricate footwork required to keep out of voice-range of loud-mouthed culture-vultures.

Make sure you take the time to study Raoul Dufy's *The Good Fairy Electricity*, a gigantic mural in praise of the beneficial progress of technology, obviously painted in an earlier age when such an optimistic view of the subject was possible. It must be admitted that there are some people who believe this mural is the biggest interior kitsch monument outside the big Paris department stores and Gaudi's buildings in Barcelona. I think this may be a rather harsh judgment. (If you want an idea of the size of Dufy's piece and you have the opportunity to visit the Philadelphia Museum of Art, take a look at the cloth backdrop Chagall painted in 1942 for the third act of the ballet *Aleko: A Wheatfield on a Summer's Afternoon*. The Dufy is five or six times larger; it is, in fact, reputed to be the largest painting in the world.)

In any case, the cafeteria is a good one, but usually jammed with the sorts of people who hang out in modern art museums (now there's a subject for Ring Lardner, Georges Bataille, or Garrison Keillor!). It's best if you can find a table outside on the terrace in the middle of the Palais with a view of the river and, if memory serves, the Tour d'Eiffel.

The other side of the Palais consists of several smaller spaces which usually show temporary exhibitions on photography and the cinema, and various donations by individuals to the French National Museum of Modern Art in the Centre Pompidou, which has not sufficient space to show most of its collection due to the fact that the Centre's architecture is so very *moderne*. This side of the structure also houses a foundation dedicated to giving courses in filmmaking and "audio-visual techniques," whatever they may be.

In fact, the Musée National d'Art Moderne began its peripatetic existence under somewhat dubious, but at the time unavoidable circumstances. The Vichy government Ministry of Education and Youth opened it in a new wing of the Palais on August 6, 1942, in a hectic attempt to fill the space before the Germans confiscated it to use as a provisional storage dump for art and cultural artifacts they stole and shipped to Germany. The Germans had already taken over the Musée du Jeu de Paume for this purpose. The pieces on display, needless to say, contained no works by Jews, no abstract art and no Picasso, perhaps the most famous name in the world of art who remained in Paris during the occupation, about whom contradictory tales floated around the city after liberation claiming him to be both a Resistance hero (he wasn't) and a collaborator (he wasn't). You can pursue the Musée National d'Art Moderne and Mr. Picasso during the occupation in Michèle Cone's valuable if scattershot *Artists Under Vichy*.

Down the street at the riverend of Avenue Président Wilson, the Place de l'Alma presented a bizarrely quaint scene worthy of a Luis Buñuel film when, two days before

271

the Germans entered Paris in June 1940, as greasy smoke from burning oil depots hung darkly over the city now empty of all but 700,000 of its inhabitants, a confused herd of dairy cows from a farm in Auteuil wandered about the square like complete unknowns without a home. How they got there and what happened to them thereafter remains a tantalizing mystery.

Further up the avenue past the Tokyo, you too can be in the movies, or at least in the fashion photographs, if you enter the **Palais de Chaillot** at the Place du Trocadéro and stand on the terrace with all the Japanese tourists to have your photograph taken with the ineluctable Eiffel Tower in the background, just like Gene Kelly, or was it Leslie Caron, or Albert Speer, or Sidney Poitier in *Paris Blues* with Diahann Carroll, Joanne Woodward and Paul Newman. The latter is a very 1950s film about putative jazz musicians and their girlfriends escaping American indifference to the country's only original contribution to music (except, of course, Harry Partch and Conlon Nancarrow) and the ever-present ugly monster racism.

The Palais de Chaillot contains the Musée de l'Homme (dioramas and stuffed animals), the Musée des Monuments Français (replicas of famous murals and sculptures for those who cannot spare the time or energy to see the real ones), the Musée de la Marine (a fine collection of navigational instruments and accessories), and the **Musée du Cinema Henri Langlois**. The latter is named after the legendary collector of films and footage in whose moviehouse the so-called Nouvelle Vague cinéastes drenched themselves in sequences of images, until they became dazed or catatonic and invented the "auteur" theory of film criticism. This contribution to cinema studies equates Jerry Lewis and Howard Hawks with Ingemar Bergman and Jean Renior, and actually credits Alfred Hitchcock with an oeuvre instead of a couple of well-made films and a lot of boring movies. To make an artist out of a solid craftsman like Samuel Fuller is no mean accomplishment, but seriously distorts the definition of both and renders debate useless. Imagine thinking *Rebel Without a Cause* (1954) is a work of art because of one 180-degree camera turn. In fairness, one must say that, in the United States, Andrew Sarris is the main culprit in making the "auteur" theory salonfähig. See, for example, his *Confessions of a Cultist* (1970) and the egregiously titled *You Aint Heard Nothin' Yet. The American Talking Film: History and Memory 1927-1949* (1998). This is not to say that Sarris and the others are not worth reading, they are, and you should.

In any case, one cannot blame Langlois for the eccentricities of his clients and, after all, they did successfully defend him against the philistines who at one point tried to shut him down. And the exhibitions in the museum are well worth your time and money.

Have you ever wondered what happened to the red jacket James Dean inhabited so coolly in *Rebel Without A Cause*? Thieves stole it from the Musée du Cinéma before the place could afford security guards. Now, the question about why a quintessential American artifact found a home in a French movie museum is another matter all together.

The Palais de Chaillot once housed an astonishing institution known as the TNP - **Théâtre National Populaire**, which the Chambre des Députés created as the Théâtre National du Palais de Chaillot in 1920. In 1951 Jean Vilar became the director and under his leadership the company's courageously imaginative productions revitalized French theater after the devastation and psychic collapse of defeat and occupation. Vilar possessed an immense amount of intelligence and energy, and in 1946 the poet René Char, and Christian and Yvonne Zervos, publishers of *Cahiers d'Art*, proposed to Vilar that he organize a summer theater festival in the Palace of the Popes in Avignon. The festival opened in August 1947, and has since become one of the finest such events in the world.

In 1952, the TNP began as the resident company of the festival, which it remained for many years even after Vilar's resignation as TNP director in 1963. Vilar continued to direct the Avignon festival until his death in 1971. Some years ago, the Avignon city government created a museum cum study center in his name, which mounted a major retrospective exhibition on Vilar's career in 1991, accompanied by an excellent catalog, *Jean Vilar par lui-même* (1991). Many highly talented actresses and actors began or broadened their careers under the wing of Vilar and the TNP, such as Jeanne Moreau, Gérard Philipe, Charles Denner, Jean Desailly, Georges Wilson, Jean-Pierre Cassel and Maria Casarés. The company is now known as the Théâtre National de Chaillot.

On April 2 and 3, 1939, ominous year, the Duke Ellington orchestra played in the auditorium of the Palais de Chaillot. Ellington expressed himself very impressed with the acoustics of the hall, which the prescient French had constructed 100 feet underground. Could they have been thinking of the Germans bombarding Paris? Only the French could consider war's interruption of musical life so unacceptable as to prepare for it. Well, perhaps the Italians....

If you are in the neighborhood and have any interest at all in Honoré de Balzac, stop at the small, half-hidden **Maison de Balzac**, at 47, rue Raynouard, to see the chair in which the Master sat, the pen he used, the coffee grinder for the stimulant that kept him awake to continue writing to pay the ever-present creditors, and whatever temporary exhibition is up at the time of your visit. We enjoyed the fine show of Robert Doisneau' photographs of writers during the 1986 international photography festival. Unfortunately for us fanatic collectors of affiches (posters), the show's poster photograph of the aged Colette in bed surrounded by her glass collection is a drag; in fact, she resembles an old man in drag. The photographer, known for his candid shots of street life in Paris, and the writer known for her exquisite word portraits of French character types, deserve better.

A recent controversy surrounding the octogenarian Doisneau serves as a cautionary tale regarding the definition of the word "candid" and the necessity for a certain amount of skepticism vis à vis any society's cultural icons. In 1950, *Life* magazine hired Doisneau to take a series of pictures of couples kissing in the City of Love, where traditionally such activity is a public event, at least according to generations of flacks for the French tourist industry. According to the legend, Doisneau prowled the city's streets snapping away and fulfilling his contract with the magazine. The most famous of the photographs he took at a café across the square from the Hôtel de Ville of a young couple who apparently have spontaneously stopped walking for an instant to express their feelings for each other with their lips, but in a non-verbal manner. In the background of the picture a man in a bêret looking both stern and somewhat baffled walks on to an unknown destination. Doisneau apparently once made over $50,000 a year from the rights to that photograph.

Late in the year 1992, a couple in their early 60s claimed the osculatory couple in the photograph was none other than themselves and they expressed their wish to participate in the reception of the largess flowing from the use-rights of the image. They threatened to sue, but then an additional claimant appeared when a woman of similar age said *she* was the girl in the photograph, that Doisneau had hired her and a young man then acting in the Louis Jouvet company to kiss in various cityscapes for the magazine series. In early January 1993, reporters located the fellow, now a vintner in the Vaucluse, who concurred that he had modeled for the photographer in that and other pictures.

Doisneau's spokeswoman said his recent cataract operation left him unable to meet the press on the matter. O yes, the man in the bêret, the typical Parisian mid-level official, turns out to be Jack Costello from Dublin on his way to Rome during that Holy Year of 1950.

The **Musée Marmottan**, 2, rue Louis-Boilly, is the third museum in Paris devoted mainly to the French impressionists and post-impressionists, the other two being the Musée de l'Orangerie and the Musée d'Orsay. The art historian, Paul Marmottan, left his house and collections of pre-19th century art to the Academy of Fine Arts. To the 1950 Donop de Monchy donation of several Monets, Michel Monet, the painter's son, gave sixty-five additional Monet paintings, and the museum built an underground gallery to hold them and works by Pissarro, Sisley and the inevitable Renoir, but neglected, due to lack of funds it is said, to install an electric security system, with the inevitable result that several years ago thieves made off with a number of pretty good Monets. The art-squad has apparently recovered most of them.

18th ARRONDISEMENT

The Montmartre Cemetery, 278 – Le Bateau Lavoir and The Mock Rousseau Banquet, 279 – Le Moulin Rouge, 287 – Le Musée de Montmartre, 292 – Le Lapin Agile, 293

The name Montmartre means martyrs' hill, so called after the mayrtrdom of Saint Denis, the first bishop of Paris, in 270 C.E., according to one tradition; according to another the original name was Mons Martis, after a temple to Mars said to have been built there. The name brings to mind many things, but mainly images of la belle époche: Mimi delicately coughing her lungs out; the dwarfish Toulouse-Lautrec peering intently upward at loosely dressed hookers, his pencil at the ready; besotted flamboyantly clothed "artistes" waving their latest oils at each other all talking simultaneously at the tops of their voices; groups of maquereaux (pimps) dressed as apaches (Parisian, not North American) leering at a line of disparately shaped women throwing their legs high into the air with squeals of artificial delight while the band huffs and puffs through yet another cancan number; the hirsute, radically thin poets lifting a last glass of cheap red wine on the Place du Tertre, manuscripts clutched tightly in palsied hand; and all the other clichés promulgated by the tourist industry and Puccini.

No doubt some of these images reflected a reality at some time during the 19th century, but by 1914 many of the artists, poets, and other denizens of bohemian Montmartre had moved down the hill and across the river into Montparnasse or to the suburbs, depending on their level of income. Indeed, the 1910 edition of the *Baedeker's Handbook for Paris and Environs* does not even mention artists or the cancan or poets when describing the quarter.

Most of the creative people left behind what had even then become a fake society of the past, a Potemkin Village organized for the tourists in buses, which is exactly what one sees today. As George and Pearl Adam so neatly put it in *A Book About Paris*: "Gaiety, like Truth, dies when it is organized."

However, this should not stop you from making a visit to the hill. The view of the city from the porch of the Sacré Coeur church is trés panoramique on the occasional day when the usual curtain of smog does not obscure the sight. Strolling around the smaller streets of the area can also be entertaining, if not educational. One summer midday, we could not help but observe a nondescript young man in a doorway pinching the nipples of an even younger scantily clothed woman, where after he gently pushed her out into the street. Within 60 seconds she strode back into the doorway, a client taking advantage of the lunch hour for une rapide in tow. Whether the erect nipples had anything to do with the quick sale, we of course did not inquire into.

The **Cimetière de Montmartre**, properly called the Cimetière du Nord, is further off the beaten path, but that is hardly reason for not visiting it. Take the subway. Get off at Place de Clichy and walk up the Rue Caulaincourt, which cuts through the cemetery's southeastern edge. A veritable roster of greats rest in eternal quietude below ground here: Émile Zola (yes, yes, he's also in the Panthéon, what can we say, he gets around), Hector Berlioz, Heinrich Heine (the city of his birth, Düsseldorf, refused for an unconscionably long time to name its university after him, apparently believing that anyone who would slander Germany by writing, in the 19th century, "Where they burn books, they'll next burn people," and was a Jew to boot, shouldn't be remembered at all), Alexandre Dumas fils, Edgar Degas, Stendhal, the finely tuned Louis Jouvet, and a host of others. You'll find some real quiet here, especially on the cold first day of the new-year.

Afterward, eat lunch in one of the unpretentious bistros on the Place de Clichy: crisp roasted chicken, hot snappy pommes frites, pieces of fresh baguette that require no butter, and a bottle of chilled Loire valley white wine. *That* is enough to get you off the Montmartre butte to the Gare de Lyon and your train to the south, where a month later, in February, snow fell on the Gard for the first time in 25 years; a veritable Provençal blizzard of three inches! Incroyable, mais vrai!

Le Bateau Lavoir and the Mock Rousseau Banquet. Even if you cannot like early 20th century modern art and poetry and prose, you certainly have heard of Pablo Picasso and you may have heard of Georges Braque and Juan Gris, if not the lovely Max Jacob, the chubby Guillaume Apollinaire, the melodramatic Amedeo Modigliani, the fashionable Kees Van Dongen, or the esoteric Pierre MacOrlan, and all this being so or not, whilst you are dawdling in Montmartre, walk over to the Place Émile-Goudeau and stop at the oddly constructed building at 13, rue Ravignan called the Bateau Lavoir. Sit in the miniscule square and think yourself back to 1908 and envisage, perhaps, those giant figures of early 20th century history.

There is some confusion about who named the rabbit warren of tiny studios and apartments inhabited since the turn of the century by impecunious painters and writers. Max Jacob may have been the first because of the washed clothes he saw hanging on the lines, or André Salmon who thought he heard a hollow echo in the building reminiscent of an empty boathouse. Both of them would have been familiar with the laundry boats tied up along the Seine called Bateaux Lavoirs.

But, look, as our friend Yannis Papastephanou would say, you do not have to be concerned with such matters. Men and women made history here! Well, actually the original structure burned down in May 1970 just as French officialdom decided to declare the building a historic monument and what you now see is the rebuilding. In a coincidence that might be termed ironic, during the same month in which the locale of his energetic and fecund youth burned to ashes, an exhibition of Picasso's recent paintings opened at the Palais des Papes in Avignon: the old man's decrepit portrayals of soulless but colorful figures engaging in a twisted mind's notion of sex and death.

Legend has it that when Picasso and Max Jacob shared a room here, they had only one bed so, P. being vehemently heterosexual with a propensity to work nights by candle light, and J. being essentially neutral in matters of gender but with Tendencies and a part time job during the day, they shared the bed as well without both being in it at the same time. Take a long look at John Richardson's magnificent first volume of a projected four-volume biography, *A Life of Picasso*, published in 1991, which prints a number of photographs of the building and gives a fine account of Picasso's years there. Indeed, Richardson's is without a doubt the best biography of the artist in any language.

Among other works, Picasso painted the "seminal" "Les Demoiselles d'Avignon" and lived here with Fernande Olivier, his first lover of any duration who wrote about her life with the volatile young Catalan in an intelligent if occasionally inaccurate book called *Picasso et ses amis* (1933).[21] And here with Georges Braque double-handedly created what we know as cubism, and helped organize in his studio the famous November 1908 whopper of a party for Henri "The Customs Agent" Rousseau. See Roger Shattuck, *The Banquet Years* (1968) and Gertrude Stein's *The Autobiography of Alice B. Toklas* (1933) for details of this hilarious event. Personally, I am convinced that Miss Toklas herself wrote that book, but only a small minority of dissidents holds this opinion. In any case, Alice helped to round up food from various charcuteries because Fernande apparently forgot, or the store forgot to deliver, depending upon whose version you chose to believe. (The "Avignon" in the title of the painting refers to a long since disappeared whorehouse in Barcelona, not our beloved city in Provence, but no one is entirely sure.) How can you pass this up?! Indeed it is incumbent upon me to add a few further words regarding the Rousseau Banquet, as it has come to be known, because the event stands as such an lucid exemplar of the intellectual sophistication and social flexibility of the period, in such contrast to the mental shallowness and rigidity, and the social stratification so prevalent off the butte then and now.

Quite a few differing narrations of the party exist written by participants (Gertrude Stein, Fernande Olivier, Leo Stein, Maurice Reynal, and André Salmon), and historians and biographers (every life of Picasso tells the story over again with varying degrees of Schwung und Wahrheit, often with more verve than veracity). Shattuck's version is a good place to begin, but the others should be consulted as well. Indeed, John Richardson's second volume of his Picasso biography (1996) contains a refreshingly revisionist picture of the affair, in which he mildly chastises those such as Shattuck for investing profound metaphysical meaning in what was in fact a joke, and a rather mean-minded one at that. As Richardson points out in no uncertain terms, all the high jinks that evening should not blind us to the "degrading plight of the guest of honor, idiot savant of art, weeping tears of tipsy joy at the mock adulation."

In any case, a complete retelling here would burst the integument of this volume, but a brief litany of images will give an indication of the hilarity of the occasion which brought together people from a truly wide range of talent and social positions.

Invited guests, in addition to those memoirists mentioned above, included Guillaume Apollinaire, who escorted the guest of honor to what was for Rousseau sort

281

of a surprise party, Georges Braque, Alice Toklas, André Warnod, Maurice de Vlaminck, Max Jacob who then had his own small studio in the building, who said he would not appear at all, but whose curiosity got the better of him, Maurice Cremnitz, Jacques Vaillant, René Dalize, Ramon and Germaine Pichot, possibly Juan Gris who also lived in the building, the sculptor Manolo, probably Wilhelm Uhde and his bride Sonja Turk (soon to be Sonja Delaunay; the homosexual Uhde married her in name to give her identity papers so she would not have to return to tsarist Russia), Marie Laurencin, then undergoing a love affair with Apollinaire (among other projects, she would illustrate an edition of *Alice in Wonderland* printed by the Black Sun Press in 1930 and who would give "art lessons" to the unfortunate Lucia Joyce in the 1920s), and the lady companions of most of the men. If questions remain about the nature of the food provided or not provided, it is clear that the party was well-watered.

Images and fragments to be made coherent by the Reader:

On what is probably November 21, a Saturday, in the early evening winter crepuscule everyone meets to enjoy an apéritif in Fauvet's corner bar at the foot of Rue Ravignan where some have enjoyed too many and have become very friendly in the loud if not boisterous manner generally associated with the consumption of apéritifs slightly beyond the point of felicity, especially the young, pale thin Marie Laurencin, a painter of thin washed canvases in a quasi-primitive style, who sways throughout the crowd, arms extended, greeting everyone with befuddled affection. This is not in keeping with Fernande Olivier's description of her as looking "like a rather vicious little girl, or a little girl who wants people to think she's vicious," but does appear to agree with Carleton Lake's phrase about the artist's "serene work and unquiet nature." In any case,

282

Mme. Olivier did not particularly like Mme. Laurencin, perhaps because of the activities narrated below.

When the crowd finally climbs the street up to the Bateau Lavoir, Fernande stands blocking the doorway to the studio preventing the gang from entering. "No! That creep will not spoil my party. This is a serious banquet. She's drunk. Pablo will not allow it." Pablo is well hidden behind Gertrude Stein and her brother, Leo, himself far from sober, who had supported the unfortunate, but ethereally happy Marie Laurencin between them all the way up the hill from the bar. Miss Stein glares into Fernande's eyes and stolidly states in no uncertain, if ungrammatical, terms: "Ma chére Madame Picasso, Fernande. Moi, I did not monte la colline engaged in la lutte to keep Mademoiselle Laurencin upright et en bonne santé pour nothing. I'll be hanged if I did! Alors, allez-y, laissez les bons temps rouler!" At this Pablo edges forward and adds "Oui, oui, certes." In tight American accents, Miss Stein notes that Apollinaire would be there shortly with the honored guest and all should be bien préparé by then. Fernande, not quite knowing what to make of the bulky, sharp-tongued Apollinaire, relents and everyone tumbles into the studio, which is dominated by the Rousseau portrait of a woman Picasso recently purchased, and a banner proclaiming "Honneur à Rousseau."

Miss Toklas (helpfully): "If the charcuterie has forgotten to deliver the food, let us telephone Félix Potin and have provisions delivered."

Marie Laurencin (indignantly): "Fernande forgot to *order* the food! And one does not telephone in France, and certainly not to a greengrocer."

Pablo Picasso (soothingly): "Fernande will no doubt find something to eat." (To Fernande menacingly): "Won't you, my turtledove?"

Fernande Olivier (unhesitatingly): "Aiieee! Aidez moi, Mademoiselle Tookla!"

And so she did, though accounts differ as to the methods applied. Everyone seems to agree on sardines and "riz à la Valencienne" prepared in one of the studios in the labyrinth of the building, in which several invited guests wander hopelessly lost until early the following day, when they arrive at Picasso's door at the same time as the dinner ordered for the previous evening.

Cooking at a boil, effervescently boiling over, Marie Laurencin falls swan-like onto a platter of jam tarts. "O pardon!" she shrieks. "Je m'excuse, n'est-çe-pas." And after a short giggle she sits quietly on a small rather unstable stool smiling to herself.

Finally, Apollinaire arrives (three loud knocks on the studio door), escorting the old man, floppy hat on his head, holding violin and walking stick, smiling tentatively, willing to accept, even desirous of, the attentions of this motley group of writers, painters and collectors, but skeptical of the evening's reality, mildly apprehensive that they might make him the butt of an elaborate joke. He soon convinces himself that they actually admire him and that Fernande is right: this is a serious banquet, hilarious to be sure, but serious. And soon to become famous, then legendary.

The honored guest dozes at intervals, elated and exhausted by the noisy babble, the abundantly flowing wine, the clouds of tobacco smoke, the adulation, mock or not, of a younger generation of artists and writers in whom he can detect no sarcasm or condescension, though it was there, but not in Picasso who truly revered the retired and practically impoverished civil servant who for years *had* painted only on Sundays - the old man nods off with a smile on his lips, his violin clutched to his chest, unimpressed by the candle wax dripping on his bald head.

In Apollinaire's presence, Marie Laurencin reverts to the tipsy waif role and becomes obnoxious just before the reading of poems, not behavior calculated to appeal to poets in their cups. Apollinaire escorts her out into the night for a few moments of fresh air not yet polluted by the gasoline engine. Shortly thereafter they return and a chastened as well as slightly bruised no longer so tipsy waif resumes her seat and quietly listens to the poems written and recited in honor of the "amateur" painter.

At some point in the evening, old Frédé, owner of the Lapin Agile, a well-known night spot nearby where he serves discounted drinks to his friends, arrives with his pet donkey, Lolo, whose tail is alleged to have painted a number of abstract pictures sold to unsuspecting tourists as le dernier cri de modrenarte. Frédé plays his guitar and several guests attempt to sing along. People come and go and the crowd thickens.

André Salmon, poet, art critic, and compulsive autobiographer, suddenly leaps upon the rickety banquet table and begins loudly in verse to proclaim the virtues of the old man. At the poem's finish, amidst the general acclaim and applause, he grabs a glass full of some alcoholic beverage, gulps it down and for an instant goes stock still (later claiming this was all an act to enervate the gathering). Then, in the depths of his throat emitting a strange growl like a tortured pit bull, he plunges off the table into the party swinging his arms in a pathetic attempted boxer imitation, flailing at anyone nearby, by now frothing at the mouth, until a number of the men wrestle him to the floor. Braque grabs two statues out of harm's way, while Leo Stein, tall, thin and swaying dangerously, protects the guest of honor and his violin. Picasso, small but wiry, leads a group to carry Salmon to the atelier being used as a ladies' cloakroom, deposit him amidst the coats, and lock the door. Later, guests find him awake and charming, but discover various things chewed up, including the yellow flowers of Miss Toklas' new hat. (One source claims Lolo ate the flowers, and a box of matches, and a petit bleu.)

285

Apollinaire sits in a corner of the studio, studiously answering his arreared correspondence, until he thinks the time auspicious, at which point he clamors to his feet and loudly recites his own, allegedly improvised, verse homage to Rousseau, in the chorus of which everyone joined: "Vive! Vive, Rousseau!"

Old Rousseau, glowing with pride, but retaining his gentle humility, plays his violin, singing his favorite song, "Aïe, aïe, aïe, j'ai mal aux dents," which might be translated as "Ow, ow, ow, my teeth ache!" Does he realize this gathering is unprecedented? Indeed, nothing like it will happen again until the rehearsed reading of Picasso's play, *Le Désir attrappé par le queue* (*Desire Caught by the Tail*), either a parody of the 1920s avant-garde or a primitive imitation of it, in the drawing room of Michel and Louise Leiris' apartment on the Quai des Grands Augustins on March 19, 1944, during the occupation of Paris. Under Albert Camus's, Simone de Beauvoir, Jean-Paul Sartre, Dora Maar, Zanie de Campan (the only professional actress among the performers), and Leiris himself read the roles. The spectators included Jacques Lacan, Georges Braque, Georges Bataille, Jean-Louis Barrault, Madeleine Renaud, Sylvie Bataille, Georges Limbour, Pierre Reverdy, Picasso, Cécile Eluard (the daughter of Paul Eluard and Gala, before Eluard gave Gala to Dali), Valentine Hugo, Jean Aubier, Armand Salacron - in short, the avant-garde of the occupied city.

But on this grand night 36 years earlier, the old man does not have to realize this, or anything like it - he is enjoying himself as never before in his long varied life. But *we* realize, and remember; almost 100 years later, we still talk about the "Honneur à Rousseau."

The Steins and Miss Toklas, assisted by their still short but wiry Spanish host, place the guest of honor in a horse drawn cab (fiacre) at five in the morning, and the Steins and Miss Toklas see him, asleep all the way, home to bed and lasting fame and very much fortune, but alas not during his lifetime.

Was it on this occasion that Rousseau leaned over to Picasso and made the now famous statement: "Picasso, you and I are the greatest painters of our time, you in the Egyptian style, I in the modern", a remark that is not as simple or as senseless at it may seem, as history has shown?

And the "unquiet" Marie Laurencin? A fascinating person, whose life reads like a romantic, if modern, fiction. The fact that the basis for Henri-Pierre Roché's novel *Jules et Jim* is the loving ménage à trois consisting of the author, the German writer Franz Hessel and Helen Grund, later Helen Hessel, is fairly well-known. More obscure to most even well-read cultured folk is the earlier ménage à trois made up of the two men and the young Marie Laurencin, whose drawings attracted Roché's attention sufficiently for him to purchase several of them and to meet the artist, then studying at the Académie Humbert with fellow-students Georges Braque and Francis Picabia. After numerous affairs, several of them with women, and several horrific abortions, she married one of the Montparnasse German painters, the bisexual Baron Otto von Waetjens, on June 22, 1914, not an auspicious time to become a German by marriage in France. Two months later, now enemy aliens, they fled to Spain, where she spent the next five years before returning to Paris. What happened to the German painter is not clear to me, but Marie continued to live a tumultuous (at least regarding her relations with men and women) and creative life until 1956, when she died. Roché remained her friend until her death.

Le Moulin Rouge. What you can pass up, but perhaps should indulge in at least once, is a visit to one of the famous nightclubs of Paris before they all shut down like the Folies-Bergère in the Autumn of 1992, and as long as you're already in Montmartre.... Not too far south of the

Bateau Lavoir, a few blocks in fact, you suddenly look up and see a brightly colored windmill on top of a low building with a sign reading Moulin Rouge (at 82, boulevard de Clichy).

The name will bring a comfortable tug of nostalgia to those who remember Pierre le Muir's book of the same name (especially the Signet paperback edition from the early 1950s with the gaudy picture on the cover!), a fictionalized biography of the near-dwarf Henri de Toulouse-Lautrec, so well-played by the late normal-size José Ferrer on his knees in the late John Huston's movie of the same name.

The traditional format for these mindless (in the positive sense) entertainment palaces has been standard for generations: singers, jugglers, standup and slapstick comedians, elaborately choreographed dance numbers, a loud orchestra and masses of uniformly packaged naked young women who prance about waving ostrich feathers, mostly in time with the music. Certain concessions to contemporary perversions of middle-class taste have been made over the years since 1918, such as unclothed women swimming with dolphins in clear-plastic water containers warbling sounds approximating the cries of terminally ruptured koala bears accompanied by sheets of brassy orchestral music.

On the whole, however, the main pillars of the structure remain in place, especially the nudes. The title of the song "Lewd Nude at the Lido" is inaccurate: we noticed nothing lewd about the seemingly hundreds of Junoesque women mincing about on five-inch high heels on a runway a few inches above the front row tables, white teeth glistening, whose feathers floated into one's champagne glass as they jiggled certain perfectly formed parts of their anatomies up and down and all around, with some delicacy it must be admitted, to the bored brassy band of professionals who can switch from Caribbean dayo to Moscow nights without a tremor of intent, thought, or hesitation.

One hundred yankee greenbacks, more or less, payable in French francs or major credit card, will get two people a two-hour show and a bottle of drinkable champagne, in 1980 that is. Has the price gone up? Surely, but not too much; nightclub boards of directors do not wish to price themselves into bankruptcy. Or so one would assume, but even this formerly fundamental notion of practical capitalist management is now apparently suspect: vide IBM, Sears and Roebuck, and the aforementioned Folies Bergère.

Has the show changed since 1980 when we last saw it? Unlikely. One hopes not. All the photographs and stories from the past reinforce the notion that such cultural institutions resist radical change, including the nudes who remain eternally aged 19. But change these days occurs at a faster pace than ever before. And the ready accessibility of hardcore pornographic displays must surely drain off some of the clientele from the palaces of "naughty" entertainment.

As evidence to support the hope that excessive change will not occur, I offer an obscure book published in London (1961) called *Paris Revue*, which contains a photograph from the 1930s of the lovely "fan dancer," Joan Warner, who possessed a shape approximating so closely the ideal figure of our western European Greco-Roman originated imaginations that she might as well be true. The photograph, alas, does not flatter her face, but classical sculptures, given the vicissitudes of time and man, do occasionally excite the synapses, even when occasionally headless. (The book, by the way, boasts a text, in addition to the lavish but black and white illustrations, in which Pierre Mariel narrates the history of Paris revues.) Another photograph of Ms Warner and her gorgeous popo taken in 1935 can also be seen in the even more obscure publication entitled *Fascination* (number 24, 1984, p. 38), but those of tender sensibilities should be warned that the magazine, whose subtitle is "Le Musée secret de l'Erotisme" (The Secret Museum of Eroticism), runs lavishly illustrated articles on such things as "Histoire et sémiologie du cunnilinctus," and the like.

One might also note that the so-called "National Alliance against Depopulation" instigated in 1935 the prosecution of Ms Warner. After a three-week trial, the Paris court fined her 50 francs for outraging public morality. By 1965, one of the more well-known practitioners of the art of public sartorial divestiture, Rita Renoir, claimed it to be a socially valuable ritual ceremony, and no one laughed, though a few smiled, and the statement outraged several. Ms Warner can thusly be viewed as a perhaps unwilling pioneer in the movement to loosen social strictures on publicly performed and socially useful eroticism.

Who knows, in the 21st century perhaps swordfish will replace the dolphins and the dances might be more savagely danced to the crack of the erotic whiplash, but the system will undoubtedly remain essentially as it always has been. Despite some, mainly architectural, aberrations to the contrary not withstanding, the French do believe the adage which advises not repairing things that remain unbroken; at least they formerly believed this and may formally still do so, but one should be prepared for anything, whilst hoping for the best.

In the meantime, if you wish to see an accurate illustration of the night side of Parisian life in the 1930s, I suggest you look into Brassaï's book *The Secret Paris of the 30s* (1976). Even if some of them are posed for the camera, the photographs reflect an authentic, at times amusing, always evocative picture of occasionally sinister and ominous, not to say unsavory aspects of urban life behind the public curtain before the war changed everything forever.

Brassaï, born Gyula Halász in Hungary, prowled the Parisian streets with his camera in the company of Henry Miller, Jacques Prévert and Léon-Paul Fargue (the archetypal pedestrian of Paris) throughout the two decades after 1918, his companions serving not only as friends, and occasionally as bodyguards. Whores, sailors, pickpockets, gangsters, hotels with rooms by the hour, sections of the city not seen by tourists and never in daylight, cesspool cleaners (from whom Brassaï learns about the various "qualities" of shit: residences where people use a lot of water for life's necessities, such as laundry and dish-washing, are easy to pump out, in office buildings "the shit is harder"), bordellos, dancehalls, dwarfs, stool pigeons, pimps, the homosexual demimonde, opium dens, criminals and their milieux, exotic, fascinating, dangerous, and now gone. In addition, Brassaï's text tells marvelous stories that reinforce and explain his images.

The raunchy dance hall called Bal du Moulin Rouge (not to be confused with the *music* hall called Le Moulin Rouge) no longer exists on the Place Blanche in Montmartre, nonetheless I cannot let this opportunity pass without another citation from Bruce Reynold's horrid excuse for a guide, mentioned earlier in reference to Harry's New York Bar. This, about the dance hall: "This, the biggest, strangest, toughest, most seething dance hall you ever were in. And the real thing. Not for tourists. Blacks and whites dancing together. And, what of it? The prettiest white girls and the blackest men and vice versa." And, then, Reynolds, warns his readers not to go there. This, seems to have been done, under the rubric of "Reverse Psychology," a term, used by those who know nothing of psychological phenomena, but who may have suffered some reverses at one time or another in their lives. Perhaps.

To show you how dependable most guides are, John Chancellor, in a book called *How to be Happy in Paris without Being Ruined*, published in London in 1926, claims the Bal du Moulin Rouge is undoubtedly "adequately wicked, but whatever work Satan commits here seems to be done in a much more surreptitious and underhanded manner than, for example, at Le Bal Tabarin," which may or may not still exist on Rue Victor Masse in Montmartre. But Chancellor says about the Bal Tabarin that any woman who has been in the Folies Bergère won't see much more here than there. And so the scurrying from place to place in search of libidinous thrills continues over the decades. There may still be joints like this in Paris, but they are either too expensive, too full of tourists from Liverpool, Frankfurt, and St. Louis, or like the Folies Bergère, closed.

The **Musée de Montmartre**, at 12, rue Cortot, is filled with memorabilia, photographs and documents reflecting the high and low times of la Bohème since the early 1800s. Yes, Puccini set his opera in Montmartre. Puccini was influenced, as so many who fell under the spell of the "bohemian" lifestyle in the 19th and early 20th centuries, by Henri Murger's fanciful book, the French equivalent of the American Webb Pierce's "There Stands the Glass," called *Scènes de la vie de Bohème* (1851). There is a bust of Murger on a stone pedestal east of the Senat building in the Jardin du Luxembourg.

In Montmartre Museum building Renoir painted the well-known picture of "Le Moulin de la Galette," which portrays a once sparkling popular dancehall now called Restaurant da Graziano, a perfect example of the cultural ambiguity increasingly present in postmodern Europe. So, too, Suzanne Valadon, her unfortunate son Maurice Utrillo, Emile-Othon Frieze, and others lived and worked here before 1914, the beginning of The Great 20th Century Cataclysm. Some cultural arbiters would have us believe the cataclysm actually started in 1907 with "Les

Demoiselles d'Avignon." Needless to say, these doomsters also tell us we have not yet gotten over the event.

The **Lapin Agile** still exists on the Rue des Saules, but for one reason or another we've never been in it despite its long history as a meeting place for the painters, art dealers, and writers who lived in or visited Montmartre from the turn of the century to 1910 or so: Paul Fort, Pierre MacOrlan, Francis Carco, Picasso, Braque, Jules Romains, the playwright George Courteline, the painter Poulbot, André Salmon, D.H. Kahnweiller, et alia. Previously known as the Cabaret des Assassins, its name changed after the popular caricaturist, André Gill, painted a sign to hang out front which depicted a rabbit jumping into a frying pan: customers began calling the place as "Le lapin à Gill," apparently a pun on "Là peint A. Gill." No doubt one would today find the low ceilings, the smoky dark walls covered with drawings and paintings by various hands, including an early harlequin by the ubiquitous Picasso, or at least a reconstruction of them, looking rather like they did in 1910. But do not look for ill-clothed, poor, but enthusiastic young artists there - they can no longer afford the prices.

While you are in the quarter, you should walk through the Place du Tertre to see the latest kitsch being bought by the tourists (are the wide-eyed kids still a big seller?) and walk around and in the Sacré Coeur basilica. The steps in front of the building afford one of the most fantastic, if by now clichéd, views of the city. When you leave the butte, walk down the steps of the Rue Foyatier and admire the stamina of the old men and women who live on the streets off the steps, who climb up and down every day.

On the way down these steps, the limping Warren Smith, former gas station owner from Saint Paul, Minnesota, half-lamed but not defeated by the savage winters in his home state, stopped to talk about the stairs with an elderly citizen of the neighborhood. Warren was nearly 70 at the time. I wish I could have heard that conversation. I know he asked the old woman how she survived the steps every day and what was her dog's name. Lynn-Marie, her mother Evelyn and I dawdled too far away to hear the talk. Warren spoke no French and the old woman had no English. They understood each other perfectly.

20th ARRONDISEMENT

Père Lachaise Cemetery, 295 – Le Musée d'Edith Piaf, 296

The largest of the Parisian cemeteries is **Cimetière du Père Lachaise**, officially the Cimetière de l'Est, where Gertrude Stein and Alice Toklas, Richard Wright, Harry Graf Kessler, Oscar Wilde, Rudolf Hilferding, William Gardner Smith (or he was until his family ceased payments on his wall-urn), and innumberable other fairly well-known French people, including Georges Seurat, Marcel Proust, Eugène Delacroix, Honoré de Balzac, Sarah Berhhardt, Louis David, Auguste Comte, Théodore Géricault, Simone Signoret and Yves Montand, as well as quite a few people (approximately one million) known only to their families, are buried. A tidy little handbook entitled *Permanent Parisians*, written by Judi Culbertson and Tom Randell (1986), or a map purchased for a few francs at the main entrance, will help guide you around the twisted labyrinth of lanes and tombstones, some of which leap out at you, others of which lay back and either invite your presence or claim to be indifferent to your gaze.

Be sure to see the several monuments to the French who died in the German concentration camps and as resistants against German and French fascism. The frightening, skeletal sculpture representing two prisoners of Buchenwald, the work of the Buchenwald survivor Louis Bancel, will rip the breath out of your lungs. On a cold winter day in April 1964, French survivors of the camps unveiled the statue, which had been paid for over the years by public subscription. (There is also a monument to the deportees on the western end of the Ile de la Cité.) One wonders, however, when the French will erect a monument to those who died in *French* camps.

In the northeast section of the cemetery, stop before the Mur des Fédérés, the wall of the federalists, at which, in the dawn's early light of May 28, 1871, French government troops executed 147 French communards, the remnants of the Commune's last stand, adding to the 20,000 Parisians deliberately killed by Frenchmen in that terrible civil war, abetted to be sure by the Germans. Civil wars, regardless of foreign intervention, are the worst: the line between love and hate is exceedingly thin and fragile.

If you need to know what the labyrinth looks like before you go, or to remind you after you, cameraless, have already been there, peruse Frederich Brown's *Père Lachaise: Elysium as Real Estate* (1973), which contains, among others, a nice photo of the tombstone of Fred Chopin. Keep in mind that some 800,000 people traipse through this necropolis each year, most of them to visit Edith Piaf; no matter what time of year you go, you won't be alone. If you aren't up to the walk, you can rent a battery-powered golfcart at the main entrance, with or without a driver.

If you are a true-blue Edith Piaf fan, you can walk up the Boulevard de Ménilmontant from the cemetery to the Passage de Ménilmontant where you turn left, then right at the first opportunity into the Rue Crespin du Gast. On the fourth floor of number 5 you will find the **Musée d'Edith Piaf**, two small rooms full of various pieces of clothing, photographs, a couch, letters, and other mementos. During your visit the concierge will play her songs on the record player, or perhaps on a CD player by the time you read this. The Museum is open Monday to Thursday from 1 to 6 PM, by appointment only, so call 43 55 52 72 first. This is only for real, that is to say, true aficionados.

Do not venture much beyond the Père Lachaise. The 20th arrondissement has sadly followed the course of the 20th century: sterile highrise buildings without character or charm are overwhelming the area, especially in the

Belleville quarter, rendering what was once a rambling neighborhood of gardens and two-story houses, poor and rundown to be sure, into a souless replicant of urban boredom in which the former inhabitants can no longer afford to live. The apartments now boast hot and cold running water and individual private toilets, which are of course necessary to a civilized life, but the structures that contain them do so without vitality or interest. In 1954, Albert Lamorisse made the marvelous film *The Red Balloon* here, in which one can see what the quarter looked like in the olden days.

Environs

Versailles, 298 – Chartres, 299 – Saint-Germain-en-Laye and Le Musée Maurice Denis, 301 – Fontainebleau, 302 – Giverny, 303 – Les Vaux-de-Cernay, 304

The 1985 green Paris *Guide Michelin* devotes twelve pages to the multitudinous aspects of the royal phenomenon called **Versailles**. We've been there a couple of times and find everything a bit much, especially the numbers of tourists, although the gardens are wonderful. Yes, history was made here not only by the royal family from Louis XIV on, but also by modern so-called statesmen in 1919 when, gathered in solemn conclave, the leaders of France, Great Britain, Italy, and the United States of America ensured the continuation beyond 1919 of the war begun in 1914; ironically this gathering was called a "peace" conference intended to formally end that war. Indeed, any number of ironies arose from this meeting, some to be realized only later, such as the creation of the federal states of Czechoslovakia and Yugoslavia and the appearance of the young Vietnamese nationalist Ho Chi Minh, not yet a communist, vainly seeking support from the Americans for his country's independence from France.

The gardens of Versailles are lovely and vast, the palaces are sumptuous, elaborate and, if you grasp their raison d'être, magnificent in their failure: architecture could not save the Bourbon monarchy from the ideas whose reification in the French Revolution smashed the tottering feudal structure out of which, over the long road of 19th and 20th century history, emerged, cantankerous and bloody, the modern French state and the economic, social and cultural foundations which support it.

While you are in Paris, if you can find the time, take the bus or the train out to Versailles one dry sunny morning and leave enough time to have lunch in one of the many cafés in town. In the mid-1980s we stayed overnight in Versailles for some reason. Having driven a long way that day, stopping at Giverny and Saint-Germain-en-Laye to see the art and landscape, exhaustion and the thought of driving on the périphérique (beltway) into the city's transportation chaos the following day nudged us firmly, if gently, toward a simple bistro dinner and an early retirement that night. I wish I could remember the name and address of the clean, well-lit, busy but nondescript bistro where a smiling waitress (unusual, that!) served us precisely what we required: a bottle of chilled Loire white wine, oeufs mayonnaise, poulet roti, salade verte, pommes frites and, at the end, tarte de pomme and expresso. Heaven it was to be alive and in France where, with any luck, even the truckstops serve food beyond the merely eatable. And to be at an age when one did not require décafiné after 18 o'clock. But you will discover your own bistro there where you will be presented with a repas both tasty and satisfying to the soul. And these days one can also find café décafiné in many restaurants.

If you don't go to Versailles, I suppose there is a chance you may regret it.

* * * *

You definitely will regret not visiting **Chartres**. On a warm May night, two decades ago, we stood on the tiny hotel room balcony overlooking the railroad station, cognac and cigarettes in hand, and softly (I think and hope in retrospect) serenaded the passengers disembarking from the last commuter train from Paris. "Que sera sera...." Ah, the bathos into which the dangerous combination of happiness and intoxication can slide.

Yes, the cathedral. This magnificent and mighty stone witness to the unconquerable human spirit and the strength of human will is further out of the city than Versailles, but we recommend, if the Fates force you to choose, that you go to Chartres. Spend the day in and around this lapidary expression of man's transcendental possibility, where endurance and obedience to a perceived highest prime cause are the main characteristics of human nature as it has evolved over the millennia. In order to participate, you do not have to be a Christian, or to have read Henry Adams' book on Chartres and Mont Saint Michel, but having read the book will vastly increase your pleasure and understanding of this living edifice, where the very flying buttresses appear to breathe before your eyes. All you have to do is match your breath-rhythm to theirs. As Adams aptly comments, "For terror or ferocity or images of pain, the art of the twelfth century had no use except to give a higher value to their images of love."

Shantih, shantih, shantih.

* * * *

There are several good reasons for traveling for a day by bus or train to **St-Germain-en-Laye**, in former times a village on its own, now a suburb of Paris: the old and the new châteaux (only the ruins of the latter remain after Charles X demolished it), the gardens, the woods around the town, the terraces, and so on. Look it up in your green Michelin guide. Incidentally, the old château suffered the indignity of being the location where the Allies and the Austrians concluded the Austrian part of the "peace" treaty in 1919.

The French cultural bureaucracy at some point converted the old château into the Museum of National

300

Antiquities, which we have not seen. We have, however, visited with much pleasure the Musée du Prieuré (Priory Museum), which started as a hospital, became a priory, then the house of the painter Maurice Denis, and is now the **Musée de Maurice Denis** (2, rue Maurice Denis).

Our 1985 edition of the green Michelin guide to Paris makes an arcane reference to a mysterious Ranson, who had a studio here in which Denis and his fellow Nabis, a post-impressionist art "movement" preceding the Fauves, met regularly to admire each others' work. Denis painted Mrs. Ranson's portrait and it is there for all to see. Mr. Ranson appears in Denis' "Hommage à Cézanne," a painting done in 1901 (that is, before Cézanne's death),[22] showing a number of artists including Denis, Odilon Redon, and Pierre Bonnard, as well as Ambroise Vollard, the unlucky art-dealer, and Mme. Denis gathered around an easel holding Cézanne's "Dish of Fruit." André Gide purchased the painting in 1902; somehow it ended up in the Luxembourg and is now, alas, in the Musée d'Orsey, where you can see it if you can find it amidst the architectural detritus clogging the building. Paul-Elie Ranson's 1895 painting, "Paysage maritime," hangs in the Petit Palais in Geneva. Mr. Ranson becomes somewhat less mysterious, perhaps, when we learn that he had another studio at 25, rue Vavin (14th) called The Temple, where he held a Saturday "salon" and operated a puppet theater for which he wrote the plays and designed the sets. His wife was known as "La Lumière du Temple." Well, yes, the light of his life, no doubt. Mr. Ranson's works appeared well hung in the exposition devoted to the Nabis at the Grand Palais during the Summer and Autumn of 1993, before the danger of falling masonry caused officials to close the building for major repairs.

One regular at the gatherings of Nabis who rarely praised anyone's work other than his own, Paul Gauguin, is undoubtedly the most well-known of the group. Who,

301

except the cultured elite remembers Emile Bernard, Henry Moret, Paul Sérusier, or, for that matter, Maurice Denis?[23] Happily, one has ready access to Pierre Bonnard's beautiful work, at least in Washington, D.C. thanks to Duncan Phillips and his museum.

In any case, we saw a marvelously detailed exhibition called "Le chemin de Gauguin" in the Denis Museum, which collected not only Gauguin's works, but also those of his colleagues mentioned above, and some of the artifacts from their visits to the Brittany coast where they spent a number of summers living cheaply and painting madly. The Museum published a catalog with some true reproductions and a detailed chronology, comprehensible even to those with only a minimal of French, entitled *Le Chemin de Gauguin. Genèse et rayonnement* (1985). Call ahead to discover the subject of the current temporary exhibition. If you do not trust your French, ask your hotel clerk to make the call. The building, the comfortable garden, and the permanent collection are worth your while even if you have no interest in the temporary exhibition.

* * * *

Fontainebleau, southeast of the city near the location of Patricia Highsmith's morally dubious protagonist, Tom Ripley, is also the venue of a popular large forest, gardens and château, a sort of junior Versailles, where the Barbizon school of painters got its name, and where the young New Zealand writer, Katherine Mansfield, suffered her final haemorrhage and died, a victim of Gurdjieff's Institute for the Harmonious Development of Man treatment for raging tuberculosis: think yourself healthy - manual labor is good for you, even if you are obviously dying from a wasting physically deteriorating disease. On the other hand, the American writer, Jean Toomer, spent much time at the Institute without any clearly visible ruinous effects.

302

Fontainebleau, however, is too far from the city to be considered a Parisian attraction.

* * * *

If you are a fan of Monet, you should not only spend time at the Marmotton museum on the Right Bank, but also take a RER train or a rental car to the village of **Giverny** outside the city. There you can walk in his garden, meander around his house, and admire his kitchen, about which at least two preciously cute and expensive volumes have recently been published, an additional indication that we have entered the terminal stage of late capitalist culture. One wonders if the words "kitchen" and "kitsch" are cognate.

On a sunny day, this place can be very pleasant, especially standing on the Japanese bridge over the pond, seeing the lilies, and realizing that the old man's cataract-plagued eye truly guided his hand almost until the end. Monet, now in danger of being too famous, that is to say too familiar, if he has not already reached that dubious point, moved from Paris to Giverny in 1883.

One hundred years later, Monet having died in 1926 deep in old age, the Centre Culturel du Marais mounted an exhibition under the name "Claude Monet at the Time of Giverny." At any rate, this is the name of the English language version of the dense, lengthy catalog containing more than you will ever wish to know on the subject unless you write a dissertation about it. A series of black and white photographs of the artist, with his biblical white beard and panama hat in his garden should motivate you to visit the place yourself and see the glorious colors of the flowers.

In June of 1992, the Musée Americain Giverny, built next door to Monet's property on the land formerly owned by his American friend, Lilla Cabot Perry, opened as an "expression of American gratitude to France" to "celebrate the historic connection between French Impressionism and the art it inspired, particularly in America." The inaugural exhibition, entitled "Lasting Impressions [out!]: American Painters in France, 1865-1915," included the works of Mary Cassatt, Winslow Homer, John Singer Sargent, James McNeil Whistler, and "a slew of others."[24]

According to an article in *The Washington Post*, the title of which recalls the motivation for urban youth's gang wars ("An American Museum on Monet Turf," May 8, 1992), the Musée Americain project cost $19 million and the exhibition space is mainly underground, except for a "terrace restaurant for 200," an all too typical example of current art appreciation: the Impressionists moved painting out of the studio into the open air and filled their canvases with explosions of brilliant sunlight and bright color; this museum will drag the paintings back into the crepuscular interior - underground. An additional caution: mass tourism has long since discovered Giverny.

* * * *

We have never been to the small village of **Les Vaux-de-Cernay** just beyond Versailles in the Chevreuse valley, described by one writer as "a remote country village"; one wishes to know remote from where? Be that all as it may be, a brief narration of the events that took place here and on the road to Paris on June 27, 1929, would not be completely out of place here.

In the last decade of his life, James Joyce's friends and sycophants regularly arranged various kinds of fêtes in his honor and to take his and Nora's minds off the increasingly visible tragedy of their daughter Lucia's mental illness and his own increasing blindness. To celebrate the publication, at last, of *Ulysses* in French, and to commemorate, late, the twenty-fifth anniversary of Bloomsday, June 16, Adrienne

Monnier organized a luncheon, known in the literature as "Déjeuner Ulysse," for a select few in this village, chosen only because a hotel there was named Léopold. A photograph of the event exists, an image curiously similar to the pictorial arrangement of Leonardo's Last Supper with, however, many more apostles in it. Dimly pictured are the Joyces, including George and Lucia, Sylvia Beach, Helen Kantor Fleischmann (George's future first wife), Jules Romains, Léon-Paul Fargue, Paul Valéry, Jean Paulhan, Philippe Soupault, André Chamson, Pierre de Lanux, Édouard Dujardin (whom Joyce considered the creator of the stream of consciousness technique), Thomas McGreevy, Nino Frank, and assorted other friends and colleagues, but not Samuel Beckett, who definitely attended but who may have already been too drunk to stand or sit up straight, or perhaps this notoriously shy person has not eaten his Powdermilk Biscuits that morning. Joyce particularly regretted that the translators of *Ulysses* into French remained conspicuous by their absence: the strains put on the relations among Stuart Gilbert, Auguste Morel and Valéry Larbaud during the long and extremely difficult task turned out to be too intense for all of them to continue to socialize together.

The menu, to turn our attention to the most important part of the event, contained six courses and various liquids:

Le paté Léopold
Les Quenelles de veau Toulouse
Le poulet de Bresse rôti
Les pommes nouvelles au beurre
La salade de laitue mimosa
Les fromages variés
La tarte aux fraises du jardin
Vin blanc, vin rosé, vin rouge
Passe-tout-grain de nuits
Moulin au vent
Café filtre

According to most accounts, including Nino Frank's detailed story in Willard Potts' compilation, *Portraits of the Artist in Exile* (1979), the liquids contributed to the outstanding quality of the day, although one would think that a gathering of so many major writers of English and French literature in one place simultaneously would be significant in itself. What did they talk about? Royalties, the perfidy of publishers, the stupidity of editors, and physical ailments, no doubt.

Joyce had a well-known penchant for white wine, particularly the Swiss Fendent de Sion, and it is thus not surprising that the younger members of the entourage, Frank, Beckett, McGreevy and Soupault, readily found a partner for their "antics," as Frank called their behavior. The older members of the gathering viewed the others with varying degrees of annoyance and distain, except Nora, who by this time had accustomed herself to her husband's eccentricities and thus remained aloof if not mildly amused. In the bus Miss Monnier rented to carry the group from the Rue de l'Odéon and back again, Beckett importuned the driver to make frequent stops at cafés and bars allegedly to allow the youth cohort, Joyce among them, to relieve their wracked bladders. The stops became longer and longer and the inebriation increased geometrically. Finally, Miss Beach succeeded in keeping Joyce on the bus, but Beckett, according to a somewhat hypocritical Joyce, finally had to be "ingloriously abandoned by the wagonette in one of those temporary palaces which are inseparably associated with the memory of the Emperor Vespasian."

Mention of Beckett brings to mind what one can call a "typical" Paris story. Beckett and Alberto Giacometti sit one evening on the terrace of a café enjoying a drink and the crepuscule, quietly chatting. One of the neighborhood hookers who knew both of them passed by and seeing them on the terrace, strode into the café to inform the proprietor that two great men graced his establishment and that he was thus both lucky and honored. The proprietor's reaction to this news is unknown, as, in fact, is the validity of the story, mais c'est belle, n'est-çe pas? Joyce, of course, must be considered one of the great peripatetic writers of all time; especially in the last half of his life he unceasingly moved his exiled family across the map of Europe like a pendulum twisting in the wind; here, there and everywhere. This not the place to analyze the reasons for his constant movements and changes of residence, shifts of locale, which wrecked any chance his children might have had for a stable environment in which to grow up or his wife to feel at home. Perhaps not incidentally, his parents had followed a similar pattern of address changes in and around Dublin during Joyce's youth. After the he and his family moved to Paris in 1920 at the behest of Ezra Pound, this agitated lifestyle continued within the city itself. Fortunately, one can trace Joyce's residences in Paris because Richard Ellmann, in the second volume of Joyce's letters (1966), thoughtfully provides a list of all Joyce's living places. We have found it pleasant to walk the streets following the family's history, so to speak, and the list below will allow you to do the same. (The gaps in the chronology indicate absences from Paris.)

December 3-22, 1902 - Hôtel Corneille, 5 rue Corneille (6e)
January 23 - April 11, 1903 - Idem
July 8-15, 1920 – 9 rue de l'Université (7e)
July 15 - November 1, 1920 – 5 rue de l'Assomption (16e)
November 1 - December 1, 1920 – 9 rue de l'Université
December 1, 1920- June 3, 1921 - 5 boulevard Raspail (7e)
June 3 - October 1, 1921 - 71 rue du Cardinal Lemoine (5e)
October 1, 1921 - August 12, 1922 - 9 rue de l'Université
September 19 - October 19, 1922 - Idem
November 13, 1922 - June 14, 1923 - 26 avenue Charles Floquet (7e)

307

August 15, 1923 - July 7, 1924 - Victoria Palace Hotel, 6 rue
    Blaise Desgoffe (6e)
August 18 - September 5, 1924 - Idem
October 5-12, 1924 - Idem
October 12, 1924 - May 31, 1925 - 8 avenue Charles Floquet
    (7e)
December 1924 - Clinique des Yeux, 39 rue du Cherche-Midi
    (6e)
February 15-25, 1925 - Idem
June 1, 1925 - April 10, 1931 - 2 square Robiac, 192 rue de
    Grenelle (7e)

During this period Joyce and one or another family member
were away from Paris on approximately 20 occasions.

April 11-19, 1931 - Hôtel Powers, 52 rue François Premier (8e)
September - October 14, 1931 - La Résidence, 41 avenue Pierre
    Premier de Serbie (8e)
October 14, 1931 - June 1932 - 2 avenue St. Philibert (Passy)
April 20 - May 1932 - Hôtel Belmont et de Bassano, 28-30 rue
    de Bassano (8e)
October 20 - November 28, 1932 - Hôtel Lord Byron, (8e)
November 28, 1932 - July 12, 1934 - 42 rue Galilée (8e)
February 1, 1935 - April 15, 1939 - 7 rue Edmond Valentin (7e)

During this period the Joyces absented themselves from Paris
approximately eleven times.

April 15 - August 1939 - 34 rue des Vignes (16e)
October 15 - December 23, 1939 - Hôtel Lutétia, 43 boulevard
    Raspail (6)

On December 24, 1939 the Joyce family, minus Lucia
who remained in an asylum elsewhere in France, moved
from Paris in the panic of war and never returned.

Biographical Notes and Other Matters

> Paris beamed upon me through
> her open shop windows; the
> Odéon itself seemed to nod
> affably towards me, and the
> white marble queens of the
> Luxembourg ... appeared to
> bow graciously and welcome my
> arrival.
>
> --Alphonse Daudet

Would that all of us might experience such a welcome when coming to Paris. Enough of us apparently do, for we keep returning year after year, bemoaning the fact that we do not live in the city, hoping that someday we might be fortunate enough to do so.

While you are there, remember that, as opposed to government or state museums in Washington DC and the Minnesota Museum of Art in Saint Paul, one pays an entrance fee to pass through the portals of French museums. Always check the days the museums close, otherwise you may be annoyingly disappointed, swell with frustration and snap at your loved ones, not behavior to be recommended on vacation.

I hope the ghost and the estate of Irving Berlin will forgive my tampering with the exact lyrics of his lovely song "Marie" (copyright 1928).

I am aware that Rick's statement to Ilse about the duration of Paris in their memories may not be precisely, that is to say entirely accurate, but accuracy to the contrary not withstanding, I prefer that he have said it this way because the line scans better so.

The source of much of the information on the American community in France at the end of the Ancien Régime and

309

the upheavals that followed is to be found in Yvon Bizardel's well-researched, but inadequately dated *The First Expatriates. Americans in Paris during the French Revolution* (1975). The translation from the French reads smoothly, which is certainly an advantage, and Bizardel sprinkles a sufficient amount of gossip throughout the text to make it palatable even for those who depended upon Cliff-Notes to get through Western Civ.

Now, about this Gouverneur Morris fellow (see pp. 118 and 126, above), what should one say? Something brief, no doubt: perhaps best known for his amatory adventures in Paris, he represented the fledgling American government with more success than he represented Americans suffering the slings and arrows of outraged French fortune. This randy, but conservative American businessman-diplomat lost one of his legs at some point and wore a wooden prosthesis, which, given his elegant dress and haughty demeanor, made him an easily recognizable figure in the streets and drawing rooms of Paris. He successfully seduced and became the "unofficial" lover of Adédaïde, Madame de Flahaut, whose "official" lover was the clubfooted but nimble survivor of very different political regimes and social systems, Tallyrand, bishop of Autun. The fact that both men suffered what might be considered by some as podiatric defects is a matter for speculation vis à vis Madame de Flahaut's private amusements, but not of course here. Morris ended his days among the landed gentry of Upstate New York, where at the age of 57 he married, sired a son to carry on the name, and took up gentleman farming. His great-granddaughter, Beatrice Cary Davenport, edited and published his truly uninhibited diary in 1932 entitled *A Diary of the French Revolution*, a perusal of which will amuse as well as edify.

The reason Hemingway's name appears so often in these pages may be explained as follows: few major writers have written in English as beautifully or as much, if

310

mendaciously, about Paris; few writers have had as much written about them and their relationship to the city. (It will be salutary for anyone fascinated by Hemingway's prose on Paris to remember Chester Himes' warning about "all that untrue crap Hemingway wrote about Paris...") At least three books in English alone are devoted to "Hemingway's Paris" or "Walks through Hem's Paris" and countless others about the city mention Hem in Paris. In addition to which we have the proliferating numbers of Hemingway biographies and novels in which he is the main character, which in total devote thousands of pages to his Paris years. Avoid the novels, but dip into Michael Reynold's *Hemingway: The Paris Years* (1989). Read the Hemingway letters and his novel *The Sun Also Rises* (a.k.a *Fiesta*) for the writer's original reactions to the city. Even "The Snows of Kilimanjaro," written in the late 1930s, is overlaid with the mist of nostalgia for a simpler, younger era. Speaking of *A Moveable Feast*, George Wickes avers in his book about Americans in Paris that for the writer of fiction reality is raw material to be reworked, not recorded. "Verisimilitude is his test, not veracity." Well, that is one way of looking at it.

The best of the "walkers," by the way, is Noël Riley Fitch's *Hemingway in Paris: Parisian Walks for the Literary Traveller* (London, 1989) and published in 1992 in the USA as *Walks in Hemingway's Paris*. Ms Fitch is also the author of *Sylvia Beach and the Lost Generation: A History of Literary Paris in the Twenties and Thirties* 1983), which I recommend to all who are interested in the subject, despite the cumbersome, academic and mythicizing title.

Perhaps the strangest book, and thus one of the more interesting, about Hemingway was created by Dick Matena as a French language "adult" bande dessinée (comic book) in hard covers entitled *Sartre & Hemingway* (1993, the ampersand is in the title). It tells a lengthy complicated story about a maid named Ève in the young Sartre's parental home, where of course she seduces the overly intellectual thirteen year-old prodigy. Later she becomes a hooker in Paris. In 1924, the young boxer manqué Hemingway provisionally saves her from a suicide death motivated by the brutal treatment she receives at the hands of her vicious cigarette smoking greaseball pimp. Hemingway insists they go for a drink to a café-bar, the same one in which her pimp hangs out. Hem knocks the pimp about after the latter punches Ève in the face, but a thug bashes the hard American head with a chair from behind and they toss him into an alley. With leather straps the pimp beats the naked Ève to a bloody pulp. The now somewhat older Sartre, at this point an overly intellectual student prodigy in plus-fours, finds the would-be boxer moaning and offers him a drink to dull the pain. Then they begin the adventures that make up the bulk of the book, all of which in some way involve the misfortunes of Ève.

All the usual suspects appear: where Sartre is can de Beauvoir be far way? Scott and Zelda, the latter of whom causes a mini-riot by making pipi in public; Ezra Pound; Miss Stein and Miss Toklas; James Joyce; Salvador Dali (whom Hemingway tosses out of the Stein-Toklas apartment because the deranged Spaniard smashed the salad on the wall calling it art, and punched Joyce in the bargain!); and Picasso, all appear and act out both the fictional storyline and the mythical stories that have grown like moss encrusting the people and the times. The story of Ève ends very badly at the liberation of Paris in 1944 ... but, I will not spoil the experience by telling you how it all turns out. This comic book is definitely not for children.

For those who either remain children past the time for that innocent age, or who in fact are still in that age, I heartily recommend Tomie dePaola's book called *Bonjour, Mr. Satie* (1991), which tells about the Parisian adventures of "Mr. Satie, world traveler - and his companion,

Ffortusque Ffollet, Esq." (a rather humanoid cat and mouse odd couple), who regale Mr. Satie's American niece and nephew with stories of their adventures among their friends Gertrude and Alice, Pablo and Henri (Matisse), Sylvia, Ernest, Ezra, Mr. Joyce, Scott and Zelda, and all the rest. Experience has shown this volume to be a fine aid in teaching three-year olds like Lynn-Marie's goddaughter, Nina Vore, about art, literature and the ability of some non-human animals to readily and unobtrusively mix socially with human animals, at least in Paris, France.

For those more obsessively interested especially in the American-British expatriate experience, Arlen Hansen's *Expatriate Paris. A Cultural and Literary Guide to Paris of the 1920s* (1990), has a full, if not exhaustive, bibliography, which contains a number of references to Hemingway, but Hansen does not inquire about the odd fact of Hem's influence over the way so many view the city and the attention paid to his life there. Hansen's text is, alas, not completely reliable, but it is a good read.

The Hemingway business is a curious phenomenon in light of the fact that other foreign writers and artists lived longer in Paris; a book on Ford Madox Ford's Paris, however, does not exist (even he himself didn't write one and he wrote about everything else!), or James Jones', or Eugene Jolas' (although Yale University Press finally published a heavily edited version of his memoirs, *The Man from Babel* in 1998 long after his death in 1952) or Harold Stearns' (although he wrote of his exhilarating and often depressing years in Paris in *Confessions of a Harvard Man,* published by Paget Press in 1984, long after his death in 1943). Gisèle Freund published a book entitled *James Joyce in Paris: His Final Years* (1965) and Stuart Gilbert's diary of his early life in Paris appeared in 1993 as *Reflections on James Joyce. Stuart Gilbert's Paris Journal* long after his death in 1969. On the other hand, Howard C. Rice, Jr. wrote a fine and entertaining book entitled *Thomas*

Jefferson's Paris (1976), which will repay your attention to it.

Henry Miller wrote a number of books and stories with Paris as the setting, including the scabrous *Quiet Days in Clichy* and the liberating *Tropic of Cancer.* Do not waste your money on the expensive glorified pamphlet by Robert Cross, entitled *Henry Miller. The Paris Years* (1991), essentially an amateur's compilation of chunks of text from Miller, Durrell, Alfred Perlès, Michael Frankel, and a few others, but not Anaïs Nin, which is curious given the amount she wrote about her love affair with Miller in Paris. Read the writers' own books. Miller's letters to his childhood friend, Emil Schnellock, entitled naturally *Letters to Emil* (1989), contain his most rapturous yet simultaneously realistic descriptions of the city.

The essay Miller wrote about his friend, the artist Beauford Delaney, appears in the collection of Miller's fugitive pieces entitled *Remember to Remember* (1947), not in *The Air-Conditioned Nightmare* (1945), as the book *Against All Odds* has it. It is indeed unfortunate that this latter volume contains so many errors; the artists in the book deserve more studious and attentive research.

If you wish to see what many people mentioned in this book actually looked like, definitely do not avoid Billy Klüver and Julie Martin's coffee table production entitled *Kiki's Paris. Artists and Lovers 1900-1930* (1989). The fabulous Kiki, née Alice Prin, is the crux around which the authors construct a history of Montparnasse during the first 30 years of the century. If you are at all interested in art, literature and gossip in Paris during this period, you must browse your way through this intoxicating volume, which contains not only photographs of people, but also street scenes, maps, memorabilia, old menus, art works, *and* an incredible Man Ray photograph of the incredible nude Meret Oppenheim, a German-Swiss artist whose presence makes one grateful for the invention of the photograph

314

camera. Indeed, most of the volumes of Man Ray's photographs contain one or more of his Oppenheim images made in the mid-1930s, but she is perhaps most remembered today for the fur-covered cup and saucer purchased by the Museum of Modern Art (New York City) in 1936. Born in Berlin in 1913, she spent most of her youth in Switzerland, moved to Paris at the age of 18 to study at the Académie de la Grande Chaumière, which she soon left to work on her own, she exhibited with the Surrealists from 1933 to 1937 and continued to work throughout her life making bizarre objects, finally, beginning in the early 1960s, enjoying one-woman exhibitions, prizes, and fame in Europe. A number of books containing her writings and sketches, as well as several volumes about her work, have been published since 1970. Meret Oppenheim died in Basel in 1985.

Curiously, the American-French-British memoirs of the period just after the end of the first half of The Great 20th Century Agony only rarely mention what Nicolas Slonimsky, in his pungent memoir *Perfect Pitch* (1988), calls "an invasion of the city by Russian émigrés" of "astronomical proportions." One might in this regard profitably read Simone Signoret's novel, *Adieu, Volodia* (1985) for a fascinating account of émigré Russian-Jewish families living in Paris over a good part of the century.

For the post-1945 period of English language speakers living in Paris, the interested reader should consult Christopher Sawyer-Lauçanno's *The Continual Pilgrimage. American Writers in Paris 1944-1960* (1992), in which a photograph of George Whitman, Richard Wright and Peter Mattiessen appears indicating Mr. Whitman's role as cultural liaison among the generations; William Styron's *This Quiet Dust and Other Writings* (1982); "The *Paris Review* Sketchbook" in *The Paris Review*, 79 (1981); and Sylvia Beach Whitman's pamphlet to raise funds to repair her father's burned second floor library, *Shakespeare &*

Company. Biography of a Bookstore in Pictures and Poems (n.d.). The memoirs by and biographies of the participants may also be of interest.

There are, of course, a number of books about the city by French Parisians. One of these is the classic Jacques Hillairet (pseudonym of Jacques Coussillan), *Dictionnaire historique des Rues de Paris*, 2 vols. (1963, 1985), which is indispensible if you are a true aficionado of the city. For those interested in a shorter version of the biographies of Parisian street names, see Bernard Stéphane's *Dictionnaire des noms de rues* (1988 edition), which I have found to be most helpful and entertaining.

The *Guide Littéraire de la France - Paris et sa proche banlieue* published in 1963 by Hachette is worth the money, if you can find it. We searched all over Paris and other French cities for this book; in no store did anyone know anything about it. Clearly long out of print, the total ignorance of it on the part of the French book trade nonetheless surprised us. One evening, whilst checking a reference in Karl Voss's *Reiseführer für Literaturfreunde: Paris*, published by Verlag Ullstein in 1975, a work I've owned and used for years, I noticed in the publication data that this marvelously knowledgeable compilation of literary addresses is, in fact, a translation and revision of the *Guide Littéraire*! I'd never noticed this previously.

In any case, do *not* buy or bother to read the book on "walks" in Gertrude Stein's Paris, not a paragraph of which is free of errors and unaccountable inaccuracies. Gertrude Stein herself wrote a book entitled *Paris France* (1940), but the work is really more about Gertrude Stein and her painter friends than about the city.

If you locate a copy of Léon-Paul Fargue's *Le Piéton de Paris* (1932), consider yourself lucky and read it with enjoyment. In lieu of that volume, which apparently has never been translated into English, try to find a copy of André Beucler's *The Last of the Bohemians. Twenty Years with Léon-Paul Fargue* (1954), which comes with a laudatory introduction by Archibald MacLeish, who notes that Fargue was never the *last* of anything and he certainly was *not* a bohemian, though invariably late for his appointments. Indeed, MacLeish makes beauty out of description when he writes that Fargue "lived into old age with his memories, but his active life was spent at the forefoot of the glacier where the ancient ice turns into green water and the future begins." Which may not make much sense, but is lovely.

Beucler gets a couple of things wrong, such as Adrienne Monnier's bookshop name, and might, in a more cynical time, be accused of inventing dialogue, but his book does offer a taste of what it must have been like to know and have been befriended by the super-garrulous Fargue. And Beucler does give us various statements that Fargue published in books now hard to find (not that Beucler's book is easy to locate!), such as this one:

> These [quotidian events and typical people] are the favors Paris has in store for those who go on foot and who wish to warm themselves in the folds of the quartiers. If these humble images were supressed, leaving us only our monuments, what a loss it would be to our senses and our illusions.

For those who read French, Jean-Paul Goujon published a fine biography of Fargue in 1997.

The intersection of the Boulevard du Montparnasse and the Rue de Sèvres, site of the Café François Coppée, a large bistro which served as Fargue's last Stammlokal, over which he had his last apartment, is named Place Léon-Paul Fargue. A badly eroded plaque on the wall of 1 Boulevard du Montparnasse reads:

ICI MOURUT
LE 24 NOVEMBRE 1947

317

LÉON-PAUL FARGUE
POÉT ET PIÉTON DE PARIS

And speaking of public plaques and naming streets to honor cultural figures, some readers may think I have been unfairly severe on American society for not so honoring its bearers of the torch of high culture in comparision to the French. Rest assured this is not the case at all. To put an even finer point on the épée, there follows a list of writers, painters and musicians for whom the French have named public places in Paris *only between 1982 and 1989*. The list does *not* include those in other professions (such as actors, physicians, explorers, and so on) who have been thus honored during this time.

Albert Camus
Albert Marquet
André Derain
Aristide Maillol
Blaise Cendrars
Charles Tournemire
Edgar Varése
Francis Jammes
Georges Brassens
Henri Matisse
Henri de Montherlant
Jean Cocteau
Jongkind (J. B.)
Lautréamont
L. N. Clérambault
Marc-Antoine Charpentier
Marcel Aymé
Maurice Denis
Pablo Picasso
Paul Eluard
Paul Léautaud
Pierre Bonnard
Pierre-Jean Jouve

Albert Londres
André Breton
André Gide
Bernard de Ventadour
Boy Zelensky
Christine de Pisan
Federico Garcia Lorca
Francis Picabia
G. F. Haendel
Henri Tomasi
Jacques Prévert
Jean Paulhan
Jules Supervielle
Louis Aragon
Louis Vierne
Marcel Achard
Marie Laurencin
Pablo Casals
P. de la Tour du Pin
Paul-Jean Toulet
Paul Paray
Pierre Emmanuel
Pierre MacOrlan

Pierre Reverdy
Raymond Queneau
Robert Desnos
Saint John-Perse
Simone Weil
Tristan Tzara
Vincent Scotto

Piet Mondrian
Rémi Belleau
Roger Bissière
Serge Prokofiev
Tino Rossi
Victor Ségalen

The fact that Walt Whitman has a toilet with a cafeteria attached to it named for him on the New Jersey Turnpike speaks volumes.

Washington DC has a park named for Lafayette, and a sterile conglomerate of inhumanly proportioned fascist buildings and space with subway station called L'Enfant Plaza. The French have named Parisian public thoroughfares for the Americans Woodrow Wilson, Benjamin Franklin, the poet Stuart Merrill, Franklin Delano Roosevelt, the physiologist Brown-Sequard (whose father was American), George Eastman, Edgar Allan Poe, Thomas Edison, Dwight D. Eisenhower, George Washington, the inventor Robert Fulton, Myron T. Herrick (Ambassador to France), John F. Kennedy, Abraham Lincoln, Avenue de New York (City), and Edward Tuck (1842-1938, according to the *Dictionnaire des noms de Rues* a "philanthropist and collector").

One more example should put the last nail in the coffin, so to speak. The French city of Pau, situated in the Pyrenees near the Spanish border, with a population of 82,157 (144,874 if we include the environs) according to the 1996 *Guide Michelin*, has streets named after 84 poets, artists, novelists, composers, and other cultural figures, including Duke Ellington and the Wright brothers!

* * * *

Nonetheless, I must admit, too much reading about earlier decades of life in Paris can be positively off-putting.

319

When one sees the level of prices in former times, so far removed from the present astronomical heights, despite a decent exchange rate, when one sees the charming antebellum-era cityscape knowing one will be emotionally and aesthetically slammed about by today's architectural monstrosities, then the pleasantly soggy sentimental yearning for the past quickly degenerates into a bilious packet of frustrated desire for that which is beyond one's reach or recall. Best not read too much before you go.

There are also large numbers of picture books about Paris, most of which are trashy clichés, and one should approach even the good ones with caution. Falling under the spell of other people's images of this protean city, like developing an unshakeable taste for vanilla fudge icecream laced with amaretto, is a risk one takes in depending upon other's visions before forming one's own firsthand. The risk increases geometrically when one moves from texts (Émile Zola, Henry James, Eugène Sue, Louis Aragon, Henry Miller, H. L. Humes, et alia) and paintings (which are endless in number, but think of Pissarro, Manet, Caillebotte and the Impressionists as a start) to photographic images (Eugène Atget, Brassaï, Robert Frank, Robert Doisneau, Sanford Roth, Izis Bidermanas, Roger Schall, all the Ronny Jacques, and grandmother's snapshots from her 1923 trip with her Radcliff friends during which, they were convinced, they saw McAlmon buying a glass of Fendent de Sion for Joyce on the terrace of the Rotonde), and movies, because the latter two genre make no demands to stretch one's imagination. In short, one no longer has to *think* to see, one only has to look - and these are two very different categories of perception. Too much is made too easy these days: photography, television, videotape, all these "educational tools" have resulted not only in less learning, but the atrophy of the younger generations' visual capacities: those born after 1950 can no longer see, it is too strenuous and requires too much mental effort for which these people are not trained, to which they are not habituated; they can only *look* at things, and little of what they look at makes any impression unless it screams in bright simple neon technicolors and lasts less than thirty seconds.

However, books of photographs, usually accompanied by some text, often witty as well as useful when a writer of talent has penned it, are worth your attention. Those particularly deserving of your time include the André Maurois/Nico Jesse collaboration, *The Women of Paris* (1954), Maurois' text for which is so typically French one wonders about the translation, and the photographs for which, while cleverly done and in some cases striking, too often contain stereotypical subject matter obviously artificially posed, and it is always Spring in Paris, no rain, no snow, no bulky overcoats and rubber galoshes.... Nevertheless, it does enclose between its covers the photograph of the most beautiful woman in the world.

On some bleak, damp, cold late autumn afternoon, preferably a Saturday about four o'clock, if your local library is open at this hour, escape the droning wasteland of the present for a hour or so, and immerse your mind and heart in the comfy warmth of a sepia-toned past time you will never experience directly, even with your head in a "virtual reality" tureen. Ask the librarian for the four volumes entitled *The Work of Atget* (1981) and disappear into a world that, if it did not exist exactly as Atget shows it, deserves to; and in any case, you will do yourself no harm and much good by believing it did. Eugène Atget, who died in 1927, spent half his long life photographing Paris and its environs. Saved from destruction by the selfless efforts of Berenice Abbott and preserved by Miss Abbott and Julian Levy, the Museum of Modern Art purchased the collection in 1968 and supported the project to print this large beautifully reproduced selection from the collection. Miss Abbott apprenticed with Man Ray in his

321

Montparnasse studio and became a fine maker of photographs herself. Anyone who does not know her work is incompletely educated.

GLOSSARY

Abbott, Berenice (1898 Springfield, Ohio - 1991 Monson, Maine). A great American photographer and a savior of Eugène Atget's life's work.

Ace, Johnny (né Johnny Marshall Alexander, Jr. 1929 Memphis Tennessee - 1954 Houston, Texas). The exemplar of the 1950s Denver proverb: "Live fast, die young, and have a goodlooking corpse," who also had an exquisitely fine baritone for those finely toned slowdrag ballads, such as "Pledging My Love," he sang so well; killed himself accidentally whilst playing Russian roulette backstage at the City Auditorium in Houston, and never knew "Pledging My Love" became a "top hit" in 1955.

Adams, Henry Brooks (1838 Boston - 1918 Washington DC). A rather morbid American intellectual with a well-known education.

Ahlers-Hestermann, Friedrich (1883 Hamburg, Germany - 1973 Berlin). German painter in Paris before 1914; the nazis fired him from the faculty at the Cologne School of Painting; spent the years 1938-45 in Berlin.

Albers, Hans (1892 Hamburg - 1960 Munich, Germany). With golden hair, startling blue eyes, overflowing with self-assurance, he made more than 100 silent films, played secondary roles in the 1920s including in *The Blue Angel* (1929), his career fully blossomed between 1933 and 1945, where after he developed his public role as an apolitical artiste-naïf; his enthusiastic rendition of "Goodbye, Johnny" in the curious film *Wasser für Canitoga* (1939) thrills some people to this day.

Aldington, Richard (1892 Portsea, England - 1962 Sury-en-Vaux, France). Imagist poet, novelist (*Death of a Hero* [1929], *All Men Are Enemies* [1933]) and biographer of Wellington, D.H. Lawrence and, fatefully, T. E. Lawrence (*Lawrence of Arabia* [1955]) which so disturbed the British establishment that his books went out of print there; lived most of his adult life in France.

Algren, Nelson (né Nelson Algren Abraham 1909 Detroit, Michigan - 1981 Sag Harbor, New York). American writer who remained for decades enraged at a former lover who wrote about their affair; author of *The Man With the Golden Arm* (1949) and an interesting book called *America Eats* (published in 1992 based on materials he gathered working for the Illinois Writers Project in the 1930s).

Antheil, George (1900 Trenton, New Jersey - 1959 New York City). The self-styled "bad boy of music," his career as a pianist and composer began with a blaze of noise and publicity in the early 1920s in Paris, when the addition of such untraditional instruments and airplane propellers (in "Airplane Sonata") and typewriters to the orchestra appeared to some in the audiences as worth fighting about then and there; later wrote film scores in Hollywood and wrote several books to support his writing serious music.

Antonioni, Michelangelo (b. 1912 Ferrara, Italy). The creator of disturbing "novelistic" films who became so enamored of the Hollywood "style" that his last feature films lost their center and did not hold, which did not stop the Hollywood academy in 1995 from giving the speechless Italian an award for "lifetime" achievement.

Apollinaire, Guillaume (né Wilhelm Apollinaris de Kostrowitzky 1880 Rome - 1918 Paris). A much better poet that an art critic, though his publicity for the cubist works of Braque and Picasso proved important in putting the genre over (Georges Braque said Apollinaire "couldn't tell the difference between a Raphael and a Rubens"); a good friend of the lovely Max Jacob; a major participant in The Great 1908 Rousseau Honor Banquet held in Picasso's studio.

Aragon, Louis (né Louis Andrieux 1897 Neuilly-sur-Seine, Paris - 1982 Paris). A one-time Surrealist writer of considerable talent who allowed political ideology to corrode his credibility and censor his work; a French Stalinist, but also a resistant (after June 1941); his long love affair and marriage with the equally Stalinist Elsa Triolet is so well known that even *Paris-Match* took note of it, his city-book *Le Paysan de Paris* (1926; translated into English as *The Nightwalker* [1970], and again in 1994 more accurately as *Paris Peasant*), written before his political commitment, is a highly idiosyncratic exploration and evocation of the city and his mind; at the southern end of métro line number seven is a station now called "Villejuif - Louis Aragon," a singular honor perhaps explained by the fact that this is a working class part of greater Paris which consistently votes for the Communist Party and already had a station called "Le Kremlin-Bicêtre" on the same line.

Arland, Marcel (1899 Varennes-sur-Amance, France - 1986 Brinville, near Fontainebleau, France). Teacher, novelist and editor at the *Nouvelle Revue Française*, his works are noted for their attachment to and insights into his native region's people and culture; snuggled just a little too closely to the occupation authorities as he continued to write and publish during 1940-44; but who also served in the late 1920s as a second to an editor friend who challenged André Breton to a duel: Breton preferred words to armaments.

Asch, Sholem (1880 Kutno, Poland - 1957 London). Author who immigrated to the USA in 1914, but who wrote mostly in Yiddish, including a novel about Jesus of Nazareth called *The Nazarine* (1939).

Atget, Eugène (1850 - 1927 Paris). When Man Ray tried to teach him to use a Rolleiflex to make his work easier, he tried it and told the younger man, "Trop vite, enfin": "le snapshot" moved faster than he could think, he said, and he remained with his primitive equipment as he haunted the early morning streets of the city.

Auric, Georges (1899 Lodève, Hérault, France - 1983 Paris). Composer; child prodigy, who wrote prodigiously in various genres including music for the theater and movies; one of Les Six.

Aymé, Marcel (1902 Joigny, France - 1967 Paris). Writer of sophisticated, witty and satirical stories and novels, children's books and plays, who wrote for the collaborationist newspapers and journals and who began the postwar revisionist trend of exculpating the collabos and portraying the Résistants as brutes and thugs in a novel called *Uranus* (1948), later made into a movie with Gérard Depardieu.

Baker, Joséphine (1906 Saint Louis, Missouri - 1975 Paris). Led of a very complicated life and could shimmy better than your sister Kate.

Bald, Wambly (b. 1902 Chicago, Illinois). Chronicler of English-speaking Montparnasse life in the *Chicago Tribune (Paris Edition)* and its successor, the *New York Herald (Paris Edition)* column "La Vie de Bohème (As Lived on the Left Bank)" 1929-33, though officially he was a proofreader; contributor to Samuel Putnam's *New Review* and other expatriate "little magazines"; friend of Alfred Perlès and Henry Miller, in whose *Tropic of Cancer* he appears as Van Norden, after whom young Lawrence Durrell named his sailboat on Corfu.

Baldwin, James (1924 Harlem, New York City - 1987 Saint-Paul de Vence, France). American writer and civil rights activist who lived many years in Paris.

Balzac, Honoré de (1799 Tours, France - 1850 Paris). Novelist, debtor and consumer of vast amounts of coffee.

Bal Nègre, Le. Bar and dance hall formerly at 48, rue Blomet (15th), frequented by black workers from the French colonies, white artists and intellectuals found it during the craze for everything Negro during the 1920s when the place became trés chic; scene of the 1928 Bal Ubu costume party.

Barnes, Djuna (1892 Cornwall-on-Hudson, New York - 1982 New York City). Exquisite writer whose life followed the now classic, but essentially mythic trajectory of the so-called 1920s generation of American writers: small town origins, Greenwich Village cauldron of avant-garde culture, Paris "exile," and return to the native soil to popular success or neglect; Miss Barnes, alas, experienced the latter.

Barrault, Jean-Louis (1910 Vésinet, Paris - 1995 Paris). Stage and screen actor perhaps best known in the USA for his portrayal of the mime in *The Children of the Paradise* (1944-45); the history of post-1945 French theater is unthinkable without him.

Basler, Adolphe (1876 Tarnow, Poland - 1951 Paris). Now forgotten Polish writer on modern art who spent 20 years in Montparnasse, but did not quite get it and sadly soured on it, but nonetheless wrote a number of works on it (those he wrote in German might be in fairness credited in part to Rudolf Levy).

Bastien-Lepage, Jules (1848 Damvillers, France – 1884 Paris). A painter who took the established Salon techniques and styles out into the open air and, thus attempted to resolve the conflict between the Impressionists and the older generation; not everyone shared the elder Pissarro's opinion of his work: at his untimely death Jules Breton wrote that "France has lost her Holbein."

Baudelaire, Charles (1821 Paris - 1867 Paris). Decadent poet whose volume *Les Fleurs du mal* (1857) was tried for obscenity; introduced Edgar Allan Poe to the French.

Beauvoir, Simone de (1908 Paris - 1986 Paris). Writer of novels, essays, and autobiographies, and sometime lover of Nelson Algren; reading her letters to him, which she wrote in fluent if idiosyncratic English, is quite a trip: *A Transatlantic Love Affair: Letters to Nelson Algren* (1998).

Bechet, Sidney (1897 New Orleans, Louisiana - 1959 Paris). One of the fine American musicians of the 20th century, in whose honor the French placed a massive sculpture of his head in the park at Juan-les-Pins, and about whom Jean Cocteau wrote that he never repeated himself, "he never blabbered on and on, he spoke, and his talk was always touching and powerful," meaning Bechet's music; lived much of his adult life in Europe, especially in Paris where he became a mighty icon with whom one could nonetheless jam.

Beckett, Samuel (1906 Foxrock, Dublin - 1989 Paris). An Irish writer who wrote much of his work in French; almost affianced to Joyce's unfortunate daughter, Lucia; joined the Resistance, for which the French awarded him two medals, and spent most of the war in hiding and in a serious depression in the South of France; lived most of his adult life in Paris.

Benét, Stephen Vincent (1898 Bethlehem, Pennsylvania - 1943 New York City). Writer of such message-laden works as *John Brown's Body* and *The Devil and Daniel Webster*, and the radio play, "They Burned the Books," performed on the NBC network in 1943 on the 10th anniversary of the nazi book burnings in Germany.

Benjamin, Walter (1892 Berlin - 1940 Portbou, Spain). An occasionally marxist literary critic, essayist, philosopher, translator, and lover of true urbane environments, about whom much nonsense has been written in the last two decades; committed suicide on the Spanish border rather than fall into the slimy and fatal clutches of the Gestapo and its French assistants; the tragedy is, had he lived another 24 hours he probably would have been able to cross the border and use his visa to the USA.

Bernard, Émile (1868 Lille, France - 1941 Paris). Painter who worked with Gauguin and others at the turn of the century whose work became overshadowed by the increasingly popular interest in the man who went to the South Seas and died there among the swaying palms and sensual young females.

Bernhardt, Sarah (née Henriette Rosine Bernhard 1845 Paris - 1923 Paris). *The* French actress of the modern acoustic theater.

Bing, Henri (1888 Paris - 1965 Paris). Painter and art dealer who opened his own gallery in 1925, and who clearly went out of his way to help his less well-off, allowing, for instance, Jules Pascin to stay at his apartment on Rue Lauriston; in 1907, Bing, having been introduced to her by Rudolf Levy, asked Hermine David to bring some of her work to his apartment to see if he might represent her, Pascin opened the door dressed in a kimono and the corset into which her mother had sewn Hermine did not long deter the two, who later married; this Bing is apparently not related to the following Bing.

Bing, Siegfried (1838 Hamburg, Germany - 1905 Paris). Writer on art styles and history; owner of the Salon de l'Art Nouveau and the art dealer responsible for bringing that style to the attention of the rather inattentive French, who seemed not to appreciate it except for subway entrance decoration, although certain French painters fell under its influence and created what we know as art nouveau; a naturalized French citizen, his gallery at 22, rue de Provence on the corner of Rue Chauchat also introduced Japanese art to Van Gogh and others; received the Légion d'Honneur in 1890..

Black Maria. *See* **Panier à salade**

Blanche, Jacques-Émile (1861 Paris - 1942 Auteuil, France). A wealthy society painter who wrote a generous amount of memoirs; known for his portraits.

Bondy, Walter (1883 Prague - 1940 Toulon, France). His father, Otto, moved the family to Vienna shortly after Walter's birth (Otto is perhaps meant by the reference to "the Czech Jew Oscar Bondy" whose art collection the nazis stole, in Lynn Nicholas', *The Rape of Europa. The*

Fate of Europe's Treasures in the Third Reich [New York, 1994] a fascinating book); lived at 205 bis, Boulevard Raspail in 1910 and 3, rue Schoelcher in 1912, two doors from number 5 into which Picasso moved the next year remaining until 1916, which may not appear to be very exciting, but think of the times, then visit the locales!; committed suicide by ceasing to take the insulin his severe diabetes required, rather than let the German and French nazi swine take him.

Bongard, Germaine. Designed clothes, operated her own dressmaking shop, in which she held exhibitions, organized by her lover, Amedée Ozenfant, during the 1914-18 chapter of The Great Twentieth Century Sado-Masochism, the first of which she opened in December 1915 showing Léger, Matisse, Picasso, Kisling and Modigliani; after the belligerents temporarily ceased killing each other, she opened the Gallery Thomas in her house in the Rue de Penthièvre (8th); one wonders what became of her.

Bonheur, Rosa (1822 Bordeaux, France - 1899 Château de By, Fontainebleau, France). A painter who admired the painter Stubbs; crossdressed for comfort and security; first woman elevated to the rank of officer in the Légion d'Honneur.

Bonvin, François (1817 Vaugirard, France - 1887 Saint - Germain-en-Laye, France). A painter who no doubt liked fine wine and studied at the Académie Suisse (apparently misidentified by Milner as "Louis").

Bouguereau, William-Adolphe (1825 La Rochelle, France - 1905 La Rochelle, France). A very successful genre painter, who taught at the Académie Julian and lost money each time he mincturated.

Bowen, Stella (1895 Adelaide, Australia - 1947 London). A fine, if uninspired artist; for many years the companion of Ford Madox Ford, life with whom she did not always enjoy but did not want to do without, though in the end she did; she contributed much, emotionally and materially to Ford and others; spent many years in Paris during the roaring era, when she and Fordy partied with the best and the not so best, and in Provence with and without her companion; wrote about her life in *Drawn from Life* (1940, Virago edition 1984).

Brancusi, Constantine (1876 Pestisani, Romania - 1957 Paris). Sculptor and photographer in the modern but graceful style, whose name is invariably mispronounced by non-Romanians; his "Boy's Head" evokes memories of Augusta Savage's "Gamin," an interesting speculation on a previously unknown influence, if true in either direction.

Braque, Georges (1882 Argenteuil, France - 1963 Paris). A gentle man who actually got on well with the volatile Spaniard for several crucial years during which time they created cubism; Picasso never forgave him for being so talented and wounded in the war.

Brassaï (né Gyula Halasz, 1899 Brasso, Transylvania - 1984 Nice, France). A great walker of Paris nightbeat streets accompanied by his camera and certain friends; author of several memoirs.

Brel, Jacques (1929 Brussels - 1978 Paris). Poet, song writer, actor, singer, film director, his brilliance lit up the cities of the western world; buried in the Atuona cemetery, Hiva Oa, Marquises Islands, a few meters from Gauguin's grave.

Breton, André (1896 Tinchebray-sur-Orne - 1966 Paris). The pope of surrealism, for more about whom, see Mark Polizzotti's massively detailed *Revolution of the Mind: The Life of André Breton* (New York, 1995).

Breton, Jules Adolphe Aimé Louis (1827 Courrières prés Arras - 1906 Paris). A painter who believed, with apparent sincerity, that marriage and a family were dangerous to all concerned when one of the partners was an artist; author of *The Life of an Artist* (London, 1891).

Bricktop (née Ada Smith du Conge or Ada Beatrice Queen Victoria Louise Virginia Smith, 1894 Alderson, West Virginia - 1984 New York City). American redheaded Negro singer who sang in various Montmartre clubs (including Le Grand Duc at 52, rue Pigalle, where Langston Hughes washed dishes and waited tables in 1924 to finance his stay in the city) before opening a popular eponymous nightclub in 1926 probably at 1, rue Fontaine (down the street from André Breton's longtime apartment at 42), where everyone went except Joséphine Baker; she and an assistant wrote her not completely fictional memoirs entitled *Bricktop's* (New York, 1983).

Brunelleschi, Umberto (1879 Monteunerlo near Pistoria, Italy - 1949 Paris). After leaving his natal land he became quite well known for his illustrations in magazines and books in the new art style; also designed costumes and sets for the theater.

Buñuel, Luis (1900 Calanda, Teruel, Spain - 1983 Mexico City). Filmmaker; creator of some of the most horrifyingly beautiful images in world cinema; a deadpan jokester of great stature.

333

Butts, Mary (1890 Salterus, Dorset, England - 1937 Sennen, Cornwall, England). Roisterous English expatriate novelist with hair, according to McAlmon, "which looked as though it had been soaked in red ink"; his Contact Editions published her *Ashe of Rings* in the early 1920s; part-time resident of the Hôtel Foyot; a stormy petrel, she never stayed in place for very long and seems to have been everywhere during the 1920s including a sojourn at the black magic temple on Celafu; her writings achieved something of a renaissance in the 1990s.

Caillebotte, Gustav (1848 Paris - 1894 Gennevilliers, France). Painter at one time known for his donation of Impressionist painting to the French state, but now known for his large painting of a rainy Paris intersection (in the Chicago Art Institute), underwent a revival with major retrospectives in Paris and Chicago in 1994-95.

Calvino, Italo (1923 Santiago de Las Vegas, Cuba - 1985 Rome). A writer of exquisite sentences of metaphysical and moral weight, but whose stories are also very funny on occasion, especially when the translation is good if one cannot read the original Italian.

Camus, Albert (1913 Algiers, Algeria - 1960 on the road near Petit-Villeblevin, France). A writer who exemplifies the French tradition of men of letters who write novels, essays, journalism, plays, criticism, short stories and philosophy who deserve the sobriquet "intellectual," as his death deserves the descriptor "absurd"; his tombstone in the Lourmarin cemetery needs refurbishing.

Carco, Francis (né Francis Carcopino-Tusoli, 1886 Nouméa - 1958 Paris). Poet, journalist, novelist; incredibly prolific and perceptive writer of memoirs (rivaling André Salmon, who entitled his *Memoirs sans fin*) and other works about the underworld milieu of La Bohème (alcoholism, prostitution, violence, disillusionment) out of which some art and much human wreckage emerged, such as *Jésus-la-caille* (1914) and *Brumes*.... (1935); his collected memoirs, in which he analyses the connections between the criminal and artist elements in Montmartre, are called *Memoirs d'une autre vie* (Geneva, 1943).

Carné, Marcel (1909 Paris – 1996 Clamart, France). One of the finest practitioners of the "poetic realism" style of cinema mise-en-scène, certain of his films will always be in anyone's list of the Best Twenty.

Carolus-Duran, Émile-Auguste (properly Charles-Auguste-Émile Durand 1837 Lille, France - 1917 Paris). Formerly well known French painter with too many dashes in his name.

Cézanne, Paul (1839 Aix-en-Provence - 1906 Aix-en-Provence). The originator of 20th century modern painting who hated Paris and loved rural Provence.

Chagall, Marc (né Moyshe Shagal 1887 Vitebsk, Russia - 1985 Saint-Paul-de-Vence, France). If you like floating fiddlers and the color blue, you'll like this painter.

Chamberlin, Dean (b. 1949 Hempstead, New York). Author's brother, a good companion in Paris, or elsewhere, but a severe literary critic.

Chambers, Robert W. (1865 Brooklyn, New York - 1933 New York City). Prolific and forgotten American writer-illustrator enraptured with Paris before The Turn of the Century.

Chapu, Henri (1833 - 1891 Paris). Yet another sculptor for a while en mode with a studio on the Rue Nôtre-Dame-des-Champs; commissioned to create a memorial to Balzac, fortunately he died before he could implement his maquette and Rodin got the commission by default.

Char, René (1907 L'ile sur la Sorgue, France - 1988 Paris). A Surrealist-influenced poet in his early years; a friend of Paul Eluard; his later poetry became increasingly dense and incomprehensible (called "hermetic" in the lit-crit trade), but he lived most of his life in a beautiful town blessed with canals and a fantastic Sunday market in the Vaucluse.

Chevalier, Maurice (1888 Paris - 1972 Paris). By 1908 this song and dance man of tremendous talent had come up from the streets to play the Folies Bergère with Mistenquett, from where he went on to a career whose success in France and the United States is unparalleled to this day, though Yves Montand came close, the difference being that the latter was an intelligent man and the former was not, though both remained epitomes of professionalism, which is how Chevalier explained his entertaining the Germans during the occupation.

Claudel, Camille (1864 Villeneuve-sur-Fère, Aisne, France - 1943 Montfavet, Vaucluse, France). Brilliant sculptor, unfortunate woman.

Cocteau, Jean (1889 Maisons-Lafitte, France - 1963 Paris). Protean cultural personality whose incessant dabbling produced several lasting works in a several media; has a museum in Menton on the Mediterranean Sea near the Italian border, which is worth a visit if you are near the town, and his color drawings decorate the Menton town hall marriage room, not really worth a visit unless you are already in town; took the famous photographs of the Famous August 1916 Photography Session.

Colette, Sidonie Gabrielle (1873 Saint-Sauveur, France - 1954 Paris). Led a very avant-garde, not to say unconventional life; wrote "light" novels and stories such as *Gigi*, *Chéri* and the Claudine series; her first rather domineering husband edited her early stories and published them under his own name; later in life she became a frizzy-haired litry monument who remained in bed with cats and jewels.

Comte, Auguste (1798 Montpellier, France - 1857 Paris). A misanthropic genius of sorts who insisted he really have died before being buried, who devised the positivist theory of the study of human behavior and who, it is said, loved mankind but abhorred humans as individuals.

Cottet, Charles (1863 Le Puy, Haute-Loire, France - 1925 Paris). A painter inspired by Gauguin and Puvis de Chavannes; painted mainly in Brittany; Jacques-Émile Blanche painted his portrait.

Craig, Edward Henry Gordon (1872 Harpenden, England - 1966 Vence, France). The son of Ellen Terry and Edward Godwin who founded a theatrical school at the Arena Goldoni in Florence, Italy, and whose theater archives Hitler wanted for his own, and who is alleged to once have said, "The thing I want most at present is a complete collection of the records by Ethel Waters," which, since he allegedly said this in the late 1920s, shows a prescient appreciation for an unfortunately forgotten, marvelously inventive voice.

Crosby, Caresse (1892 New York City - 1970 Rome). Sometime publisher and owner of The Black Sun Press with her husband, Harry (1898 Boston, Massachusetts - 1929 New York City), who ran off with a younger woman with whom he ended in a midtown Manhattan hotel room where he shot her in the head before killing himself; author of an unreliable memoir of the period.

Cullen, Countée (1903 New York City - 1946 New York City). American Negro poet who wrote about black life in America, whose books include *The Ballad of the Brown Girl* and *The Black Christ*; when in Paris he hung out with a group that included Hale Woodruff and Palmer Hayden, whose Paris social headquarters was Augusta Savage's studio.

Cunard, Nancy (1896 Leicestershire - 1965 Paris). Owner of The Hours Press, wearer of large baubles, who died an unnecessarily lonely death.

Dardel, Nils (1888 Bettna, Sweden - 1943 New York City). After studying at the Stockholm academy in 1909-10, moved to Paris where he fell under the influence of Matisse, Cézanne, the Japanese and the naive painters (whether sequentially or simultaneously is not clear from the sources); often chose (according to one source) "bizarre" themes to paint.

Dardel, Thora (née Klinkowström, 1899 Strafsund, Sweden - 1995) Swedish sometime sculpture student at the Académie Colarossi who posed for one of Modigliani's last paintings, married for the first time to the Swedish painter Nils Dardel, and worked as a journalist in Paris for Swedish newspapers and magazines during the 1920s.

David, Hermine (1886 Paris - 1971 Paris). Student at the Académie Julian; painter with a great deal of patience; long-term lover, wife and widow of Jules Pascin.

338

David, Louis (1748 Paris - 1825 Brussels). The painter who created the two images by which we bets know Emperor Napoléon I; his support of the Emperor's return in 1815 cost the painter his residence in France.

Davidson, Jo (1883 New York City - 1952 Bercheron, France) American sculptor and memoirist who had to demolish his largest work for the usual reason.

Delacroix, Eugène (1798 Charenton-Saint-Maurice, France - 1863 Paris). The painter with a heavy responsibility for bringing "orientalisme" in deep bright colors to French art, who painted the symbol of Liberté as a half-naked harridan striding flag in hand over a pile of corpses.

Delaney, Beauford (1901 Knoxville, Tennessee - 1977 Paris). A marvelous American painter, plagued with great visions and menacing voices, who did not live to enjoy his current success and renown. See David Leeming's biography, *Amazing Grace: A Life of Beauford Delaney* (1998).

Denis, Maurice (1870 Granville, France - 1943 Saint-Germaine-en-Laye, France). Student at the Académie Julian; one of the founders of the Nabis group; wrote the first Nabis manifesto, "Définition du Néo-Traditionnisme" (1890), which included the bald statement "A painting, before it is a war-horse, a naked woman or an anecdote of some kind, is essentially a plane surface covered with colors assembled in a certain order"; not surprisingly, this painter wrote a number of books of art criticism.

Depardieu, Gérard (b. 1948 Chateauroux, France). Ubiquitous actor and vintner, currently en mode.

Derain, André (1880 Chaton, France - 1954 Garches [some sources say Chambourcy], France). Considered by some in the late 1920s to be one of the main practitioners of "the French tradition" in painting, no doubt a chauvinist reaction to the work of certain Jewish colleagues from Eastern Europe and beyond; the 1914-1918 years of The Great 20th Century Hurt seems to have debilitated his inspiration, and his behavior during the German occupation is thought by some to have been at a minimum ill-advised.

Dickens, Charles (1812 Portsmouth, England - 1870 Godshill, England). English writer who may not belong here, but is.

Diriks, Anna Maria (née Westerberg 1870 Uppsala, Sweden -1932 Drobak, Norway). A Swedish artist usually referred to as Karl Edvard's wife, but with her own entry in the *Norsk Kunstner Leksikon* (Oslo: Universitetsforlaget, 1982); lived in Paris for two decades (1899 - 1921), during which time one hopes she enjoyed herself beyond words.

Diriks, Karl Edvard (1855 Oslo - 1930 Horten, Norway). Norwegian painter; husband of Anna; lived for 20 years (1899 to 1921) at 18, rue Boissonade near the Closerie des Lilas, where Paul Fort edited the first issues of the journal *Vers et Prose*.

Dodge, Mabel. *See* Luhan, Mable Dodge

Dos Passos, John Roderigo (1896 Unknown - 1970 Baltimore, Maryland). American novelist and painter who exemplified the notion that anyone who is not a socialist when young is inhumane and anyone who is not a conservative when older is a fool.

Dreyfus, Alfred (1859 Mulhouse, France - 1935 Paris). A soldier who only wanted to serve what he thought was his country, not become a cause célébre in the labyrinth of French nationalism and antisemitism.

Drieu La Rochelle, Pierre (1893 Paris - 1945 Paris). The sad case of a writer of talent who is known more for his collaboration with the nazis (he edited the *Nouvelle Revue Française* 1941-44) than for his works; after the liberation of Paris he went into hiding and committed suicide before he could be tried and probably shot.

Dubas, Marie (1894 Paris - 1972 Paris). One of the stars of the Parisian music hall scene for much of the century; the only rival Mistinguett both admired and respected.

DuBois, William Edward Burghardt (1868 Barrington, Massachusetts - 1963 Accra, Ghana). Negro intellectual, scholar, Communist, and pioneering civil rights activist, who also advocated the separation of the races.

Duchamp, Henri-Robert-Marcel (1887 Blainville, France - 1968 Neuilly-sur-Seine, Paris). Rrose Sélavy when in drag.

Dufy, Raoul (1877 Le Harve, France - 1953 Forcaquier, France). A painter whose career followed the classic path from Impressionism in his youth to a deep plunge into "fauvisme" under the influence of Braque and others from which he barely rose to the surface to paint some wildly colored pictures that continually give pleasure.

Du Maurier, George Louis Palmella Busson (1834 Paris - 1896 London). Progenitor of Eliza Doolittle and Henry Higgens, sort of; definitely grandfather of Daphne du Maurier.

Duncan, Raymond (1874 – 1966). Sometime manager of Pablo Casals' concerts; vegetarian; an urban William Morris who nonetheless possessed a strong desire to be a business executive and dominate others; purveyor of handmade leather sandals in Paris and environs; lived in the Rue de Seine during the 1930s where he hosted meetings of anti-fascist exiled intellectuals and writers and operated an art gallery.

Dunning, Ralph Cheever (1878 Detroit, Michigan - 1930 Paris). Student of debilitation and sometime poet and protegé of E. Pound; apparently lived on no financial income and about whom not much is known, except that he seems to have died because he did not particularly like to eat; but did like his opium, and writing poems in distinctly "unmodern" idioms, which endeared him to the fragmented mind of the same E. Pound; rarely talked to anyone but Pound, Samuel Putnam and a few others; lived in "virtually a wooden box" (Wambly Bald) with only a cot, a stove, a bookcase and a straight-backed chair; hell, what else does a poet need, except good food and someone to love?

Durey, Louis Edmond (1888 Paris - 1979 Saint-Tropez, France). Composer; a sixth of Les Six; joined the French Communist Party in 1936 and changed his way of living and composing; active in the resistance against the Germans and Vichy thugs; more known now for his politics than his music.

Durrell, Lawrence George (1912 Jullundur, India – 1990 Sommières, France). An extreme example of the myopia of the Nobel Literature Prize Committee.

Ehrenburg, Ilya Grigoryevitch (1891 Kiev, Ukraine - 1967 Moscow). Sometime Bolshevik Russian writer and publicist, one of the few prominent Jews to live through the Stalin era and die of natural causes.

Eluard, Nusch (née Maria Benz, 1906 Germany - 1946 France). Lovely and sensual muse to her husband, Brassaï, Picasso, and Man Ray; photocollagist in the mid-1930s.

Eluard, Paul (né Eugène-Emile-Paul Grindel, 1895 Saint-Denis, France - 1952 Charenton, Paris). First husband of Gala Dali, only husband of the lovely Nusch and, after Nusch's death, of Dominique; member of the Resistance; authored a poem praising Stalin and remained too close to the Moscow-dominated French CP when he should have known better; subject of a fascinating exhibition at the Centre Georges Pompidou entitled *Eluard et ses amis peintres* (1982).

Ernst, Max (1891 Brühl, Germany - 1976 Paris). Part-time chess player, saved from the Gestapo's clutches by Peggy Guggenheim and Varian Fry; the French named a Parisian thoroughfare after him in the 11th arrondissement.

Famous Braque Dinner of January 14, 1917, The. Braque suffered a severe wound at the front and, after a lengthy convalescence, returned to Paris with his wife Marcelle to face a banquet prepared by Marie Vassilieva, who ran a canteen the police considered a private club and thus exempt from the curfew, and the increasingly saintly pederast, Max Jacob, in honor of his discharge from the military; to say the event turned into a brawl would be to claim too much, but the night had its moments, especially when Modigliani, not quite sober and having been warned not to be there, poured through the door with a disparate bunch of "artists and models," which would probably have been fine, but one of his former lovers was there with her current lover, who tried to shoot his fellow Italian with a pistol; trying to hustle Modi out the door Madame Vassilieva discovered that those fine Hispanic jokesters, Picasso and Ortiz, had locked everyone in the place and hidden the key; but before she throttled both of them, Matisse diplomatically retrieved the implement, Modi and his crew found themselves on the street again, and the participants turned to the turkey and to toasting the honoree.

Famous August 12, 1916 Photography Session, The. Cocteau scheduled a lunch with Picasso at a restaurant on the Carrefour Vavin in order to convince him to undertake the backdrop and the costumes to the ballet *Parade*; Picasso brought a number of then and subsequently talented and/or famous people with him, and others joined the group later; Cocteau by happenstance brought with him his mother's camera which contained a roll of unexposed film; the rest is history, which you can see in Billy Klüver's very expensive little book, *Un jour avec Picasso. Le 12 août 1916* (Paris, 1994) and the somewhat less expensive American edition published several years later. Klüver and Martin's *Kiki's Paris* also has several pages about the event; the names of those involved alone should motivate you to look into this: Picasso, Pâquerette, Max Jacob, Moïse Kisling, Marie Vassilieva, Ortiz de Zarate, André Salmon, Modigliani, and Henri-Pierre Roché; imagine going out to pick up a baguette and a bunch of carrots and meeting all these people on the street corner!

Fargue, Léon-Paul (1876 Paris - 1947 Paris). The ultimate French Parisian pedestrian; author of *Le Piéton de Paris*.

Fauconneir, Henri le (1881 – 1946). French painter; member of the loosely associated group often linked as "second generation" cubists, most of whom possessed little idea of what cubism actually meant; indeed, based on his most famous painting, the massive "Mountaineers Attacked by Bears" (1910-1912 at the Rhode Island School of Design), he was no cubist at all, but a painter of very interesting modern images.

Fäy, Bernard (b. 1893). A historian and biographer of Benjamin Franklin and George Washington; born to a well-connected ultra-Catholic family; friend of many writers and artists including Gertrude Stein whose *Autobiography of Alice B. Toklas* he translated into French; Stein submitted a positive reference for him during his purge trial after the nazi occupation; sentenced to life in prison despite this, but in 1948 the court commuted the sentence to 20 years; as Vichy-appointed director of the Biblioteque Nationale and with his old connections, during the occupation he could indeed have protected the Jewish Miss Stein and Miss Toklas, as he later claimed he did, but he was also a vicious opponent of Freemasonry; escaped from prison in the spring of 1951, fled to Spain where he joined the history faculty at the University in Madrid, later moving to the university in Freibourg, Switzerland, where he remained even after being pardoned, traveling to Paris only occasionally.

Feuchtwanger, Lion (1884 Munich, Germany - 1958 Santa Monica, California). A very popular, but fine German novelist during the 1920s, 1930s and 1940s who, having been saved by Varian Fry and the Emergency Rescue Committee from his biological fate as a Jew when the nazis infested the South of France, promptly gave an interview upon landing in New York which detailed the secret path over the Pyrenees through which he had been rescued; a rather naive fellow who believed everything the Stalinists told him during a visit to Moscow during the 1930s and wrote a book about the glories of the Soviet system to counteract the truth published by André Gide a year previously.

Fidler, Eugène (1910 Balti, then Russian Empire, now Moldova - 1990 Roussillon, France). An artist of many talents whose work should be in more museums than it is; member of the Resistance in the South of France, he went into hiding in Roussillon where Samuel Beckett taught him English and where he remained after the war; his studio in that village provided a meeting place for all kinds of interesting people from the 1960s until his death, a tradition carried on by his wife, Edith, and daughter, Natacha, both ceramicists of high talent and ingenuity.

Fitzgerald, Francis Scott Key (1896 Saint Paul, Minnesota - 1940 Hollywood, California). American writer who did not believe in second acts for his countrymen and did not live to see his own.

Flanner, Janet (a.k.a. Gênet) (1892 Indianapolis, Indiana - 1978 New York City). American writer who discovered a method of making a living by writing about the city while living in it, a circumstance some of us have yet to achieve.

Flechtheim, Alfred (1878 Münster, Germany - 1937 London). German art dealer, publisher of *Der Querschnitt*, and boxer fan.

Ford, Ford Madox (né Ford Hermann Hueffer, 1873 Merton, Surrey - 1939 Deauville, France). English writer, who suffered from overproduction and now suffers from underappreciation.

Fort, Paul (1872 Reims, France - 1960 Paris). Poet (indeed, at the death of Léon Dierx in 1912, those in charge of such things voted Fort into office as "prince des poètes";

one of the electors, Old Fred Mistral, himself, noted after the election, "J'ai nommé Paul Fort, la cigale du Nord," which coming from Freddy was a high compliment); editor; friend of painters; lived at 24, rue Boissonade, a few doors from his friend, the tall Norwegian painter, Edvard Diriks; back issues of his journal crowded the apartment to the point where his family used them as tables and chairs; founder of the first Symbolist theater; author of the multitudinous *Ballades françaises*; close colleague of the only American member of the Symbolist group, Stuart Merrill, who wrote his poems in French, wore a cowboy hat, and rolled his own.

Frampton, Sir George James (1860 London - 1928 London). English sculptor, possibly related to Peter.

Fry, Varian Mackey (1907 New York City- 1967 Easton, Connecticut). With Lincoln Kirstein co-founded the literary magazine *Hound & Horn* in 1927, whilst both were undergraduates at Harvard, the title coming from an early Ezra Pound poem "The White Stag" ("Bid the world's hounds come to horn!"); a non-fiction Scarlet Pimpernel, he headed the Emergency Rescue Committee's office in Marseilles 1940-1941, about which he published a fascinating memoir, *Surrender on Demand* (1945, reissued 1997). See also Andy Marino, *A Quiet American. The Secret War of Varian Fry* (1999).

Gabin, Jean (né Jean-Alexis Moncorgé 1904 Paris - 1976 Neuilly-sur-Seine, Paris). Actor in French vaudeville and light operetta before beginning an incredibly successful career in the movies during which he captivated Marlene Dietrich and much of the western world, spending the war years frustrated in the USA, but thereafter played Maigret perfectly and acted at the end of his career with Jean-Paul Belmondo and Alain Delon.

Gauguin, Eugène Henri Paul (1848 Paris - 1903 Atuana, Marquesas Islands). Main character under a different name in Willy Maugham's racy exposé of the world of modern art called *The Moon and Sixpence* (1919).

Gautier, Théophile (1811 Tarbes, France - 1872 Neuilly-sur-Seine, Paris,). Writer of macabre and morbid but almost perfectly formed poetry; exponent of the l'art pour l'art doctrine.

Gérome, Jean-Léon (1824 Vesoul, France - 1904 Paris). Painter, owner of the monkey Jacques; vehement opponent of the Impressionists' work.

Giacometti, Alberto (1901 Borgonovo near Stampa, Switzerland - 1966 Chur, Switzerland). Sculptor.

Gide, André (1869 Paris - 1951 Paris). A complex man of literature, one of the few to achieve the highest levels of European culture with his works and his life, the latter of which was relatively open in its bisexuality; never really played the role of Grand Old Man of French Letters, but could have; instead kept up with what was New through friendships with people such as Adrienne Monnier, Sylvia Beach, Klaus Mann, and Roger Martin du Gard and other relative youngsters; was active in the anti-nazi Popular Front movement until he published a book critical of the Soviet Union.

Goetz, Richard (1874 Ulm, Germany - 1954 New York City). German painter who came to Paris in 1901 and moved into Whistler's studio at 86, rue Nôtre-Dame-des-Champs in 1902 (according to one source; according to Klüver and Martin he lived here 1911-1914); showed at the Salon des Indépendents; left Paris in August 1914, but returned after 1919, this time as a collector of French art no longer himself interested in painting (because "one can never paint better than Cézanne"); before 1911 in his apartment on the corner of Rue du Cardinal Lemoine and the Quai de la Tournelle occasionally served roasted geese to the artists who hacked at it "with saws and hatchets," according to Fernande Olivier; lived in New York from 1939 till his death; became a naturalized American citizen and died of a raging brain tumor which had wiped out his memory.

Goldfarb, Shirley (1925 Altoona, Pennsylvania - 1980 Paris). American painter who lived most of her all too brief adult life in Paris; author of the posthumously published *Carnets. Montparnasse 1971-1980* (Paris: Quai Voltaire, 1994).

Goncourt Brothers, The. Edmond de (1822 Nancy, France - 1896 Champrosay, France) and Jules de (1830 Paris - 1870 Auteuil, France). A literary prize is named after these two indefatigable writers of, literary history, biography, plays, naturalistic novels (veritable forerunners of Zola in their subject matter then considered degenerate: whores, poverty, nasty health conditions in hospitals, and the like), and a marvelously gossipy diary.

Gottlieb, Léopold (1883 Drohobycz, Poland - 1934 Paris). An artist whose sensitivities resulted in an early morning duel with his colleague, Kisling; unknown today, André Salmon published a book about him in 1927.

Graß, Günter (b. 1927 Free City of Danzig, now Gdansk, Poland). The postwar German writer who finally received the Nobel Prize for Literature in 1999; author of the classics *Die Blechtrommel* (1960), *Hundejahre* (1963) and *Der Butt* (1977), among others.

Guggenheim, Peggy (née Marguerite Guggenheim 1898 New York City - 1979 Venice, Italy). A rare personage, who did much to make our lives more enjoyable, often through coldblooded wheelerdealing in the cutthroat art dealer world.

Guillaume, Paul (1891 Paris - 1934 Paris). Art dealer and collector deeply involved in the Parisian art world; editor and publisher of the influential journal *Les Arts à Paris*; with Thomas Munro wrote the path finding book *Primitive Negro Sculpture* (1926).

Hamnett, Nina (1890 Tenby, South Wales - 1956 London). English painter and writer about whom many stories of outlandish behavior are told, who would eagerly disrobe and dance in sketching class if asked, because she knew she had a very displayable body; not without reason did she entitle her memoirs *Laughing Torso* (New York: Ray Long and Richard R. Smith, 1932), must reading; lived for some time at 8, rue de la Grande Chaumière; memorized a large repertoire of bawdy songs, such as "Bollocky Bill the Sailor" and "She Was Honest But She Was Poor", which she often sang at Pizzuti's Italian restaurant across the street from the Dingo Bar; according to one source she liked sailors a lot, occasionally large groups of them, but this is tawdry phallocentric gossip from an era before "political correctness" began its reign of censorship; reputed to have a fine drawing hand which resulted in many direct and meticulous paintings; fell or threw herself out of her apartment window whilst drunk and died; there is, of course, much more to be said about her, but in another place.

Harlem Renaissance. A misnomer for a not very exact period of time during which American Negro artists and writers, many of who lived or worked in Harlem, flourished.

Harrison, Alexander (1853 Philadelphia, Pennsylvania - 1930 Paris). American painter known in his last years during the 1920s as The Grand Old Man of Montparnasse, who studied and worked in Paris during the late 19th century and into the 20th, when, at the end of his life, almost 80, he sipped a nightcap with the younger crowd at the Closerie des Lilas before returning to his Rue du Val-de-Grace studio; painted the pastoral nudes in a curious arbor entitled "En Arcadie," and at one point all the European capitals knew his work; one of the first plein-air painters to move his nude models out of the studio into the open countryside.

Hartley, Marsden (1877 Lewiston, Maine - 1943 Corea, Maine). American painter with a taste for laborers clothing; Gertrude Stein put him in a play; in the end a difficult man to know.

Hawks, Howard (1896 Goshen, Indiana - 1977 Palm Springs, California). An antisemite adventurer who found work in Hollywood.

Hayden, Henri (1883 Warsaw - 1970 Paris). Arrived in Paris in 1907, but lived in relative isolation until 1914 when he moved to Montparnasse; worked with Eric Satie and Les Six; became a French citizen in the early 1920s; fled Paris to the South of France in June 1942 hiding in the Auvergne, Mougins, and finally in the perched village of Roussillon (Vaucluse), where he met the ceramicist and collagist Eugène Fidler, also in hiding from the Gestapo, as was Samuel Beckett; returned to Paris in the autumn of 1944, he discovered his studio and works he'd left there destroyed, so he began again.

Hayter, Stanley William (1901 Hackney, London - 1988 Paris). Etcher who worked for the Anglo-Iranian Oil Company 1922-25, after which he survived Surrealism to become one of the great innovative printmakers of his day; ran his own printmaking school, named Atelier 17, at 17, rue Campagne Première 1933-39, after which he moved to New York City to escape the Huns.

Héburtene, Jeanne (1898 Paris - 1920 Paris). Art student; lovely, but unfortunate lover of Modigliani and mother of his children: leapt to her death from the top floor of her nasty parents' apartment building at 8 bis, rue Amyot behind the Panthéon a day and a half after the artist died.

Heine, Heinrich (né Chaim Harry Heine 1797 Düsseldorf, Germany - 1856 Paris). Torn between a real love for his fatherland, expressed in some beautiful lyrics and some sentimental verse, and a profound abhorrence of certain German characteristics and institutions, expressed in sarcastic but witty journalism, he spent the years between 1831 and his stoical death in Paris where he became a cultural monument to all that is admirable in a human being at the same time as his countrymen banned his writings and heaped calumny upon him; he never surrendered his efforts to reconcile the two cultures, an enterprise in which he obviously but sadly achieved no success; alas, he also accepted a "pension" from the reactionary French government when he really did not need it, and his credibility suffered.

Hiler, Hilaire (1898 Saint Paul, Minnesota – 1966 Paris). Played the piano accompaniment to Kiki's boisterous songs in his nightspot, The Jockey, for which the outside American aborigine motif decor he designed himself; for someone as well-known in Paris at the time, there is little biographical information to be found about him now.

Holbein, Hans (the Elder) (c. 1460 Augsburg, Germany – 1524 Isenheim, Alsace). Painter of various parts, mainly altars, of various churches, and portraits of those who could afford such things; painted in the "Flemish-influenced style" for most of his career.

Honegger, Arthur Oscar (1892 Le Harve, France - 1955 Paris). Composer; one of the three well-known members of the quasi-group Les Six; wrote "Pacific 231," a train piece, among other works for the ballet, theater, movies, and radio as well as the concert hall.

Howard, Wil (a.k.a. Wil de Vray 1879 Leipzig, Germany - 1945 Mittenwald, Germany). Apparently a better German photographer than a German Impressionist landscape painter, who studied at the Académie Julian (1903-1911) after leaving art school in Leipzig, since we know him for his photographs of the Germans and their friends in the Dôme before 1914, and not for his paintings, though he did exhibit at least once at the Salon d'Automne; Pascin painted his portrait (as "William Howard") in 1909; lived after 1932 mainly in Mittenwald (Oberbayern); at least four of his linolium prints are in the Museum des bildenen Künste in Leipzig.

Huchette, Rue de la. Fabled street in the 5th arrondissement about which Elliot Paul wrote two books, now nothing like it was, but what is?

Humes, Harold Louis (1926 Douglas, Arizona - 1992 New York City). A possibly great American writer whose history is mysterious with unasked questions.

Jacob, Max (1876 Quimper, France - 1944 Drancy transit camp, Paris). Gentle poet whose conversion to Roman Catholicism many years before did not save him from the fascist beasts' definition of being a Jew.

Jacques. Pet monkey who sat at table in a formal white cravat with the guests unless he misbehaved, in which case he was banned until he put on a rag pickers rags, then he could return to the meal, suitably chastened one supposes.

Jardin du Luxembourg (also known as the Luxembourg Garden). One of Paris' pigeon hunting areas for poor struggling hungry writers and their families.

Jolas, Eugene (1894 Union-Hill, New Jersey - 1952 Paris). Proponent of the "Revolution of the Word" and literary assistant to James Joyce; author of the posthumously published autobiography *Man from Babel* (1998), which also describes his service as a cultural affairs officer in the American zone of occupation in Germany 1945-47.

Jones, Lois Mailou (1905 Boston, Massachusetts – 1998 Washington DC). American Negro painter who studied in France and returned there many times, and to Haiti to recharge her creative energies.

Jouhandeau, Marcel (1888 Guéret, France - 1979 Rueil-Malmaison, France). An example of the terrible ambiguity in French culture when it comes to writers and antisemitism, he wrote a brochure entitled "The Jewish Peril" and scurrilous articles for the notorious *Je Suis Partout* and *L'Action Française,* while simultaneously writing for the pre-occupation *Nouvelle Revue Française* being a close friend of the NRF group's undeclared leader, Jean Paulhan.

Joyce, James Augustine Aloysius (1882 Rathgar, Dublin - 1941 Zürich, Switzerland). A Dublin writer who wrote only about Dublin while living all his adult life on the Continent.

Joyce, Lucia (1907 Trieste, Italy - 1982 Northampton, England). A possibly brilliant woman whose father rather believed her clairvoyant than demented; her life cannot even be imagined.

Julian, Rodolphe (1839 La Palud, Vaucluse, France - 1907 Paris). Painter and art teacher; founder of the Académie Julian and its many branches throughout the city, all of which brought him wealth if not taste.

Kaelin, Martin. Painter and director of the Académie Colarossi during the summer of 1915 when he refused to allow the continuation of the concerts, so successful the past winter, for reasons still not clear to me.

Kafka, Franz (1883 Prague - 1924 Kierling, Austria). Wrote exemplary modernist fiction, but never heard Lee Konitz play.

Kahnweiler, Daniel-Heinrich [Henry] (1884 Mannheim, Germany - 1979 Paris). Twenty-three years old when he opened his first gallery in Paris, this German Jew, who preferred to be French despite their absurd treatment of him as a German, died at 93 still actively involved in the trade, defending his artists and their work as he perceived they required defending against the onslaught of the barbarians and philistine schools of "art" he deemed unworthy of the name; perhaps the greatest art dealer of the benighted 20th century.

Kantorowicz, Alfred (1899 Berlin - 1979 Hamburg). A leftist writer and literary critic as a young man who left the left for the middle ground for sufficient reason later in life; alas, this turnabout also influenced his memoirs and his scholarship on the period of his exile and he played down his communist affiliations during his time in Paris and an antifascist activist; served in the International Brigades in Spain 1936-38, about which he wrote in *Spanisches Tagebuch* (1948); 1941 fled to the USA via Martinique; 1946 return to Germany (East) and in 1957 fled to the West.

Kickert, Conrad (1882 The Hague - 1965 Paris). Netherlandish artist who could not follow the cubist path; had a studio near the Montparnasse railroad station which he kindly gave to Mondrian, the place now obliterated by human greed and indifference; lived for much of his life in Paris beginning in 1909, where after he inhabited 33, avenue du Maine (1912), 26, rue du Départ, and 18, rue Boissonade (1925-36) and 33, rue Boissonade (1937-65).

Kiki de Montparnasse (née Alice Ernestine Prin, 1901 Châtillon-sur-Seine, France - 1953 Paris). A well known serious person with extraordinary pizzazz.

Kisling, Moïse (1891 Krakow, Poland - 1953 Sanary-sur-mer, France). A painter about whom many stories are told, most of them true, such as his early morning duel in the Parc des Princes on June 12, 1914, with his countryman, Léopold Gottlieb, concerning an unidentified "question of honor," after which both claimed victory since each cut the other with cavalry sabers during the heated exchange of The Old Thrust and Parry.

Klément, Rudolph (1910 Hamburg, Germany - 1938 Paris). Unfortunate secretary to Leon Trotsky in France.

Koestler, Arthur (1905 Budapest - 1983 London). Prolific writer of fiction, journalism, and idiosyncratic scholarly works, and immensely complex human who moved from being actively involved in Zionist, then Communist causes to an independent leftist stance and withdrawal from the mundane world to the study of ethics, esoteric biological and other scientific matters; wrote about his reprieve from a Franco fascist death sentence in *Spanish Testament* (1936), also wrote the classic investigation of totalitarian ethics and morality, the novel *Darkness at Noon* (1941), *The Scum of the Earth* (1941) about his internment in the French concentration camp Le Verne, and *The Invisible Writing* (1954) about his profound disillusionment with and loss of faith not only in communism, but the prospects for the future of mankind; terminally ill, he took his life in a double suicide with his perfectly healthy wife who apparently decided life without him was simply not worth living.

Konitz, Lee (b. 1927 Chicago, Illinois). One of those modern figures the general public has never heard of, but without whose contribution today's music would sound much worse, as difficult as it may be to think such a thing possible.

Knudsen, Grethe (b. 1955 Tonder, Denmark). Danish artist, Paris resident and fine dinner companion.

Kramstyk, Roman (1885 Warsaw - 1942 Łódź Ghetto, Poland). Polish artist who lived in Paris for many years and was still there in 1925, which bit of information we know because he appears in photograph of a group on the terrace of La Rotonde taken at the time; his painting "Deep in Thought" is in the Chicago Polish Museum.

Krohg, Christian (1852 Aker near Oslo - 1925 Oslo). Broadminded fullbearded patriarch and Norwegian painter and journalist; father of Per; second husband of Oda; moved back to Oslo from France in 1910 to become head of the new Academy of Fine Arts.

Krohg, Lucy (née Cecile Vidil 1890). Model, muse, mother, wife, mistress, magnetically sensual, and a great dancer of the tango.

Krohg, Oda (née Othilia Lasson 1860 Asgardstrand, Norway - 1935 Oslo). Painter; freespirited wife of Christian, mother of Per and other children, lover of a number of acquaintances and friends long before such a style of living became something other than utterly outrageous.

Krohg, Per Lasson (1889 Asgardstrand, Norway - 1965 Oslo). Painter; king of the Scandinavian tango; husband of Lucy and father of Guy (b. 1917 Oslo), a painter; later husband of Ragnhild Helene Andersen and father of Morton (b. 1937 Oslo), also a painter.

Ladd, Alan (1913 Hot Springs, Arkansas - 1964 Palm Springs, California). Actor who embodied, among other forgettable fictive persons, one short cowboy, one short assassin, and several quasi-detectives, the portrayals of the cowboy and the assassin being fine performances.

Landshoff, Fritz (1901 Berlin - 1988 Amsterdam, Netherlands). Editor and publisher; forced by the nazi regime into exile, he founded the German branch of the Querido publishing house in Amsterdam to publish writers who could no longer be printed in Germany, thus keeping many impoverished authors alive and their works in print; barely escaped to New York as the nazis and their collaborators shot out all the lights in Europe plunging the continent into a new dark age.

Laurens, Jean-Paul (1838 Fourquevaux, France - 1921 Paris). Painter with a studio in the Rue Nôtre-Dame-des-Champs; painted the Théâtre de l'Odéon ceiling; taught among others Alphonse Mucha at the Académie Julian.

Léautaud, Paul (1872 Paris - 1956 Paris). Noted for his sordid lifestyle and the 16 volumes of his *Journal littéraire,* a stewpot into which he threw whatever happened to him or didn't and what he thought about everything.

Léger, Fernand (1881 Argentan, France - 1955 Gif-sur-Yvette, France). Tubist painter with a museum in Biot, near Grasse, in the South of France.

Leiris, Michel (1901 Paris - 1990 Paris). A mystic Parisian anthropologist-poet and creator of aphorisms who played the role of Big Foot in Picasso's play, *Le Désir attrappé par la queue* in its first reading in the occupied Paris Spring of 1944, one of those magical nights that no one believes happened the next day; knew everyone and all knew him; perhaps most well-known for his several volumes of memoirs, *L'Age d'homme* (1939) and *La Règle du jeu* (4 volumes, 1948-1972), the latter title he seems to have got from Jean Renior.

Lenin, V.I. (né Vladimir Ilych Ulyanov 1870 Simbirsk, Russia - 1924 Gorki, Russia). According to some a close competitor with A. Hitler for the title of Greatest Evil of the 20th Century, but also a habituée of cafés before 1917 when he had the time, which on occasion he did.

Les Six. Essentially a public relations creation of brief duration consisting of several French composers (Darius

Mihaud, Francis Poulenc, Georges Auric, Germaine Tailleferre, Louis Durey, and Arthur Honegger) who reacted against the elaborate heaviness of Romanticism by combining elements of popular and folk music in their creations; they looked to Erik Satie for inspiration and the ubiquitous Jean Cocteau served as their spokesman; they did not form a school and developed their own individual styles.

Levy, Julien (1906 – 1981). As a young man was lucky enough to marry Joelle, daughter of Mina Loy; owned an art gallery in New York and Paris where he knew everybody; wrote a book about it all entitled *Memoir of an Art Gallery* (1977); in 1927 he first saw Atget's photographs in Man Ray's studio in the Rue Campagne Première and began to buy as many as the old photographer would sell; he assisted Berenice Abbott in saving the glass plates for posterity after Atget's death later that year; one of the few men who turned Kiki down, upon which incident she told him "Vous n'êtes pas un homme, mais un hommelette".

Levy, Rudolf (1875 Stettin, Pomerania, Germany - 1944 en route to Auschwitz, probably in the transit camp Carpi near Modena). German painter who managed the Matisse Academy for a brief period; forced by the nazi regime out of Berlin in 1933 his life became a debilitating odyssey that wound its way through the South of France, Rapallo, to Mallorca until the civil war after which he went to the USA for a brief period, then in 1937 to the Yugoslavian island of Sipanska Luka by Dubrovnik, whence he moved in early 1938 to Ishia, and finally to a form of hiding in Florence where he could occasionally sell a painting and where his former wife, the actress Genia Morelli in Munich, could send him money orders; denounced to the Gestapo which arrested and deported him for his three-fold offense against "aryan blood:" being a Jew, a homosexual, and a modernist painter.

Lewis, Harry Sinclair (1885 Sauk Center, Minnesota - 1951 Rome, Italy). Renegade Minnesotan.

Lipchitz, Jacques (né Chaim-Jacob Lipchitz 1891 Druskieniki, Lithuania - 1973 Capri, Italy). Sculptor who arrived in Paris in 1909; studied at the École-des-Beaux-Arts with Injalbert, the Académie Colorossi and the Académie Julian; became a French citizen in 1924; forced to flee the nazis in 1940-41; spent the war years in the USA.

Lissitzky, El (né Lazare Morduchovitch Lissitzky 1890 Potchinok, Russia - 1941 Schodnia, near Moscow). A modern artist who seems to have been everywhere when it counted and to have tried every school and style of the century, in many of which he excelled.

Lord, James (b. 1922 Englewood, New Jersey). Biographer of Giacometti and gossipy memoirist.

Loren, Sophia (b. 1934 Rome, Italy). Soaked dress poster idol in the late 1960s.

Loy, Mina (née Mina Gertrude Lowy 1882 Hampstead, London - 1966 Aspen, Colorado). Trained as a painter in Paris before 1914 when she had a studio at 17, rue Campagne Première in 1905; married an English artist with whom she had the first of her two "raving beauty" daughters, the second of whom she had in 1919 with her second husband, Arthur Craven, Oscar Wilde's putative nephew, some months after he disappeared at sea off Salina Cruz, Mexico, and she returned to Europe and eventually to Paris, living with the girls at 9, rue Saint-Romain (6th), where she wrote poetry and made lampshades of her own design; author of *Lunar Baedecker* (1923), misspelled by her publisher, Robert McAlmon; published an interesting critical interpretation of Gertrude Stein's style in the *Transatlantic Review* (1924); appears as Patience Scalpel in the risqué *Ladies Almanack,* written by Djuna Barnes and published anonymously in Paris (1928); her collected poetry was published as *The Last Lunar Baedeker* (1982); one of her more notable lines reads "Pig Cupid, his rosy snout rooting erotic garbage," which, according to William Carlos Williams, everyone remembered; her technical experimentation in style and feminist subject matter kept readers away in droves, alas; she continued to write poems, paint, and make constructions from found objects and materials (assemblages) until she died; subject of a biography by Carolyn Burke, *Becoming Modern: The Life of Mina Loy* (1996).

Luhan, Mable Dodge (1879 Buffalo, New York - 1962 Taos, New Mexico). A welloff hostess with a yen for writing memoirs about her life with artsy types throughout a good part of the 20th century; contributed to the popularity of Taos, New Mexico.

MacOrlan, Pierre (né Pierre Dumarchey 1882 Péronne, France - 1970 Saint-Cyr-sur-Morin, France). Writer who was a member in goodstanding of the Bateau Lavoir crew and a good friend of Max Jacob and Apollinaire; Pascin painted his portrait; among many other books, he wrote *Quai des brumes* (1927) from which Jacques Prévert crafted the screenplay for Marcel Carné's film (1938); his works tremble between dream and reality.

Maillol, Aristide Joseph Bonaventure (1861 Banyuls-sur-Mer, France - 1944 Banyuls-sur-Mer, France). Randy

French sculptor who insulted his wife and liked the Germans too much.

Malet, Léo (1908 Montpellier, France - 1996 Paris). Poet, anarchist, creator of "found" art, and writer of detective novels featuring the anarchic private eye, Nestor Burma.

Mann, Klaus (1906 Munich, Germany - 1949 Cannes, France). Member of the German literary family who lived a complicated life, possessed a tremendous talent, spent a good deal of his short life working for the benefit of others, and killed himself out of despair; posthumously his books became well-known in reprint editions, including his memoirs, including his 1943 book on André Gide which he wrote and published in English.

Marcuse, Herbert (1898 Berlin - 1979 Starnberg, Germany). A part-time socio-politologist in California for a long part of his life.

Masurovsky, Gregory (b. 1929 The Bronx, New York). American artist and teacher resident in Paris since 1954, where he has created a unique oeuvre of drawings with pen and ink; his work deserves a major retrospective exhibition.

Matisse, Henri (1869 Le Cateau-Cambrésis, France - 1954 Nice, France). One of the founders of 20th century modernism in painting.

Matthiessen, Peter (b. 1927 New York City). Risk-taking writer, environmentalist, and co-founder of *The Paris Review*.

Maupassant, Henry-René-Albert-Guy de (1850 Château de Miromesnil près Dieppe - 1893 Paris). One of the creators of the modern short story; a sufferer of constant arousal; *The Reader's Encyclopedia* (1948) notes that "as a result of overwork he became insane near the end of his life," but it was rather more complicated than that, having to do with syphilis, among other things.

Maurois, André (né Émile Salomon Wilhelm Herzog 1885 Elbeuf, France - 1967 Neuilly-sur-Seine, Paris). Novelist, biographer, philosopher; admirer of the women of Paris; elected to the Académie Française in 1938; a good man.

Mayakovsky, Vladimir (1893 Bagadadi, Georgia, Russian Empire - 1930 Moscow, Stalinist Empire). The most prominent Soviet poet who began his career as a Futurist; traveled to Paris in October 1924 hoping to obtain a tourist visa to the USA; Elsa Triolet, who knew him earlier in Moscow and Berlin, then living at the Hôtel Istria, got him a room there ("it's the cheapest and the cleanest"); his visa application denied, he returned to Moscow at the end of December, alas; remained a free-thinking spirit who really believed in the Revolution's promises, all of which (in addition to the usual destructive emotional entanglements of Russian poets) made his life intolerable where he lived, and he shot himself rather than continue to be disillusioned.

Mayo, Flora Lewis (b. 1900 Denver, Colorado). Art student, who came to Paris in 1925; at the age of 27, became passionate about and for a time influenced the style of her fellow student Alberto Giacometti, who, tiring of the passion after five years, advised she return to the USA, which she did after unfortunately destroying all her own work; according to James Lord, "she ended her days in demented solitude." Giacometti's flattened head of this poor woman is in the Association Alberto et Annette Giacometti, Paris, and is shown at exhibitions from time to time.

McAlmon, Robert (1896 Clifton, Kansas - 1956 Desert Hot Springs, California). Indirectly received a considerable sum of money from England's richest man, with which he subsidized Joyce and published younger writers in his Contact Editions, also writer of some good, if hasty short stories.

Mercader, Ramon (a.k.a. Frank Jacson 1914 - 1978 Havana, Cuba). Léon Trotsky's murderer.

Mérimée, Prosper (1803 Paris - 1870 Cannes, France) Sometime inspector-general of historic monuments in France; writer of potboiler historical novels.

Merrill, Stuart Fitzgerald (1863 near Whitman's birthplace on Long Island, New York - 1915 Versailles, France). American poet who wrote mainly in French; member of the Symbolist journal *Vers et Prose* circle around Paul Fort and the Closerie des Lilas, at a time when poets could afford to drink and eat there; disinherited by his father for supporting the Haymarket Riot defendants, he left the USA in 1892 in bitterness and never returned; helped subsidize several avant-garde journals such as *La Révolt* and the very influential *La Revue Blanche*; his volumes of poetry include *Gammes* (1891), *Petits Poèmes d'automne* (1895), *Quatre Saisons* (1900), and *Une vois dans la foule* (1909); author of the frightening sentence "The Symbolist is the anarchist of literature," which would have been more appropriate to the Dadaists, but remains scary; nonetheless in 1927 city officials named a square after him in the 17th arrondissement.

Milhaud, Darius (1892 Aix-en-Provence, France - 1974 Geneva, Switzerland). Composer and teacher (for many years at Mills College in California where he began as an exile during the 1939-45 conflagration), whose immense output contains a large number of pieces worth listening to.

Miller, Henry Valentine (1891 Brooklyn, New York - 1980 Los Angeles, California). The most American of Parisians.

Mills, Mariette (b. ca. 1909 Morristown, New Jersey). American sculptor; her husband Heyworth built and repaired model ships; friend of Satie, Duchamp, Brancusi, Picabia, Léger, Mina Loy, McAlmon (her bust of whom was shown in the Louvre in 1923), and many other writers and artists of various nationalities; their Montparnasse studio formed one of the social and artistic focal points during the Interregnum between the sessions of The Great 20th Century Dark Age, about whom very little else can be discovered in the usual reference works.

Mirbeau, Octave (1850 Traviers, France - 1917 Cheverchemont, France). Something of a revolutionary journalist and novelist whose behavior resulted in a tedious history of duels, but who also wrote the charming *Journal d'une Femme de chambre* (1900), which both the "American" Jean Renoir and the "French" Luis Buñuel made into films.

Mistinguett (née Jeanne-Marie Florentine Bourgeois 1875 Enghien, France - 1956 Bougival, France). Possessor of a legendary set of legs even into old age; star of stage and music hall, she introduced a number of young singers to audiences such as Maurice Chevalier and Jean Gabin; an icon symbolizing the city of Paris for decades; Joséphine Baker annoyed her because Miss Baker was so good at the same métier.

Mistral, Frédéric (Frédéri) (1830 Mas du Juge prés Saint-Remy-de-Provence, France - 1914 Maillane, France). Nobel Prize winning poet and scholar who refused to believe that Provençal was a dead language or that Provençal culture only existed for the archeologists; established a museum in Arles for that culture's artifacts with his Nobel money.

Modigliani, Amedeo (1884 Livorno, Italy - 1920 Paris). Painter of lengthy unshaven naked women; lover of Jeanne Héburterne and others.

Mondrian, Piet (1872 Amersfoort, Netherlands - 1944 New York City). Netherlandish painter of hip squares.

Monocle, Le. Famous lesbian bar near the hetero whorehouse Le Sphinx on the Boulevard Edgar Quinet, both no longer extant.

Monnier, Adrienne (1892 Paris - 1954 Les Déserts, France). Publisher and bookstore owner in Paris (see also Beach, Sylvia).

Montand, Yves (né Ivo Livi 1921 Monsummano, Tuscany, Italy - 1991 Senlis, France). Born into a communist worker's family, he held on to the faith until he could no longer justify his fellow-traveling; a hysterically popular singer and film actor; in 1982 the first pop entertainer to play the Metropolitan Opera in New York; a giant of 20th century culture, so bursting with talent it is a wonder he did not explode.

Moore, George (1852 Ballyglass, County Mayo, Ireland - 1933 London). Irish journalist and novelist who spent his youth in Paris, wrote in French at the beginning of his prodigiously productive career and knew everybody one should have known; also studied "art" for a short while in Montparnasse.

Moreau-Vauthier, August-Jean (1831 Paris - 1893 Paris). Now forgotten, once fashionable doublenamed ivory sculptor who did the oversized figure of La Parisienne for the monumental gate at the Exposition Universelle of 1900; his book on the painter Gérôme (1906) describes the bucolic cityscape of the Rue Nôtre-Dame-des-Champs around the year 1860: "...paths of beaten earth fringed with grass...."

Mucha, Alphonse Marie (1860 Ivancice, Bohemia - 1938 Prague). Student of the art nouveau poster style who shared his first name with Al Capone; achieved fame if not fortune after Sarah Bernhardt "discovered" him in 1897; his poster of La Grande Sarah as Medea (1898) is still known today; recently a museum in his name opened in Prague.

Mühsam, Erich (1878 Berlin - 1934 Oranienburg concentration camp, Germany). Bisexual German anarchist poet who felt comfortable in Paris and should have remained there; having survived being beaten almost to death, during his incarceration 1919-24 in the Niederschönenfeld prison in Bavaria for having participated in the Bavarian Soviet Republic, his fellow Germans later viciously tortured him in the Brandenburg penitentiary, where after they hanged him in the camp; his wife Zenzi survived both the German and the Soviet gulags, which is a book in itself.

Nadelman, Elie (1882 Warsaw - 1946 Riverdale, Bronx, New York). Came to Paris via Munich in 1904 to study at the Académie Colarossi; met Picasso in 1908 through Leo Stein; in 1911 Helena Rubinstein began to but his work and in 1914 helped him to emigrate to the USA where he lived from then on, becoming a citizen in 1927.

Nancarrow, Conlon (1912 Texarkana, Arkansas – 1997 Mexico City). Composer who studied with Walter Piston, Nicolas Slonimsky and Roger Sessions; joined the Lincoln Brigade in 1937 to fight the fascists in Spain; harassed as a premature antifascist by US government agencies on his return in 1939, he went into exile in Mexico City where he lived the rest of his long life; the major part of his oeuvre is written for the player piano, the rolls for which he himself punched out; if you are fortunate you may with some effort find recordings of the music by this American Original.

Nerval, Gérard de (né Gérard Labrunie 1809 Paris - 1855 Paris). A poet of curious sensibilities and talents who, at the age of 20 and with only rudimentary German, translated Goethe's *Faust* to the older poet's satisfaction; both the Symbolists and the Surrealists claimed him as a precursor; Heinrich Heine claimed him as a best friend among the French; he relied on intuition and inspiration, denigrated reason and rationality as epistemological methods, suffered from mental instability, wrote a number of what he called "super-naturalist" poems, and hanged himself from a street lantern on a cold January morning in the Rue de la Vieille Laterne.

Ney, Michel de la Moskova, Prince (1769 Saarlouis, France - 1815 Paris). French general who supported Napoléon I at the cost of his life; much admired by Ernest Hemingway.

Olivier, Fernande (née Amilie Lang 1881 Paris - 1966 Paris). Picasso's first longterm female companion; possessed a certain talent for drawing and a remarkable memory, which may or may not be trusted; later wrote down everything; and convinced the painter to ensure she had no material need to publish the second volume of her *Souvenirs intimes*, which appeared anyway after the two protangonists died.

Ortiz de Zarate, Manuel (1886 Como, Italy - 1946 Los Angeles, California or New York City). Chilean painter and art teacher who participated in The Famous Photography Session on August 12, 1916, at the Carrefour Vavin, and took the key at The Famous Braque Banquet of January 1917.

Ozenfant, Amédée (1886 Saint-Quentin, France - 1966 Cannes, France). Another of the second generation cubist painters; moved to Paris in 1905; hovered on the fringe of the dadaist's activities, but in 1917 developed the "Purist" school of painting which consisted of him and Charles-Edouard Jeanneret (Le Corbusier) demanding a totally rational approach to painting; edited art-ideological journals, wrote books on modern art; taught at the Académie Moderne and at his own studio-schools in London (1935-38) and New York City (1939-55), after which he returned to France.

Pach, Walter (1883 New York City – 1958 New York City). American artist, printer, and writer; desultory student at the Matisse Académie in 1908; translator of Elie Faure's 5-volume *History of Art;* author of a book on Renoir and one entitled *Queer Thing, Painting* (1938).

Pâquerette (née Emilienne Pâquerette Geslot 1896 Mantes-sur-Seine). A fashion model for the famous Paul Poiret; met famous artists and writers in Montparnasse before, during and perhaps after the first chapter of The Great 20th Century Abattoir; one of Picasso's lovers 1916-1917 and an attendee at the Famous Braque Dinner in

January 1917; married Dr. Alexandre-Raymond Barrieu, Kisling's second in The Famous 1914 Duel.

Panier à salade. *See* Black Maria

Partch, Harry (1901 Oakland, California - 1974 San Diego, California). An American Original in the tradition of Paul Bunyan and the sculptors Korczak Ziolkowski (1908-1982, creator of the great unfinished mountain sculpture of Crazy Horse) and Harry Jackson (b. 1924, who has painted and carved archetypal images of the American West), whose music is so personal he had to create the instruments on which to play it; listen to *And on the Seventh Day Petals Fell in Petaluma* (1966) and *Delusion of the Fury* (1963-69).

Pascin, Jules (né Julius Mordecai Pincas 1885 Vidin, Bulgaria - 1930 Paris). A self-destructive painter with a singular style and continually fulfilled healthy obsession with young female bodies.

Paul, Elliot Harold (1891 Malden, Massachusetts - 1958 Providence, Rhode Island). Author of mystery novels in which the characters sit a lot in the Café du Dôme.

Perlès, Alfred (1896 Vienna - 1990 Wells, England). Polylingual writer known as Joey to his pals Henry Miller and Lawrence Durrell.

Piaf, Edith Giovanna (née Gassion 1915 Paris - 1963 Plascassier, France). The tawdry life of this quasi-dwarf with one of the great voices of 20th century popular culture is as well known as her greatest hits.

Picabia, Francis Marie Martinez (1879 Paris - 1953 Paris). Painter and writer; at one point just after 1918

371

(according to some) considered to be the big daddy of Dadaists, as famous as Picasso; lover of expensive motorcars and fast women; publicly broke with the Dadaists in May 1921 to protest their increasing ideological rigidity and French dadist leader André Breton's ex-cathedra behavior; thereafter painted in an eccentric style unique to himself; moved to Mougins, Provence, in 1925; in the 1930s became friendly with Gertrude Stein; returned to Paris at the end of the Second Chapter of the Great 20th Century Suppuration and took to abstraction again.

Pissarro, Camille (1830 St. Thomas, Virgin Islands - 1903 Paris). An Impressionist painter with a mind so fine but flexible that pointillisme penetrated it.

Pissarro, Lucien (1863 Paris - 1944 Heywood, Somerset, England). Son of Camille; a fine engraver and woodcutter in his own right.

Plimpton, George (b. 1927 New York City). Compiler of experiences for successful books, sometime supplier of banned schnapps, perhaps.

Poe, Edgar Allan (1809 Boston, Massachusetts - 1849 Baltimore, Maryland). American creator of the classic police procedural; sometime poet and substance abuser.

Poiret, Paul (1879 Paris - 1944 Paris). A very well-known designer of female clothing who dabbled in The Arts and designed camouflage patterns for the French army during the 1914-1918 chapter of The Period of Self-Delusion; not able to find a place for himself in his milieu after 1918; died in poverty.

Pomeroy, Frederick William (1857 London - 1924 Clintonville, England). English sculptor.

Pongy, Liane de (née Anne-Marie de Chassaigne ca. 1870 near Rennes, France - 1950 France). One of the last grand and beautiful courtesans, who said if she could afford it she'd never let a man touch her; she couldn't, but allowed the relentless Natalie Barney to seduce her into a passionate affair plagued by Miss Pongy's financial necessities; wrote autobiographical novels which shocked Paris society and appeared as the star in shows at the Folies-Bergère and the Olympia.

Porter, Katherine Anne (1894 Indian Creek, Texas - 1980 Silver Spring, Maryland). Author of the wonderfully titled book of novellas *Pale Horse, Pale Rider* (1939) and one somewhat popular novel *Ship of Fools* (1962), who left her papers to the University of Maryland.

Poulbot, Francisque (1879 Saint-Denis, France - 1946 Paris). Artist whose drawings of children led to a characteristic type being called "poulbots," the silhouette of which became "world-famous" with its large helmet of hair and trousers held up by one suspender strap; the image has always sold well.

Pound, Ezra Loomis (1885 Hailey, Idaho - 1972 Venice, Italy). One of the vital midwives of 20th century English language literature, a fine, if all too often obscure poet, composer of an idiosyncratic music, an economic theory crank, and, unfortunately, a suburban antisemite.

Presley, Elvis (1935 Tupelo, Mississippi - 1977 Memphis, Tennessee). A self-destructive American pop cultural phenomenon, who could actually sing the blues quite effectively in his youth.

Prévert, Jacques (1900 Neuilly-sur-Seine, Paris - 1977 Omonville-la-Petite, France). A writer whose talent knew no boundaries between poetry and prose, but who never wrote a novel, confining his prose to film scenarios for some of the greatest movies of all time, whilst his poetry continues to appeal to a smaller circle that spans the generations.

Purrmann, Hans (1880 Speyer, Germany - 1966 Basel, Switzerland). First studio assistant in the Matisse Académie at 33, boulevard des Invalides, one of the many Germans associated with this school, which he directed in its last year; subject of a "word portrait" by Gertrude Stein; in 1935 emigrated to Florence, Italy, where he became director of the Villa Romana, a private German institution to support painters, and where he gave haven to non-Jewish artists who couldn't stomach the nazis, until he had to escape in the Swiss consul's motor car to Switzerland in the Autumn of 1943 after the Germans occupied northern Italy (there could be no question of offering refuge to Jews: Purrmann had to meet his good friend from the Paris days, Rudolf Levy, in secret until the Gestapo got him).

Putnam, Samuel (1892 Rossville, Illinois - 1950 New Jersey). American writer who lived in Paris and wrote about it; founded *The New Review* in 1931; became well known for his writings on Brazilian literature and culture.

Puvis de Chavannes, Pierre (1824 Lyon, France - 1898 Paris). A very famous and successful painter, yes, but to his credit official Salon circles and the successive avant-garde movements' popes never fully accepted him; received a bit of recognition at the end of his life; some of his murals are in the Panthéon.

Rachel (née Elisa Félix 1821 a roadside inn in Switzerland - 1858 Le Cannet, France). An actress who has been credited with saving the great French plays by Corneille and Racine from the dusty obscurity of literary history's academic attic where the French Romantics preferred to store the French Classicists; recognized as a great actress in her time despite the efforts of antisemites to discredit her French heritage; one of the wonders of early photography shows her in a two-handed nose-thumbing pose that Barbra Streisand might envy.

Radiquet, Raymond (1903 Parc St. Maur, Paris - 1923 Paris). A prodigy whose bisexual distribution of his favors found appreciation and scorn, but whose two lyrical, sardonic novels of requited adolescent passion for older women (*Le Diable au cours* [1923] and *Le Bal du Comte d'Orgel* [1924]) have continued to enchant readers.

Ranson, Paul-Émile (1864 Limoges, France - 1909 Paris). A once fairly well known painter associated with the Nabis; little has been written about him in many decades.

Rattner, Abraham (1895 Poughkeepsie, New York - 1978 New York City). A far too unknown American painter.

Ray, Johnnie (Dallas, Oregon 1927 - 1990 Los Angeles, California). A mostly deaf, white blues singer whose explosive wailing style brought him fame and fortune in the early 1950s, but whose indiscreet bisexual lifestyle brought him ruin (trying to pick up a policeman while dressed in pumps, nylons and a ball gown was not quite the thing to do in Detroit in 1952); anyone who saw him perform at his peak will never forget the event.

Ray, Man (né Emmanuel Radnitsky 1890 Philadelphia, Pennsylvania - 1976 Paris). One of the more incredible

American multi-media artists of the 20th century, who lived most of his adult life in Paris.

Rilke, Rainer Maria (1875 Prague - 1926 Valmont, Switzerland). German lyric symbolist poet and cultural icon of the 20th century who loved Paris even at its most difficult ("Paris is hard. A galley."); served as Rodin's secretary for several years before the 19th century ended with a bang and a scream in August 1914; loved Balthus' mother and wrote a foreword to the painter's first published work.

Roché, Henri Pierre (1879 Paris - 1959 Paris). A great traveler who always came back to Paris; studied at the Académie Julian and though he allegedly never stopped painting, he spent the rest of his life as a private dealer in art works; author of *Jules et Jim* (1953), *Deux anglaises et le continent* (1956), both of which François Truffaut (1932 Paris - 1984 Paris) made into films; one of the great donjuans of the 20th century, who shared two unique women, Marie Laurincin and Helen Grund Hessel (1886 Berlin - 1982 Paris) with the German writer Franz Hessel (1880 Stettin, Germany - 1941 Sanary-sur-mer, France), the Jules to his Jim.

Rodin, François Auguste René (1840 Paris - 1917 Meudon, France). Sculptor and womanizer for whom the term "male chauvinist pig" was appropriately coined.

Rollins, Theodore Walter "Sonny" (b. 1930 New York City). A colossal saxophone colossus.

Root, Waverley (1903 Providence, Rhode Island - 1982 Paris). Writer of evocative books on food and a longtime resident and lover of Paris; not to be confused with

Wambly Bald, who also loved and wrote a great deal about Paris.

Rossi, Tino (1907 Ajaccio, Corsica - 1983 Ajaccio, Corsica). Singer who began his career in Marseille 1927, moving up to Paris three years later where he discovered his light tenor to be a perfect instrument for the radio and recording technology of the day; continued to be immensely successful after 1944 despite being brushed with the tar of collaboration.

Roth, Moses Joseph (1894 Brody, Galicia, now Ukraine - 1939 Paris). A German-language man of letters whose life is a perfect example of the history of Central European Jewish writers who formed the core of literary life in that region before the German nazis and their collaborators began hunting them down and killing them; his addiction to alcohol and work resulting in his early death saved him from the Gestapo's clutches.

Russell, Morgan (1886 New York City - 1953 near Philadelphia, Pennsylvania). One of the few American painters to use the cubist vocabulary to develop an individual style.

Sage, Robert (1899 Detroit, Michigan - 1962 Paris). Literary journalist and editor who, with his French wife, remained in Brittany in hiding during the German occupation; returned to Paris to continue work for the *New York Herald*, for which he'd worked before the war and when it was called the *Chicago Tribune (Paris Edition)*; published a well-received volume on Stendhal.

Saint Gaudens, Augustus (1848 Dublin, Ireland - 1907 Cornish, New Hampshire). Formerly popular American sculptor of garden and funerary works.

Saint-Pol-Roux-le-Magnifique (né Paul Roux 1861 Saint-Henri, Bouches-du-Rhône, France - 1940 Brest, France). Poet who flamboyantly proselytized a personal school of poetry he called "magnificisme"; threatened to drop from the balcony upon a crowd of non-appreciates during a Symbolist theater "performance" at the Théâtre Moderne on December 11, 1891, when he yelled "If you don't stop laughing, I'll let myself fall on your head!"; honored by a dinner turned into a raucous shindig by the Surrealists; German soldiers broke into his house in Camaret, Brittany, during the night of 23-24 June 1940, shot the family servant, gravely wounded one of his daughters, and burned the house down, destroying a large number of unpublished manuscripts, shortly after which he died.

Sainte-Beuve, Charles-Augustin (1804 Boulogne, France - 1869 Paris). One of the great French literary critics, who lived with his mother; reputed sometime lover of Mrs. Victor Hugo; wrote about their love-affair in the scandalous *Le Livre d'Amour* (1843).

Salmon, André (1881 Paris - 1969 Sanary-sur-Mer, France). Literary journalist and groupie who wrote a great deal about artists and writers he had known, including about the painter Henri Hayden, whose life is interesting enough to deserve a full-length biography; one source says this about Salmon: "...began as a cubist disciple of Apollinaire, later joined Dadism, and distinquished himself as a critic of modern painting," none of which is true, but it does give me the opportunity of mentioning Apollinaire again, something one cannot do too often.

Salomé. A female threat to the stability of certain male egos and heads.

Sargent, John Singer (1856 Florence, Italy - 1925 London). Expatriate American painter of "Madame X" and other daring portraits.

Sartre, Jean-Paul (1905 Paris - 1980 Paris). Refused the Nobel Prize for Literature, probably whilst on amphetamines.

Satie, Erik [-Alfred Leslie] (1866 Honfleur, France - 1925 Paris). Often described as an "unorthodox" composer, whose music, he said, should be as furniture: there but not prominently so, but it is, for which we can be grateful; collaborated with Jean Cocteau and Pablo Picasso on *Parade*, a visually cubist ballet organized by Sergei Diaghilev, a famous impresario of the ballet who is buried in an island in Venice near Ezra Pound and Eager Strawskinski; Satie gave his pieces such names as "Sports et Divertissements," "3 Morceaux," "Jack-in-the-Box," and "Préludes flasques (pour un chien)"; whose composition "Socrate" Roger Shattuck described as an attempt at "a new balance between monotony and variety," which led him to become the putative father of the minimalist composers of today's ultra boring but lengthy stuff they still insist on calling music.

Schjerfbeck, Helene (1862 Helsinki - 1946 Saltsjöbaden, Finland). A much underrated Finnish modernist painter.

Schmeling, Maximilian (b. 1905 Klein Luckow, Brandenburg, Germany). Well known boxer, from whom I've never heard a pronouncement on 20th century art; celebrated his 96th birthday on September 27, 2001.

Seberg, Jean (1938 Marshalltown, Iowa - 1979 Paris). American actress whose best role was herself in *A bout de souffle* (1960) by Jean-Luc Godard (b. 1930 Paris), in which she played with the formerly ubiquitous Jean-Paul Belmondo (b. 1933 Paris); it is rumored that her corpse was found locked in the trunk of her car, leading to the suspicion that someone murdered her.

Seiki, Kuroda (1866 Kagoshima, Japan – 1924 Tokyo). Japanese art teacher at the Tokyo Art School's Division of Western Painting; in the 1880s lived in Paris where he studied at the Académie Colarossi.

Sélavy, Rrose (? - ?). Marcel Duchamp in drag, two of whose sayings are "From our line of idle hardware, we recommend a faucet that stops dripping when one stops listening" (though the puns are lost in the translation) and "My niece is cold because my knees are cold" (this originally written in English).

Sérusier, Paul (1863 Paris - 1927 Morlaix, France). Post-impressionist Nabi painter who created the famous landscape called "Talisman" following Gauguin's instructions about color and exemplifying Maurice Denis' dictum on the definition of a painting before it is a recognizable image.

Service, Robert William (1874 Preston, England - 1958 Lancieux, France). English-born North American writer of verse known, no doubt to his chagrin, as the Canadian Kipling; sometime art student.

Shakespear, Dorothy (1886 London - 1973 near Cambridge, England). Married Ezra Pound in their youth and never found the energy to leave him, except occasionally; her loyalty is admirable; Pound gave her son his name; she made the woodcuts for the long since forgotten work of fiction by the long since forgotten B. Cyril Windeler (a nom de plume, perhaps?) entitled *Elimus*

(Paris: Three Mountains Press, 1923); a lady whose drawings and paintings need to be publicly exhibited, if they can be found.

Shanghai Gesture, The. One could continue to think of this as the 1942 movie by the ever-exotic/claustrophobic Josef von Sternberg; indeed with the cast made up of a motley gang of exiles from various European societies then under the metal-studded feet of the German occupation and Hollywood regulars, including Ona Munson, Albert Bassermann, Maria Ouspenskaya, Eric Blore, Ivan Lebedeff, Mike Mazurki, Mikhail Rasumny, Michael Delmatoff and the eternal croupier Marcel Dalio, in addition to the unbelievably satiny Gene Tierney, The Great Conman of Movies Walter Huston, and the simply unbelievable Victor Mature, with all of this one might be forgiven for thinking of this as just a movie, but a more mind-expanding approach would be to ponder on that look in his eyes as Mature lifts his cape to shroud the illicit kiss he is about to plant on the upturned mouth of the lovely Tierney in the middle of the biggest, busiest saloon cum gambling casino in town, and simply *know* that *this* is The Shanghai Gesture!

Soupault, Philippe (1897 Chaville, France - 1990 Paris). Dadist then surrealist poet and another Joyce assistant, who abandoned this kind of literature, though not surrealist principles for novels of political and social analysis, and books on Joyce, Charles Chaplin and William Blake; he wrote about being imprisoned by the nazis in *Le temps des assassins* (1945).

Sperber, Manès (1905 Zablotów, Galicia, Poland - 1989 Paris). Writer, psychologist, premature anti-fascist activist, and public intellectual who joined the German Communist Party in Berlin in 1927; jailed and moved to Vienna 1933;

worked for Komintern in Yugoslavia and Paris 1934-1937; director of "ideology" for the Institute for the Study of Fascism in Paris, an agency founded by German communists (including Arthur Koestler) at the behest of the Komintern 1934-35; broke with the Party in 1937; editor in chief of the independent leftist *Die Zunkunft* (a post-break-with-the-Komintern Willi Münzenberg publication in 1938); served in the French army 1939-1941; fled to Switzerland 1942 where the Swiss interned him; returned to Paris after the war where he resumed his writing and scholarly careers.

Stein, Gertrude (1874 Allegheny, Pennsylvania - 1946 Paris). Writer companion of Alice Toklas.

Stein, Leo (1872 Allegheny, Pennsylvania - 1947 Settignano, Italy). Gertrude's brother, whose mind may have been finer than his sister's had he been able to focus it on itself as she did hers; sometime student at the Académie Julian and an important champion and purchaser of early 20th century modern art.

Stein, Michael (1865 Allegheny, Pennsylvania - 1938 Palo Alto, California). Oldest Stein sibling and the "corporation's" financial manager who, with his wife, Sarah (Sally) Samuels Stein (d. 1958 Palo Alto, California) and Leo and Gertrude, were the first Americans to seriously collect modern art in Paris starting ca. 1903; Sarah and Michael also became close friends with and bought many works by Matisse and helped found his art school in 1908.

Stephens, James (1882 Dublin - 1950 London). An Irish poet of small stature but largish talent whom Joyce picked to finish *Finnegans Wake* if the latter died before the former, one of the latter's curious jokes, one hopes; author of the novel *Crock of Gold* (1912).

Sterne, Laurence (1713 Conmel, Tipperary, Ireland - 1768 London). One of those writers whose lives are sufficiently uncomfortable emotionally, spiritually and economically as to render them devoid of humor, but who somehow possess the wherewithal to invest their writings with lightness and whimsy, touched with acid, it is true, but full of wit and ironic retort, in Sterne's case, overlaid with an eccentricity of style and baroque expression dense enough to make the prose difficult to penetrate, but well worth the effort.

Strindberg, Johann August (1849 Stockholm - 1912 Stockholm). Moody misogynist playwright, who really disliked women.

Styron, William Clark (b. 1925 Newport News, Virginia). Commonly accepted as one of the leading postwar (that is, post-1945) American novelists.

Tailleferre, Marcelle Germaine (née Taillefesse 1892 Parc-Saint-Maur, near Paris - 1983 Paris). Composer; the only female member of Les Six aside from Cocteau and he was only an associate member; he appropriately compared her music (for the ear) to Marie Laurencin's paintings (for the eye); unfortunately not much of her work is currently available for the ear.

Tanner, Henry Ossawa (1859 Pittsburgh, Pennsylvania - 1937 Paris). American painter longtime resident in France.

Thirion, André (1908 – 2001 Paris). One of the culturally-minded young Communist activists who fell deeply under the sway of Surrealism and the debonair Aragon during the late 1920s; one isn't sure whether in the end he was more of one or the other, but he wrote an interesting book about his lives and time called *Révolutionaires sans révolution* (1972).

Toklas, Alice Babette (1877 San Francisco - 1967 Paris). Longtime resident of Paris, writer, gardener, cook and the subject of much speculation.

Trauner, Alexandre (1906 Budapest – 1993 Omonville-la-Petite, France). A set designer who worked on many of the finest films ever made including Orson Welles' *Othello* (1952).

Treize, Thérèse (née Thérèse Maure 1900 Paris). Intimate friend of Kiki's who passed the hat while the rapturous Kiki sang her heart out in the Quarter's clubs and cafés; worked in her own gymnastic studios on the Rue Denfert-Rochereau and elsewhere; accepted the change in her name by the poet Robert Desnos, her lover for a brief time, in order to pursue her life in anonymity (and so as not to embarrass her family); kept a small mouse in a small cage which she carried around the cafés; involved one night in a punchup outside The Jockey with Pascin who had somehow insulted her; engaged in an erratic love affair with Per Krohg, whose wife Lucy could not break with Pascin until the latter forced the issue by killing himself; in 1930 worked as Alexander Calder's assistant during performances of his wire circus until Calder married Louisa James, a student a Treize's gymnastic studio, who thereafter took over the assistant's position; at Pascin's funeral on June 7, 1930, asked in despair "What's going to happen to all of us now?"; married the Cuban painter Manuel Cano de Castro; responded with amusement to André Breton's intellectualized but earnest attempt to have an affair with her in the desperate days of 1938.

Triolet, Elsa (née Elsa Kagan 1896 Moscow - 1970 Paris). Wrote novels and polemics in French; a number of the novels remained surprisingly free of marxist-leninist-stalinist cant; the French CP's controller of the asset Aragon.

Trotsky, Léon (né Leib Davydovich Bronstein, 1877 Elisavetgrad, Russia - 1940 Mexico City). Failed revolutionary intellectual, whose first meeting with André Breton in Mexico in 1938 resembled that of Sartre-Marcuse decades later in that Breton left Trotsky's well-guarded house convinced the revolutionary knew the Surrealist's work very well, when in fact Trotsky had barely skimmed a few volumes.

Twydsen, Lady Duff (née Dorothy Smurthwaite, a.k.a. Mary Duff Stirling Byrom Twysden King 1892 Yorkshire, England - 1938 Santa Fe, New Mexico). Well known in the Montparnasse Quarter during her sponge-lush phase when she met Hemingway and the others; she appears under the name Brett Ashley in *The Sun Also Rises* (1926).

Tzara, Tristan (né Samuel Rozinstock 1896 Moinesti, Romania - 1966 Paris). Moldo-Wallachian Dadist.

Uhde, Wilhelm (1874 Friedeberg, Germany - 1947 Paris). Gay German art dealer and writer; longtime resident of Paris; an early admirer and friend of Picasso whose works he showed in his art gallery called Nôtre-Dame-des-Champs in 1908; the nazis took away his citizenship and he suffered accordingly, living during the war under a false name in the South of France.

Van Dongen, Kees (1877 Delfshaven, Netherlands - 1968 Monaco). After beginning his career with the avant-garde in the Bateau Lavoir before 1914, he used his considerable talents to develop into the most sought-after portrait painter in the city.

Vassilieva, Marie (née Mariia Ivanova Vasileva, also known as Vassilieff, 1884 Smolensk, Russia - 1957 Nogent-sur-Marne, France). Manager of her own art académie in the mews at 21, avenue du Maine, in whose sketching class Nina Hamnett would feel compelled to dance a few impromptu steps in the nude; opened her studio in February 1915 as a canteen to provide inexpensive food and drink to penurious artists, the locale of The Famous Dinner to celebrate the return of the wounded Georges Braque in January 1917.

Verlaine, Paul (1844 Metz, France - 1896 Paris). About whom one source notes that as a Symbolist poet his work is distinguished for its musical qualities and his life for being disreputable; he did write some beautiful as well as some intensely erotic poems, and he did like his regular snort of absinthe.

Vian, Boris (1920 Ville d'Avray, France - 1959 Paris). Born with a defective heart, he ignored the disadvantage to organize his life according to the old Denver guideline about the speed of one's life, one's age at death, and condition of one's corpse; he remains today the icon and male-symbol of the postwar era in Saint-Germain-des-Prés which formed the palimpsest from which developed international pop culture, a subject seeking its analyst.

Vigny, Alfred de, Comte de (1797 Loches, France - 1863 Paris). Successfully played the role of stoic martyr to his melancholy art; a Romantic poet who retired from the world after an unhappy love affair and about whom the phrase "ivory tower" was first used.

Vivian, Renée (née Pauline Mary Tarn ca. 1877 England - 1909 Paris). An ethereal youth who wrote and published poetry and an autobiographical novel in French; addicted to alcohol, drugs and death, she drifted wraith-like through the upper class Paris lesbian world of money (of which she had none), talent and beauty (of which she had an abundance) until she finally embraced her desire for oblivion; her own epitaph on her tombstone speaks of her "ravaged soul."

Vollmoeller, Mathilde (1876 Stuttgart, Germany - 1943 Munich, Germany). Painter; student at the Matisse Academy 1909-10, in whose studio at 17, rue Campagne Première the poet Rilke lived for a few months in 1908 from where he moved into the studio in the Hôtel Biron (77, rue de Varenne) of his sculptor wife Clara Westhoff-Rilke who had studied with Rodin; married Hans Purrmann in 1912 with whom she returned to Germany after the birth of their second child and after the French confiscated their personal property in 1914.

Washington, Booker Taliaferro (1856 Franklin County, Virginia - 1915 Tuskegee, Alabama). No relation to George or the pop song singer.

Weisgerber, Albert (1878 St. Ingbert bei Saarbrücken, Germany - 1915 near Fromelles, Ypres, France). German artist; student in Munich; lived in Paris for several years from 1906; his short life ended in the trenchslime of the western front.

Welles, George Orson (1915 Kenosha, Wisconsin - 1985 Los Angeles, California). On a sunny May 1987 afternoon, following his instructions, his daughter Beatrice placed a small blue urn holding his ashes in a shallow brick well, which was then sealed, at the country house of the retired bullfighter Antonio Ordonez in Ronda, Spain.

West, Nathanael (né Nathan Wallenstein Weinstein 1903 New York City - 1940 El Centro, California). American small game hunter and novelist who married someone's sister Eileen.

Whistler, James Abbott McNeill (1834 Lowell, Massachusetts - 1903 London). American painter, whose work suffered through four simultaneous exhibitions in Washington DC during the summer of 1995.

White, Stanford (1853 New York City - 1906 New York City). Architect who designed the Washington Square Arch and loved unwisely.

Williams, William Carlos (1883 Rutherford, New Jersey - 1963 Rutherford, New Jersey). One cannot quite decide whether his work lives on because of its originality and independence of "schools" and "theories" or his presence and influence at the right place and time throughout his long and prolific life as both poet and physician; author of the book-length poem *Paterson*, several prose works, hundreds of published poems, an autobiography, a collection of essays and collection of letters, all worth reading despite his often harebrained and cranky notions and opinions.

Wrangel, Count F. U. (b. 1853). Swedish lord chamberlain to the Swedish queen (until he gambled away her travel allowance at Nice in 1906) and writer of memoirs; settled in Versailles in 1908 where he acted as advisor and father-figure to the young Scandinavian artists who flowed into Paris before 1914; a habitué of the Café de Versailles on the Place du 18 Juin 1940 (formerly Place de Rennes) (6th, 14th and 15th) several blocks west of the Carrefour Vavin; remained in Paris until well into the

1920s with his painter wife, with whom he first lived in Paris 1888-91.

Zawadowski, Wacław (Zawado) (1891 – 1982). Polish painter who arrived in Paris in 1912 and stayed for many years; friend of Kisling and member of the Polish contingent in Montparnasse; moved into Modigliani's studio after the Italian's death in 1920; Nina Hamnett moved in with him in 1921.

Zadkine, Ossip (1890 Smolensk, Russia - 1967 Paris). A sculptor who studied with Injalbert at the École des Beaux-Arts, whose museum, where he lived from 1928 until his death (except the period 1941-45 when he lived in exile in New York City), in the 6th arrondissement, is well worth visiting.

Zervos, Christian (1899 Argostoli, Greece - 1970 Paris). Publisher of books of and about modern art.

Zola, Émile Edouard Charles Antoine (1840 Paris - 1902 Paris). Novelist exemplar of the "naturalism" school of fiction (i.e., "warts and all"), sometimes also referred to as "realism"; debtor and friend of Cézanne's youth; his remains seem to be both in the Panthéon and the Montmartre Cemetery.

Zuckmayer, Carl (1896 Nackenheim, Rheinhessen, Germany - 1977 Visp, Wallis, Switzerland). Playwright of no particular innovative talent, but whose works are driven by strong delineation of their main characters; his first big success, *Der fröhliche Weinberg* (1925), motivated him out of the Heidelberg bohemian life into the bourgeoisie; his great comedy satirizing the German propensity toward the worship of militarism and regimented bureaucracy, *Der Hauptmann von Köpenick* (1931), and his Jewish mother, ensured his place on the nazis' unwanted list and he went into exile, spending seven years in the USA during which time he wrote the popular anti-nazi piece *Der Teufels General* (*The Devil's General* 1946); his autobiography, *Als wär's ein Stück von mir* (1967) (tr. *A Part of Myself* [1970]), is worth reading.

Endnotes

[1] All the names are explained in the rarely found *Au fil des lignes du métro. L'encyclopedie des stations* by Dan Sylvestre with illustrations by Siné (Paris: L'Itinérant, 1997).

[2] For a well-written account of Mrs. David's life, see Artemis Cooper, *Writing at the Kitchen Table: The Authorized Biography of Elizabeth David* (New York: The Ecco Press, 1999).

[3] Anything Mrs. Fisher has written is worth reading. A good place to start would be *The Measure of Her Powers: An M.F.K. Fisher Reader* (Washington DC: Counterpoint Press, 2000), and *A Life in Letters: Correspondence 1929-1991* (Washington DC: Counterpoint Press, 1998).

[4] In *The Richard Wright Reader*. Edited by Ellen Wright and Michel Fabre (New York: Harper and Row, 1978).

[5] For the academically-minded, the short title stands for *Publications of the New Sydenham Society: Lexicon of Medicine and Allied Sciences* by H. Power and L.W. Sedgwick, 1879-1899.

[6] For a fascinating and wildly inventive modern "take" on these Alexandre Dumas creations, see Arturo Pérez-Reverte's novel *The Club Dumas*. Translated from the Spanish by Sonia Soto (1993).

[7] The GI-bill was an arrangement under which former servicemen and women could attend college and university with government financial assistance, of which many young people took advantage to support a longer or shorter sojourn in one European city or another. Most remained in the USA and went to college and, no doubt, became productive members of American society. Many took off

for Paris as soon as the first check arrived in the mail and continued to sign up for classes to ensure additional checks continued to arrive. Did you know that Lawrence Ferlinghetti has a PhD from the University of Paris? He spent several years there actually working at his education. The city had such an effect on him that he called his own bookstore and publishing house in San Francisco "City Lights."

[8]The Library of America series finally published the uncensored texts of Wright's books in 1991. "Uncensored" must be understood relative to the fact that Wright agreed to the alterations demanded by the publishers in the 1940s. Nonetheless, the books did not originally appear in the form Wright intended.

[9]A revision of a 1992 publication entitled *A Street Guide to African Americans in Paris* appeared in the spring of 1996, with Michel Fabre and John A. Williams credited as editors. "Credited" because there are so many errors in the book that it is hard to believe that these two meticulous craftsmen really had much to do with its production. For example, the plaque noting Richard Wright's presence at 14, rue Monsieur-le-Prince is quoted as reading "Richard Wright, écrivain afro-américain" when it clearly does not say this; Sonny Rollins appears as Rollinson; the index page references are often wrong or non-existent; Albert Camus is André; La Chope Danton on the Rue de Condé is not on that street; the Jockey Club said to be at 127, boulevard de Montparnasse isn't (at least not at the end of May 1996); the Café de la Suisse is surely the Petit Suisse; and so on. Nonetheless the book is indispensable for anyone who wishes to see where Americans of color lived and worked in Paris; it is fascinating in its details and should be available at the Village Voice bookshop on Rue Princess and elsewhere. Or one could write to Cercle

d'Études Afro-Américaines, 12 Square Montsouris, 75014 Paris, the organization that produced the volume.

[10]The letter is cited by John Rewald in his *Cézanne in America. Dealers, Collectors, Artists and Critics 1891-1921* (Princeton NJ: Princeton University Press, 1989), pp. 73 & 85.

[11]For more about that Morris character, see below under "Envoi."

[12]You can see it on page 189 of Christopher Sawyer-Lauçanno's book *The Continual Pilgrimage* (1992) and in *The Paris Review*, 79 (1981).

[13]"Rast angesichts der Zerstörung" in *Das Neue Tagebuch* (Paris), 25.6.1938, reprinted in *Im Bistro nach Mitternacht* (Cologne: Kiepenheuer & Witsch, 1999).

[14]The diaries have recently been republished in the old translation by Charles Kessler (no relation), with an introduction by Ian Buruma replacing the one by Otto Friedrich, and under a different title: *Berlin in Lights: The Diaries of Count Harry Kessler (1918-1937)* New York: Grove Press, 2000. Nowhere in this volume is there any reference to the earlier edition.

[15]Joseph Breitenbach is not to be confused with the writer Joseph Breitbach (1903-1980), who also lived for many years in Paris, writing in both French and German for French and German publications; he wrote several novels including *Bericht über Bruno* (1962), perhaps his best known work.

[16]After his death, Polygram Distribution released a collection of his most popular songs originally recorded on

the Barclay label, including a duet with Juliette Gréco ("Je prends les choses du bon cote").

[17]Many denizens of Montparnasse and Montmartre, including Picasso, kept such common Mediterranean tortoises as household and studio pets during the period. The animal appears notably in Matisse's "Bathers with a Turtle" (1908).

[18]For an extremely comprehensive examination of this issue, see Anthony Julius, *T. S. Eliot, Anti-Semitism, and Literary Form* (Cambridge University Press, 1995).

[19]Plimpton note to the author, ca. 15 June 1998. For a recent study relevant here, see Henry Fountain, "Secrets of Fuel for Creative Fires Unlocked," in *The New York Times* (April 18, 2000), which reports on recent work by chemists to explain the attraction of the stuff for artists. For a description of the London craze for absinthe in the last year or two of the 1990s, see Amanda Hesser, "A Modern Absinthe Experiment" in *The New York Times* (May 31, 2000).

[20]Plimpton note to the author.

[21]Recently an English-language compilation of Fernande Olivier's writings about her life has been published under the title, *Loving Picasso: The Private Journal of Fernande Olivier* (New York: Harry N. Abrams, 2001).

[22]On 5 June 1901, Cézanne wrote to Denis "Dear Sir, In the newspapers I have learned of the demonstration of your artistic sympathy toward me that has been shown at the Salon of the Société Nationale des Beaux-Arts. Please accept this expression of my deep gratitude and relay it to the artists who have joined you on this occasion." Paul

Cézanne, *Letters*. Ed. by John Rewald (New York: Hacker Art Books, 1984), 272.

[23]The only book now (1999) in print on Sérusier is Caroline Boyle-Turner, *Paul Sérusier. La Technique, L'Oeuvre Peint* (Lausanne, 1989).

[24]The citations come from a publication of the French Embassy in Washington, "News from France," Vol. 92.06 (April 3, 1992).